D0891941

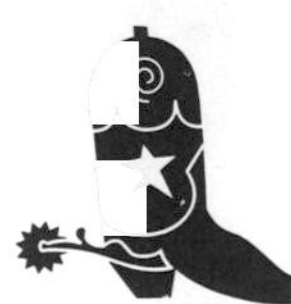

New Westers

New West

The
West in
Contemporary
American
Culture

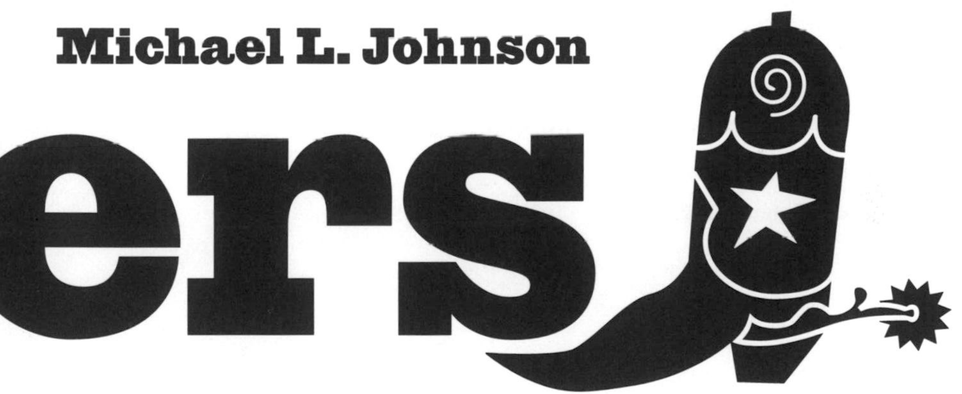
Michael L. Johnson
ers

University Press of Kansas

Published by the University Press of Kansas (Lawrence, Kansas 66049), which was organized by the Kansas Board of Regents and is operated and funded by Emporia State University, Fort Hays State University, Kansas State University, Pittsburg State University, the University of Kansas, and Wichita State University

The paper used in this publication meets the minimum requirements of the American National Standard for Permanence of Paper for Printed Library Materials Z39.48-1984.

Library of Congress
Cataloging-in-Publication Data
Johnson, Michael L.
New westers : the west in contemporary American culture / by Michael L. Johnson.
p. cm.
Includes bibliographical references (p.) and index.
ISBN 0-7006-0763-3 (alk. paper)
1. Popular culture — West (U.S.) 2. Popular culture — United States. 3. West (U.S.) in mass media. 4. West (U.S.) — In literature. I. Title.
F596.J49 1996
978-dc20 96-426

British Library Cataloging in Publication Data is available

Printed in the United States of America

10 9 8 7 6 5 4 3 2 1

FOR KATHLEEN

who got me back in the saddle

Suppose we say that wilderness invokes nostalgia, a justified not merely sentimental nostalgia for the lost America our forefathers knew. The word suggests the past and the unknown, the womb of earth from which we all emerged. It means something lost and something still present, something remote and at the same time intimate, something buried in our blood and nerves, something beyond us and without limit. Romance — but not to be dismissed on that account. The romantic view, while not the whole of the truth, is a necessary part of the whole truth.

— Edward Abbey, *Desert Solitaire: A Season in the Wilderness*

We lived two different lives, your mother and I. I came from a people who held the wind as brother, because he is free, and the horse as companion, because he is the living, fleeting wind — and your mother, well, she came from men who hold the earth as brother. They are a steady, settled people. We have been at odds all of our lives, the wind and the earth. Perhaps it is time we gave up the old differences.

— Gabriel Márez in Rudolfo Anaya, *Bless Me, Ultima*

Contents

Preface, xi

Acknowledgments, xiii

Introduction
Westering Again, 1

Chapter 1
A Vertical Ride: Cowboy Chic and Other Fashions of the New West, 14

Chapter 2
Manifest Diversity: Turning Turner on His Head, Retelling Western Histories, 55

Chapter 3
Rewriters of the Purple Sage, Part 1: Trails to New Western Literature, 102

Chapter 4
Rewriters of the Purple Sage, Part 2: A Gathering, 135

Chapter 5
Crossed Over: *Unforgiven* and Other Revisions, 199

Chapter 6
Garth and Friends: Resinging the West, Dancing to the Cowboy Beat, 260

Chapter 7
The New West: A Sense of Place, 303

Conclusion
Staying Put: The Future of the New West, 342

Notes, 365

Suggested Readings, 385

Index, 391

Preface

In south-central Missouri, on Interstate 44, once part of celebrated Route 66, America's Mother Road, lies the town of Lebanon. I lived there before I went off to college in Texas and California and finally wended my way back to the heart of the Midwest in Lawrence, Kansas. As a child, I played cowboys and Indians—a lot. In grade school, during rest periods, my teachers—all of them, year after year, it seemed—read from Laura Ingalls Wilder's books. Those stories about experiences in the so-called settling of the West registered more deeply in me than I knew. Rheumatic fever kept me from rough-and-tumble fun during the fourth and fifth grades, so I spent considerable time listening to the radio (that was the *early* 1950s). My favorite shows were Westerns, and in my mind's ear I can still hear the sound effects and voices, especially those of the Lone Ranger and Tonto.

Then, recovered, I began to ride and for several years wore the withers off a succession of my family's horses. And I took up shooting—BB guns, rifles, shotguns, bows, you name it. I traveled the maze of section roads through Laclede County with one weapon or another across the pommel of my saddle—or across my lap if I was riding bareback, hoping I had the air of an Osage warrior. Sometimes I imagined myself one of the notorious outlaws—Jesse James, Cole Younger, and others—who originated in Missouri.

Little did I suspect that such activities and fantasies were planting a seed that, after over three decades of dormancy, would germinate into a full-blown fascination with the West and with the rampant desire to return to it at the end of the twentieth century. I could hardly have guessed—though I belonged to 4-H and once even raised a few cattle—that the average kid in Lebanon High School's vocational-agriculture program was learning lessons that I would have to wait till my middle age to learn, avidly but less directly. Nor did I quite foresee that a boy I hung out with whose surname was West would become a lifelong friend, largely because he embodies qualities I associate strongly with the West and admire: wry sense of humor, skeptical optimism, patience, philosophical resilience, dependability. And I sure didn't know that, after half a human span given to molding myself as a self-determined person, I would come round to so much resembling my own father, definitely a Westerner at heart. You are where you're from. I'm from the eastern edge of the West. It's okay to say that now.

Acknowledgments

I have no idea how many people have helped me write this book. Some are living. Some are dead. Some are Old Westers, and some are New Westers. Some are both. Some aren't Westers at all. But let me single out several people for special thanks: my wife, Kathleen Johnson, who got me started and encouraged me all the way through; Beth Sullivan and Stephen Evans, who proved themselves peerless research assistants; Jon Blumb, who worked photographic wonders; all those who read various versions or portions of the manuscript and offered helpful advice, especially Tony Hillerman, Kim Wiar, Stephen Tatum, Fred Woodward, Carolyn Doty, Donald Worster, and Richard W. Etulain; the formidably competent staff of the College Word Processing Center at KU, who again and again transmuted low-quality handwriting into high-quality fair copy; and the enthusiastic, assiduous, and imaginative people at the University Press of Kansas.

New Westers

Turn around. We'll make a westerner of you yet.

—Hunt Thatcher in Doris Betts, *Heading West*

INTRODUCTION

WESTERING AGAIN

Yeeeeehaaah!

That sound, with variations, is the primal scream of the American West. It's a noise not too far away from the rebel yell I learned in high school in south-central Missouri, which itself doubtless was much the same sort of yell many young men from the South took with them after the Civil War when they headed west to become cowboys. With some vocal tinkering it might be shaped into the whoop of a Plains Indian. Hard to freeze on the page, it's rooted in the raw dynamics of chest and throat, meant to blast out into the dry, climbing air of the big sky beyond the 98th (some say 100th) meridian. It's a lot more like the neigh of a mustang in a desert canyon than like a high note from a diva, a holler on the floor of the New York Stock Exchange, or even a cheer from a football fan in Dallas. It's an out-of-doors sort of racket, distinctively exuberant, exorbitant, unhampered. It's a brief song of freedom, of the lusty drive to get on with the day's work or the night's play. To plunge pell-mell into whatever wildness is left in the world. To stop puling about the chaos of things and head out for the territory. When properly executed, it's a proud belch of the wide-open spirit.

Yeeeeehaaah!

It's a male utterance, of course, but you can discover women who make it. At the end of the twentieth century, you might have to venture well into the outlands to find some wizened and born-to-the-saddle old-timer who can really perform it well. Who can do it the way it used to be done in the days before the Wild West turned into movies and television, before urban corporations took over ranches, before rodeos with riders trained in clinics became the hottest thing on ESPN and PSN since the Olympic competitions. Still, though, you may hear a vestige of it breeze out from under a Stetson during a line dance at one of the boot-scootin' bars with names like Cadillac Ranch or Stallions & Stars or Cactus Moon springing up like mushrooms from coast to coast.

Nowadays a lot of people — an increasing number, from Prozac-popping fern-feelers to regenerate closet cowpokes — frequent such places. They wear clothes ordered from Sheplers, learn to line-dance and two-step, drink beer from long-neck bottles, grow Western plants like manzanita and yucca, acquire the language by reading books like Edgar F. "Frosty" Potter's 1986 *Cowboy Slang*. They decorate their Mission-style coffee tables with Western knickknacks, attend cowboy poetry gatherings or powwows, take pack trips in Yosemite, hang their walls with Western-theme paintings, collect San Ildefonso pottery or Navajo trade blankets, view Western movies, play Wild West arcade games, cook Mexican. They drive pickup trucks, whether or not they have anything to haul. They vacation in the West, move to the West, try their damnedest to go Western, to save the West, to turn *into* the West or what they think is the West. In all those people the yeeeeehaaah, smothered in the routines of quiet desperation or close to the surface on a Saturday night, longs unquietly to come out.

Most of those many postmodern Roy Rogerses and Dale Evanses probably never have sat a horse, much less participated in or even seen a roundup. They've never fired a Colt .45, watched a sand painting blossom under expert hands, or panned for gold. But they want to do all that, one way or another. They want a personal West, to whatever extent it may be merely mental, Walter Mittyish. They hunger for its heritage near the end of a century — and a millenium — adrift in confusing change. They're ready to redo the Old West — or what they consider the best of it — into a refreshed worldview, a more elemental lifestyle, less

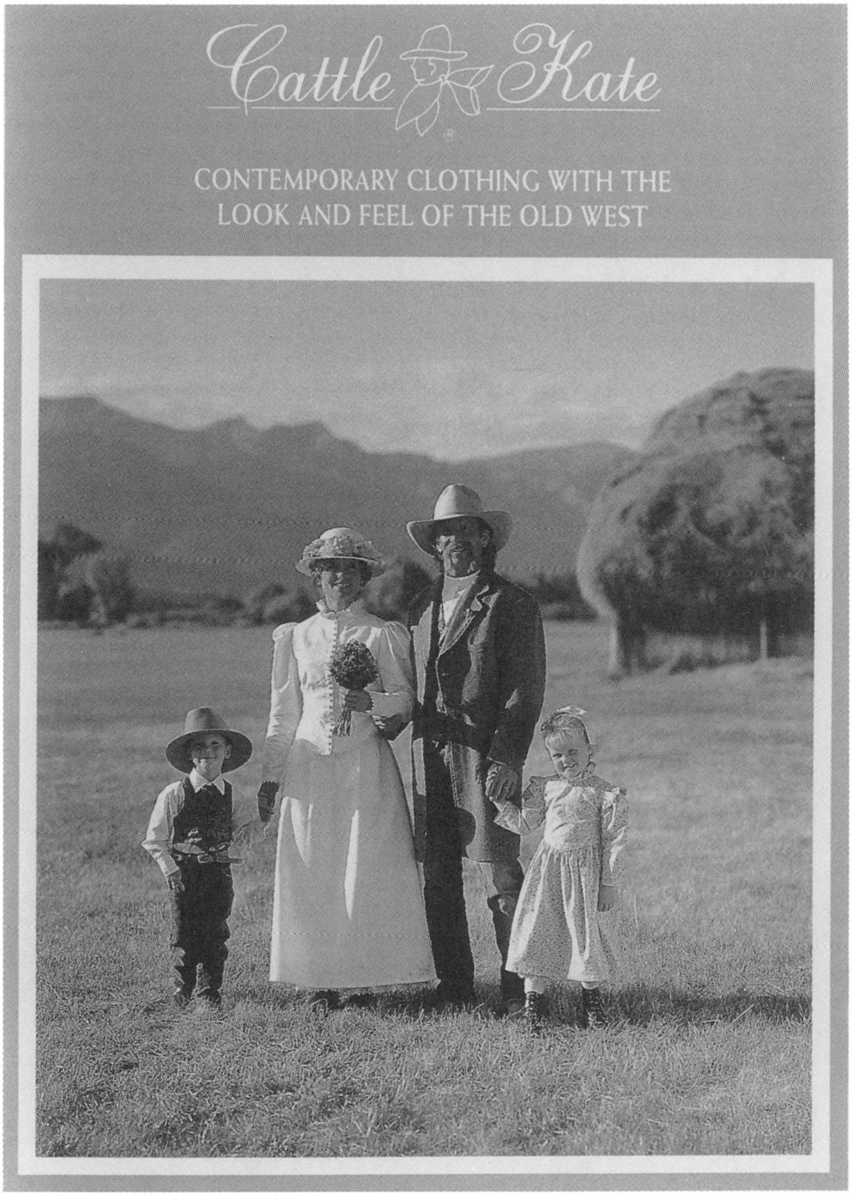

The front cover of a 1993 Cattle Kate catalog: postmodern westering as a quest for a more elemental lifestyle. (Courtesy of Cattle Kate)

Arcade games like Mad Dog McCree *provide a vicarious experience of the Wild West. (Courtesy of American Laser Games)*

frantic but more colorful lives. They want back the dream of the West — but on new and different terms.

So the West is now in once again, once again reimagined. But the new fans of the West can't perform the yeeeeehaaah with the same sincerity, the same fire in the belly, as the old-timers. A sense of the contrast may be gained from two cinematic reimaginings of the West. Listen to the yeeeeehaaahs of John Wayne and his tough company before they head north with their herd on the Chisholm Trail in Howard Hawks's 1948 film *Red River*. Then listen to those of Billy Crystal and his New York cronies, in a parodic echo of the *Red River* scene, before they head their herd, along with dude-ranch hands, north into Colorado out of New Mexico in Ron Underwood's 1991 film *City Slickers*. Even in these two illusionary worlds of film, the latter just isn't as *auténtico* as the former and couldn't be. And yet, of course, both casts of characters wind up — with differences — committed to and absorbed by their Western experiences.

That kind of contrast both oversimplifies and complicates the discussion here, though it may prove helpful. But let's try another approach to distinguishing Western generations, one that leads right to the title of this book.

In a special 1993 issue of *Life* devoted to "The Wild West Yesterday and Today," mystery novelist Tony Hillerman suggests further dimensions of the distinction I'm exploring and supplies a nomenclature for it. He begins his article, "The Wild West Will Never Die," with a consideration of what the Old West means to him. He defines it as "a certain kind of people and certain kinds of places — mostly places that are almost empty. The two tend to go together. When you find them, you find the Old West alive and well." Because of the distances involved, "people live too far apart to get on one another's nerves" and gladly salute each other when they do occasionally meet.[1]

Those people, whom Hillerman calls Old Westers, he characterizes by one of his many generalizations: "If you have car trouble out in the empty West, no Old Wester will pass without stopping to help." And then he inserts the gig: "If somebody does drive by, you can with certainty accuse him of being an easterner or, worse, a New Wester," a type Hillerman plainly doesn't cotton to. For him, "the term 'New West' . . . describes much of the territory west of the 100th Meridian, including 99.9 percent of California and most settlements everywhere of more than 3,000 folks. Santa Fe, for example, became irreparably New West about 1962 (the year I gave up and left)." He backs off briefly and then condemns with a shade more specificity: "It remains a lovely place, but it has been flooded by the same folks who turned Aspen into a national demonstration of what happens when yuppies get too much money." Still, he observes, "a salting of Old Western types survives" in such places.[2]

Beyond the differences in how they treat stranded motorists, how much money they have and how they use it, ubiquitous New Westers and vestigial Old Westers may be distinguished also by the divergence in their political attitudes, according to Hillerman. One of his anecdotes illustrates that divergence. It concerns a meeting of the New Mexico chapter of PEN, the socially conscious international printers' and editors' association, in Santa Fe in 1992: "The first speakers were fairly typical of the New West, upwardly mobile newcomers with expensive educations, abundant talent and good intentions. Racial and sexual insensitivity were attacked. A woman bared her soul for us in the language of the touchy-feely movement. We heard from the New Age version of transcendentalism. All was politically correct." Then, that transplanted Southern California folderol finished, there "arose Max Evans, his gnarled knuckles showing why the bar fights one finds in his fiction are so knowingly described and his face proving he is a man who has dismounted many a rodeo horse earlier than intended and headfirst."[3] Standing tall, Evans plays the avenging Old Wester in this rhetorical showdown at the I'm-O.K.-You're-O.K. Corral.

Author of *The Rounders* and other well-known Western novels, Evans, in Hillerman's anecdote, presents himself as "both a white male and a cowboy," thus "a member of two of America's most loathsome and contemptible minorities, and justly so." Thereupon he shares an account of "that moment of epiphany when, as a boy, he witnessed the event that led to wisdom." It concerns an old cowhand who, after being kicked in the stomach by a horse he's saddling, slowly gathers himself up off the ground, finishes saddling the animal, and then gives it a swift kick in the stomach. When Evans asked him why he did that, the cowhand answered, " 'A horse has to understand it's a horse.' " Hillerman explains the point of his anecdote in terms of a contrast between the "wisdom" of the Old West and that of the New: "About 26 percent of the audience roared with delighted laughter, and about 74 percent produced polite smiles and puzzled looks. That is the ratio of Santa Fe population between Old West and New West — New Westers being those who feel it politically incorrect to kick a horse, even when common sense dictates that it needs to be done."[4]

The contrast inheres not only in a difference of political attitudes and wisdom but also in the difference between the Old West's unquestioned, action-mandating "common sense" and the New West's self-conscious, self-serious "good intentions." It's much the same difference that operates between the way of thinking (wry, straightforward, practical) dramatized in Don Cook and Chick Rains's song "Cowboy Logic," made popular by Michael Martin Murphey on his 1990 album *Cowboy Songs*, and the way of thinking that informs ads for amulets and the like that you find in catalogs for New Age products.

Moreover, from Hillerman's point of view, New Westers don't understand Old Westers very well — and understanding, I'd throw in, is probably equally flawed in the reverse direction. In his characterization, the former seem to believe that the latter are sort of Will Rogers types, but the latter know by inured ironies that they are more like Won't Rogers antitypes. For instance, horses aren't romantic pets for them: they're horses, critters through which Old Westers do their hard work; they're "relatively reliable," but they can bite, kick, endlessly irritate, or even kill you. Old Western realism about horses, which suggests a good deal about Old Western philosophy in general and its differences from New Western philosophy, is amply illustrated by another of Hillerman's anecdotes: "Once somebody failed to show up for a panel at a Western Writers of America convention, and I was sent in as a sub. A New West type in the audience asked us about our horses. I am happy to report that not one of us: a) owned a horse, b) would ride a horse if alternate transport would get you there, c) considered horses more intelligent than the average fence post." Thus, he concludes, "The WWA is still dominated by what remains of the Old West," whose "last outpost," he predicts, will be Taos, New Mexico — because, despite the fact that the town "probably has more boutiques, art galleries and tourist traps per capita than Santa Fe," it is inconveniently distant from the Albuquerque airport and has "an odd mystique" whereby "it seems to change people more than they change Taos."[5] New Westers may strive to change the

Old West, to remake it to conform to their worldview and answer their needs, but for Hillerman something of it will endure, intransigently, indefinitely — and justly so.

Well, let's hang around the Taos area and see what a New Wester who lives there thinks of Old Westers. After all, turnabout is fair play, though we need to remind ourselves that, as in the case of Hillerman, we're dealing with one person's perspective — and generalizations. In this case the person is John Nichols, the novelist and essayist who has lived since 1969 in Taos, where for some time he has been involved in local struggles over land and water. The struggles figure fictionally in his much-praised 1974 novel *The Milagro Beanfield War*, as they do also in his 1986 memoir *On the Mesa*. Like a number of Taoseños, he is worried about the destruction of the Taos Mesa, a sagebrush plain west of his home that has so far escaped development.

In the first chapter of *On the Mesa*, Nichols lyrically evokes "this spare, bony plateau" on which he frequently wanders and meditates like a Southwestern Thoreau. He begins by speculating about why the area has become "so hallowed" to him: "It has to do, I suppose, with the lack of clutter. Here, my imagination is free to take off because there are no impeding structures. I crave the wild silence it offers . . . the aloneness I am bequeathed as I wander across the becalmed sagebrush expanse." He comes to the mesa "deliberately, asking for succor," relief from the monumental disasters and frantic anxieties of postmodern civilization.[6] All that falls away as he surrenders himself to the mesa, breathes its clean air, ponders the subtle economies of its life-forms.

"But," as Nichols announces his sudden wrench of perception, "nothing remains perfect for long." A man approaches across the space Nichols has been enjoying as his own, a man he's quick to size up with his cultural calipers as a certain breed of Old Wester: "This bowlegged fellow wears a tan cowboy hat, a white shirt (whose sleeves are rolled up on thick arms), purple double-knit slacks, and western boots. . . . When he speaks, the accent is good ol' boy and right friendly: 'Helluva day, ain't it? Hot enough to fry the devil.' " It turns out the good ol' boy has an Old West–flavored name: I. J. Haynes. And he's "a petroleum landman for the William Castle Drilling Company outta Shreveport, Louisiana."

He's looking for property to buy so he "can make you rich."[7] He drives a Chrysler, its metallic spread of bright yellow incongruous on the mesa.

So is Haynes as Nichols portrays him with a hint of affectedness and more than a little self-righteousness: "Oh dear, I think: Just what the doctor ordered — a mastermind of megabucks, a plump little hayseed dervish of Progress American Style . . . and I shudder: Is no place sacred?" Exactly the kind of reaction an Old Wester might attribute to the kind of New Wester who wears jogging shoes (as Nichols does in his jacket photo) and agonizes over the disruption of an ecospiritual moment. But the incident is more intricate than such an observation implies. Just as Haynes hardly comes on as a veteran of the range, so Nichols soon discloses to the reader that he's not simply a Nike-shod tenderfoot, either. Haynes represents — or pretends to be — a familiar type of displaced Old Wester, a wrangler of horsehead oil wells rather than horses, a more modern exploiter of the West; but Nichols, though he is polite to his visitor, confesses to the reader that he harbors within himself, stifled, a distinct Old Western type exaggerated by the cinema: the gunfighter. He may "bow and scrape and smile" when confronted with his "enemies," but, he declares, "often I would like to cast rude insults, or perhaps blow their brains out — à la Clint Eastwood — with a .357 magnum."[8]

Nichols may caricature Haynes as an oil *gazapo* who cares no more for the land than a cowpuncher finally cares for a herd that gets carved into steaks, but the contrast between the two men, short of caricature, reveals plenty. It's the contrast between New Wester and Old Wester, each with a touch of the other, Haynes perhaps more alienated from the land than his self-knowledge allows him to discern, Nichols perhaps bearing more of the Wild West in his bones than he would wish. Still, Nichols winds up at the end of his chapter caricaturing himself — though unconsciously, I believe — when his diction reveals him as an overly precious descendant of nineteenth-century nature writers like John Muir. After Nichols explains to Haynes that he doesn't "want to be rich," Haynes opines, predictably, that "money isn't everything, I reckon . . . but it's sure way ahead of whatever's in second place." Nichols then invokes an ecological judgment: "With that he guffaws — ho ho ho! — slaps his thigh . . . and on cue I'll bet another hundred species go extinct." Nichols backs away, waving goodbye, exclaiming "drop dead" under his breath, feeling "panicked little desert flowers atremble" around him.[9]

All of which isn't to say that we should ridicule Nichols's praise of Western nature's power to heal and inspire or vindicate corporate depredations of its beauties and fragilities. Rather, it is to say that distinguishing Old Westers from New Westers can be tricky. As much as he represents certain aspects of the Old West, Haynes represents also less "kinder and gentler" aspects of the New West. Likewise, Nichols, for all his defensive stridency about environmental issues, nurtures more sympathy for some aspects of the Old West (ranching on a small scale, for instance) than he does for more questionable aspects of the New West. And he's as much an elbow-room seeker for his purposes as Old Westers were and are for theirs.

Elsewhere in the special issue of *Life* that features Hillerman you find all manner of New West/Old West distinctions that echo those in Nichols's chapter, along with similar complications. For instance, we are reminded of the brevity of the Wild West and of its displacement by many succeeding different Wests, each retaining, transformed or distorted, residues of that yesteryear:

> Born during the Gold Rush of 1849, the Wild West of wagon trains and Indian raids and range wars and fast-draw artists faded into history as the 20th century arrived with its civilized amenities: government regulations, special interests, local, state and federal taxes — and lawyers. Passels of lawyers, pardner. But the legend lingered on in Buffalo Bill Cody's Wild West extravaganzas, in hundreds of penny dreadfuls, in thousands of movie and television westerns. And the spirit of the Wild West is still alive.[10]

There were earlier Wild Wests too, of course, before the one that gave up gunplay for legal finagling. But that span of a few decades, with its enduring imagery, holds a fascination for many people far greater than that of the preceding ages of the mountain men and trappers and traders and scouts or of Native Americans before the centuries of the Spanish entrada into their territories and cultures — though lots of New Westers are increasingly interested in such ages and their survival in some form. For such people the Wild West is still wild, however much its millions of acres, its multicultural and natural richness, are held hostage by one kind of developer or another.

Another piece in the magazine concerns the sheriff of Cochise County, Arizona, a man with some of the mettle of the Old Western lawman but who spends much of his time in the executive-bureaucratic realm of fax machines and public relations. Another concerns a Lakota medicine man who must do part of his shamanistic work in the technological surroundings of the Cheyenne River Indian Reservation hospital. And there's one about Western women living out revised versions of Old Western roles: a Wyoming rancher who tends her Charolais herd by pickup, operates the High Plains Press, probably could perform a respectable yeeeeehaaah, and whose pluck recalls that of many a pioneer; a brothel owner in Ely, Nevada, a businesswoman whose enterprise is updated by her establishment's requiring condoms; and so on — a gallery of successes not wholly sanctioned by postmodern feminism but exemplary of a New West distinct from but still entangled with the Old West.

And you can make a game out of categorizing the differences between Old and New Westers, soon moving far beyond Hillerman's anecdotal distinctions and the preceding historical and biographical sketches. Old Westers eat meat, mostly beef. New Westers tend to avoid red meat; some are vegetarians. Old Westers are lusty conservatives. New Westers are neopuritan liberals. And so on. It's hard to stop. Old Westers crave habaneros — at the top of the Scoville scale of hotness. New Westers don't get more adventurous than jalapeños in catering to their addictions to capsaicin (the chemical that makes chiles hot). Old Westers believe the West was *won*. New Westers are concerned with how it was *lost* — or is being lost or will be.

The more I think about such distinctions, the more I can cite exceptions to them or discover contradictions in them. A lot of New Westers have some Old Wester in them and vice versa, as I've already implied. Most Westers are partly dissonant, partly harmonious combinations of the two, not pure types, certainly not caricatures. And hardly all Caucasian. Maybe there never were any *real* Old Westers besides the Native Americans before the Spanish came, but weren't they too New Westers at some point before horses were brought to this continent?

Well, logical enigmas aside, a couple of things hold true. The first is that non-Westers are easy to spot. In one of his personal essays in the *American Scholar*, Aristides (pseudonym of Joseph Epstein, the editor of the journal) confesses to being such a person, "an anti-western kind of guy," almost a caricature: "Whenever I find myself in the West . . . I feel a distinct if ineffable sense of discomfort, no matter how glorious the day or how splendid the surrounding scenery. Only recently have I understood why this is so: the American West is about life lived outdoors, where, as it turns out, none of my fantasies takes place — and in none of these fantasies, it ought to be added, am I wearing jeans."[11] That nails the opposite, the type who's out of the Western loop entirely and not interested in re-anything-ing the West but in booking his flights to other parts, apparently destinations with plenty of buildings. So we can feel fairly confident about the term *Wester:* it refers to a person whose fantasies do take place in the West, who enjoys the scenery there, wants to live life outdoors, wears jeans. You get the idea.

The second thing that holds true is that, in spite of whatever qualifications you offer, the term *New Wester,* like *Old Wester,* is useful, particularly when applied more expansively — and more forgivingly — than Hillerman applies it. In my adaptation it refers to any person who more or less recently has developed (or redeveloped) an extraordinary interest in the American West. As we'll see in the chapters ahead, that widespread and burgeoning interest covers a lot of territory and varies in its emphases from individual to individual. It involves a spectrum of fads and fashions — from cowboy memorabilia to contemporary Western clothing, from Santa Fe–style architecture to Native American kitsch. It involves retelling Western histories, so that many neglected or suppressed stories — cultural, economic, ecological, personal — are now being told and thus changing greatly — enlarging, pluralizing, complexifying — our sense of the West as places, attitudes, and lifeways. It involves rewriting Western literature to include more realistic characters and situations, to take into account more attentively the glories and dilemmas of the Western environment, to reread or reconstruct Western myths, to spin whole new tales of the region or save old ones. It involves revisionist Western films that allow us to "resee" a West that many people know only as depicted in earlier films, and it involves reinterpreting Old Western art to find new meanings through it. It involves a revitalized music industry whose artists are both singing the New West and resinging the Old West. It involves a vigorously expansive and, in numerous ways, destructive impulse to travel in and move to the West. And more — exploring and exploiting frequently cheek by jowl, New and Old West often in conflict and almost always in a precarious give-and-take that has high stakes.

New Westers in their increasing numbers, passions, and activities constitute an event of the first magnitude. Scholars with a cultural-studies slant might call it Neowesternism. That's all right, of course, though the word has an abstruse nasal buzziness. And I may theorize or moralize about the event and what it says about us, but mostly, since God is in the details, I want to deal with its particularities and peculiarities, its voices, gestures, textures, colors, contours, twists — thick knowledge. I want to adduce whatever seems most helpful to understanding and appreciating the New West.

Such a survey of New Western doings should prove worthwhile to anyone intrigued by or caught up in the ongoing explosion of Westerniana. But risks are involved. People like me who deal with "new" happenings need, besides a love of the subject, familiarity with its background and context. I hope I have enough. They also need good crap detectors. I have mine on board and try to keep it sharply tuned. At any rate, I believe that New Westers have much to teach us Americans about ourselves. So — onward.

As a country, we have become nostalgic, indulging our latest craving for the Old West. Weary of mean inner cities and air-headed suburban malls, we romance the idea of freedom in nature, in wide open spaces. The West is a hot ticket now: Montana writers, adobe architecture, cowboy bars, the two-step. That is in itself not unusual: Americans routinely go through periods of infatuation with the West, often after unsettled times when a mythic-identity check feels in order. These days, we find ourselves going to the American myth well even more often. — Joseph Hooper, "Finally Cowgirls Get Their Due: New Thoughts on the Old West"

A VERTICAL RIDE: COWBOY CHIC AND OTHER FASHIONS OF THE NEW WEST

A few snapshots, if you will.

It's 1993 in the United States, where most of the presidents for decades have been Westerners and used the rhetoric of Western passions for political ends. *Vogue*, with typical anorexic haughtiness, seems still not to have noticed the New Western eruption. *Yippy-Yi-Yea*, on the other hand, celebrates its first anniversary. This magazine has caught on to what's happening and tackles the gamut of Westerniana. The anniversary issue contains pieces on the High Road to Taos, Florida as the original cattle-ranching state (and still a competitive — and swamp-polluting—participant in the industry), the cowboy poetry of Greg Monacelli, badge collecting, the painting of Navajo artist Allen Mose, the role of dime novels in creating Western heroes, and spittoon etiquette. It reviews books concerned with firearms of the Old West, Hopalong Cassidy memorabilia, and Western toys of the 1960s and 1970s. It offers ranch recipes (for grilled beef tenderloin, peanut-butter pie, and the like). It features ads for everything from a Wyoming cattle-drive vacation at the High Island Ranch & Cattle Company to faux-suede fringed cowgirl getups from some clothier in Bayonne, New Jersey. The magazine makes a yeeeeehaaah all its own. Not for yuppies, pardner, but for yippies.

The Playmate of the Month for April 1993 is Nicole Wood. In her layout she variously lolls in shot after shot arrayed with Western trappings: pickup, saloon furniture, obligatory Stetson and boots, bolo tie, even a nightie constructed from pieces of a denim jacket and dotted sheer. " 'I really love cowboys and the West,' " she is quoted as cooing. But she's more New Wester than Old, because "the first time she rode a horse, she ended up on her rear—and decided to leave riding to cowboys."[1] (This in the same issue with an article on ecowarriors, like the Choctaw monkey-wrencher Crazy Coyote, who are the spiritual descendants of Edward Abbey, the now-legendary deep ecologist of the West.)

In the July 1992 issue of *Playboy*, which magazine from time to time urges us to acquire handmade goodies like calfskin-and-kidskin cowboy boots or all-wool cowboy hats prestained around the band, Asa Baber, in his "Men" column, sings the praises of "shit-kicker redneck women," a phrase he has lifted from a Lyle Lovett song, "Give Back My Heart," on Lovett's album *Pontiac*. It "tells the story of a cowboy who falls in love with a country girl." As Baber notes, it also "tells the story of my life." So what are the virtues of these women? They are such stuff as Western (sexist-male) dreams are made on. Shit-kicker redneck women love men and "saved my precious gonads from shriveling up and blowing away during these cold years of gender wars." They are "sweet country mamas in tight-fitting baby-blue jeans" who live in "wide-open spaces." These self-confident cowgirls can flip a man "like a grain sack and ride him like a bucking bronco," and, glory be, they know "how to make grits and gravy" in this age of timid fiber-eaters.[2] No litigious prudes, they're half mother-ranchera, half playmate-dominatrix.

Perfume counters in the 1990s offer an abundance of more or less sagey skin scents with names like Santa Fe, Chaps, Stetson, Wild Heart, New West.

USA Weekend regularly includes full-page ads for limited-edition collector plates illustrated with kitschy portraits of Western figures, often generic Native Americans. An example — typically, to borrow a word from Choctaw-Cherokee-Irish author Louis Owens, ethnostalgic — from the Bradford Exchange: "The Noble Quest," "a portrait of a Blackfoot warrior at prayer by artist Harry Schaare . . . re-created on fine porcelain" that invites us to "walk in the footsteps of the brave."[3]

Or have another look at that special issue of *Life* I discussed in the Introduction. Among the ads are four that concern the West. The first is for a framed Franklin Mint collection of twelve "Official Badges of the Great Western Lawmen," crafted in sterling silver, with Pat Garrett's Lincoln County sheriff's badge electroplated with gold. The second, from Northwestern Mutual Life, centers on a black-and-white photo of a gunfight, a guy in a white hat blazing away with dual six-shooters at three bad guys. The pitch is for both the company and "The Wild West," the 1993 documentary miniseries of which Northwestern was a sponsor: "Tune in to a time when a little life insurance might have come in handy." The third touts the companion volume to the miniseries, from Time-Life Books, as "a true story of real grit and courage." The fourth offers a set of videocassettes of episodes from the "Maverick" television series, so that once again you can "watch James Garner (Bret Maverick) bet, bluff and blast his way out of every possible danger the Old West could ante up!"[4]

Any number of television ads for Miller beer follow a general scenario: a cowboy figure intrudes into the relatively under-control situation of a striking young woman who quickly takes to him and by the end of the ad appears more than willing to admit that, to borrow the title of Pam Houston's best-selling collection of short stories, "cowboys are my weakness." And, of course, there's an award-winning Miller Lite ad in which bar customers fantasize about being rodeo cowboys who chase and rope lawyers instead of calves.

The preceding snapshots instance the contemporary fashionability of the West. They entail fantasies of the West, curiosity about it, longing for it. Certainly, they suggest the extent to which the West has been mythologized, fetishized, stereotyped, commodified. That's been going on for quite a while and is headed for a new peak, though there are other, more complicated, and opposing processes increasingly in effect as well. But the snapshots speak of a popular fixation on the West whose intensity, variety, and scale are greater than and perhaps otherwise different from fixations associated with earlier Western vogues. Hard-core Eastern types aside, it may be becoming epidemic. It's been rushing toward its present pitch since about 1985. To a large extent it has to do with the American cowboy, but it takes in much more.

The cowboy thing. For a moment, let's stay with that. In his 1989 book *Cowboy Culture: A Saga of Five Centuries*, David Dary dedicates himself to an encyclopedic treatment of "the culture of the cowboy" as a "frontier institution" that "died when the frontier died." He finds himself, over and over, debunking. But still, at the end, he has to admit the durability of a myth that writers of all kinds — journalists, screenwriters, novelists, and some historians — continue "by omission and default" to perpetuate. It's an admission that leads him to key questions:

> The real American cowboy *was* colorful. He *was* a romantic figure, even before writers embellished his life and culture. . . . His culture developed out of the conditions of his time and place, and it should be recognized for what it really was — an important page in the history of the settlement of the American West.
>
> But a mythical cowboy culture still survives alongside the real one, and it is in evidence today in cities and towns across America. . . . More and more young people and even many of their elders have adopted the fashions of the cowboy — western hats and boots, western-cut clothing, western belts and buckles actually unlike those worn by real cowboys a century ago. More and more Americans seem to be grabbing for bits and pieces of this mythical cowboy culture.
>
> Why?
>
> Are they trying to avoid becoming a cog in a machine over which they have no control? Are they searching for some satisfying identity that suggests rugged individualism in our highly legislated society? Are they seeking the frontier experience through imitation? Are they looking for a new frontier?[5]

Dary's claims about the pervasiveness of mythical cowboy culture have certainly been justified since 1989, and his questions are pertinent indeed.

Dary also ventures responses to those questions. They tend toward ominousness, but they do illuminate some issues concerning the current fashionablity of things Western.

First, Dary is rightly suspicious of new frontiers and the rhetorical baling wire that holds them together. He points to the failures of the new frontiers proposed by Henry A. Wallace in 1934 and John F. Kennedy in 1960 and remains dubious about any other "substitute frontiers" that politicians might quilt together from national yearnings. If the proposing of new frontiers "has become an American tradition," that may be due not so much to a myth as to a reality: "Americans are dissatisfied with the trappings of modern civilization — big cities, masses of people, man-made pressures and problems, and the frustrations of a mechanical society." In contradistinction to that mess stands the cowboy, who "symbolizes the free life, closely tied to the out-of-doors and Nature." But for Dary irony resides in the desire that many overcivilized people have for cowboy culture because "the very thing that destroyed the real cowboy's culture during the last century was the culture of the man in business and industry, deeply rooted in the East." And there's a paradox as well — in "that the business culture that now stretches from the Atlantic to the Pacific still believes in the mythical culture created by its writers, and too many Americans are shaping their lives after the images of that mythical culture, one that never existed."[6] Of course, that same "business culture" now busies itself marketing the fashionable New West to people so alienated from the "real" West that even the "Nature" of sexuality must suffer the intervention of a plastic coating. The craze for the West, now as before, involves a cyclical entanglement of myth and money.

Well, let's not get too bleak just yet. Any fashion phenomenon is bound to have a furtive side where the capitalist elves do their manipulative promising and count their cash. Other perspectives need to come into play before we can get a fuller sense of the extent and significance of that phenomenon.

Let's visit the Crybaby Ranch, a store in Larimer Square in Denver, Colorado, that "encores Old West style with fresh spirit" — a phrase that captures the essence of at least part of New Western style. The store was started up in 1989 by two women, one "an aspiring cowgirl" and the other "an interior designer." They're intent on accumulating and selling "ranch and rec-room relics of the '40s and '50s — memorabilia from the days when that independent icon, the cowboy, was king."[7] You enter their store through bold-red double doors that open onto a treasury of vintage furnishings: horseshoe lamps, boot vases, colorful saddle blankets and serapes, Roy Rogers clocks and lunch boxes, classic Western-movie posters, hand-tooled leather mirrors, carved-pine furniture, Indian-theme pillows, a bucking-bronco this, a wagon-wheel that, you name it — all at prices to flatter the egos of a well-heeled clientele. Business is booming. Why?

Roxanne Thurman, the aspiring cowgirl, offers her explanation:

> Cowboy chic, Roxanne says, is more a back-to-basics, put-your-feet-up lifestyle than it is a trend. "It's cowboy with a different twist. It's cowboy that goes into the homes of the nineties — done with a touch of class," explains Roxanne. . . .
>
> "Whatever their home is — Southwestern, country, or whatever — people are starting to incorporate bits and pieces of the Old West, which is a real heritage for Americans," she says. "I see people who like the idea of cowboys being heroes to their children. They like the idea of watching westerns, the idea of the Old West. They love the appeal of it, because it was the good against the bad, and the good always triumphed. It was a very good time in people's lives, and they're remembering that time."

That makes most of the customers, as she remarks, baby boomers. And some want "custom projects" in which an artisan has been able to "improve upon the original, replacing — for instance — stiff Naugahyde with soft leather in reproduction seating pieces."[8]

There you have one of the hallmarks of New Western style in its commercial mode: unlike a number of historians, writers, and filmmakers who are attempting to expose and move beyond the conventional myths of the West, many designers cling to them, nourish them, exploit them by contemporarily redoing them. They shamelessly cater to the desire for a kitsch version of a myth of a myth. The Crybaby Ranch is aptly named, for it appeals to a child's sense of the West. The name derives from a disappointment suffered by Thurman's four-year-old son, but you can read into it overtones of self-indulgence or other kinds of disappointment.

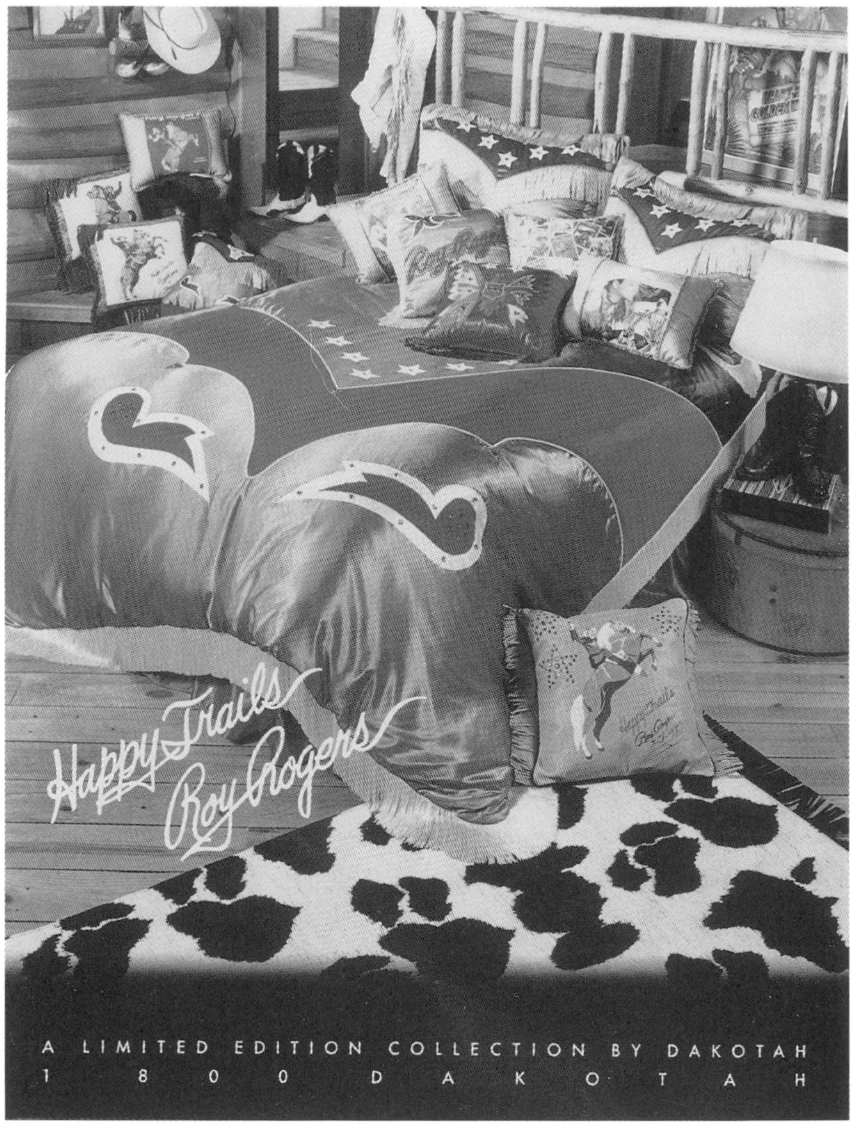

Crybaby Ranch-type decor, here done to excess, of course. (Courtesy of Dakotah)

And yet, if you take that refinished paraphernalia and bric-a-brac a little less seriously, it's fun—even if the prices kite up to absurdity. Simple folk find nostalgic pleasure in it. Sophisticated postmodernists recognize its pretense. The Old West may be "real heritage for Americans," but surely Thurman's customers know that she's selling a somewhat different heritage. Or do they? Many of them, however pathetic the effort appears, may really be looking for something important as they browse through the Crybaby Ranch.

Though its embodiments may be faddy (or as crazy as the articles available from Ruby Montana's Pinto Pony, Outfitters for the Cosmic Cowpoke), we might indeed call that something "real heritage." Or, remembering Dary's questions, we might call it "historical identity," Norman O. Brown's term for the sense of self "made out of identifications: ancestral figures we identify with." The notion is one that Brown develops in a psychoanalytic direction, but it strikes me as immediately pertinent here. So does his emphasis on *reseeing* historical identity: such "revisioning as I have experienced it is not a luxury but life itself, a matter of survival; trying to stay alive in history; improvising a raft after shipwreck, out of whatever materials are available."[9] New Western Historians "do it better" perhaps, but customers at the Crybaby Ranch—or at Sheplers, Vanderbilt's, wherever—may also be revisioning their historical identities, more as a matter of survival after cultural shipwreck than they would or could readily acknowledge. The same holds for people ordering from the Bradford Exchange or God's plenty of catalog outlets or ogling cowgirl playmates.

In a time of drift, the world of Western fashion, for a lot of Americans, provides the only identification with ancestors, the only connection with heritage, they can find. It's not sufficient, maybe, but it seems to be necessary. As for the business end of the thing: you may despise the pimps of "whatever materials are available," but they know a need when they see one.

Tom Averill, a fiction writer and editor of *What Kansas Means to Me: Twentieth Century Writers on the Sunflower State*, gets at that need in a 1992 interview. He's discussing William Least Heat-Moon's contribution to the collection, an essay about crossing Kansas:

> He talked about this negative image [of Kansas], and about how people travel across Kansas at night, partly to beat the heat, partly because there's nothing to see anyway. . . . He delves deeper than that, and says two things. One is that people do that also because at night they can imagine the difficulty and the dangers of the crossing.

> He says if they went through during the day, they'd realize that it was just a fairly normal place . . . , but when you cross at night, it's like a major excursion. . . . Really what you're doing there is sort of pretending still that Kansas is the place that it once was — a place that many people had to cross under very dangerous circumstances, and that people want it to be that way because they still want it to be a part of that great Western experience.[10]

Which is to say, those travelers try to identify with their westering ancestors. Whatever the negative image of Kansas, the state's growing tourist industry testifies to a contagious desire for that historical identification. More and more people each year visit (even in the daytime!) restored versions of nineteenth-century Abilene and Dodge City or follow the Santa Fe Trail on its long diagonal route.

But Averill sees cause for concern about what he calls a "*too* positive" image of Kansas and its region, along with related phenomena over the last twenty-odd years — "the rise of magazines like *Midwest Living* and the way country sort of took over the decor of so many little frou-frou shops, and all the films that started being made about farmers and farm life." His concern is specifically about the Midwest, but by implication it carries to the larger West as well. It has to do with fashionability: "One of my theories is that as soon as we start paying attention to some aspect of our culture, that probably is a death knell; it's a signal that it's on the way out. We want to explore that, or we want to understand it, or we want to grasp at it one last time before it dies."[11]

In other words, what's too much *in* fashion is headed *out* of existence. In regard to the West, such prophecy may be too dire, but it does echo Dary's contention that twentieth-century business culture destroyed nineteenth-century cowboy culture. So one might ask if twenty-first-century business culture, with its global regulation of fashions, will destroy even the remnant mythical aspects of that culture — or change them to the extent that they no longer bear any significant relation to the Western past.

A certain kind of "attention" to the West surely does involve destructive forces. The peaks of Western fashionability over the last century or so have occasioned all manner of havoc. No more than a half-critical beholding of Los Angeles, Denver, Phoenix, and other hypertrophied urban cancers west of the Mississippi will verify that. It makes for acute awareness of the distance between us and what once was, a distance that continues to grow.

In the late 1960s, before the 1970s incremental dry spell of popular interest in the West and its mid-1980s resurgence, Larry McMurtry wrote tellingly of that distance, at least of its version in Texas. For him, then and probably now too, it was "movement, from country to subdivision, homeplace to metropolis, that gives life in present-day Texas its passion," he remarks in the introduction to his 1968 book *In a Narrow Grave: Essays on Texas*. That kind of movement had contributed mightily to establishing "a complex distance from those traildrivers who made my father and my uncles determined to be cowboys to the mechanical horse that helps convince my son that he is a cowboy, as he takes a vertical ride in front of a laundromat." It was a distance that McMurtry wanted to—and did—cover in his book: the distance between "Old Man Goodnight, Teddy Blue, Uncle Johnny and all they stood for" and that vertical ride on a mechanical horse.[12]

However you think of it, such distance has increased since 1968, but the vertical ride still seems a suggestive metaphor for our remote experience of the Old West. It's an emblem for the kitschy artifice of a lot of New Western fashion. It also sums up the relatively sedate, touristic involvements of the New West—compared to the dynamic, horizontal ride that was the historical sweep of the Old West. (And it correlates with the 1960s rhetoric of outer space as the last "upward" frontier.) But if we ride the mechanical horse of fashion, what do *we* "stand for"? To put the question another way, what is it about the vertical ride that helps us feel we are cowboys—or cowgirls or whatever? What are we after?

Well, the West, of course. And what is the West, exactly? One answer I've heard is that it's the part of the United States where most of the states are square. Some people say it's everything west of the Mississippi River and east of the Pacific Ocean, north of the Mexican border and south of the 49th parallel, with diverging opinions as to whether Texas or California, especially their big cities, should be included. Some people stop at the California Sierra Nevada or quibble other demarcations. Interior states like Utah and Nevada are never excluded from anyone's definition. The 100th—or 98th—meridian seems as good a cutoff as any, for it has the advantage of dividing two areas with dramatically different rainfall, the West being dominantly dry. (So you encounter a lot of welcome oases with names like Sweetwater and Crystal Springs.) The West is also an open space of the spirit, as much a mental as a geographical landscape. As the commonplace goes, it's a state of mind. And, however static a mechanical-horse state of mind might seem compared to the state of mind entailed in driving cattle a thousand miles or praying in a kiva in the twelfth century, the West has been and continues to be changeful. Furthermore, the state of mind promoted by the vertical ride involves, to borrow a term from the frontier of computerized-video gadgetry, a kind of "virtual reality" — and thus, to an extent, virtual meaning, virtual heritage, virtual values. A facsimile, something as far from the original as video war games are from actual military combat.

But that's not how it starts, of course. Nobody looks around and says, "By God, I've had enough. Think I'll ride out to the Beaumont Club and round me up some virtual Western reality." McMurtry's son rode that mechanical horse because he wanted to be a cowboy — and that imitation was the best he could do for the one indispensable vehicle of cowboy identity. Likewise, when in the late 1980s a lot of men and women began tentatively putting on Western duds, they were responding to something deeper than a need for virtual reality. Some part of them wanted *the real thing*. Their need, whether or not they could have articulated it, was for a more livable reality than the one they found themselves in. They were dealing with fundamental impulses: a desire to escape the fouled nest of city life, to simplify, to participate in a culture somehow older and more solid than the makeshift of evanescent contemporaneity that whirled about their distracted daily skittering. They wanted cleaner, less anxious, more tangible and immediate, and *less* virtual lives. As feasibly as they could, like McMurtry's son, they wanted to head west, go back, do it better. They still do.

New Westers ultimately want the experience of what non-Indians thought of as virgin land, their own version of Boone Caudill's journey up the Missouri River in *The Big Sky*, that realistic novel of fur-trapper days in the upper West written by A. B. Guthrie, Jr., half a century ago. Or they want their version of Ántonia Shimerda's difficult but direct life on the Nebraska frontier in Willa Cather's 1918 novel *My Ántonia*. Or they want to be like Eddie Swimmer, a Native American hoop dancer who enacts a vision of life's unity and wholeness. Or they want what Jane Tompkins argues that readers of formula Westerns want: escape from “triviality, secondariness, meaningless activity” and into “the fully saturated moment” beyond “the sense that life . . . isn’t going anywhere,” into the “boundary situation” of the Louis L’Amour hero “where everything he’s got is the necessary minimum.”[13] Or they want to know the triumphal moment of the rodeo champion. But what New Westers get is probably only a vertical ride on a mechanical bull, their bar sport of choice, instead — or armchair rodeo on ESPN. Largely spectator fans, most New Westers achieve nothing more than a mood, a taste, an attitude, or, yes, a fashion — though some may well go further than that.

So desires that start out with a measure of sanguine clarity wind up at times fuzzy, diluted, disappointed. Indeed, that’s almost the story of westering. Why? The answer has to do not just with the distance that concerns McMurtry or with the shiftingness of postmodern realities juggled by fashion designers and other magicians of cultural imagery — though they or their earlier avatars are implicated quite a way back, certainly in nineteenth-century rain-follows-the-plow bombast. The answer has to do also and more essentially with the fact that the West has never been simply just *there:* it was, is, and will be, as Richard White puts it, “a historical creation.”[14] In the next chapter we’ll explore that insight at length, but for now I want to think about its relevance to the West as a matter of fashion.

In one of his eloquent essays, the late Wallace Stegner observes that “history builds slowly, starting from scratch, and understanding of a new country depends upon every sort of report, including some that are unreliable, biased, or motivated by personal interest” — an observation true in spades for the West. He lists dozens of such “reports” in a variety of verbal and other media — the journals of Lewis and Clark, geological surveys, dime novels, Currier and Ives prints, photographs, stories from Owen Wister and Zane Grey, on and on. Finishing his inventory, he reaches the main point: “True or false, observant or blind, impartial or interested, factual or fanciful, it has all gone into the hopper and influenced our understanding and response at least as much as first-hand acquaintance has.” He notes moreover that “it took a long time. Even learning the basic facts — extents, boundaries, animals, ranges, tribes of men — took a long time.” As a consequence,

Mechanical-bull operator Craig "Harley" Eddis takes a ride at the Cadillac Ranch in Lawrence, Kansas. (Photo by David Doemland, courtesy of the Lawrence Journal-World *and David Doemland)*

delusion abounded, especially "in the marginal zone between humid Midwest and arid West" where "the individualism of the frontier, the folklore and habit learned in other regions, the usual politics and boosterism, and land speculation encouraged settlement on terms sure sooner or later to defeat it."[15] And, of course, delusion has flourished — and continues to flourish — in other parts of the West subjected to overblown agribusiness or mining, real-estate development, what have you.

But if history is built up "from scratch," it's also true, as Stegner argues elsewhere, that "history is an artifact. It does not exist until it is remembered and written down; and it is not truly remembered or written down until it has been vividly imagined." He speaks here of the role of "novels, works of the imagination," in their interrelations with history "touched . . . with a novelist's imagination" — specifically, literary works like *The Big Sky* and histories like Bernard DeVoto's *Across the Wide Missouri* — as sharing "a characteristic western impulse: they are intent on creating a past, firming up a ground on which the present can stand and by which it can be comprehended."[16] Yet historians and novelists, as Stegner noted earlier, aren't the only people who write and rewrite the Western past. To borrow from Robert Frost's poem "The Gift Outright," "the land" may still be "vaguely realizing westward," but it never was really "unstoried, artless, unenhanced." Rather, it has been storied, artful, and enhanced as far back as you can look, with that looking itself being necessarily reconstructive. It's hard to imagine a time when there wasn't someone, even if only the first human stepping onto the continent, already reimagining the West. In that sense, if no other, "The land was ours before we were the land's."[17]

The people who lived in the West prior to the arrival of the invaders now referred to as Euro-Americans seem to have imagined it in a way that, not without exceptions, ensured a close, consistent relationship to its environment. Euro-Americans, on the other hand, have never really established such a relationship. For them the West, as Stegner puts it, "is less a place than a process" and the Westerner "less a person than a continuing adaptation."[18] That process and the adaptation interlocked with it, from the earliest explorations of land that could be understood only through ideas grounded in previous lifeways, have never been comfortable for those strangers in a strange land. Such unsettled and unsettling people were never likely to "settle" anything. The West was — and in some ways still is — a colony of the East whose identity inheres in endless ambiguous and, increasingly, contradictory stories, in various forms, about itself.

Thus, the West as generally experienced, by Old or New Westers, exists, willy-nilly, as a self-fashioning and self-imitative affair. In that respect it differs little from the cowboys of the late nineteenth century who already had come to see themselves (and represent themselves in their songs and poetry) more and more in terms of popular images of what cowboys were like, images they themselves promoted to some extent — or from Indians who similarly learned to conform to Euro-American stereotypes. For all its emphasis on naturalness and authenticity, the West has a made-up feeling. Even the dominant traditions of Western film and literature, despite their insistence on a certain realism, have succeeded by and large only in maintaining a conventionalized romanticism, satisfying predictable mythic expectations. And that holds true also for much collecting of "realistic" memorabilia, antique gear once used by real cowboys, miners, Pony Express riders, chuck-wagon cooks, whores, gamblers, Indians, whomever.

As surely as *buckaroo* is an Anglo rewriting of *vaquero*, the originality of the American West has always been derivative, patched together out of scraps of cultural cloth both at hand and brought from somewhere else. It has always depended on a contingent reinvention of itself, so no one should be surprised that people, Anglo-Americans especially, have immigrated into the West to reinvent themselves, to bootstrap a new identity that somehow both (re)defines and is (re)defined by what was there before them. That's as true of senior citizens now moving into Sun City, Arizona, as it was of hippies flooding into San Francisco or precariously back to the land in the late 1960s, the rich and famous in their ongoing mania to buy up land in the interior West, or battalions of Easterners seeking a new life in the nineteenth century. Think how many personalities traditionally associated with the West headed there in order to reinvent themselves — Owen Wister, Zane Grey, Wyatt Earp, Teddy Roosevelt — and how dime novels and newspapers then reinvented them again.

To get an idea of how far the process of reinventive bootstrapping can go, rent a video of Robert Altman's 1976 film *Buffalo Bill and the Indians, or Sitting Bull's History Lesson*, based on Arthur Kopit's play *Indians*, first performed in 1968. It's an almost cartoonlike movie, set during winter camp of Buffalo Bill Cody's Wild West show, that entails Cody and his company dealing reflectively with the myth of Cody and his company. It's a less hallucinatory collage than the play, but it makes vivid enough its argument that popular Western history (at least before New Western History picked up momentum) and its typical heroes are more inventions of flamboyant, pretentious showmanship than recovered realities. The further you get into the movie, the more the West feels like Chinese boxes: a movie based on a play based on an absurdist view of the mythic personality who did in fact exploit and help to propagate the myth of the West by running a Wild West show whose carefully arranged events bore little relation to the actual events that Sitting Bull and other Indians who were co-opted into the spectacle had once experienced. I know Old Westers who walked out on the movie in disoriented disgust when it was first shown. It wasn't successful at the box office. Still, intentionally or not, it quite likely contributed to the birth of the coming generation of New Westers, for there were many viewers who understood why, in a synoptically revealing scene, Cody (well played by Paul Newman), in the midst of a huggermugger of props and wardrobe, is flustered because he can't find his "real" buckskin jacket.

On the other hand, a lot of more naïve New Westers now don't seem to recognize the Chinese-boxes ironies of the West that attracts them. They don't see — or don't want to see — how revised, rewritten, redesigned, recommercialized, just downright re-ed, it has been, again and again. (Or, Old Westers might argue, rediluted, reperverted, reruined.) That re-ing, acceleratively fiercer now than ever before, makes problematic any belief that the West is a place or mindset of innocence, uncomplicated values, new life. It also, paradoxically, highlights the necessity to rethink the presence of the West in contemporary culture, American and otherwise, and to reimagine its possibilities — a project that less naïve New Westers don't take lightly.

Perhaps the most cogent reason for the West's being so susceptible to fluidities of identity may be discovered in its lack of what historian Gerald Thompson calls "an overarching historical or cultural experience that crystallizes its identity." For him, two regions may be contrasted in that regard to the West: "the South, whose identity is delineated by slavery, secession, and defeat; and New England, whose identity is defined by Puritanism." The West has no "such common cultural underpinnings" but instead "would seem composed of a series of overlapping characteristics," which he goes on to suggest by listing broad categories that the West usually brings to mind — cowboys, Indians, aridity, "Hispanic influence," mountains, "long territorial experience," and so on.[19]

A signal result of that regional complexity and multiplicity — of history, geography, and culture — is a self-uncertainty that belies the idea of the West as a men-are-men-and-women-are-women place. It also makes a bit silly the practice, to which I have been subjected, of judging whether or not a given person is a "true" Westerner — as if a Zen master were testing a student to determine whether or not he had reached satori. As White argues, refuting the undying notion of "an essentialist West," "there has never been a regional type."[20]

But out of that welter of variability and uncertainty, types, in a range, have emerged, more or less fictitious identities that Westerners and others can assume or use in other ways. They have a feeling of detachability, however, so that it's been possible, for example, for television to reduce the aggregate "modern West," in White's formulation, "to something called life-style, a sort of cultural costume that could be replaced by another costume without changing anything fundamental." Because of that reduction, series like "Dallas" and "L.A. Law," though "being set in the West," were not "of the West, and they were certainly not 'westerns.' They were stories that depended on the West only for accessories: ranches, oil wells, palm trees, and beaches" — trappings like Cody's buckskin jacket. Those stories "communicated the generic joys and tribulations of people who possess large sums of money."[21] They could just as easily have "put on" other regions.

And therein lies the possible joke in the recent fashionability of the West: that it's merely a quickly passing thing, just another opportunity to "accessorize" or collect profitably, another direction in which historians and literary scholars can expand their careers, another mechanism for selling movie-theater tickets and clothing and food and real estate. Only a fool would believe that that couldn't turn out to be the case, since the possibility always comes with the territory of fashionability. I believe nonetheless that it won't — at least no more than partially — for reasons that will become clearer and more convincing in the coming pages. Toward that end, let's have a closer look at some specific phenomena of New Western fashion.

A good place to begin is a special issue (June 1993) of *Architectural Digest*, an expensive interior-design monthly with an international circulation, devoted to the American West. Paige Rense, the editor-in-chief, introduces the issue by invoking a prominent Western personality and offering a teaser for the next issue:

> Last March Clint Eastwood won two Academy Awards for *Unforgiven*, a film that reconfigured our ideas about what the western genre could be. Given his ability to breathe new life into a timeworn form, it's not surprising that Eastwood was able to work a similar alchemy on the Mission Ranch in Carmel, California, which we feature in our July issue. The 1850s farmhouse, set on a twenty-two-acre site with unmatched views of the Pacific and the Monterey coastline, needed help when he acquired it. Since then it's become something of a personal obsession ("I don't buy anything I don't love," he tells contributing writer Susan Cheever), and Eastwood has had the property meticulously restored, transforming it into one of the country's most scenic inns.[22]

Now there's a text that fairly bristles with implications: that a wealthy New Wester like Eastwood can "reconfigure" Old Western architecture into New as readily as he can update Western cinema; that, however much the property has been "meticulously *restored*," it has really been *transformed* into an inn; that the purpose of that transformation is surely as much to make money from the well-to-do who hang their hats there as it is lovingly to preserve the Old West.

Unsurprisingly, the whole issue of the magazine deals with wealthy people who have been similarly — and with increasing zeal — busy reconfiguring or restoring/transforming the designs of the Old West in terms of New Western visions. The intent appears to be to get the reader with extra cash and a hankering for Western spaces on the bandwagon. That's not all bad, of course, and well-off closet cowpokes need to come out with panache. But even a developer as environmentally conscientious as Robert Redford, "a devoted student of the authentic" profiled in the issue who "loved the West long before he became a movie star," admits that it's tricky to control the destructive forces that have come into play with the swelling of New Western greed. As the founder, in 1969, of Sundance, a ski resort and arts community in the mountains above Provo, Utah, he has tried assiduously, he claims (many locals would disagree), to minimize his operation's adverse impact on the environment. But "opportunists on both coasts," among whom he doesn't count himself, " 'attached themselves to me like barnacles, paid lip service to the concept of an area without development, and the minute my back was turned, went about quietly buying up the land.' "[23]

What did Redford expect? Like it or not, he's helping drive the bandwagon and started doing so with the release, in 1969, of *Butch Cassidy and the Sundance Kid*, one of the most commercially successful Westerns ever made, a film that, even as it poked fun at the Western, romanticized and glamorized the West for a whole generation. Its cheerful images of youthful outlaws have persisted on the mental screens of New Westers now middle-aged but affluent enough to get in on the grab, to bring the land in line with their romantic, glamorous visions of "the authentic." Sundance, of course, now has a catalog and offers a collection of home furnishings, clothing, and accessories, much of it in the mode of Redford's more recent film *A River Runs Through It*.

Still, Redford does profile as a person among the most intelligent and realistic of *Architectural Digest*–brand New Westers. Director of the film version (1988) of Nichols's *Milagro Beanfield War*, he "is as famous for his resistance — and his activism — as he is for his movies," Judith Thurman notes, "and has been an aggressive champion of the environment, and not only from on high." He's done his homework, as he demonstrates in a quotation from her portrait of him:

> "Nostalgia is futile. I'm impatient with the armchair romantics who content themselves with the Ralph Lauren version of the Old West. And I'm impatient with a certain kind of idealism. It doesn't do any good to take the high moral ground with people who feel their livelihoods are at stake. They need a financial incentive. The African wildlife preservationists have arrived at the same conclusion. They have to give the farmers an incentive to protect the game, and tourism is that incentive. The same is true of the wilderness. I would have loved to leave Sundance the way I found it, and the way it looked a hundred years ago, but that was impossible — there are no more private nature preserves. We've tried to strike a balance between guarded development and realistic preservation, and to some extent, though I don't like it, it means putting nature under a bell jar. The struggle is

to accept the new terms that overpopulation and overcorporatization have imposed on us."[24]

Though Redford does have a sense of the delicacy of the balance involved and its paradoxes, he completely sidesteps the question of why he didn't just leave alone the area encompassed by Sundance. I guess a man's gotta do what a man's gotta do. Born in working-class Los Angeles, he too was responding to the westering craze now inspiring his financial peers.

Still, if they gotta go West, better by Redford's example than by many others — for some of his peers' pursuits featured in that issue don't seem as enlightened as his. There's a hideaway designed to look like a classic false-fronted Western whorehouse that's tucked ruinously into an opening in an outcrop in the middle of the canyonlands outside Moab, Utah (" 'It's real Marlboro country,' " says one of the owners, who keep a tape of R. Carlos Nakai's flute music "running twenty-four hours a day up on the balcony").[25] There's a house out in the middle of the Santa Ynez Valley in California that's a rebuilt barn brought piece by piece all the way from New England because, as one of the owners puts it, " 'I wanted something that looked as if it grew out of the ground, something that belonged.' "[26] And so on — you get the idea. Some of the habitations featured don't affront my sensibility or the landscape as much as these do, and most of them are maybe even livable. But all of them are reserved for the socioeconomic elite, and I wonder about the costs hidden from the eye devouring their laid-back luxury.

Then look at the articles on collectibles, the objects that you use to decorate the interior spaces of the reconfigured West. In this issue particolored kachina dolls — wooden Hopi representations of the spiritual forces that infuse natural processes, most of them dating from the turn of the century — and cowboy memorabilia receive special consideration.

The former embody a style of carving, observes Ramson Lomatewama, to which "some contemporary carvers have reverted . . . , employing tools common to the times along with natural pigments. This 'old-style' carving may be a statement, a way of reminding us that perhaps life was meant to be plain and simple, and that there is a danger in digressing toward the complexities of modern life." Whatever that reversion to an earlier authenticity means, "kachinas and kachina dolls will continue to play significant roles in Hopi religion and the art world."

That world is governed far more by the flow of electronic money than by the flow of animistic energy, but it's hard to distinguish the two in Lomatewama's New Age enthusiasm: "It will be fascinating to see where they take not only the Hopi people but others as well."[27]

The cowboy memorabilia, on the other hand, are dealt with in a more overtly financial way. Christopher Finch, as they say on the television news, reports:

> Though the classic era of the American West lasted only a few decades, it bred a legion of myths. Yet in many ways the reality was even more dramatic than the hokum propagated by pulp novelists and Hollywood moviemakers. Styles of clothing that originated in the Old West — from blue jeans to cowboy boots — remain current throughout the world, . . . and increasingly collectors are seeking out the artifacts that inspired these fashion trends.
>
> "Nothing is more American than a great pair of wooly chaps or a turn-of-the-century stockman's hat," says Sandy Winchell of Fighting Bear Antiques in Jackson, Wyoming. "The generation that grew up on John Wayne and *Bonanza* now has disposable income available," adds her husband, Terry, "and it's been very natural for members of that generation to turn to western memorabilia." Whatever the reason, the artifacts of the cattle-drive era, and of the later dude ranch period, are enjoying a renaissance among collectors that has not been encountered since the 1950s.[28]

Little mention here of the hokum (or crookery) propagated by collectors, of course, or of how "natural" it is to spend disposable income on spurs that cost, to pick an example from the article, $5,000 to $8,000.

In any case, the revival of interest in Crybaby Ranch–type kitsch obviously has both enlarged and shifted into a boom, as Finch defines it, "in the field of authentic western antiques and high-quality western craft objects of the more recent past (such as bits and saddles custom-made for Hollywood cowboys)." That takes in clothing, bridles, branding irons, and so on — besides items like handcuffs, mining equipment, firearms, and whatnot that comprise other categories of collecting, as well as Western furniture like horn chairs and hat racks. Such items are attracting collectors nearly as strongly as Southwestern items have been for several years. And appalling prices don't cause any flinching overseas, either, where Germans and Japanese appear to have an insatiable interest in cowboy collectibles. Still, the market remains hottest in the United States, most notably in the West itself. As Terry Winchell explains this regionality, " 'In this part of the country, people collect cowboy boots or branding irons because it's part of their heritage. If an item comes into the store that's marked "Wyoming Territory"—which means it was made before 1892—then there's a huge local interest.' "[29]

Finch elaborates on this theme, arguing that "many forms of collecting derive, in part at least, from the desire to forge a link with some past period and culture." He discerns "a special urgency" in that regard in collecting the West "because the past it represents was just the day before yesterday, and the culture it binds us to evolved right here, on the North American continent. . . . The world of the cowboy still resonates in contemporary American life. . . . Small wonder, then, that collectors will pay $250 for a marshal's badge or $2,500 for a fancy bridle. Such objects come loaded with meaning for most Americans."[30] Indeed, those memorabilia have come of age at exactly the right time and in the context of an unprecedented appetite for a certain kind of meaning.

That meaning may not be free of ambiguities. A lot of collectors seem more like just dealers in anything that generates high profits; some seem more interested in escaping history than in verifying it. And doubtless more inauthentic items move through the market than collectors would like to acknowledge. But many people, a growing number, "don't buy anything they don't love," and what they do love is perhaps as close to the real thing as time allows and "forges a link" to a past way of living that, even if half mythical, means more to them than the floating confusion of their present daily routines. That holds as well not only for collectors of Western kitsch but also, more troublingly, for the gullible millions who order Heartland Collection plates that feature cats decked out as "The Dalton Gang," "sculptures" of Sacajawea from the Hamilton Collection, or bargain-price Western-theme collectibles from QVC.

But you can collect Western memorabilia or contemporary items in a manner that's financially safe and honorable—and that will allow you to explore and enrich your sense of connection to the West and its past. Read *Collecting the West: Cowboy, Indian, Spanish American, and Mining Memorabilia*, a 1993 book by William C. Ketchum, Jr., that well fulfills its purpose as, in his words, "a guide to the vast number of new collectors who have, over the past decade or so, entered the area of Western antiques and collectibles."[31] He offers useful advice about

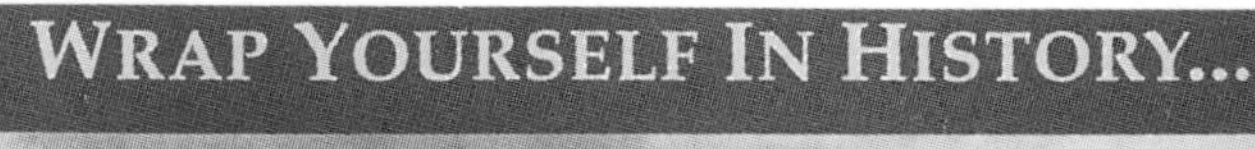

64" x 80" Hopi Trail™ Design© 1993 Ramona Sakiestewa

Honoring the Hopi way of balance and harmony, the HOPI TRAIL™ blanket features a bird and bat motif from 14th century Sikyatki pottery. Designed by renowned Hopi artist Ramona Sakiestewa.

SOUTHWEST TRAILS BLANKETS®
A SERIES
Exclusively from Santa Fe Pendleton / Dewey Trading Co.®

TO ORDER CALL 1-800-645-4434

The Hopi Trail Blanket™ supports the Hopi Foundation in its efforts to promote self reliance within communities and to give voice to universal Hopi values.

An ad for Southwest Trails Blankets: collecting the West as a way to forge a link with the past. (Courtesy of the Dewey Trading Co.®, Santa Fe, New Mexico)

An ad for Bryan Moon's plate "The Dalton Gang": the epitome of New Western kitsch. (Courtesy of Hadley House. ©1994 Bryan Moon. Prints available through Hadley House, 11001 Hampshire Avenue South, Bloomington, Minnesota 55438-2425)

fraud, an analysis of the markets, and a wealth of cultural and historical information about the techniques of hide painters, the various styles of quillwork and beadwork, the spectrum of cowboy kitsch and its relation to movie props and costumes (cowboy funk). And he includes an up-to-date treatment of Spanish American crafts and the limited amount of authentic work (*bultos*, *retablos*, and so on) that has survived.

If you're interested in contemporary Indian crafts and arts, order work from the Southwest Indian Foundation (P.O. Box 86, Gallup, N. Mex. 87302-0001), which provides free catalogs and sends its profits back to the Indians to support schools, homes for battered women, and other such worthy institutions. Or do your shopping directly from the artisans under the portal of the Palace of the Governors in Santa Fe, at the monthly auctions of Navajo textiles held by the Crownpoint Rug Weavers Association in Crownpoint, New Mexico, or in similar situations that eliminate middleman exploitation and foster acquaintance with the people who actually make what you buy.

Above all, learn more about whatever kind of collectible has caught your eye and about the context of its production. If it's jewelry of the Hopi, Zuñi, or other tribes of the Southwest, read Dexter Cirillo's elegant and authoritative book on the subject, *Southwestern Indian Jewelry* (1992), which deals not only with the jewelry itself but also with exemplary artists and their cultures. If it's trade blankets, read the bible on the subject, *Language of the Robe: American Indian Trade Blankets* (1992), by Robert W. Kapoun with Charles J. Lohrmann, a book brimming with historical and practical specifics. Such resources recently have become bountifully available.

If I were asked to pick one place that has been and continues to be the main hub of New Western fashion, it would be Santa Fe, New Mexico, the City Different, almost a living museum. There you can find the obsession in spades. Though it's true that the Southwestern focus of much contemporary enthusiasm about Westerniana has opened out to take in the larger West—an event nicely indexed in the early 1990s by *Southwest* magazine's altering its name to *West: The Spirit of the Frontier Home*—the Southwest still manifests principal aspects of that enthusiasm (witness how Sheplers gradually has acquired a stronger Southwestern accent), most intensely in Santa Fe. That centuries-old town marks the end of the Santa Fe Trail, a crucial passage in the "conquest" of the West militarily, commercially, and otherwise. It's a town of special importance to New Western Historians because its evolution exemplifies a pattern that Old Western History can't readily account for. The words *Santa Fe* printed on a label attached to furniture, a bottle of salad dressing, or practically anything else will cause it to sell like magic; that commodified name has a mantra's power to invoke a New Western mindscape. Santa Fe annually hosts one of the best rodeos around (in terms of ambience, anyway), and it serves as a central marketplace for Indian crafts and arts of all kinds, Western and Southwestern art in general, and Western collectibles. Santa Fe also is justly famous for serving the best of the New Mexican food that figures in many people's concept of the New West. And the distinctiveness of its Pueblo-like architecture has contributed to making it one of the most inflated real-estate markets in the world.

All of that in its particulars — kiva fireplaces, *ristras*, squash-blossom necklaces, tin mirrors, real or simulated earthy-pastel adobe walls, viga ceilings, coyote fences, Saltillo tiles, Nambé metalwork, images of the humpbacked flute-playing fertility god Kokopelli, posole and blue-corn tortillas, annual burnings in effigy of Zozobra (Old Man Gloom), *farolitos*, hollyhocks, chamisa, crisp air, cyanic sky, piñons, contrastive washes of sunlight — all of that and more constitutes what has come to be called Santa Fe style, a style that has reached the point of self-parody.

The high priestess of that eclectic style is Christine Mather, author of *Native America: Arts, Traditions, and Celebrations* (1990) and *True West: Arts, Traditions, and Celebrations* (1992) and, especially, along with Sharon Woods, *Santa Fe Style*, a 1986 book featuring gorgeous photographs and informative commentary and from which the two later books follow as *West* follows from *Southwest*. Mather doesn't define the style rigorously, however, and her reluctance to do so probably has prevented the book from dating during the ensuing changes in Santa Fe. In some ways, though, maybe not that much has changed since 1986. Immigrants to the town find now largely what they found when they first came to appreciate it in the middle of this century: a soulful culture and lifestyle that reflect and are one with what Mather and Woods characterize as "the plain, integrated human setting of Santa Fe and its environs," "the interwoven harmony" of mixed Spanish-peninsular and Native American architectural elements, a sense of landscape "brought into human scale," decorative "spareness," functionality — quintessentially what New Westers in flight from the mire of postmodern dissonance, heritagelessness, and dysfunctional complexity are seeking.[32]

And come to Santa Fe New Westers do, more and more, in part, ironically now, because of books like *Santa Fe Style* that celebrate among others things the town's not being too clotted with tourists and

The Indian Market in Santa Fe: the good-time Charlies are back.

new immigrant population. But here they come: wanna-be cowboys and cowgirls, artists (though many choose Taos instead), New Agers with their crystals and hopes of hooking into a spiritual vortex, phonies and self-reinventors of various ilks, and even a smattering of Old Westers as well. Some care deeply about the heterogeneity. Some, particularly old-timers, find it jarring. They may increasingly long to leave a place that, oddly enough, tends toward suburban homogenization, in attitude and also in the architectural dittoing of outlying developments. They may find Santa Fe too tolerant, even predictable, in its multiculturality.

So things *have* changed since 1986 under the pressure of inrushing New Westers. In that year John Ehrlichman, who moved to Santa Fe in the wake of his implication in the Watergate scandal, spoke too soon about its recovery from the previous time it was rediscovered: "In the mid-Seventies *Esquire* and *Women's Wear Daily* splashed news of Santa Fe all over their pages. With its pop debut, the old town saw an unreal real estate boom and an influx of trendy folk who preempted all the tables in the good restaurants, ran up the price of our turquoise jewelry and made it impossible to find a place to park downtown 'in season.' " But, he adds, "the good news is that the debutante has been jilted by all those good-time Charlies."[33] Now, that's a dated assessment! The good-time Charlies are back, and they certainly jam up the downtown area. Some of them, especially Californians, put off locals with their big-city rudeness, ostentation, and hypocritical environmentalism. They are, at any rate, dominantly New Westers. They want something that's already there — but frequently in terms of needs different from those entangled in the fashions of the less desperate mid-1970s.

Still, just as interest in the larger West supplements that in the Southwest — or even, to an extent, supplants it — Santa Fe style is being supplemented by — or even countered by — a more macho Western style. Montana and Wyoming are really in. If nothing else, the uneasy kinship of the two styles dramatizes the diversity of sensibilities that typify New Westers. The macho style contrasts to Santa Fe style as male does to female, steak-eater to vegetarian, shit-kicker redneck woman to yuppie feminist, the more leathery fetishism of Mather's *True West* to the design niceties of *Santa Fe Style*, or (to an extent) Old Wester to New. In a 1992 piece published in Santa Fe's *New Mexican*, Jura Koncius of the *Washington Post* gets at the distinctions:

> Macho Style is here.
>
> Country Western might be the decor of the moment for Real Men (and Real Women). Think cowboy. A chair big enough for Clint Eastwood to kick back with a glass of whiskey. . . .
>
> It's pony-skin sofas, blanket plaid chairs and wagon-wheel chandeliers. . . . Simpler, gutsier, more-rustic home furnishings are riding high. . . .
>
> It's put-your-feet-up furniture, although preferably feet clad in pointy-toed, snakeskin Tony Lama boots.
>
> Call the look *Northern Exposure* gone chuckwagon. It's distressed leathers, bandanna prints, fringed suede upholstery and funky 1930s style cowboys-on-horseback fabrics. It's the Old West mixed with a bit of backwoods hand carving and the unadorned lines of Mission oak.
>
> This is not sissy stuff. The more bullet holes, knots or barbed wire nicks in the pine, the better.

Koncius's frenetic phrasing embraces here a universe of furniture, and its "buckaroo look" correlates with other facets of New Western fashion, like gun collecting, that hint at a Baber-like masculinist backlash, an inclination that tempers a diffuse New Western tendency to feminize

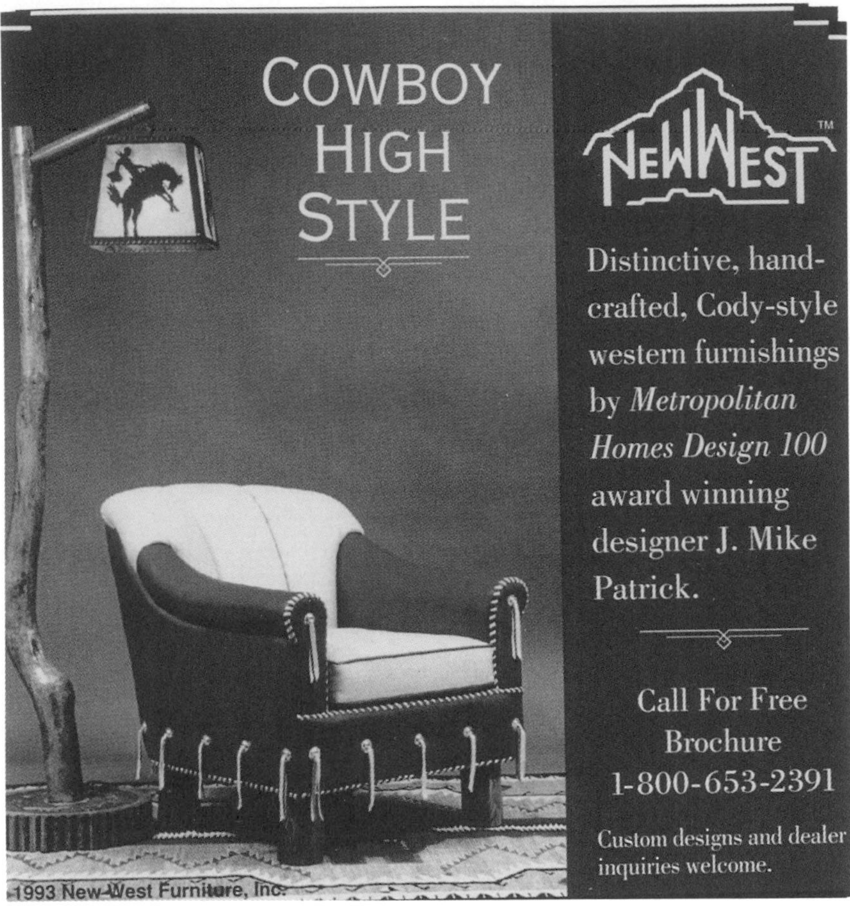

Macho style: "a chair big enough for Clint Eastwood to kick back with a glass of whiskey." (Courtesy of New West Furniture)

the West. Koncius associates the style with "macho types from John Wayne to Sam Shepard," but its redolence may be of Real Men more like the anachronistically sensitive protagonist of *Dances with Wolves*. Still, it's hardly surprising that Eastwood asked J. Edgar Broyhill, who coordinated the design of Mission Ranch, purchased in 1986 (that fateful year again), to furbish it with exactly the "large scale and weighty" kind of "Rawhide"-like furniture that Koncius sees as characteristic of macho style; and Eastwood has lent his support to the establishment of the Mission Ranch Collection as well.[34]

Then, on the other hand, lest this seem just man talk, Mary Emmerling, of *American Country West: A Style and Source Book* fame, has

A Sheplers-equipped couple ready to step out of the catalog and scoot a boot. (Courtesy of Sheplers)

worked up a collection aptly called American Country West for Lexington; and Hickory Chair, Lane, and Tell City, among other furnishers, have developed similar ones — all in counterpoint to the more delicate nuances of Santa Fe style. But it's a yang-yin counterpoint, with macho and Santa Fe styles holding strong together, at times overlapping, each responding to a breadth of needs for identity and heritage, each dependent on the other for the force of what it declares.

Beyond the relatively costly world of New Western collectibles, architecture, and furniture and its stylistic concerns — but intertangled with it — lies the more accessible and accessorizable world of New Western clothing. Wearables, mostly of natural materials, far jazzier than anything most nineteenth-century cowboys or cowgirls

Western wear: portable atmosphere, identity, transWestite statement — even art. (Courtesy of Robin Brown)

ever wore: Stetson hats, Wrangler shirts, Cattle Kate dresses, Roper blouses, Levi jeans, Justin boots, J.C. Penney whatevers. Then add on vests, bandannas, wide embossed-leather belts with dandy buckles as big as your palm, fringed gauntlets, concho earrings. Or go simple with only a band-collar cotton shirt and pocket watch. If you're bold, top it off with a duster or frock coat. Rig up matching outfits for you and the missis. For the kids too. Now in what some people regard as its golden age, Western wear, solidly traditional to costumelike, is hot. It's never really been out of style, but it's in like hell now. It's the most intimate New Western environment, whether or not you live in Wyoming in a reconfigured ranch house full of Apache basketry. It's portable Western atmosphere, identity, transWestite statement. And it doesn't cost much — unless, of course, you get into vintage boots, say, or high-dollar brand names.

Like the recent general Western rage, Western wear started its takeoff in the mid-1980s and was high in its still-rising trajectory by 1992. By that time Ralph Lauren had the hands at his Colorado fantasy ranch dressed in his own Western-look outfits. Young American fashion renegades like Marc Jacobs and Isaac Mizrahi were doing their Wild West shows, and European designers had joined the roundup, along with accessory designers of every school. Long taffeta skirts with denim or chambray shirts were in, as were Western-theme button covers. You'd see women wearing Western boots and Coldwater Creek–cutesy jewelry with couture clothes. Famous people were dressing, up or down, Western. Al Beres's Western belts were touted as instant collectibles, some going for as much as $1,500, Wall Streeters wearing them with Italian suits. Then, as now, a lot more people dressed with a touch of Western flair — belt or boots, say — than in a complete outfit, and sporting a cowboy hat, however you crimp the crown and trim the brim, continues to require more bravado of a New Wester than wearing Noconas mostly hidden under slacks or jeans.

Ah, yes, the boots. All kinds were hot in 1992. They remain so and doubtless will for some time, for they are the one indispensable Western wearable. A pair of them is front, center, dominant on the jacket of Mather's *True West*.

A thoroughgoing New Wester of almost any variety is likely to have several pairs, maybe a dozen or more, for daily or after-work or weekend wear. (The patent exception here, since boots of even minimum quality are made of cowhide or God knows what critter's skin, is New Westers troubled about animal rights. They tend to wear synthetic, athletic-looking shoes, even the kind Roper makes that accommodate pull-on spurs — not boots, at any rate.) People who don't wear cowboy boots can't comprehend the comfort of something that seems to them alien to the shape and operation of the human foot — though I wouldn't argue in favor of the practicality (for a long walk, for instance — unless you're in roper-style boots) of a covering designed originally by a Kansas cobbler (and in a plainer style than is typical today) for buckaroos who believed that Real Men don't descend from the bracing elevation of their horses unless they absolutely have to. And the bootless certainly don't see why a person would want lots of pairs.

But New Westers do want and wear their cowboy boots. From high-sheen ankle-high half-boots to vintage types with appliqués to metal-clad gonzo bronco-kickers to straightforward Acmes to distressed-leather ropers as plain as manual labor. Whether they wear their pants inside or outside (a somewhat disputatious matter of self-presentation). Whether they get duded up like electric horsemen and do a yeeeeehaaah that feels like it has quotation marks around it or just quietly take in some tube with their feet securely and decoratively holstered. They wear Mahans, Luccheses, Fryes, Muleskinners, Tony Lamas, Carson & Steeds, custom-mades of every conceivable kind of snazziness. Tan snakeskin, black lizard, green alligator, red stingray, mauve elephant, pink goatskin, duo-tone wildebeest, you name it. Toes squared off some, rounded variously, or as acute as a condor's claw. Heels downright flat or tall enough to lend a strut some acrophobic pride. Art forms. Most of the possibilities are covered in *The Cowboy Boot Book*, Tyler Beard's 1992 coffee-table tome. Once you get into the habit of cowboy boots, your other footwear tends to gather dust.

Such much-loved boots last awhile, which accounts in part for their being collectibles as well as wearables. But the interest in collecting vintage boots requires additional explanation, which Annie Woods of the *New Mexican* offers: "It seems only natural that baby boomers, reared on a dose of Roy Rogers' and Dale Evans' two-part harmony and classic black and white Western movies, are resurrecting this nostalgic icon of cowboy mystique. Vintage cowboy boots, with their funky styling, intricate hand-tooled inlays and cut-outs and vivid colors, are the epitome of trendy, retro-chic Americana." To achieve this folk-art status, boots must be at least twenty years old, and they can cost a pretty penny. The buyer needs to beware; learn to recognize 1940s boots, with their "squared toes, short tops and underslung riding heels"; and keep an eye out for hard-sought "message boots," ones with writing stenciled on them.[35]

Woods's explanation for the vintage-boot quest may not be the last word, though it's cogent enough. The last word ought to come from someone she quotes after letting others have their loquacious says about boot attitudes (rebellious, exhibitionistic, and so on) and meanings: " 'Boots are about understanding,' said a long-time boot fanatic passing through [Santa Fe] from Nebraska. 'They are totemic.' Try that on for size."[36]

What about the chuck?

By and large New Western food is Old Western food, though you can find lots of recipe variations — all the way to sonofabitch stew turned into something like nouvelle cuisine (calf innards served up expensively as stingy artwork) or chicken Anasazi and salmon Sonora, the sort of thing on the menu at the Silverheels Southwest Grill in Golden, Colorado. But it's still mostly old food cooked and eaten with new gusto: sourdough bread or sinkers, grilled wild boar flavored with mesquite smoke (to the extent that mesquite, like the piñon burned in Santa Fe kiva fireplaces, is being unconscionably overharvested), venison chili, *cabrito, fajitas, huevos rancheros,* Mescalero tacos, *nopalitos,* steaks smothered in big iron skillets, on and on. You can find recipes and other hands-on information in cookbooks like *Barbara Blackburn's Old West Cookbook* (1987) and a spate published since it came out. Much New Western food is Southwestern, borrowed from Hispanic-peasant or Native American cookery. Some is Tex-Mex. Some is traditional Midwestern. Whatever its origin, New Westers who aren't compulsively fructivorous like it served in quantity — and lay on the sauce! Many drink margaritas and Mexican beer, straight tequila with limes for solar ease on a hard night; some have a taste for single-barrel bourbon, the elixir of cattle kings. They've watched television shows like "The Art of Mexican Cooking" and "Great Chefs of the West." They frequent so-called Mexican restaurants that continue to pop up like prairie flowers all over the country. They try their own skills at Western cuisine. And they have more than a little to do with the fact that the buffalo industry (and the price of its product) is growing on the Great Plains, since they've figured out that the meat is more healthful than beef (lower in fat and calories, higher in protein) and the buffalo well adapted to land it once grazed in unbelievable numbers, land that some ecologists aver never was suitable for cattle.

Many New Westers are deeply fond of chile-spiced foods. *Comida sin chile no es comida*, as the Mexican saying goes. And the hotter, the better, for the real aficionados. Chiles provide vivid punctuation for virtually any gustatory undertaking, the wilder ones maybe even a sense of danger, for people weary of frozen dinners, fast food, low-this-or-that blandness. Chiles sharpen the perceptual edges, so that people who usually eat automatically with their heads full of citified anxieties have to pay attention to their enjoyment. (The Planters Division of Nabisco Foods has latched onto this principle in a television ad featuring cowboys in a saloon that promises that even the dull peanut, chile-laced as Heat, can provide snacking not to be forgotten. And fast-taco feederies are now providing optional hotter fare.) Chiles, though slightly salty, have no dire dietary consequences and may well promote good health. Also, in the resolution of their fire, chiles bring an easeful high as bright as Arizona sky. Chiles might well be chosen as an emblem of the kind of experience New Westers are seeking generally: something awakening, authentic, colorful, freshening, as positively immediate as can be found in a world permeated by abstractions — close and cleansing, an instant sauna. Chiles purge and open your soul.

If in all this fashionability there's a longing, however self-deceived, for a last frontier, yet another one after the several that have contributed to the realities and myths of the West, it probably has to do with the Pacific Northwest. The more I learn about that subregion, the more it reminds me of *the* frontier (by conventional thinking): a place defined as much by self-conflicted lunacy as by hope. As the fashionable West has enlarged, popular interest seems to have been flirting with another focus: not the end of the Santa Fe Trail but the end of the Oregon Trail. I began to wonder about that when David Lynch's bizarre television series "Twin Peaks" premiered its doomed run in the late 1980s. Maybe it was just a blip of interest, just as there was a blip of interest in (commercially disastrous) cowboy chic in the wake of *Urban Cowboy* in 1980. But then came "Northern Exposure," a series that, even though canceled in 1995, made for more persuasive evidence: an imaginative melodrama for the young and the Westless done in the more politically correct style of the 1990s and anchored enough in its region — with

Roslyn, Washington, serving as mythical Cicely, Alaska — to escape the criticism that White levels at "Dallas" and "L.A. Law."

Well, maybe. In any case, however much the Northwest differs from the more familiar West in history and mythology and imagery (humidity and flannel versus aridity and leather, for instance), it does appear to be a conceivable candidate for the postmodern last frontier. Timothy Egan, author of *The Good Rain: Across Time and Terrain in the Pacific Northwest* (1990), lends credence to this argument:

> Early on, the settlers in the Northwest developed a reputation for tolerance, and a certain edge. The Cascade Range and the Olympic Mountains walled them in; the jagged coast kept out interlopers. The feeling was, and still is: You could be left alone at the edge of the continent. . . .
>
> Today two types of people are still drawn to the Northwest: those seeking liberation in the scenery — the poets and idealists, the artists and tree-huggers with modems back at the cabin — and those who come here to hide and who view the mountains and raging surf as protection from a world they can no longer control. Thus, Eugene, Oregon is the center of alternative lifestyles. . . . But Springfield, its neighboring city across the Willamette River, is a hotbed of skinheads, mad-at-the-world loggers and religious fundamentalists.

Damn sure we're not in Kansas anymore but in a locale where "the very mist seems impregnated with Miracle-Gro" and from which "the gospel of plaid, grunge and latté-sipping spreads — along with the dark elements of neo-Nazi survivalism and New Age religion-by-credit card." Whether or not the Northwest feels like the old frontier, of truth or myth, it does share some of the latter's traits. It has "an indigenous streak of wacko," attracting "people who are already on the edge" and "who, having sloshed around the country, have nowhere else to go." It seems to be partly accounted for by Egan's observation that "a hundred years after historian Frederick Jackson Turner pronounced the American frontier closed, we still cannot shake restlessness from our souls." It's at once "Ecotopia" and the site for a "24-hour Church of Elvis" (in Portland), a place where "Birkenstock-clad characters" help variegate "a 'homeland' for white people with character defects." An area so riddled with extreme "contrarian impulses" persuades Egan to believe that Turner "had it wrong. The frontier is not dead."[37]

Really? I'm New Wester enough to stay alert to that possibility, even, given the world's thirty-one other flavors of piety, to be half charitable toward Northwestern New Agers. But I'm also Old Wester enough not to want, ever, to trade in my Noconas for Birkenstocks or my Wild Turkey for a cup of esoteric coffee. Still, if Barry Lopez's hints in *Arctic Dreams* prove out, one day we may realize that the Northwest was but a stage in a much more expansive shift of interest — all the way from Santa Fe to the Far North. "The Arctic," he observes, "overall, has the classic lines of a desert landscape: spare, balanced, extended, and quiet." The more he rhapsodizes about it, the more the Arctic sounds like the vast, renewing West that its nineteenth-century chroniclers praised — complete with native tribes whose traditions and very existence are endangered by so-called civilization. One day a New Norther, gussied up in the latest fashion born of Arctic nostalgia that implies profounder needs, may, like Lopez, look out across the Bering Sea and glimpse her own desire: "The landscape and the animals were like something found at the end of a dream. The edges of the real landscape became one with the edges of something I had dreamed. But what I had dreamed was only a pattern, some beautiful pattern of light."[38]

But for now we have New Westers, mostly not the Northwestern breed. And here come more snapshots to suggest the scale of their presence.

The greeting-card business is going more and more Western, with lots of cowboy humor.

Back in 1990, in *Barbie: A Trip to Santa Fe*, a coloring book, the hourglass ideal took a trip to the City Different, where she did a conference presentation on Southwestern interiors. More recently she's been ubiquitous as Western Stampin' Barbie by Mattel.

Like Frederick's of Hollywood, Petticoat County has gotten more-than-fetlock deep into the Western thing, with lingerie sets that carry names like Red Hot Cowgirl and Black Lace Outlaw.

Elderly cowboys and cowgirls can live out their last days at the Silver Spur Museum and Park, a Western-theme retirement home in south St. Louis, Missouri. Employees dress appropriately, and the residents,

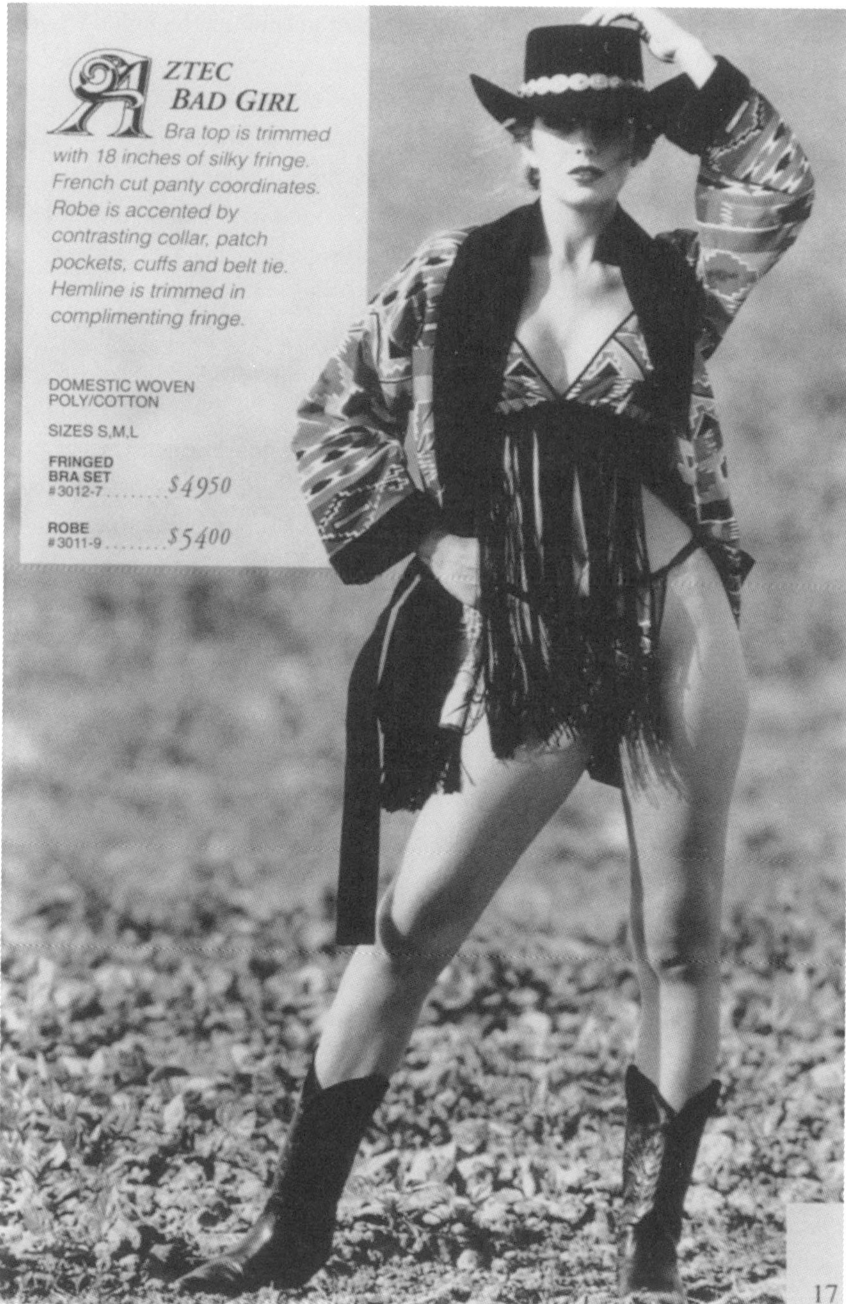

AZTEC
BAD GIRL
Bra top is trimmed with 18 inches of silky fringe. French cut panty coordinates. Robe is accented by contrasting collar, patch pockets, cuffs and belt tie. Hemline is trimmed in complimenting fringe.
DOMESTIC WOVEN POLY/COTTON
SIZES S,M,L
FRINGED BRA SET #3012-7........$4950
ROBE #3011-9........$5400
17

A page from Petticoat County's Western-lingerie catalog: perhaps one of Asa Baber's "sweet country mamas." (Courtesy of Petticoat County)

called desperados, are housed in log cabins and dine at the Gilded Lady Saloon and Dance Hall.

Horseshoeing, a calling that had almost died out a few decades ago, has been making a firm comeback. The horse population in the West is definitely up — maybe as high as it was in the middle of the nineteenth century. And if you want to acquire the farrier's art, places to do that, like the Shur-Shod Shoeing School in Cimarron, Kansas, also are coming back.

Like a spate of other Western-wear companies, which increasingly make use of rodeo and Western-film stars and country singers for endorsements, Wrangler has gone all-out national in its marketing. The result, especially on television, is some of the most magnetic ads ever put together — in terms of mood, landscape tones, the economies of word and picture.

Hardly a day goes by without yet another catalog appearing in my mailbox. More than a thousand are published by Native American sources alone. A number of them are from Miller Stockman ("Where," as the cover has it, "True West Meets New West!") and such established Western-wear sources. But even those from Childcraft, the Linen Source, and such offer more and more Westerniana. And the Quality Paperback Book Club catalog has no shortage of Western-oriented titles to sell.

The holiday season seems to be getting increasingly Westernized. *Better Homes and Gardens* demonstrated the decorative potential in an article, "Cowboy Christmas," in its issue for December 1992. The Mind's Eye featured an abundance of Western items in its 1993 Christmas catalog. That same year saw the publication of Christine Mather's *Santa Fe Christmas*. In 1994 Michael Martin Murphey's *Cowboy Christmas* album was released. Not too long ago I heard somebody on a country-music radio station singing "Don we now our Western apparel."

Western furniture, with or without a buckaroo look, from Habersham Plantation's brightly painted cowboy furnishings to pseudodilapidated pieces from Doolings of Santa Fe, is selling at the multibilliondollar level. Reporting on the first Western Design Conference, held in Cody, Wyoming, in fall 1993, Ann Wilson, managing editor of *West*, noted that furniture makers at the conference "displayed everything from lodgepole-pine beds and sofas to a buffalo-hide chair complete with head and horns to a high-style table with a six-shooter leg."[39]

When the premiere issue of the magazine *Western Styles* came out in summer 1993, on the heels of the premiere issue of the very successful *Cowboys & Indians*, newsstand and subscription sales zoomed beyond editorial expectations. The fall issue had its "Mailbag" section jammed with letters from grateful readers. A woman from Weippe, Idaho, praised the magazine as an alternative to the likes of *Elle* and *Cosmopolitan* and expressed her enthusiasm for "boots, jeans, and the swing of full Western skirts." A retired naval officer from Virginia Beach, Virginia, applauded the magazine's potential to "act as a vehicle" for the "good down-to-earth, realistic Western thinking" that accompanies the present "massive trend" of interest in the West.[40] *Western Styles* switched from quarterly to bimonthly publication in 1994, and the premiere issue of yet another Western magazine, *American Cowboy*, appeared in the spring of that year.

As a cover of *Time* announced in late 1993, it's "Boom Time in the Rockies." Handling the cover story, Jordan Bonfante documented the ongoing progression of Rocky Mountain fever:

> While most of the U.S. is suffering from the blues, or stuck in an outright funk like California, the six states along the spectacular spine of the Rockies — from Montana in the north through Idaho, Wyoming, Colorado and Utah to New Mexico in the south — are prospering happily. . . . Since 1991, economic growth has regularly exceeded 5%, compared with an anemic 1% in the rest of the country. . . . The region's population of 14,380,000 grew 346,000 last year, by far the largest percentage of any area in the country.
>
> On the strength of current migration trends, some experts believe the region may even be on the way to becoming a magnetic pole of a New West, replacing California as the ultimate, mythmaking destination. . . .
>
> The Rockies, perhaps too rosily, are increasingly being regarded as the new American heartland.

Well, such news isn't all good for locals who may not be prospering quite so happily, what with multiplying property prices, stretched-to-the-limit emergency services and water sources, and an excessive number of aroma-therapists or "right-wing cliques and go-it-alone extremists." People in once-sleepy places like Montrose, Colorado, call their invaders New Okies. On the other hand, it's true that for many immigrants "good times in the Rockies are producing a distinctive old-and-new life-style laden with a backpack of paradoxes." There's a "new ethos," as Bonfante put it, that "manages to combine the yearning for a simpler, rooted, front-porch way of life with the urban-bred, high-tech worldliness of computers and modems." With this "basic redefinition of the West," you encounter a lot of people who do remote-site work for downsized, diversified companies. So we have "the telecommuters, the modem cowboys."[41]

New Westers. Eating barbecue at a ranch-style cookout in Sweden. Shopping in a store in Paris called Cowboy Dreams. Firing six-shooters loaded with blanks at a country-music concert in Germany. Camping out in a teepee in Czechoslovakia. Looking in America for something more indigenous than the warmed-over Northern European culture of the East. Trying to save what remains, to recover what has been lost, and to rebuild what has been destroyed in the West. Experiencing the West, commodified or not, as more or less an outsider — but an ardently curious one. Learning, while driving across the Oklahoma Panhandle toward the Llano Estacado, how to lift one forefinger off the top of the steering wheel to greet a fellow Westerner in an approaching pickup, a gesture as precise in its fashion as the signature move of a gunslinger.

Inevitably, in cowboy movies, the boys made a mess. At the peak of the mess, they mounted their horses and rode away. Most of the audience rode away with them, but I stayed behind in the saloon and wondered, who is going to clean up this mess? — Patricia Nelson Limerick, interview, *University Daily Kansan*

MANIFEST DIVERSITY: TURNING TURNER ON HIS HEAD, RETELLING WESTERN HISTORIES

What kind of mess got left behind after the usual story was told? More than broken furniture, bullet holes in the walls, and shattered whiskey bottles, as we'll see. Besides the physical evidence of disorder, what got left behind was, preeminently, the silence of all the diverse stories that didn't get told in the romanticized ruckus of the usual one that did.

The usual story involves, to use the term journalist John L. O'Sullivan coined in 1845, Manifest Destiny, a repeating Old Western saga: white men, the Appalachians long behind, conquer and ride on. It's like a dream whose real landscape has been forgotten or never completely noticed. To see the landscape, you have to get through the dream. To deal with the mess, you have to hang around after the usual story and investigate what else was going on while the boys were having their day. You have to be a whole other breed of New Wester, a New Western Historian, a person who traffics in "manifest diversity," who makes different stories manifest — with a difference. And you'd better be prepared for any trouble you stir up. (A cautionary anecdote: when Ed Whitelaw, a part-time professor of economics at the University of Oregon, testified as a consultant at the widely publicized 1992 federal hearings on the timber industry, just to argue that its history has been and would be one of declining rather than increasing economic importance, he had to have a bodyguard. Westerners with an Old Western belief in the exploitability of nature, a long-ambivalent relationship with the federal government, the logic of Manifest Destiny programmed into their nerves, and their wallets at risk don't like messengers bearing divergent news.)

Who are the New Western Historians? And why are they saying such bad things about Old Western History? Let me begin to answer those questions by recalling a piece I read in the *New York Times* not too long ago. I've misplaced it since cutting it out, but I remember a few particulars. It concerned a course in the Lakota language at the University of California at Berkeley. The enrolled students were almost all white, and many gave a double reason for taking the course: to atone for the crimes of their ancestors against Native Americans and for the omissions of their history teachers. In the course they learned, for instance, that the Lakota word for *Caucasian* means something like "fat, greedy person." Coming into such knowledge, they were necessarily dealing with New Western History — the other side of the coin. They had been taught Old Western History, and they rightly wanted something else and more.

Such desire is hardly restricted to college students. In his 1992 book *Under Western Skies: Nature and History in the American West*, environmental historian Donald Worster writes of how in the mid-1970s his interests, much like those of many people recently, were "swinging back west." The result of that aggregate swing, he observes, is that "today the history of the American West is undergoing a thunderous reawakening, drawing attention from journalists, film-makers, novelists, and undergraduates as well as a new generation of scholars. People everywhere sense that this region is central to our nation's experience and identity, as well as unique in so many ways, and they want to know from historians why this is so and what it means."[1] It follows that what's at stake in the renewed historical awareness of the West, in constructing and communicating knowledge about it through historiography, what the whole debate between Old and New Western History is about, is what the West, to borrow Worster's word, means. And what it means is, beyond all doubt, "central to our nation's experience and identity," to what America means.

Thus, answering my questions as to who the New Western Historians are — what they stand for, even as they differ among themselves or assume intermediate positions in the debate — and why they are saying bad things about Old Western History requires an understanding of the high-stakes conceptual struggle between two kinds of history of a region whose past and present are complexly blurred together. Let me begin our quest for that understanding by considering, in terms of their alternative views, how several prominent New Western Historians have characterized the struggle involved. Essential to any such survey is the 1991 book *Trails: Toward a New Western History*, edited by Patricia Nelson Limerick, Clyde A. Milner II, and Charles E. Rankin. It's a richly documented gathering of position-defining papers by representative New Western Historians at a critical time in the unfolding of their enterprise. Though such papers may lack the fuller treatments of their subjects to be found in the authors' book-length works — to which, as appropriate, I'll refer — they make up for that in succinctness and unencumbered relevance to my purpose. Most of the contributions included in *Trails* are reprinted from special issues — in 1990 and 1989, respectively — of *Montana: The Magazine of Western History* and *Western Historical Quarterly* (the journal of the Western History Association [WHA]). Three are from a symposium in September 1989 with the same title as the book's, which meeting launched the tour across the interior West of the much media-ized exhibition "Trails Through Time," and one was written specifically for the collection by Limerick.

First, let me return to Worster, deemed the dean of Western environmental historians by many of his colleagues. He describes Old West-

In American Progress *(1872) John Gast emblematized in oil Old Western History's positive view of westering as Manifest Destiny. (Courtesy of the Autry Museum of Western Heritage, Los Angeles)*

ern History as grounded in an "agrarian myth" that implies, contradictorily, the possibilities of both endless progress through economic development and escape from civilization already victimized by progress. The myth "was a song, a dream, a fantasy, that captured all the ambivalence in a people about their past and future." Out of it, Worster argues, recalling Henry Nash Smith in 1950 in *Virgin Land: The American West as Symbol and Myth*, "sprang directly" Frederick Jackson Turner's "frontier thesis," articulated in his essay "The Significance of the Frontier in American History," which he presented vigorously but late in the day to a weary audience at the American Historical Association meeting in Chicago on July 12, 1893.[2] (The meeting took place at the Columbian Exposition in Chicago, which simultaneously was hosting William Cody's usual extravaganza, with its far less contemplative — but corollary — treatment of the West.)

For Worster and New Western Historians generally, Turner's thesis (a word that imparts to his ideas an unjustified nimbus of scientific rigor) formed the foundation of Old Western History. His thesis states, to capsule it, that the sequentially shifting frontier was an exceptional place, that westward expansion into its diminishing "free" land explained the American character, and that, as indicated by the population-density figures of the 1890 census, it was closed forever — with uncertain consequences for the country's future. The thesis became the locus classicus for the critique of Turner (which usually has proceeded with more respectfulness than the catchphrase "Turner bashing" suggests or than some New Western Historian bashers have shown) that would begin a few decades later and, even with the richer understanding of long retrospect, reach something like jamboree fervor in the work of New Western Historians at the centennial mark. In 1893 Turner's thesis seemed to account for a world of troubles (social unrest, closing banks, corporations going into receivership); in 1993 it was a general-purpose ideological whipping boy — and, given the political factiousness of the times, hardly a dead horse.

The problems with Old Western History are manifold, according to Worster, and they implicate not only Turner and subsequent Turnerian disciples, like Walter Prescott Webb, but also his precursors, like Josiah Royce.[3] One of those problems is that Old Western History (even that of gloomy Royce) didn't see the degree to which the development of the West early on turned into a destructive affair. New Western History does. The latter sees, among other things, what Ian Frazier sees in a passage from his 1989 book *Great Plains*, to which Worster bends our attention, that sums up the more critical and negative view adopted by New Western Historians (though Frazier doesn't regard himself as one of them). Presenting a staccato narrative description of the mess-left-behind that typically positive-minded Old Western Historians have been prone to downplay or ignore in their myth-infatuated chronicles, the passage concretely refutes the Western Edenic myth, triumphalism, and Turner's exceptionalist thesis and concludes with a sharp smack of apocalyptic warning:

> This, finally, is the punch line of our hundred years on the Great Plains: we trap out the beaver, subtract the Mandan, infect the Blackfeet and the Hidatsa and the Assiniboin, overdose the Arikara; call the land a desert and hurry across it to get to California and Oregon;

One of the photographs in the "Trails Through Time" exhibition: these Coloradoans pushing a car though mud in 1930 suggest New Western History's less positive view of westering. (Courtesy of the Division of State Archives and Public Records, State of Colorado)

> suck up the buffalo, bones and all; kill off nations of elk and wolves and cranes and prairie chickens and prairie dogs; dig up the gold and rebury it in vaults someplace else; ruin the Sioux and Cheyenne and Arapaho and Crow and Kiowa and Comanche; kill Crazy Horse, kill Sitting Bull; harvest wave after wave of immigrants' dreams and send the wised-up dreamers on their way; plow the topsoil until it blows to the ocean; ship out the wheat, ship out the cattle; dig up the earth itself and burn it in power plants and send the power down the line; dismiss the small farmers, empty the little towns; drill the oil and natural gas and pipe it away; dry up the rivers and springs, deep-drill for irrigation water as the aquifer retreats. And in return we condense unimaginable amounts of treasure into weapons buried beneath the land which so much treasure came from — weapons for which our best hope might be that we will someday take them apart and throw them away.[4]

Now, that's not your usual chamber-of-commerce y'all-come-on-out-and-visit-us inventory — self-implicating, rather, at once traditionally anti-imperialistic in tone and postmodern in perspective.

Frazier's portrait of relentless exploitation doesn't take in the whole West, but it gets close enough. It doesn't directly mention women and children, but it intimates plenty of downers for them. It fittingly highlights the baneful roles of the military and the defense industry. But it neglects to mention that, if those doomsday weapons do get thrown away, they will probably wind up somewhere in the West, in the "empty" spaces that always come to mind first when Americans need to experiment with newfangled war horrors, stash obsolescent military hardware, or dump hazardous waste or big mistakes.

So, for Worster, the much-vaunted "liberty" associated with the West has resulted in "an ambiguous achievement" of which "westerners are more aware . . . than ever before." He endorses Smith as "the first bona fide revisionist, in a sense the prophet of a New Western History, . . . for it was he who first [in *Virgin Land*] told us what was wrong with the old history and dared to call it myth." Which is to say, it was Smith who helped Westerners begin to see their region in terms of what had gone awry and wasn't taken into account by myth, which Worster defines, generically, as "the grand archetypal stories of heroic origins and events that all peoples create for themselves, a kind of folk history written by anonymous minds." As Smith himself did later in his life, Worster grants that "in truth popular belief and historical reality are joined together in a continuous circle, moving back and forth in a long, halting, jerky interplay." But he also recognizes that "there is a lot of falsity in any myth" and that "such falsity can lead people into difficult, even tragic, situations" — especially in a region beset by violence whose main myth "was a story about a simple, rural people coming into a western country . . . and creating there a peaceful, productive life." It may well be the case, I'd add, that the worse things got in reality, the more the myth was desperately embraced — a slippage that many New Westers now may be caught in, despite (or even because of) their informed skepticism. In any case, the New Western Historians are on the scene, and "for this region that was once so lost in dreams and idealization," Worster claims, "we have been creating a new history, clear-eyed, demythologized, and critical. We have been rewriting the story from page one and watching it be accepted."[5]

That's a grand claim, to be sure, since all historicizing inevitably does its own sort of more or less implicit and unconscious mythologizing — by substituting, say, the myth of a fallen Eden for that of an ideally innocent one. Furthermore, of course, given what's at stake, not everybody accepts the rewritten story or thinks it's being properly done or agrees that it's new. In the 1990s there may be few dyed-in-the-wool Old Western Historians around to assail that story, but it has had opponents from the beginning of the decade — see, for instance, Sherry L. Smith's sympathetic study of the military's problematic role in the West in her 1990 book *The View from Officers' Row: Army Perceptions of Western Indians*. Opposition ranges from qualified rejection to outright viciousness. Exemplifying the former, Gerald Thompson criticizes New Western Historians for leading a "politically correct posse" in the tricky "lynching of Turner's ghost," for being inconsistent, ignoring demographic records, and failing to acknowledge the limited but substantive revisionary inquiries of their predecessors. Though he doesn't accept "many parts of Turner's thesis," he agrees "with Turner's general proposition that moving west proved beneficial for most Americans"; and he thereby can't condone the negativity of New Western Historians, whom he judges unlikely to create "an interpretative framework that supplants the old frontier model."[6] Exemplifying the other end of the range of opposition, Gerald D. Nash stridently — and somewhat irrationally — accuses them of intellectual totalitarianism.[7]

But surely William W. Savage, Jr., has proven to be New Western Historians' most cold-jawed and wittily acidic disparager. Though always opinionated — and at times remarkably perceptive — concerning matters of the West, he vents unrestrained fury on the subject of New Western Historians, referring in one published piece to their field as "whorishly fashionable," to their approach as "self-serving" and marked by "increasingly dogmatic posturing," and to them as "cranky and mean-spirited." He admits the limitations of Old Western History (a discipline that got "mired . . . in Turner worship" after overvaluing "his haphazard thought") and the "validity" of being concerned with the histories of "ethnicities and genders," but he also argues that "nations need their myths" and apparently endorses the notion "that what people choose to believe about their past is more important than the facts of their past." If millions of Americans prefer "glory" to "gloom," so be it, he says — and New Western Historians who label them "demented" are parlously defying that preference.[8]

Larry McMurtry doubtless speaks, less rancorously, for many dissenters when he contends that the tragic dystopian version of the West has already been told — and told better — by earlier historians (Henry Nash Smith and others). Likewise when he compares the New Western Historians' eclectic revisionist project to a Herfalo, a freakish hybrid that the famous cattleman Charles Goodnight once produced by crossbreeding a Hereford and a buffalo.[9] Indeed, there has been considerable resistance — that prime mover of debate — to New Western History, though it appears to be weakening as Old Western Historians die out or are read less and the public realizes that New Western History, however much repetitive or imperfect, exposes and illuminates situations that must be addressed.

Whatever may come in that regard, when the reaction against Turner was well under way in the 1950s and 1960s, two decades of historiographical change that pivoted on the founding of the WHA in Santa Fe in 1961, there were basic problems not just with the content of Western history (in some neglect as American historians focused on pressing post–World War II national and international issues) but with its style as well, according to Worster. Historians contemporary with Smith, like Richard Hofstadter, found a superfluity of blandness in the Turnerian approach, a lack of intellectual discernment. They wanted a more academic style, one that would prove useful in treating the increasingly more complicated events of Western history in the modern period: rising multicultural immigration, deepening financial dependency on the East, metasticizing federal entanglements, technologization, urbanization. As Worster makes clear, when Western historians moved beyond the frontier, they also moved beyond the old narrative style: "The postwar generation of historians, led by scholars like Earl Pomeroy and Gerald Nash, discovered the twentieth century. The West did not suddenly end in 1890, . . . they declared, but was at that point only beginning its ascent to prominence. . . . The legendary man on horseback fighting against a horde of menacing savages, the plowman toiling alone beneath a prodigious sky, all but faded away in this nonagrarian, professionalized, heavily footnoted, technology-centered, city-based redefinition of the region's past." Those historians didn't go far enough, however. Their style also was marked by blandness but of a different kind: "Their books and articles could almost have been introductions to company reports or state tourist brochures trumpeting the arrival of a 'New West.' "[10] They had broken the spell of Old Western History, but they hadn't found a distinctively new voice — soon to become plural — or, quite yet, the darker tale — also soon to become plural — it would tell.

That situation began to change in the late 1960s or, as Worster has it, "around the year 1970."[11] McMurtry's *In a Narrow Grave*, with its candid assessments of Texas and its history, shows signs of a shift in the wind. Certainly Vine Deloria's 1969 book *Custer Died for Your Sins: An Indian Manifesto* does. It abruptly introduced a persuasive alternative viewpoint — that of a Standing Rock Sioux — into the historical conversation and anticipated Native Americans' more intense preoccupation with relating their version of Western history. But, like Worster, I find the missing voice and its darker tale emerging most significantly in Dee Brown's *Bury My Heart at Wounded Knee: An Indian History of the American West*, published in 1970. Controversial (partly because of questions concerning authenticity), that best-selling indictment of the United States' military aggression against Indians didn't outline the future course of New Western History, but it did offer an alerting taste of what it would be like.

Brown had a perspective diametrically different from that of previous official histories of Native Americans. Just as important, his audience, mostly a youthful and very interested one, was hip to the practices of America's long-denied internal imperialism. His audience saw its consequences (Indian reservations as symbols of violent intolerance, paternalistic Americanization gone haywire), its nationalistic acceptance of cultural diversity only if such didn't affect the established order, and its translation over decades into experiments in international colonialism that had turned into disasters. His audience, in other words, was more than willing to listen. Worster again:

> A younger generation, shaken by Vietnam and other national disgraces — poverty, racism, environmental degradation — could not pretend that the only story that mattered in the West was one of stagecoach lines, treasure hunts, cattle brands, and wildcatters, nor for that matter aircraft plants, opera companies, bank deposits, or middle-class whites learning how to ski. What was missing was a frank, hard look at the violent imperialistic process by which the West was wrested from its original owners and the violence by which

> it had been secured against the continuing claims of minorities, women, and the forces of nature.

The stage was set. Brown had heated up the mood. Enter the New Western Historians, ready for "confronting and understanding those radical defects of the past," for restoring "to memory all those unsmiling aspects that Turner wanted to leave out."[12]

Since 1970 — and unremittingly since the mid-1980s — such revisionist historiography has made and continues to make a cluster of "important arguments." That activity involves, as Worster explains, not a pretense of scientific objectivity but the historian's commitment to an intellectual critique of ideology, to taking an outsider's perspective, even to acting as "a self-appointed moral conscience." It involves also a willingness to assume different positions *inside* the West: "to look at the past through the eyes of an American Indian" (Brown's accomplishment) or "to look, as it were, through the eyes of the rest of nature" (what John Muir was about, a century ago, in his efforts at environmental reform). More and more it involves what Worster calls "the program of the New Western Historians," which he outlines:

> To find ourselves prefigured in our ancestors and find in them the origin of the problems and questions that plague us today;
>
> To achieve a more complete, honest, penetrating view of those ancestors as well as of ourselves, including the flaws or ironies in their achievements, to question their and our collective successes, to explore other points of view, and to discover new values;
>
> To free ourselves from unthinking acceptance of official and unofficial myths and explanations;
>
> To discover a new regional identity and set of loyalties more inclusive and open to diversity than we have known and more compatible with a planetwide sense of ecological responsibility.[13]

A daunting program, perhaps, but one to which, however it might be restated, most New Western Historians would subscribe.

Certainly that's true of Richard White, another environmental historian, who's best known for his 1991 book *"It's Your Misfortune and None of My Own": A New History of the American West*. There and elsewhere he distinguishes New Western Historians from Old in terms of vision: where the latter "see nature," the former "see the debris and consequences of human use" (not the Oregon Trail but the trash in its wake — stoves, kegs, harnesses, whatever). He disarmingly contrasts Old Western Historians, "who rode high in the saddle," to New Western Historians, who "tend to be kind of nebbishy." The former draw "bold lines" in dividing up the physical West. The latter discern nature and culture in a blurred and frequently unpredictable interrelationship. The two travel similar routes, but they have "different experiences" and end up "in very different places."[14]

White offers other points of distinction, and they foreground important issues of difference. Old Western Historians "usually write comedy" (stories with "a happy resolution"). Some New Western Historians — White mentions Worster here — tend to write tragedy, a kind of narrative not quite as "gripping and ultimately satisfying," but "most end up with the far less satisfying mode of irony," which typifies any story of achievement at odds with intention. They tend also to suspect Old Western Historical formulations of "an essentialist West that produced . . . men able to overcome and dominate a feminine nature." With their "relational outlook" they study the West not as an environment that gave rise to a certain kind of person (*man*, in Turner's and Webb's formulations) but as "a series of relationships established within that place which inevitably changed over time." By this approach, *range*, for instance, "is no more an environmental category than is a parking lot. It is a cultural category defined by how we intend to use the land." For New Western Historians, then, the West is not homogeneous but "full of diverse interests and conflicts" that interconnect through differing perceptions, goals, and transacting power structures that ceaselessly change. What White and his colleagues investigate is "a more complex West," its trails "more a maze than a simple line" and its "land and people constantly in the midst of reinvention and reshaping" rather than resolved into some timeless mythic holding pattern.[15] A fluky process. An ongoing merging of peoples and cultures, a *mestizaje*.

Another sure subscriber to Worster's program is Patricia Nelson Limerick, a recipient of a MacArthur Fellowship (a so-called genius grant) who once described herself at a lecture I attended as "Worster's Frankenstein monster" and reigns, some say, as the queen of New Western Historians. She has definitely achieved public visibility, particularly since the media coverage of the "Trails" symposium, for which she was the principal scholar, but she made a polemical splash before that, in 1987, when her book *The Legacy of Conquest: The Unbroken Past of the American West* was published. That engrossing work continues to be widely read, with plenty of New Westers sympathetic to its hardheaded study of a region simultaneously glamorized and trivialized, still cursed with the consequences of conquest, and misconstrued.

Noting that the 1989 "Trails Through Time" exhibition, with its disenchanting images of the West, "got wild fast" through publicity, Limerick depicts the two histories in intergenerational conflict by a suitably Western personification: it's "a showdown, with the Old and the New taking aim at each other from opposite ends of Main Street." But she shows kindness to Turner: though he may have overdone his thesis, he would, with his call for new hypotheses in his later book *The Frontier in American History* (1920), surely comprehend the rationale for the "Trails" symposium. And she reminds those people prone to forget the cycles of things that his thesis was "quite solidly trounced in the 1930s and 1940s," only to be salvaged at mid-century by Ray Allen Billington and other scholars — so we're really talking about a "Restored Old Western History" under attack.[16] Like Worster, she dates the beginning of action back to the late 1960s, at which time the paradigm of that history began to crack, though its adherents tried to incorporate, peripherally, some of the left-out stories that threatened its premises.

Limerick, rehearsing the predicament that all historians face, the tension between ideal objectivity (history as pure facts) and hopeless relativism (history as incompatible points of view), judges that Restored Old Western Historians had worked out a predictable and familiar reconciliation: "They had in fact placed their sympathies with English-speaking male pioneers and then called that point of view objectivity." She argues that New Western Historians abjure such conflating and typically believe that the emotions and values in play in the writing of Western history shouldn't be veiled by an illusory objectivity but put "on record," up front.[17] Worster's monster indeed, she strongly advocates New Western Historians' candid expression of pride in their region and what they espouse for it. For her, that's simply a matter of taking the West as a real place with a complex and momentous history.

Westerners, according to Limerick, frequently seem quite open to the frank, personal judgments that that approach entails. Finding New Western Historians less dour than they expect, they also find a realism about economic to-and-fros, land-management struggles, and intercultural difficulties. If New Western History is disillusioning, it seems to be so to a degree that many New Westers — and Old — reckon appropriate. Though some critics may be disappointed that the activities of that history don't adhere to "a party line of 'political correctness,' " those with an appetite for disputation rejoice in its being "fundamentally a free-for-all."[18]

Limerick construes that ongoing discussion as "the finest opportunity imaginable to revive the role of the western public intellectual." It's an important role in these confusing times of limited public thought, in the perspective of which New Western History may be classified as "part of a much broader regional movement" whose several aspects suggest the extent of New Westers' interests and involvements: "In fiction, in poetry, in landscape photography, in painting, in architecture, in legal thinking, and in environmental sciences, westerners are taking the West seriously, putting together a firm, grounded sense of where we really live, how we got here, and on what terms we can continue to live here in each other's company." Limerick praises that movement for its potential to make the 1990s "a decade in which westerners might become settlers, and not unsettlers, of the region."[19] Contrary to media images of New Western Historians as merely grim reapers of Old Western myths, Limerick presents herself and her colleagues as affirmative and hopeful contributors to that movement.

The orientation that Limerick brings to the study of Western history derives in many respects from her own past. Now a professor of history at the University of Colorado, she grew up in Banning, California, a town on the edge of the Mojave Desert. There she experienced a respectable variety of Western phenomena: cattle business, forest fires in the mountains on either side of the San Gorgonio Pass, the aridity of the desert, the manifold multiculturality of the town (home to Cahuilla Indians, Hispanics, African Americans, Filipinos, Caucasians of sundry backgrounds). It's no surprise that her awareness of the West would differ from that of Turner, who grew up a century earlier in water-rich Portage, Wisconsin, far from a milieu of such diversely Western character.

Nor is it a surprise, therefore, that Limerick, in *The Legacy of Conquest* and other works, would come to perceive the geographical boundaries of the West as "fuzzy," its processes of change as not unique but similar to those elsewhere, the term *frontier* as useless or counterproductive, Western "progress" as thoroughly mixed up with regress. If she shows impatience toward those people who would preserve the image of the Western public as "cheerful fools" trapped in "appealing and colorful legends," that's understandable: she knows that public to be largely not so. Furthermore, the region isn't all "dilemmas": it has "its charms" as well, and New Western Historians cherish them. They also work at "dissolving the great divide between the 'Old West' and the 'New West,' " for them as troublesome a gap as that between frontier and postfrontier eras. Their study of the West, as Limerick sums it up, "simply does a better job of explaining how we got to where we are today" than does Old Western History.[20]

Elliott West, a historian who emphasizes demographics and has authored, among other books, *Growing Up with the Country: Childhood on the Far Western Frontier* (1989), would agree. Arguing that "the prevailing view of the western past has changed more in the last ten years [the 1980s] than in the previous ninety," he notes that new themes (diversity, the relation of the West to the rest of the world, and so on) are weaving a history that "feels different," one that shows less interest in top-down romantic heroism and more in the somber data of "cultural dislocation, environmental calamity, economic exploitation, and individuals who either fail outright or run themselves crazy chasing unattainable goals." For him, much is gained by that bottom-up perspective: it allows "a fresh look at particulars."[21]

In the old view, "adult white males" *are* Western history; in the new view, "the story of settlement is finally going coed" and taking into account the whole family as a powerful force in populating and physically and culturally shaping the West. The story tells of single women who homesteaded and ran ranches or businesses, of wives who held households together, of children. It tells also of Indian women, Chinese, Basques, and others "not all blue-eyed sons of Albion." The new view affords a way of looking back to the very beginning of Western settlement, a 25,000-year span, and forward to contemporary immigration from the South. In that stretched vista, "Indians and Hispanics may have been militarily subdued, but when we start to reconstruct the details, we find that, contrary to the usual 'triumphalist' view, those cultures have been remarkably resilient"—and have endured through intricate interrelations with the people who labored to conquer them.[22]

West engages also another kind of view: the one, which Worster's program includes and West's book on childhood adopts, that "looks from the inside out." A concern of ethnohistorians and others, it deals with how the varied peoples in the West have experienced it, what it *means* to them, to recall that crucial word. How did Native Americans perceive their Euro-American invaders? How did women size up the new country in relation to what they had left? What did African Americans migrating after the Civil War make of it? To wrestle with such questions, West and other New Western Historians turn to all manner of documents: diaries, journals, and the like, as well as "the region's literary and visual iconography." West is very much aware that "a 'new fiction' . . . has grown up alongside the new history," that it offers "emotional insights quite in line with recent historical works" — a matter to which I'll return in the next chapter — and that both are part of what he terms "a maturing understanding of the West."[23] Life-writing, biography and autobiography, figures more and more in this West-as-a-state-of-mind history, which can encompass everything from speculative psychohistory to Robert Utley's *Billy the Kid: A Short and Violent Life* (1989).

That last development appears ironic since Western history suffers the slights of many academic historians because it "has been characterized as glorying in narrative at the expense of analysis," in the words of Brian W. Dippie. Dippie, author of books on Custer, Western painters, and U.S. Indian policy, would contend, however, that the irony is only apparent, given the more analytical feel of much recent historical narrative — though such a change risks alienating a public, including more than a few amateur historians, enamoured of "the colorful and peripheral" that enjoys reading stories about Calamity Jane and Liver-eating Johnson. And Dippie has a sophisticated position regarding the ends of such narrative. He understands the appeal of Turner, who read his fateful paper in Chicago at exactly the time when the frontier seemed closed. (Sitting Bull had been killed in 1890 shortly before the Wounded Knee tragedy; Chicago's own urbanization hinted at the end of Jeffersonian agrarianism; and so on.) He understands also the appeal of history written in terms of "a coherent, self-flattering vision of the American past," a thesis whose "sweeping imagery and elegiac tone nicely matched the nostalgic mood that, in the twentieth century, would make the mythic Wild West a global phenomenon." He insists, however, by an amplification of Worster's program, that that vision/thesis should be not only recognized and taken seriously as a myth but also (and here is Dippie's most astute counsel) intensively *studied* as such. In addition, "frontiering" should be seen not as a special American process but as "a global phenomenon," that of colonizing, in which America itself once served as a sort of West for Europe. In that regard, he underscores the role played by Earl Pomeroy in placing frontiering in the larger contexts of other myth-laden quests for "fulfillment in some elusive Elysium" and of Western history "as a continuation of eastern development."[24]

Territorial studies of the kind Dippie advocates construe the West thus contextualized not as the wilderness of the self-reliant wanderer but as a dependent colony of the East controlled by its tycoons, cowboys not as romantic knights but as hands hired into the service of cattle kings, gold rushes not as adventures of individual prospectors but as enterprises of corporate capital (much of it British). Western history thereby becomes less a coherent story and more a dispersal of topics under investigation. The myth of the Wild West as the American dream looks more and more like what Webb said it was decades ago: an image manufactured by "outsiders meeting outside needs." The myth of Old Western History generates the more self-conscious "anti-myth" of New Western History, a situation in which Dippie calculates more profit than loss because the two can function as "keys" to the pasts and presents of both the West and America.[25]

Yet, in spite of the professional excitement accompanying such analytical advantages, Dippie discerns "a persistent malaise" among Western historians, New and Old. It derives, according to him, from an inferiority complex haunting and exacerbating their conceptual struggle, an anxiety that the discipline that has too often been labeled "the 'cactus and sagebrush' school of history" has reached a "crisis," with "the last roundup imminent." The Harvard that once was Turner's academic home found little of interest in Limerick's intellectual passions when she was at the Charles Warren Center there and evidently holds open no door to Western historians and their parochial "glorified antiquarianism." There's a discouraging dismissiveness in that colonialist attitude, according to Dippie: "Easterners . . . dismiss the yokels 'out there' in 'flyover country' with their cowboy hats, red necks and empty faces designed, as Leslie Fiedler reported years ago after escaping from the horrors of intellectual isolation in Montana back to the safety of New York, principally for squinting into the setting sun."[26] But, with all respect to Dippie, that attitude is beginning to change saliently as New

Western Historians grow in their professional self-assurance and enlarge the perspectives through which they study the West, as the economic and demographic center of the nation shifts west, as New Westers escape from the horrors of New York to the safety of Montana. The West is less and less dismissed — by snobbish historians or anyone else.

Michael P. Malone, a historian who is president of Montana State University and has written several books on Montana history, along with *Historians and the American West* (1983) and, with Richard W. Etulain, *The American West: A Twentieth-Century History* (1989), maintains a less worried hope for Western historians than Dippie. In many ways critical of New Western History, he nonetheless believes that there's ample cause for celebration since the founding of the WHA in 1961. He even quotes a Western historian from Yale (where Limerick, under his mentorship, received her doctorate), Howard Lamar, to that effect. Though Malone acknowledges that many historians still confuse "the West as a defunct frontier process" with the West as a region and neglect the study of it as the latter, he's most sanguine about the possibilities of "a revised approach to interpreting the region and its history."[27]

Malone thus acknowledges also the durability of Turner's thesis, especially as modified by Billington and others, as well as the contributions of its adherents to "good narrative history" with broad appeal. But he faults that history's ignoring Western urbanization and industrialization, intentness on cultural assimilation instead of differences, and so on, and he commends the recent corrective efforts of historians like Walter Nugent and Paul Kleppner who have brought "social-scientific rigor" to the study of the West without losing the ability to write accessible prose. He gives his blessing to a number of innovative approaches, but he finally insists on the logical necessity of an "interpretive model" based on the factors that bond the West together as a region. He proposes four: "(1) the abiding aridity of the West, (2) its exceptional reliance upon the federal government, (3) the recency and residual aura of its frontier experience, and (4) its still heavy dependency on extractive industries." The list hardly sounds as exciting as tales of cowboys and Indians, and it might serve as a hide-out for New Western essentialism or exceptionalism; but Malone makes a cogent, if not exciting, case for those factors, and his cosmopolitan wielding of his model allays fears about hidden isms.[28]

The warrants for Malone's case are, with a qualifier or two, unequivocally New Western in emphasis and might strike many people with the force of revelation. The crucialness of aridity is scarcely a new matter, and Worster has dealt with it influentially in his *Rivers of Empire: Water, Aridity, and the Growth of the American West* (1986); but it assumes fresh meaning in a West that Malone dubs "the most urban part of America," where obtains the incongruity of "great cities surrounded by endless desert expanses." The extent of federal ownership likewise makes for a waker-upper, with Nevada, for instance, at 87 percent and "no state of the Far West" at less than 29 percent (whereas such ownership in Eastern states never exceeds 12 percent).[29] The implications, historical and otherwise, astonish.

Though Malone concedes the value of Limerick's "presentist approach," he disagrees with her emphasis, especially in *The Legacy of Conquest,* on the role of regional conquest and urges concentration on how "a major part of the region's shared cultural heritage lies in the drama and recency of the frontier's passing . . . and in the very fact of the region's preoccupation with it." Like Dippie, he advises the study of cultural aspects of the frontier, more or less mythic, that haven't passed at all. What he calls "this 'Old West' syndrome" is hardly strange to New Westers. As Malone observes, you find it "everywhere west of Kansas City and Dallas, particularly in the rural interior: cowboy clothes, music, art, food, and jargon; pickups with rifles in the rear window; . . . a 'Mint,' 'Longbranch,' or 'Stockman's' bar in every gulch; round Skoal cans in the backpockets of ragged jeans. For good or bad, it *is* what most westerners think is their heritage. It is what they mean by 'West.' " Well, you find that syndrome more and more in plenty of elsewheres too, and it has to do not just with a Western but with a distinctly American sense of heritage. But Malone's point is that the historian's problem with the frontier is *not* its "unreality" (refuted by its refusal as a way of thinking to vanish); rather, it's the fact that "the Frontier school tilted toward Filiopietism, exclusivity, and insularity and away from cosmopolitanism and multicausal contexts." The trick for Western historiography is to get a better fix on "the frontier phenomenon" by putting it "in better regional and global focus," by doing what Malone's own work on the northern West exemplifies, what Pomeroy started doing in the 1960s.[30] And that better focus demands not the squinted John Wayne eyes of the Old Western Historians but the wide-open eyes of the New.

Malone's consideration of the West's dependency on extractive industries makes a distinction between two types of frontiers that recur globally. Of those two types, "Type I (stable-agricultural) and Type II (unstable-extractive)," as depicted by Nugent in his statistical-demographic research, Malone conceives the second to be more applicable to the study of the West than the first, which carries Turnerian, even Jeffersonian, connotations. Though you might well argue that agriculture has played a plentifully significant role in the West, not always as a force for stability and maybe, given soil depletion and aquifer consumption, more and more as an extractive enterprise, his choice still seems justified. The West has relied heavily and widely enough on what are conventionally termed extractive industries — lumber, copper, petroleum, coal, and so on — for them to constitute a regional bond. Moreover, because the West has depended on those unstable industries more than other regions, it "has paid the price in a long succession of boom-and-bust cycles" that have run through one "collapse" after another: "of placer mining in the early 1870s, of open-range cattle ranching in the 1880s, of silver mining in the 1890s, and of homesteading in the 1890s and the years following World War I." On and on — maybe more to come. In Malone's view, the study of those industries and their destructive cycles has been disregarded for two reasons: "the persistence of a frontier interpretation that for decades has shunted historians away from post-1890s developments and a failure to see that old-time frontiers and continuing exploitations of resource bounties are really two aspects of the same process."[31] Doubtless I speak with the arrogance of hindsight, but I'm amazed at the failure to see the connection.

Whatever the ocular disorders of past historians, their successors have a potent tool of vision in Malone's interpretive model. Unlike Turner's, it "is not singular" but is constructed as "an amalgam," and its use demands (recall Limerick here) a tolerance for relativism, for understanding the West as simultaneously both "*place*" and "*processes*" — much as physicists understand the subatomic realm as simultaneously both particles and waves. It allows us to understand better how, for instance, the closing of the frontier (or whatever you want to call that event) "did not come with the 'last stands' of Sam Peckinpah's aging heroes but rather with World War I and the global [migration] quota systems of the 1920s" — or how the West suffered in the 1970s when America's economic preeminence declined with the rapid evolution of a global economy of unprecedented intricacy. Malone properly situates his model in the constellation of "a broadening synthesis," one that he believes would at least attract the sympathies of Turner and Webb but that nonetheless "must surely replace the older interpretations." Even if "less appealing to romantic appetites and far more challenging to comprehend," it does enable "a fuller and richer understanding of what makes the West the truly fascinating place that it is."[32] Malone may be an unromantic synthesizer, but he's also a bona fide New Wester.

Though New Western Historians in general—and by and large the ones I've been discussing—would subscribe to Worster's program outlining their goals, some of them are more preoccupied than others with the theoretical underpinnings of work being done toward accomplishing those goals. One such is William G. Robbins, author of a number of books on the history of political economy and industry in the Northwest. In various respects, he has much in common with his colleagues. Like most of them, he judges that New Western History has "served to refashion and redefine discourse about the place we call the West." Like Limerick, especially, he's not just engaged in that discourse: he's enthusiastic about it. He endorses White's argument that the growing significance of the Pacific Rim "has placed the West at the physical center of events in the larger realm of national affairs." He approvingly shares in an awareness of how multifaceted the shift from Old to New Western History has been: from anti-intellectualism to poststructuralist methodologies, from "utopian" nostalgia to an "apocalyptic" presentism with a sometimes Joan Didion–like interpretive temper, from a single smugly coherent story to a file cabinet full of fragmented and macaronic texts. Robbins applauds that variegated change, even in its grimmer tones. But, unlike some New Western Historians and their critics, he applauds also the increasingly successful effort to keep New Western History "firmly and empirically grounded within a larger theoretical construct."[33]

Robbins spots signs of that grounding all over the field of Western history. In the work of environmental historian William Cronon, a somewhat uneasy neo-Turnerian member of the "Gang of Four" (with White, Limerick, and Worster), who ingeniously argues for a transformational continuity between West-as-frontier-processes and West-as-region approaches. In Harold Simonson's *Beyond the Frontier: Writers, Western Regionalism, and a Sense of Place* (1989), which provides systematic evidence that New Western Historians' "tragic vision" isn't new but intrinsic to the imaginative literature of major American writers from the mid-nineteenth century on, thus anticipating McMurtry's and others' criticisms of those historians' claims. In an impressive assortment of "recent monographic building blocks — centering on studies of the borderland/Southwest and the northern West."[34]

Robbins's inventory demonstrates that New Western History, even as its province grows more comprehensive, is learning to moderate and refine its claims and, indeed, to keep many of its against-the-grain narratives "solidly framed in theoretical argument." (Of particular interest in that regard, given my speculations in chapter 1 about the Northwest, is his detection of "a progressive 'greening' of scholarly work on the northern West." Such work is quite different from the large body on the Southwest, where the United States shares a "border" with Mexico rather than a "boundary," the conventional term for the line dividing it from Canada.) Optimistic about the future of Western historiography, he ranks the publication of Malone and Etulain's 1989 book *The American West* "as the capstone to the renewed efforts at synthesis in western history," and he finds cause for cheer in the ideological implications of White's "*It's Your Misfortune and None of My Own*," a portrayal of cultural and economic competitions through time that doesn't even mention (except bibliographically) either Turner or the frontier. Perhaps White's elision is wholly appropriate since, in Robbins's opinion, the question of victory over the avatars of the Turner model now "is the wrong question." For him the field of Western history isn't in need of that victory so much as it's in need "of fresh perspective, of greater cross-disciplinary analysis, of scholars who would think about the region as part of a larger world order." What Robbins calls for here abstracts the ongoing agenda of New Western History, and he anticipates elaboration of White's approach when he speaks of the "virtue to rethinking the past unencumbered by Turnerian or frontier apronstrings."[35]

If New Western History has had an annus mirabilis so far, probably, as Robbins suggests above and as I suggested earlier, it was 1989. Several events in that year brought the work of its historians into conjunction or into a larger public arena and have encouraged much work since: the "Trails" symposium in Santa Fe and the traveling exhibition it launched; the October meeting of the WHA in Tacoma, Washington, at which Cronon, White, and Worster confronted a packed house in a heated debate on the topic "What's Wrong and Right with Western History"; and the publication of *The American West* as well as Simonson's book and at least one state-of-the-art collection, *Major Problems in the History of the American West*, edited by Clyde A. Milner II.

I could cite more such events, and it would be easy to list books published in the wake of them — or conferences held, like the one at Utah State University in 1992, "A New Significance: Re-envisioning the History of the American West," or the one in Colorado Springs, Colorado, in 1994, "Voices of the New West: Multicultural Issues and the Western Story." But let's briefly revisit the "Trails" symposium, surely the most controversial event of that watershed year, and allow one more drubbing of Turner.

Santa Fe again. Why? Because, as Limerick argues, it made the "ideal location" for the symposium, both retrospectively and prospectively:

> It is . . . the core of my hopes for western American history that any future models for the field will be inclusive and expansive enough to take places like Santa Fe into account. The old concept of the frontier — that bipolar opening-and-closing operation — never looked sillier than it did when applied to New Mexico. When, for instance, would one say the frontier opened in what would become New Mexico? When the Athapaskan Indians came into Pueblo territory? When Coronado made his failed exploration in the 1540s, or when Oñate planted his precarious colony in 1598? Did the successful Pueblo Revolt of 1680 close the frontier or prolong it? Or does the concept of the frontier require the presence of Anglo-Americans?

And so on, through another half-dozen questions. In Limerick's view, Restored Old Western History "totters" when confronted with the complexity of such questions, but New Western History is thereby "in its element." And she hopes that "the whippersnappers" grappling with that kind of diverse complexity "will not turn back on the trail leading western history to a full reckoning with Santa Fe" and will not, as many historians have, "retreat to the university" but keep the public involved in the conversation on that trail.[36]

The whippersnappers haven't disappointed her. Many with a public voice and a yen for ructious colloquy, they were determinedly headed down that trail before the symposium occurred and surely have been since, as a survey of some exemplary areas of inquiry and examination of several key works will show.

At the beginning of *The Great Gatsby*, F. Scott Fitzgerald's narrator, a Midwesterner named Nick Carraway, tells the reader that "the intimate revelations of young men, or at least the terms in which they express them, are usually plagiaristic and marred by obvious suppressions."[37] Much the same might be said of the stories written by Old Western Historians, which tended uncritically to echo one another. If they grew in passing from pen to pen, the purpose typically was to embellish rather than to take account of something suppressed. Indeed, by reason of cultural blinders, their authors may hardly have been aware of suppressions more or less obvious to us now. But Limerick's whippersnappers, whether or not they would classify themselves as New Western Historians, are out to demythologize those stories, expose their biases, and tell what has been suppressed. They are out to set the record straight, and yet the wisest of them know that their own stories will appear to future historians as "plagiaristic and marred by obvious suppressions"—because of "the terms in which they express them," their own blinders. Be that as it may, what have the whippersnappers been up to?

In the late 1960s a number of historians began in real earnest to set the record straight on cowboys, maybe most notably Gene M. Gressley in *Bankers and Cattlemen* (1966) and Robert R. Dykstra in *The Cattle Towns: A Social History of the Kansas Cattle Trading Centers* (1968). The undertaking, uphill against the tenacity of myth and nostalgia, has continued, through Richard W. Slatta's *Cowboys of the Americas* (1990) and even Blake Allmendinger's provocative but question-begging study *The Cowboy: Representations of Labor in an American Work Culture* (1992), until the present. Today anyone who wants a fix on something as close to the unvarnished truth about cowboys as humankind can achieve should have little trouble getting it. But setting the record straight on the other end of the cowboys-and-Indians pairing has proven more difficult.

Needless to say, Vine Deloria and Dee Brown opened a brimful can of worms at the close of the 1960s. Deloria has since written more books on the legal history of Native Americans, with the fervor to correct of a

Ralph Nader, and Brown, of course, has rewritten a lot of Western history, sometimes less innovatively (see his 1994 book *The American West*), concerning Native Americans and other matters, since then. And more voices joined the chorus of correction during the 1970s. Robert F. Berkhofer, Jr., and P. Richard Metcalf strived to inaugurate "a new Indian-centered history," as Berkhofer puts it, "that follows Indian peoples from before white contact to their present lives on reservations, in urban ghettos, and on rural farms."[38] There was an all-around effort, by both historians and anthropologists, to deal with what Reginald Horsman calls "the dilemma of Indian escape from a white straitjacket" and to reconstruct "the Indian past in its true complexity," projects that some ethnohistorians had been pursuing, less radically, since the 1950s. White values were entangled in much of that work, "but traditional moral judgments were often reversed." Still, by the late 1970s, as Horsman observes, though interest in Native American history had "never been greater," historians on the whole were "still bound by the frame of white history." He laments a situation that remains the case even today: "In spite of a number of historical studies that demonstrate a new richness in source material and a new sensitivity to the complexities and continuities of Indian societies, most of the writing by historians on the Native American past continues to be dominated by the history of white-Indian relations."[39] Since most of the historians have been and are white, the situation is understandable — as is the fact that books like Dippie's admirable 1982 study *The Vanishing American: White Attitudes and U.S. Indian Policy*, however much they may have helped in numerous ways, have contributed to it.

Most of the historians but hardly all. The real New Western History of Indians began, in the wake of Deloria's and Brown's books, when, in Horsman's words, "the development of an Indian power movement and the search for a usable Indian past . . . produced a renewed interest in Native Americans' own depictions of their past." He amply documents the proliferation of such depictions, many of them drawing on oral tradition (though not as "filtered through white anthropologists"), in the 1970s. Those "internal" Indian histories, commissioned or published by increasingly autonomous tribal organizations and others, continued to appear during the 1980s, as they still do — see, for example, Joe Sando's *Pueblo Nations: Eight Centuries of Pueblo Indian History* (1992). Their recovery of a past "stolen . . . by white historians" and its public presentation from an Indian viewpoint reached almost a frenzy in the anti-Columbus sentiments of 1992.[40]

Justifiable for a number of reasons, the near-frenzy had at least two significant consequences: it left the American public with a disturbing consciousness of the significance of cultural relativity, and it prepared the way for the 1993 airing, on Discovery, of "How the West Was Lost," surely the most moving presentation of Indian-centered history ever on national television. Telling the victims' stories of Western expansion, the miniseries — harbinger of others, like CBS's "500 Nations" in 1995 — placed the white viewer in a position not unlike that of a non-Jewish German watching a documentary on the Holocaust. Sobering as a slap in the face, it dealt not with "Indians" but with the Nez Perce, Navajo, Sioux, the nations — and persons — that expansion cost, mostly through disease and military campaigns. Voice-overs from Native Americans' nineteenth-century accounts of events, archival photographs, descendants' tearful recitations of narratives passed through oral tradition — all combined to counterbalance poignantly the Old Western History of white victors. However dubious hard-nosed historians may be about the veracity of some of the material or its mode of presentation, great merit inheres in the public's learning, for example, how the Navajos see Kit Carson: not as a hero after whom thousands of acres of national forest are named but as a mean-minded Anglo, bent on genocide or close to it, who used scorched-earth tactics to herd native people brutally from holy land to Bosque Redondo. Even after Indian atrocities are weighed in — and they were — the programs comprise a startling portrait of indefensible policies and occurrences.

It may be true, as Worster asserts, that the bulk of Native American and other minority history of the West "is still where Frederick Jackson Turner's history was in 1893" — that is, it amounts to "a celebration of 'my people,' a record of what 'we' have accomplished, a lament for how 'we' have been neglected or oppressed or underappreciated." But it's also true, as he hopes, that such activist history is beginning to broaden.[41] The substantiation of separate racial and ethnic identities — originating with the acknowledgment that westering has involved a great deal of "eastering" and "northering" and even "southering" as well as, in the case of Native Americans, trying to stay put — is probably an unavoidable step toward a more global and balanced view of cultural interrelations. Native American historiography, though still not attentive enough to early-modern and post-Vietnam events, seems to be headed beyond it. Likewise Hispanic historiography, if David Montejano's *Anglos and Mexicans in the Making of Texas, 1836–1986* (1987) and a handful of other studies can serve as dependable indicators. My sense of Asian-American historiography is that much — though far from all — of it remains stuck at that step. African-American historiography, particularly that concerning women, is too limited in quantity for a secure judgment. But a great deal of revised minority history is in progress — resulting in publications like *Peoples of Color in the American West*, multiculturally edited by Sucheng Chan, Douglas Henry Daniels, Mario T. Garcia, and Terry P. Wilson (1994) — and New Western Historians have prepared a spacious context as a target for its impact.

The history of women in the West — that's a different matter. The whole enterprise has been very fruitful, mostly since about 1979, in which year Julie Roy Jeffrey published her groundbreaking study *Frontier Women: The Trans-Mississippi West, 1840–1880*, and recently, under the aegis of organizations like the Western Association of Women Historians and the Coalition for Western Women's History, has been moving into a full-blown interrelational revamping. You can watch the pattern build. Start, for example, with Joanna L. Stratton's *Pioneer Women: Voices from the Kansas Frontier* (1981), a book that artfully tessellates selections from a "rediscovered" collection of reminiscences written by hundreds of stalwart and intriguing women — homesteaders, circuit riders, on and on. It's a trove of the sort of primary material that has been dug up in the last two decades and helped enrich understanding of women's experiences (from childbirth to captivity to locust plagues and shootouts) in the West.

Then, for your next text in the recent evolution of Western "herstory," consider Sandra L. Myres's 1982 study *Westering Women and the Frontier Experience, 1800–1915*. She takes account, to an extent, of Hispanic, Indian, and African-American as well as Anglo-American women. Her book weaves together a tremendous amount of overlooked primary material, gives it historical (albeit quasi-Turnerian) coherence, and thereby illustrates the principal roles that women (from Elizabeth Custer to those whose names endure only because they left some record of their lives) played in what Myres writes "not as women's history but as frontier history." The distinction is an important one, for it signals her intention to avoid Worster's "we" syndrome and tell "of women's *participation* in a unique human experience."[42]

I think Myres fulfills her intention, by and large. She avoids also some of the pitfalls of presentism by relying strongly on the primary material and not excluding evidence that qualifies her main arguments, which concern how "women's preconceptions about the frontier" were modified by their living there. You learn about Anglo westering as "primarily a middle-class activity" (it wasn't cheap) and the unreliability of reminiscences that exaggerate or include formulaic elements (men weren't the only tellers of tall tales). Myres's investigation inventories, questions, and revises the stereotypes of frontier women: the Anglo woman as "the weary and forlorn frontier wife, a sort of helpless heroine" who guarded the values of civilization, or the Calamity Jane–like "bad woman"; the Hispanic woman as a cult-of-the-Virgin ranchera-saint or "the seductive señorita"; the African-American woman as the ignored and passive sufferer; the Indian woman as a treacherous redskin, Pocahontas-like princess, "sensual Indian maiden," or abused squaw; and so on. Myres is wary of both "the old nineteenth-century myths and the more recent feminist stereotypes of frontier women." She acknowledges the extent to which the old stereotypes were in fact embodied in some women, but she strives to reveal her subjects in all their less-presupposed variety and to show, more specifically, how "the *reality* of women's lives changed dramatically as a result of adaptation to frontier conditions while the public *image* remained relatively static." Scarcely slavish in their obedience to "Eastern-dictated models of femininity," the women she studies "stepped out of woman's place with few regrets," Myres argues. Though she allows that later generations of Western women tried to embrace such models, she adjudges them not very successful at it — with the consequence that those women continue to be "better educated," more independent of mind, "open to change," and egalitarian in gender terms than their counterparts in other regions of the country.[43] However mythical it might seem, Myres proclaims, the heritage of the pioneer woman's spunky self-sufficiency lives on in 1982. Still does, I'd say.

So, I suspect, would Teresa Jordan, author of another early-1980s book, *Cowgirls: Women of the American West.* It's less formal than Myres's, even freewheeling, and Jordan's subjects, except for cursory glances backward, are her contemporaries. Though equipped with an elaborately annotated bibliography, her study is arguably more journalistic than historical, but her aim — to write the real cowgirl into the story of the West — has much in common with the purposes of New Western History. At the beginning of the book, Jordan sets the tone for her exploration as both revisionary and entertaining with a comment on the *Madonna of the Trail* statue in Lamar, Colorado: "This image of the frontier woman as earth mother pervades our sense of women in the West. She took care of the house and children while father tamed the land . . . but she had more adventurous sisters."[44]

Those sisters have a tradition going back well over a hundred years that counts ancestors among the thousands of single women and widows who headed west after the Homestead Act of 1862, the shit-kicker redneck women of their day. Some were married to cowboys and cattlemen when they migrated and took over spreads after their husbands died. Some with ranch experience joined rodeos or Wild West shows. Jordan summarizes that history of cowgirls, whom she strictly defines as women who know all the physical aspects of herding cattle and "work outside, on ranches or in the rodeo, on a regular basis" (cooking and the like don't count), and yet she observes that "they are invisible." They're overshadowed not only by their male counterparts but also, historically if not contemporarily, by prairie madonnas and desperadas. In Jordan's assessment the invisibility has to do with a general cultural willingness to accept boys' growing up to be cowboys but not girls' growing up to be cowgirls — they're supposed to go on to other, more proper things. So she's out to undo the suppression involved and promote the cowgirl's "equal canonization." Her book, written after 60,000 miles of travel in the West and nearly a hundred interviews between 1978 and 1980, strives persuasively to accomplish both goals. Still, she admits that these women of hardy self-respect who have always "felt more comfortable in the world of men" — whose history long absorbed them — have been and remain relatively few.[45] Of course, there aren't that many real cowboys, by her definition, around these days, either.

But, however vehemently Jordan argues, she never loses sight of context. She's not out to make a case for any kind of feminist separateness of Western women or their history. Turner bashing, maybe, but not male bashing. Much the same could be said of other publications on through the 1980s concerning the history of women in the West, from recovered

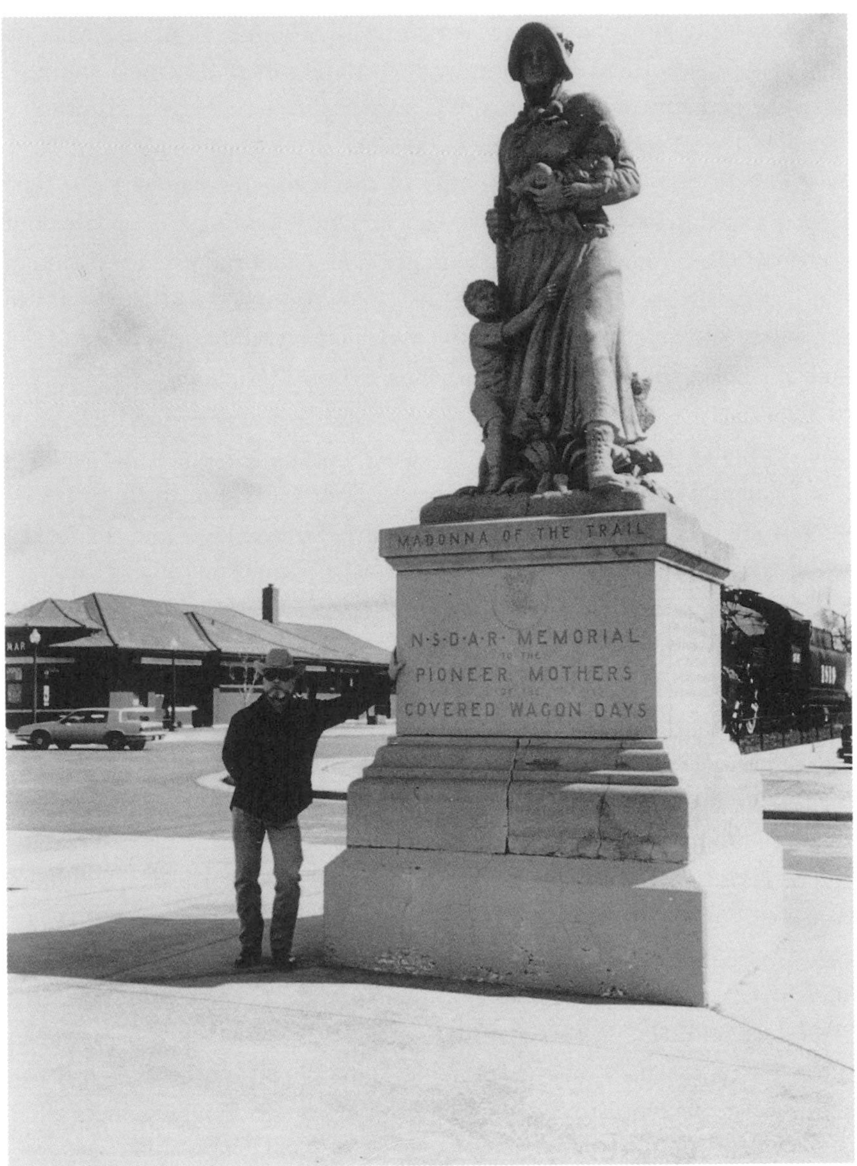

The Madonna of the Trail *statue in Lamar, Colorado: a pervasive historical stereotype now subject to substantial revision.*

primary material like that presented in *Plains Woman: The Diary of Martha Farnsworth, 1882–1922*, edited by Marlene Springer and Haskell Springer (1986), to Glenda Riley's broad-based study *The Female Frontier: A Comparative View of Women on the Prairie and the Plains* (1988) or Cheryl J. Foote's more localized study *Women of the New Mexico Frontier, 1846–1912* (1990). Certainly no undue ideological narrowness characterizes Sarah Deutsch's *No Separate Refuge: Culture, Class, and Gender on an Anglo-Hispanic Frontier in the American Southwest, 1880–1940* (1989) or Peggy Pascoe's *Relations of Rescue: The Search for Female Moral Authority in the American West, 1874–1939* (1990), both carefully documented intercultural studies. Though the last two books have stirred up troublesome controversy, Robbins rightly mentions them as examples of the kind of projects to be found at "the vital points of inquiry" in the recent study of the West, projects that "will contribute to the further integration of the gender issue as part of the larger mosaic that is western history."[46]

Pascoe, for one, surely would agree that the 1980s were the takeoff decade for a new history of women in the West, a decade that ended with "an increasing number of calls for a broader, more 'multicultural' approach to the history of western women," as she remarks in her paper in the *Trails* collection. She encourages the continuation of recent studies of how gender is "embedded in depictions of western landscapes," for instance, but she also urges more effort, building on the work of Vicki Ruiz and others, toward "the study of western women at the cultural crossroads" of the West rather than on its frontier as "a geographic freeway." Unsurprisingly, she sees New Mexico as "the center of new research" on Western history in terms of "intercultural relations as well as . . . multicultural diversity."[47] Beyond any doubt, given the work of White and others, women and men, her urging foreshadows much of the important activity of New Western History in the 1990s.

The drive for scope and diversity in the retelling of Western history — and in connecting it to ordinary lives — has prompted also recent studies of children in the West. Elliott West's *Growing Up with the Country*, cited earlier, is a good example. So is Elizabeth Hampsten's *Settlers' Children: Growing Up on the Great Plains* (1991). An interesting assemblage of primary material is *"A Funnie Place, No Fences": Teenagers' Views of Kansas, 1867–1900*, edited by C. Robert Haywood and Sandra Jarvis (1993). Such books represent yet another aspect of the New Western Historical endeavor to evidence the tremendous effect of the family on the West.

Related to that endeavor is New Western life-writing, and there's a lot of it. As has long been the circumstance, some is narrative that straddles the categories of the historical and the imaginative. But much of it seeks assiduously to fulfill New Western Historical goals: to tell a life (and not just a heroic Anglo-male one) absent its mythology (or with its mythology in an analytical perspective) and set in a context inclusive enough to energize its significance in terms of the larger cultures in which it occurs. That operation was performed over and over again on Columbus around 1992, and it's easy to find, for instance, life-writing from early in the nineteenth century or before that does something like it on a famous cattleman or less famous cowboy. Any attempt to pinpoint the first New Western example is liable to raise questions, but Dee Brown's 1974 collection of brief biographies *The Westerners* seems a defensible prototype, if not the definitive candidate.

Brown describes his book as "the story of the West told through the experiences of a few representative Westerners from the sixteenth to the twentieth century" (among them Francisco Vásquez de Coronado, George Catlin, Brigham Young, Sitting Bull, Charles Goodnight), some well known, others not. This biographical collage isn't romantic Old Western History by a long shot. Brown makes clear in the introduction what his narratives illustrate: that the history of the West "is a tragedy relieved by interludes of comedy" and concerns a region whose first explorers "were driven by elemental greed" and which from the beginning of exploration was "treated . . . as a storehouse to be exploited for personal gain." Though he ascribes freedom as a motive to a few of his subjects (and knowledge as that to Lewis and Clark) and admits that some loved the land or came to love it, greed rides through his narratives like a leitmotif. In a passage that anticipates the one I quoted earlier from Frazier, Brown totals up the achievements of his Westerners and others before he even begins the business of biography:

> In their march to the Western Sea, they and many of the thousands who followed them destroyed a native civilization and obliterated innumerable species of animals and birds. They ripped apart the delicate balance of Plains grassland, they gutted mountains for metals and poisoned the earth, they leveled forests and created wastelands.

> They raped, stripped, and plundered the land as if they hated the Garden of the West with a violent passion. They built large cities in waterless places where even the primitive tribes knew that cities should never be built.

From there he goes on to catalog "the litter and refuse of the conquerors."[48]

Though a phrase like "primitive tribes" indicates that Brown precedes the full swing of New Western History and its more sensitive ethnography, he's got the basic steps of the dance down. Though he speaks of what "they" did instead of what Frazier's more presentist and morally engaged "we" did, his judgments have a New Western Historical ring to them. So do his assays of his subjects in their gray-hat ambivalences that reflect their cultural worlds. Read, for a splendid example, his portrait of "Teddy the Rough Rider," "the first cowboy to enter the White House." Brown reveals him as, among other things, a lover of stuffed trophies, a Western dandy, an owl-faced joke, an imperialist, a hero of sorts, a bankrupt rancher, a preserver of the Western wilderness, finally "an anachronism, a windbag." Above all, Brown paints him as a man who went West and invented himself as a typal incarnation of frontier epithets with predominantly positive meanings for the progressive Anglo-American society of his time (and, in some respects, for good or ill, our own): "voluble, energetic, ebullient, overconfident, self-reliant, . . . righteous, messianic, contradictory, avaricious and generous."[49] Like the West, a tapestry of dramatic features both concordant and conflicting.

Since 1974 both academic and commercial presses have been very much committed to publishing Western biographies that recall the disposition of Brown's book or otherwise and increasingly share goals with New Western History. Though its voices are all male, Clarus Backes's collection *Growing Up Western* (1989) presents telling remembrances of Western childhoods in the early twentieth century by some of the finest modern writers in the West — Wallace Stegner, Frank Waters, A. B. Guthrie, Jr., and several others. Roxana Robinson's *Georgia O'Keeffe: A Life* (1989) does an impressive job of writing the story of a woman who was perhaps *the* Western, certainly *the* Southwestern, artist of her time, dealing deftly with the subtleties of a feisty genius whose major work was rooted in the West but inextricably tangled with the whole history of modern art and culture. Also, older autobiographical material continues to be recovered and interpreted in a more encompassing context. A good example is Salvador Guerrero's *Memorias: A West Texas Life*, edited by Arnoldo De Leon (1991), a diary that fleshes out with touching personal details De Leon's previous research on Southwestern migration in the first half of the twentieth century.

The environmental history of the West is a protracted, immensely complicated story of intractable troubles. As the national media regularly remind us, the story not only trudges on but also is being forcefully retold by new voices, many of them embodied in or enabled by New Western Historians. A September 1991 issue of *Newsweek*, centered on "The War for the West: Fighting for the Soul of America's Mythic Land," suggests that the "war" involved won't end for some time, if ever. The land-use battles highlighted there grind along unabated: Native Americans and the government going at it over water in Arizona and New Mexico; miners, bikers, and ranchers in California opposing legislation to protect the East Mojave Desert; everyone at odds with everyone else over timbering in Oregon and Idaho; and more. All such contentions star two bedfellows each far too long sleeplessly heedful of the other for them to be strangers: ecology and economy.

In one of the pieces he wrote for that issue of *Newsweek*, Tom Mathews connects the whole melee to an old habit, well exemplified by Custer at the Little Bighorn, of misjudging the Western landscape. Thus Mathews calls it "the Custer syndrome," which he nutshells this way: "At its heart is a vain and deadly attitude. The West is mine. I'm going to fight you for it. And only one of us is going to get out of here alive." It's not just an Anglo attitude, he's careful to explain, noting that, after all, the Sioux who fought Custer took the Black Hills from the Crow. Mathews's recognition of the persistence of the Custer syndrome leads him to fundamentals:

> To see the West is to lust after it. . . . The basic question is, "Who owns the West?" The correct answer is, "Everyone," or if you take a geological view of the problem, perhaps, "No one." But very few people ever get it right. This is because Westerners and Outsiders always get themselves so badly tangled in The Myth of the West. To rustle an insight from William Kittredge, . . . white Westerners tend to think they own the place because they settled it, brought law to it,

suffered and shed blood over it and survived, earning the right to do with it as they see fit.

That's quintessentially an Old Western way of thinking, of course, and it's bound up, as Mathews soon admits, with more than one myth — and a lot of dire truth that tends to get suppressed. For him the Custer syndrome is the "curse of the West. You could write a history of the region on the theme: a tragedy with no permanent winners."[50] That, of course, is exactly what a lot of New Western Historians specializing in environmental or economic history or both have been up to.

As lawyers, environmentalists, politicians, realtors, and others have it out over issues of wise use, those historians have been telling of the long-term consequences of the Custer syndrome. Their advocacy tends to be patent: New Westers at their best, they embrace the Everyone/No-one philosophy of ownership. They toil to document and explicate the hard-to-accept reality that, in Mathews's words, "as the old, rural West enters the information age, ranching, timbering and mining are heading the way of the family farm in the Midwest and the steel mill in the rust belt." They know that the conflicts involved are "too hot" and that "what's needed is a new spirit of the West" — a spirit not of independence but of cooperation that preserves the West and takes care of the losers.[51]

New Western Historians have written shelves of books about the Western environment and economy. A tenable precursor to more recent work might be Gressley's *Bankers and Cattlemen*, a study of how Eastern capital controlled Western ranching in the last third of the nineteenth century. By the time of White's *Land Use, Environment, and Social Change: The Shaping of Island County, Washington* (1980), a book with implications much wider than its title suggests that counts Indians too as ecological invaders, environmental history of the West clearly was changing gears. Another book of the time that signals the shift is Malone's boom-and-bust study of political corruption, *The Battle for Butte: Mining and Politics on the Northern Frontier, 1864–1906* (1981). By the end of the 1980s, New Western History had gone into overdrive in its production of texts with subregional focuses but proliferative implications — Robbins's *Hard Times in Paradise: Coos Bay, Oregon, 1850–1986* (1988), for instance, and Andrew Gulliford's *Boomtown Blues: Colorado Oil Shale, 1885–1985* (1989). Lots of books on "hydraulic history" were then in print — Worster's *Rivers of Empire*, for instance, and Marc P. Reisner's *Cadillac Desert: The American West and Its Disappearing Water* (1986) — and many more were on the way.

By now New Western History has turned into almost a minor industry, and we certainly know more diverse stories about the West than Old Western History could have made possible. Limerick's mess is getting cleaned up. Our knowledge of the West is becoming more globalized as New Western Historians help us understand how we have come to a time when cowboys still wear Stetsons but livestock auctions are controlled by cellular phones, rodeos are planned, down to who wrestles what steer when, by computers, and 90 percent of Westerners live in metropolitan areas. The work of those historians amounts to a multifaceted lens through which we can see more fully the West's undying gambler's belief in future prosperity, gradual movement away from excessive individualism and localism and toward cooperative regionalism, multiplying need for less and less water, increasingly complex and ambiguous relationships to the East and the Pacific Rim, and growing political influence.

In spite of the negative implications of much of their research, New Western Historians on the whole don't come off looking addicted to gloom. They probably would agree with Gressley's conclusion, in 1979, that "the West, with its new economic power, its population influx, its open spaces, and its brilliant atmosphere, has substantial advantages with which to move into the twenty-first century." But, like Gressley, they also would betray some pessimism, still well justified, about the region's ability to achieve quickly a more balanced relationship with Eastern money and government toward "the preservation of the West's environment and life-style."[52] Perhaps, to use a word that's in the air, "postregional" New Westers with less ingenuous ideas about preservation and a more studied understanding of the nonlinear mutability of economic and ecological systems will be able to do it better in the years ahead. If that happens, much credit will be due their larger view of Western history, their awareness of its cautionary tales of light and darkness, freedom and responsibility, boom and bust, what is hoped for and what comes unexpected.

So, enough of sitting around the campfire and telling sad stories of the death of kings. The West has been comedy as well as tragedy, with as much irony inherent in the former as in the latter — and not just happy-ending comedy but funny comedy too. Right now in the Southwest, the home of the Bomb and the Jornada del Muerto, there are people, especially in and around the Four Corners area, spooked to jumpy dread by a *mysterioso* piece of protein called the Sin Nombre hantavirus that's carried by rodents, frequently turns its human victims' lungs into soup, and at a peak of activeness in 1993 appeared to be slowly spreading all over the nation. There's terrible drought, on and off, in parts of the interior West. And you can find other disasters that past historians either couldn't predict or foresaw as being as recurrently certain as a metronome. But tug your boots off, pull up your blanket, rest your head on the seat of your saddle, and enjoy the entertaining side of Western history for a second.

Let your mind move at a slow gait through Dee Brown's *Wondrous Times on the Frontier* (1991), a thoroughly researched book that portrays the Old West with both a gentle sense of humor and a New Western Historical sense of realism. It's about vanity and hardships, folly and catastrophe, myths and legends, and it proves the less-known truths of the West to be at least as fantastic as its well-known tall tales. It's about diversity but with a grain of salt. Or read the late C. L. Sonnichsen's *Roy Bean: Law West of the Pecos* (1986), another humorous book that benefits from careful factuality and yet keeps in play the much-legendized aspects of its subject. Or read David Dary's *True Tales of Old-Time Kansas* (1984). Or, if you're up for pursuing some historical trivia, have a gander at Rod Gragg's informative grab-bag *The Old West Quiz and Fact Book* (1986), which here and there will surprise even the best-versed Old or New Wester with an odd datum. All of which is to say, don't lose track of the great fun of Western history.

And don't take too seriously any New Western Historian who wants that history wholesale denuded of its myths. In an age when there's apparently a mandate for humanist academics to be compulsively "political" even in their sleep — and a kind of vague suspicion that if you aren't beating the devil over the head all the time, then you must be of his party — it's possible to go too far: you can throw out the baby of truth with the bathwater of myth. As many of those academics are discovering, you can theorize politically to the extent that you've lost all the vivid, however mythological, particulars of experience — a lesson that some more theoretical New Western Historians may still have to learn.

Truth itself ultimately answers mythic needs. Myth tells its own truth about the teller. And about the believing listener.

The multiplex myth of the West may well be a big part of the West's problem of survival in the postmodern age, as Gressley and others argue. But its accoutrements need to be rethought to decide what ought to be retained and what has to go. That's a New Western mission that Old Westers may not like, but it concerns an important paradox: if things are going to stay the same, then things will have to change. In essence, the mission entails studying the myth itself through its successive manifestations, the sort of research that Robert G. Athearn, for instance, does in his 1986 book *The Mythic West in Twentieth-Century America.*

Or the kind that, more ambitiously, Richard Slotkin does in his three-volume study of the myth of the frontier in American literary, popular, and political culture from the colonial period till the early 1990s. In *Regeneration Through Violence: The Mythology of the American Frontier, 1600–1860* (1973), he analyzes how warfare experiences on the nation's early frontiers were transformed into narrative lore and how that in turn was codified into symbolic myth by historians and fiction writers. Then, in *The Fatal Environment: The Myth of the Frontier in the Age of Industrialization, 1800–1890* (1985), he traces the myth as it's adapted to fit the ideology of a country rapidly changing from an agrarian republic into an industrial nation-state. Finally, in *Gunfighter Nation: The Myth of the Frontier in Twentieth-Century America* (1992), he explores the cultural translations of the myth, bereft of significant reference to geography, into metaphors that have become almost purely — but with potent historical resonances — expressions of modern and postmodern ideology.

The last volume is particularly germane to the New West, for it demonstrates at great length how those metaphors, conventionalized into clichés, have been used, selectively and very much politically, to interpret, rationalize, falsify, mystify, and promote supposedly redemptive violence from the time of Turner and Teddy Roosevelt to that of the so-called War on Drugs and the Gulf War. Though Slotkin's conclusions testify to his uneasiness about how such politicized metaphors continue to govern the material lives of millions of people, his exploration nonetheless emboldens him to believe not only that critical study of mythic discourses affords better understanding of history but also that the American multiculture now has the opportunity and ability to alter a myth no longer validated by the world it ostensibly represents.

Let me return to Dippie, who deliberates the methodological specifics of this approach. He supports a suggestion from Roger Nichols that Western historians might improve their professional lot by being less concerned with who fired first at the O. K. Corral and more concerned with the social and economic processes through which such an incident came about. But Dippie proposes that another step be taken: asking why such "a relatively minor incident . . . has seized and held the American imagination for over a century, and why figures like Wyatt Earp and Doc Holliday still command attention." He cites numerous works that illustrate "an established tradition in western history of separating fiction from fact to get at the truth behind such storied individuals and episodes," and he compliments Ramon Adams on his assiduousness "in exposing the legends surrounding Billy the Kid in *A Fitting Death for Billy the Kid*" (1960). He notes, however, that "cultural historians find the legend more arresting — and revealing — than the facts" and that facts can be bought at too high a price: "Strip Billy the Kid of his myth and little of historical consequence remains, as Robert Utley has ably demonstrated." Thus Dippie applauds Stephen Tatum's *Inventing Billy the Kid: Visions of the Outlaw in America, 1881–1981* (1982) because it "accepts myths and legends as facts for a different kind of history — the study of how people conceive the past in mythic patterns that define a culture and its value system."[53]

The investigation of such patterns — in literature, paintings, film, memoirs, journalism, historical writing itself, wherever — therefore provides the historian with potent information, according to Dippie, who goes on to present probing questions:

> Since cultural values shift over time, myths, in order to remain relevant, shift their meanings as well. If, as most would agree, the major challenge facing western history is to relate past to present in a meaningful way, the mythic approach has much to offer. It accounts for continuity *and* change. Custer is dead, his Last Stand long over. Why then do people continue to refight it? . . . We may dismiss Custer as a minor figure historically. But he was once a national hero. . . . His defenders still think of him as a paragon if not a saint, and he has been

> compared to Jesus, who died on *that* hill. His detractors regard him as a racist villain, fit symbol for America's mistreatment of its native peoples: "Custer died for your sins." . . . In either guise, hero or villain, Custer continues to function as a vital presence in the public's imagination. Why?

Dippie doesn't answer those questions in this text, though he cites several studies, including his own book *Custer's Last Stand: The Anatomy of an American Myth* (1976), that try to. Such studies, along with broader ones by Slotkin and others, make convincing Dippie's argument that "far from glorifying old verities, myth analysis can offer a searching perspective on American development."[54] Perhaps it can even help us understand how and why New Westers, with their drive to hold on to the West and at least some of its traditional mythology (and associated images, symbols, values), have come about.

Following the basic nature of most tellers of the past, New Western Historians won't have a lot to say about New Westers (themselves included) until more time has gone by. They've said little about them so far, at least in print. Doubtless, much of what they say will be prefaced or contextualized by recitations about other, earlier New Wests. So be it, but they'll find significant differences when they get down to the nitty gritty, I suspect. And they won't discover much of depth if they don't keep the imaginative play of ever-shifting Western myths in view. It has to do with situations and needs both perennial and contemporary, both fundamentally human and peculiarly American.

Much of the groundwork for understanding New Westers in such terms has already been laid. Go back to the 1960s again, to Kent Ladd Steckmesser's 1965 study *The Western Hero in History and Legend.* With compendious documentation he analyzes the intermingled histories and legends of four figures — Kit Carson, Billy the Kid, Wild Bill Hickok, and George Armstrong Custer — in order to define the "common hero-type" they represent and "to explain how and why these heroes were created." Through his analysis emerge several interlinked and useful insights. The contradictions in heroic roles (between purity and dissolution, for example) "facilitate the growth of legends, because every Western fan can create a hero after his own ideas"; as a consequence, "many of the sordid episodes in Western history become heroic." Much Western biography is thereby inflated to epic proportions and cleansed by "sins of omission" in order to give "Eastern readers narratives . . . based upon Eastern preconceptions and expectations rather than upon the facts." Moreover, the stature of Western figures in such narratives depends greatly on whether or not they have been well processed through the cycle of popularization from dime novels to television scripts; thus "Hickok surpasses Wyatt Earp as a legendary figure because Earp was never a dime-novel hero"—and subsequently, even taking recent movie portrayals into account, never treated as fully by Hollywood, the ultimate determiner of who gets legendized. All culpability aside, "professional hero makers . . . have simply supplied what the people have demanded," and the people have generally demanded "the beautiful" rather than "the true"—though now, with revisionist Westerns in various media and the advancement of New Western History, that insistence is letting up. Through most of the twentieth century, in any case, it derives from projected needs, "aspirations." Especially in the case of the cowboy hero, another of many "American equivalents of Ajax and Hector," it derives from the fact that "Americans have generally cast themselves in idealistic roles." The predilections entailed here are enveloping, seductive, densely networked through the national culture. It's no surprise that New Westers, even when they most cynically "peer into the dark shadows of a hero's life," don't so much shake off such predilections as modify, qualify, update them.[55] And they do so in terms of their own, postmodern needs for "truth" of another kind.

Jump from the 1960s to 1979, by which time a more sophisticated and perhaps even more forgiving perspective on the Western myth was possible—at least for William W. Savage, Jr. After a brief discussion of the function of dude ranches and "the conventions of playing cowboy" safely, he declares the obvious: "The West is a place for fantasies." Why? Because its history—both "brief" and "bizarre," words he borrows from Walter Prescott Webb—"has no power to temper reveries." (Though, as Savage notes, Webb "could hardly have foreseen . . . the proliferation of imagery that could allow nearly everyone to become, however briefly or superficially, a cowboy.") But, not stopping there, Savage pursues deeper "becauses":

> The West is a place for fantasy because it is remote in time and space. If its history is brief and bizarre, its landscape is vast and bizarre,

> often isolating the individual through extremes of geography and climate and forcing him to depend solely upon his own physical and psychological resources. . . . In the face of an overwhelming experience, history is initially irrelevant simply because so many other data must be assimilated first. The problem of the West is that the assimilation is seldom ever complete, and consequently the confrontation between the individual and history is often indefinitely postponed. Fantasy is an early step in the process of assimilation, and it appears to constitute a psychological island upon which the popular mind is marooned and to which history is as a message in a bottle, cast about by the tides and currents of image and myth and unable to make much headway in any direction. If Webb is correct, that message is an inadequate instrument of salvation anyway. But such a view posits fantasy as a normal state of affairs and ignores the possibility that images and myths may have histories of their own that, in juxtaposition to "real" history, can facilitate the assimilation of otherwise troublesome data.

Plenty of New Western Historians might take exception to that line of argument, but they would sidestep its implications at their professional peril. They may yet write the " 'real' history" of the cowboy, but they'd better not forget his enduring "refusal to accept revisions of his image" and at least one of the reasons why "people play cowboy: by dressing the part and playing the role in an extravaganza for which no script exists, Americans are preserving a bit of the past until something worthwhile can be done with it." Playing such a role, we "anticipate substance," which is at least part of what New Western Historians have the task of delivering. Still, "the image of the cowboy is less bizarre than other images roaming the West" (for instance, the ahistorical Western phantasms of Disneyland). As Savage argues in words and through pages of photographs (of old-time Wyoming cowboys, William Cody, singing cowboys, on and on), the "numbers alone" of people who bear that image "confirm their normality."[56]

Then jump from 1979 to the early 1990s, at which time those numbers of people were unprecedented. By then some New Western Historians were indeed beginning to investigate the full complexities of the interdependencies between the Western myth and "real" Western history all the way up to the present — a changeover after their rigorous push to demythologize, during which they had denied the relevance of such an investigation or avoided it or just put it off.

White recapitulates that sort of maneuver in "*It's Your Misfortune and None of My Own*" when he comes to his last chapter, "The Imagined West," and confesses to an inevitability, asks a burning question, and immediately problematizes it:

> This imagined West has not . . . overtly intruded on this text until now because it would have been potentially confusing to interrupt each chapter to analyze how various imagined Wests have shaped the topics of discussion. I have postponed the issues of the mythic West until, having nearly reached the end of this book, I can delay no longer. What is, then, the relationship between the variety of publicly imagined Wests — the mythic Wests — and the historic West? Even the question is misleading, for it implies that the two can be easily separated.

They can't be, as White well knows. But the real problem implied here is that he and other New Western Historians haven't quite figured out how to explore and discuss effectively the richness of the interactions entailed. They have to become more than afterthoughts. White says as much when he speaks, just before his confession, of a "gluttonous consumption of fictions about the West" (which he suspects may have brought about "the decline of the Western in the 1970s and 1980s" by "a severe case of cultural indigestion") and of how "Americans have also actively imagined their own Wests" to the extent that, through metaphors of showdowns and last stands and roundups and the like, "the imagined West [has] intruded constantly on everyday American life."[57] More and more New Western Historians, following, especially, Slotkin's example, will, I predict, study that intrusion — and with increasing theoretical and methodological subtlety.

Though I may fault White for not going further in treating myth and history together, I grant that his follow-up on his misleading question gives intriguing glimpses of the mythic-historic territory that future historians will travel. Distinguishing between "folkloric" imaginers of the West, whose influence is local, and the professionals, who write novels and make movies that have a much more suffused influence, he observes that the fictions of the latter also have tremendous impact locally:

> So powerful is the influence of this imagined West that its fictional creations and personas become symbols of the West, and real westerners model themselves after fictional characters. In the late 1970s a journalist for the *New Yorker*, Jane Kramer, wrote an account, entitled *The Last Cowboy*, of a ranch foreman on the Texas Panhandle. The hero was a skilled working cowboy who was disappointed in the realities of life on a cattle ranch. He viewed his actual modern West of absentee ranchers and agribusinesses as a declension from a truer but vanished West. His true West, however, was an imagined West, and he knew it from Westerns: real cattlemen were John Wayne in *Chisum*, or Chill Wills in *The Rounders*. His own sense of himself, and how he acted, were informed not just by the West he lived in but also by a powerful cultural image of the West he *should* have lived in. The actual West and the imagined West are engaged in a constant conversation; each influences the other.

Or consider White's commentary on an anecdote concerning Kit Carson — an ambiguous figure, to be sure — brought to his attention by Limerick, who, like Cronon and others, is keenly interested in how the meaning of West has been verbally constructed. It concerns Carson's search, in 1849, for a white woman captured (that archetypal American mytheme) by Jicarilla Apaches. His party catches up with the Indians too late, and the woman has been killed; but in the Apache camp Carson discovers a book, the like of which he's never seen before, that portrays him as a great Indian-slaying hero. White comments:

> This actual event in New Mexico in 1849 could be a scene from a novel by Italo Calvino: the actual Carson confronts the literary Carson. And in a sense the literary Carson proves the stronger of the two. Carson's reaction to finding the book, probably Charles Averill's *Kit Carson, Prince of the Gold Hunters* (1849), was to lament his failure to live up to his fictional reputation. The fictional Carson became the standard for the real Carson, and the connection between the two goes beyond this, for the story of the incident comes to us in a book, written by the actual Carson, to capitalize on the market the mythic Carson had created for him. . . .
>
> What Kit Carson confronted in the deserted Jicarilla camp, westerners have in a sense been confronting ever since. There are cultural visions of the West, constantly changing but always present, that de-

> fine both for westerners and others what the western experience means.[58]

Thus, for the *new* New Western Historians, not only the histories of the region are competing to define what the West means but the myths as well. And the conversation between the two kinds of stories, each shaping the other, positively or negatively, makes for dialogue as interwoven as what must have occurred between the two Carsons but writ as large as the West itself. Such historians are learning how to read and re-present that dialogue in the drama of the West as the interactive process it always has been, no longer, as it were, separately gathering up all the lines from one speaker and then all the lines from the other to make two monologues. They're starting to get both sides of that constant conversation together.

To counterbalance that highfalutin play of tropes and carry the chapter toward its close, I'd like to show hospitality to a point of view that has a more Old Western feel and let McMurtry, who is far from always friendly to the Western myth, tell us why we need to hold on to it in one form or another. At the end of his critique of New Western History, to which I alluded earlier, he reminds us that, though Charles Goodnight "gave up on the Herfalo," he "kept his buffalo." That reminding opens the way for another story that McMurtry, who has written so many novels about the desolation of modern men bereft of the Western myth, passes on, along with some interpretive reflection. It concerns, as you might expect, Goodnight and his buffalo:

> He once was persuaded to give one of them to a straggling band of Kiowas, who had slipped off their reservation and come to the only place where they might still find a buffalo, which was Goodnight's ranch. He thought they wanted to eat it. What they really wanted to do was to chase it on their skinny horses and kill it with lances, in the old way, one last time. (John Graves has a fine story, "The Last Running," based on this incident.) Goodnight watched the last running from his porch. Or at least that's the story that is still told in the Texas panhandle.
>
> There is no finer or sadder moment with which to illustrate the Quixotism at the core of the Western story. And the Quixotism was

> there almost from the beginning. The very explorers who began the destruction of the Garden could not bear to admit that the Garden had been destroyed — that it could be so lost, and in only a single lifetime, that the Kiowa Indians would have to beg a buffalo from the Old Man of the Plains, a man who had fought them for fifty years and won. From Zebulon Pike to Louis L'Amour, no Westerner has wanted to think that the West of the imagination was lost. For if that West is lost, then it's all just jobs. The West of the imagination is the West upon which the revisionist Sancho Panzas now wish to shine the sober light of common day. Fair enough. Still, it might interest a few of them to read the end of *Don Quixote*, to consider what happens when the crazy old Don surrenders his fancies and lets the tough little realist have his way.[59]

It may be that in a time when believing in the future of the West is hard you have to believe in a past when it was easier. Or at least some people have to. Maybe, after all, to use Savage's word, that's one "worthwhile" thing to do with a bit of the past — though, of course, there are others.

Late in 1994, in an article in the *Magazine of History*, which is published for teachers of history by the Organization of American Historians, Walter Nugent remarked how, "in the last several years, the field of western American history has become more vibrant and visible." He attributed much of its vibrancy and visibility to the fact that New Western Historians were telling their story "in a fresh way" less because of an interest in "entertainment" than because of one in "national self-explanation." And he compared such trafficking in the meaning of America to tinkering interpretively with the Dead Sea Scrolls: "Research into either the Scrolls or the American West constitutes a high-risk process of shedding light on matters of fundamental belief. In the case of the West, the belief in question is the cultural bedrock of American nationality. Everything we like to think of as 'American' — flattering things that Turner said best: individualism, democracy, progress — are things widely considered western and as having developed out of the frontier and westering experience." It's scarcely surprising, therefore, that Nugent took due note, in a time when the national political mood was turning increasingly conservative and some New Western Historians (Cronon, for example) thought the assault on Turner had gone too far, of the myriad people protective of their nostalgia and willing to oppose any narrative that "literally beggars their belief."[60]

Nor is it surprising, given all the polemics within and about New Western History during its rapid ascension, that Nugent spoke of "something of a Thermidor," a counterrevolutionary propensity, that "by early 1993 . . . had set in." He pegged it accurately, for he was looking back to a year that had seen not only Savage, Thompson, and similar detractors launch some of their severest criticisms but also, according to his own survey, many historians, writers, and journalists of the old dispensation reaffirm their "Turnerian and Webbian categories," a few adamantly. On the other hand, he acknowledged that Western historians, "while not accepting the 'New Western History' as a full-scale paradigm shift," were already incorporating "many of its points into their teaching and research." Such a muddled polarization prompted him to conclude that where the Thermidor will lead "is not fully clear."[61]

Still isn't. But it's a good bet that New Western History will continue, uphill at times, to be more accepted — not just piecemeal but as the formative base of a different paradigm. It's a good bet also that the story of that acceptance will continue to be a ripsnorter.

Somehow, despite the fact that many of its patterns continue unchanged, the West seems to be coming of age. Its people, and its contemporary writers in particular, I think, seem to realize that our mythic history — call it our cowboy heritage — simply isn't enough to hang our hats on forever. — Russell Martin, *New Writers of the Purple Sage*

REWRITERS OF THE PURPLE SAGE, PART 1: TRAILS TO NEW WESTERN LITERATURE

Before I earnestly thought out this chapter, I had what struck me as a clever idea for a title: "New Balls for an Old Canon." But then I realized that two things were wrong with it: (1) there really isn't any such thing as a Western literary canon — that is, a generally agreed-upon list of great, seminal works — and (2) even if some such list of past works could be agreed upon, many (maybe most) of the writers recently contributing works that could defensibly be added to it aren't men but women. So my double pun, briefly treasured, was laid aside — though I've sneaked it back into play here, where its falsehood has helped get me started on New Western literature, who's writing it (and what it is), and why.

Let's scout the territory before riding into that thicket. The relationship between Western history and Western literature has always been close, one way or another. Gaspar Pérez de Villagrá's 1610 *History of New Mexico* is a narrative in verse, for instance. Max Westbrook, a well-known scholar of Western literature, notes in his preface to *A Literary History of the American West* that the book at hand surveys those artists who "chose to write honestly about the American West, believing that experiences long known to be of historical importance are also experiences that need and deserve a literature of importance."[1] Even the most formulaic Western fiction adheres to a principle of historical consistency whose violation its readers won't abide (a story set in the 1870s had better not feature a protagonist armed with a Model '94 carbine). And in his 1990 mystery novel *Coyote Waits* Tony Hillerman spins a plot whose crux concerns a wanna-be New Western Historian's research on Butch Cassidy and the Hole-in-the-Wall Gang.

That close relationship has recently grown closer — and thicker. With the new awareness of the West has come an increasing demand for truth, fact, authenticity, a demand that holds not only for prose fiction but also for poetry, nature writing, memoirs, film, painting, television series, music, all genres and media. But there seems to be an especially acute responsiveness to the demand in the world of fiction writers, publishers, and readers. In his 1992 book *Living the Dream: An Outline for a Life in Fiction*, Michael Seidman, discussing popular Westerns, observes that though "the bad guys are sociologically correct according to today's mores" (an anachronism that turns up in film and on television as well), "the stories are no longer the simplistic tales of the pulp era. Characters are becoming more fully developed and well rounded. History plays more of a role." Thus his advice to aspiring writers: "While the basic storyline of a confrontation (cavalry vs. Indians; sheepherder vs. cattle baron; sheriff vs. rustler; railroad vs. everyone) remains a must, the writer has to be careful in terms of description. . . . The readers now know what a cattle drive was like, what a herd of stampeding buffalo might have looked and sounded like, what a Lakota warrior wore into battle. If you're using elements like those, make certain that you know what you're talking about." Though Seidman may grant his typical hypothetical readers more historical sophistication than I would, he's dead right in a number of particulars that support his basic argument: female characters are more realistic (in the newest work some are "leads," and editors are searching for "female writers" to address "the apparent growth of popularity of the category among women readers"); publishers now foresee an expanding market for "so-called 'adult western' series" that break away from the "asexual" traditional Western; and so on. Move over, Louis L'Amour — though no one New Western author "has been crowned king" to take his place.[2]

A year after Seidman's book was published, Susan Porter, in a column, "The Markets," in *Writer's Digest*, corroborates him but carries the argument further: "After a ten-year drought, the western has shown signs of making a comeback, but it's not the same animal that rode off into the sunset with the Lone Ranger, Roy Rogers or even Little Joe Cartwright. . . . Today's tombstone-territory tales are complex. Many involve social issues, including the role of women and minorities on the frontier. Dale Evans and Tonto would no longer be mere sidekicks." Characters "are more three-dimensional." The genre includes more stories of Native Americans, contemporized settings, and elements from other genres like science fiction and mystery fiction. (The bimonthly *Louis L'Amour Western Magazine*, which premiered in January 1994 and soon enjoyed soaring subscription figures, is intent on publishing short stories about both epic and everyday heroes, both the overstated and the understated West.) "Nonfiction western tales are also doing well," Porter notes, and there is "a resurgence" of cowboy and cowgirl poetry — thanks to Gibbs Smith and other Western presses, small and almost large, that have tapped into a mother-lode market. Magazines like *West*, *Old West*, *True West*, and literary quarterlies like *Red Clay* seek more and more work from writers. And that, with some exceptions, isn't really the Serious Literature of the West, but even so — especially in the genre of Western fiction — "one aspect . . . remains unchanged: historical accuracy is a must."[3] Now, however, such accuracy involves a larger scale, more detail, finer sympathies for issues of culture, race, class, and gender.

Why has Western literature been so obsessed with history and historical accuracy? How does that obsession square with its obsession, pro or con, with myth? And why have both obsessions apparently intensified in recent years, along with a mixed determination not only to retain Western tradition, at least some of it, but also to revise it or even completely transform it? This is complicated territory. God knows, it's been visited before, by critics and scholars and others. The "facts" of the West and the fictions about it, realistic or otherwise, have long had a relationship as tangled with hate and love, with divergences and affinities, as an enduring but crazy marriage. Mutually distorting mirrors. You can get some sense of that relationship just by reading *Owen Wister out West: His Journals and Letters*, edited by Frances Kemble Wister (1958), side by side with his famous 1902 novel (or is it a romance?) *The Virginian: A Horseman of the Plains*: the "actual" West described in Wister's journals and letters differs considerably from, while still serving as the basis of, the "imagined" West of his fiction. But, as my questions suggest, that differing has changed since Wister's time, most notably within the last decade or so. I may not be able to answer such questions definitively, but I'll take a shot at doing it tentatively. Let's start into the thicket. We'll need to be strong readers/riders, willing to cope with lots of subtext/underbrush.

Richard White shows us an accessible point of entry. Speaking of the function of "local legends," tall tales and parodies especially, he classifies them as "a form of local chauvinism that identifies the local people with the place and its peculiarities." That's obvious enough in the case of "places with cultures rooted for hundreds or thousands of years," but in the case of the West, where, "except among Indians and Mexican Americans, personal roots rarely went back more than a generation or two," there's a twist: since such legends can't function to preserve long traditions for people who don't have them, they function, by derision and denigration, to clear away what preceded those people (nature, other cultures) and thus "exalt the pioneers." Extrapolate that process across a few years, and you get a bootstrapped heritage embodied in both oral and written literature, a "blood bond" created through "a common past and a pattern of shared memory" that "was often very much an invention." Likewise — though White doesn't make the connection explicit — the people displaced by the pioneers, dislocated from "cultures rooted for hundreds or thousands of years," whom he calls "the marginalized and subordinate, . . . could also imagine the West." Or, maybe, *had to*. So, for example, Hispanics accomplished that through "*corridos*, the folk ballads that created a popular past" and "also reworked popular memories to locate emblematic events" like those involving "Mexicans cheated of their just rewards."[4] Local history and myth, fact and fiction were a muddle from the start. Throw in the West imagined on a national scale, the West dreamed up by a whole new rootless country in need of chauvinistic identity, and it's clear that we're all in the muddle together.

Over time what we get out of that muddle, among other things, is literature with a centaurlike mythical-historical makeup: supposedly authentic accounts of heroic masculinity endlessly repeated in terms of romanticized formulas, with the truth suppressed by racism and sexism not that hard to find in the interstices. A contradictory literature that has trouble deciding whether Billy the Kid was a good guy or a bad guy, whether it wants to treat him straight or play out some version of the myth of him. More and more, recently, it's a literature that insists on achieving fuller historical accuracy of one kind or another and on doing something about the standard Western myth — avoiding it, inverting it, putting spin on it, anything to keep from being programmed by it. The authors of that literature want to rewrite both history and myth.

Gnarly matters. Maybe Richard W. Etulain, a historian with a thoroughgoing knowledge of Western literature, can help us gain some clarity. "Serious study of western American literature" did not come about, he instructs us, writing in 1979, until the 1960s. That decade saw the founding of the Western Literature Association (WLA) and its journal *Western American Literature* in 1965, the Popular Culture Association and its *Journal of Popular Culture* in 1967, and the Southwestern Literature Association and its journal *Southwestern American Literature* (the former now defunct) in 1970 — all of which "provided a powerful impetus for students and scholars interested in doing research on western authors and their works." He argues that by the end of the 1970s — and his argument applies to the present as well, I think — scholars of such literature hadn't come to much agreement on "the nature of the literary West" and related questions. Still, he ventures to "distinguish a few points of view that dominate" such research. One sees Western literature as the product of a provincial or colonial culture. Another sees it as the embodiment of recurrent mythic themes — the West as garden, as passage to India, and so on — first laid out in Henry Nash Smith's *Virgin Land*. Another, "increasingly popular since 1960," sees it as "primarily a land-oriented and nonrational literature," philosophically somewhat Native American, its works, in Richard Chase's critical terms, "more often mythic *romances* than realistic *novels*." And yet another, exemplified by Wallace Stegner, sees that literature as a response to "an arid and spacious environment."[5]

Etulain is surely right in his claim that these points of view have been significant, each productive of much worthwhile scholarship and criticism. But he's right also in proposing that his outline needs to include a point of view that recognizes "another significant emphasis in western fiction, one that has not received sufficient attention. This is the noticeable tendency among many western novelists to search for a useful or usable past." The tendency has become more intense since 1979, I'd argue, as has attention to it, in part doubtless because of stimulus from New Western History. The other points of view and their approaches remain much in evidence and interrelate considerably, but this one has become increasingly more relevant. In some respects, in fact, it may be subsuming the others. Though stressing Western writers' "concern for understanding the western past and for communicating the connections or continuities between past and present," Etulain nonetheless warns that "it would be incorrect to argue that this is the most important theme of western literature."[6] His warning rings true for literature written before 1979. For literature written since, it doesn't. That theme, understood broadly enough, is preeminent in the work of New Western writers, Euro-American and otherwise, of the last decade or so in their search for a cogent imaginative vision of the West, just as it is in New Western Historians' quest for the diverse truth of the past in relation to the present and in the multiform attempts of New Westers in general to scare up a meaningful heritage.

You won't have much trouble turning up predecessors to this flourishing. Etulain mentions in a note a handful of novelists who make much "use of history"—Willa Cather, Ole Rølvaag, Frederick Manfred, and others—and he treats three at length in his text: Vardis Fisher, A. B. Guthrie, Jr., and Wallace Stegner. Certainly Fisher and Guthrie are appropriate in that regard. But Etulain hits the bull's eye dead center when he argues that it's Stegner who "takes the giant step," for in his 1971 novel *Angle of Repose*, which won a Pulitzer Prize in 1972, "he has produced a western novel that is more than *about* history; he has written a first-rate fictional interpretation *of* the historical development of the West." Etulain was convinced, in 1979, that "an examination of the significant relationship between western history and the western novel will open new vistas of research for historians and literary scholars." Time has proved him correct. Though he argues that *Angle of Repose* "is a model for subsequent novels written about the West," he couldn't entirely foresee what Stegner's giant step was moving toward: not just more interest in writing fictional interpretations of Western history but a deepening and concerned fascination with them both in prose fiction and in other literary genres.[7]

Let's talk about that step for a moment, beginning with Etulain's overview of *Angle of Repose*:

> On one level the novel is the story of an eastern woman, Susan Burling, who marries another easterner, Oliver Ward, goes west, and tries to acclimate herself to western ways. On another level the book is about Susan's grandson, Lyman Ward, a retired history professor, who is an amputee and alienated from his world of 1970. By shifting back and forth between the late nineteenth century and events and ideas of the 1960s, Stegner deals with a full century of western history. It is a huge task and one that Stegner accomplishes through two major themes of western history: (1) What is the relationship between East and West? Should the emphases be placed on continuities or on differences? and (2) What comparisons and contrasts can be made between the frontier West and the New West of the 1960s?

As Etulain later remarks, this is sure not " 'just another western' " in the vein of Zane Grey, Luke Short, and Max Brand.[8] Though Lyman Ward serves as the author's agent in making present sense of the past from an attic full of his grandmother's letters, drawings, and publications, the real "hero" of the story isn't a man but a woman, Susan Ward. She's a character stronger in her clear-eyed way than any of the myth-tranced males in traditional Western novels. "When frontier historians theorize about the uprooted, the lawless, the purseless, and the socially cut-off who settled the West," Lyman proclaims, "they are not talking about people like my grandmother." For her, having given up so much in leaving the East, "the West was not a new country being created, but an old one being reproduced; in that sense our pioneer women were always more realistic than our pioneer men."[9]

Nor, to go further, were Old Western novelists talking about people like her. In constructing one of the most compelling female characters in

Western literature — certainly, at the time, *the* most compelling from a male novelist — Stegner broke from a long tradition of characterization, much as, in dealing with the spatial axis of East and West and the temporal axis of Old West and New West, he broke with the long tradition of fictionally writing about "the frontier West" as an isolated never-never land locked in the backward abysm of time. His novel isn't just historical: it wrestles with *issues* (environmental and economic, particularly) of Western history and identity in exactly the era in which New Western History was preparing for its own giant step.

Thus, just as *Bury My Heart at Wounded Knee* gave a taste in 1970 of what was to come in Western historiography, so *Angle of Repose* gave a taste in 1971 of what was to come in Western literature. Stegner's enlarged geographical context of the West; his extended view of its problems and values; his care in portraying Lyman's sympathetic reliving of his ancestors' lives and Lyman's sensitivity to the seductions of the past "as a refuge from an oppressive present"; his characterization of Susan; his stress on Lyman's need to learn from history "as it was, not as he wishes it had been," and to "comprehend fully the relationship between the Old and New Wests" — all figure in Lyman's studious attempt "to discover how they [his grandparents] achieved an angle of repose ["the incline at which rocks cease to roll"] in their lives." In many ways he's a New Wester exploring the Old Wester in himself in order to find his own sense of place through how his ancestors found theirs. A lot of New Western writers since have been engaged in their own versions of such an exploration, whether we think of it as Lyman's or Stegner's. Doubtless the quality and quantity of their work, along with urgings from Etulain and others, as well as the rise in the 1980s of New Historicism (a critical movement intent on the detailed historical analysis of literature), have encouraged Western historians to counter their "decreasing interest . . . in utilizing literature in their studies" in 1979.[10] And that work may well have had something to do with the fact that since 1987 we've had a comprehensive history of Western American literature, now being supplemented.

Stegner died in spring 1993. By that time he was much respected by historians, and several — Etulain, Elliott West, Patricia Nelson Limerick — honored his memory with presentations at a symposium in tribute to him at the University of Montana in September of that year. Such respect and tribute recognize that throughout his writing — fiction, biog-

Wallace Stegner, the grand old granddaddy of New Western writers. (Photo by Leo Holub)

raphy, history, essays — "he worked," as Jackson J. Benson put it in the issue of *Western American Literature* that appeared just after Stegner's death, "to increase our understanding of the West — its history, its geography, and its social dynamics — and to expose the myths that all too often had contributed to its exploitation." Benson offered several examples, among them "his Mormon histories" that "displayed the fallacy of a West created by the lone horseman and demonstrated how important cooperation was to its actual development."[11] There he's getting at the core of Stegner's revolution in *Angle of Repose* and other work, at the essential differences between Old Western literature and the New Western literature whose growth Stegner animated: an emphatic attention to history as what did happen rather than as what should have happened, to the *staying* of Western people rather than their going, to their efforts at community rather than their individualistic spirit, to the possibility of stewarding the land rather than destructively exploiting it (in regard to which possibility Stegner seems to have moved gradually from a conservationist to a preservationist position).

In the introduction to his last book, *Where the Bluebird Sings to the Lemonade Springs*, a collection of essays, Stegner reflects that shift of literary attention in expressing a preference for a certain breed of Westerner. Remarking how, "against probability, some sort of indigenous, recognizable culture has been growing on western ranches and in western towns and even in western cities," he argues that "it is the product not of the boomers but of the stickers, not of those who pillage and run but of those who settle, and love the life they have made and the place they have made it in. There are more of those, too, than there used to be, and they know a great deal more, and are better able to resist and sometimes prevent the extractive frenzy that periodically attacks them." In "the stickers" he speaks of New Westers at their best. And the writers among them — the ones he discusses in his book (Norman Maclean and others) as well as "all the new ones, the Ivan Doigs and Bill Kittredges and James Welches, the Gretel Ehrlichs and Rudolfo Anayas and John Daniels, the Scott Momadays and Louise Erdrichs and many more" — all inspire in him "the inextinguishable western hope." In his view those literary artists of different races, cultures, and genders are no longer really interested in the mythic Anglo "lone horseman," the "boomer" riding irresponsibly on, but in the larger human family hanging on in a preserved Western environment. "It is a civilization they are building," he says, "a way of looking at the world and humanity's place in it," and he believes "they will do it."[12]

The subtitle of his last book is aptly *Living and Writing in the West* because for Stegner living and writing there are bound together and interanimate each other. Thus, in a 1987 essay in the collection, he offers advice about what sort of society to look for in the contemporary West and the writer's role in maintaining it:

If I were advising a documentary filmmaker where he might get the

> most quintessential West in a fifty-six-minute can, I would . . . send him to just such a little city as Missoula or Corvallis, some settlement that has managed against difficulty to make itself into a place and is likely to remain one. . . . It would do no harm if an occasional Leslie Fiedler came through to stir up its provincialism and set it to some self-questioning. It wouldn't hurt if some native-born writer, some Doig or [Richard] Hugo or Maclean or Welch or Kittredge or Raymond Carver, was around to serve as culture hero — the individual who transcends his culture without abandoning it, who leaves for a while in search of opportunity and enlargement but never forgets where he left his heart.

For Stegner and, as we'll see, for the writers of whom he speaks, the stakes involved in such connectedness — of writer to place, of way of writing to way of living — are high:

> It is in places like these, and through individuals like these, that the West will realize itself, if it ever does: these towns and cities still close to the earth, intimate and interdependent in their shared community, shared optimism, and shared memory. These are the seedbeds of an emergent western culture. They are likely to be there when the agribusiness fields have turned to alkali flats and the dams have silted up, when the waves of overpopulation that have been destroying the West have receded, leaving the stickers to get on with the business of adaptation.[13]

And, he may as well have said, leaving the sticker writers to get on with the literature of that adaptation.

Now here's a terminology that within limits may be useful: New Western literature is sticker writing; Old Western literature — from before James Fenimore Cooper to Louis L'Amour — is boomer writing. The latter is written largely by Anglo men and published in the East, the former written more and more by non-Anglos and women and, with increasing frequency (though mostly early in their careers), published in the West. Returning to Elliott West, we could add another distinction. It's found in his description of the " 'new fiction' that has grown up alongside the new history," and it concerns the sobered-up and ironic view of the West associated with much sticker writing:

> The novels and short fiction of Douglas Unger, James Welch, Patricia

Henley, Craig Lesley, Kent Haruf, William Kittredge, Louise Erdrich, and David Quammen are stories of disappointment and persistence, grudging accommodations, the ghosts of traditions. Just as the new historians look hard at the romantic idealism of earlier works, these writers break with the easy heroism of the traditional western novel. There is little about promise but much about costs. Dreams have become obsessions and comic lusts. The characters — whether snake-farm proprietors, rodeo Indians, or over-mortgaged turkey farmers — are bound to the country by a bitter affection, a connection that is hard earned and as inescapable as blood kinship.[14]

Boomer writing is happier stuff, prewritten in a sense, easier to pull off. It ignores a lot of consequences. Sticker writing deals with the mess left behind after the boomers ride away. It takes on the task of rebuilding a hardscrabble world. Writing romantically about a myth-misted Custer is a piece of cake compared to writing realistically about Chippewas in the North Dakota of the 1980s.

Such distinctions aren't absolute. You can cite exceptions. Neither booming nor sticking, nor either of their literatures, exists in a pure form. Still, there's a remarkable difference of emphasis. All nature might be defined in terms of the ceaseless interrelations of stationary and mobile organisms, homers and roamers, those that stay rooted and those that exploit and move on. But in terms of physical exploitation the West is pretty near boomed out. Its Pacific extreme is silted up with people who have moved on as far as they can. So most recent Western writers realize that it's time to look around, put down some roots, take care of the place — and get on with writing its new stories of endurance. The feeling of that shift of attitude is as palpable as, in Stegner's words, "the feeling in a football game when the momentum changes, when helplessness begins to give way to confidence, and what looked like sure defeat opens up to the possibility of victory. It has already begun."[15] Indeed, it has. Stegner won't witness the stickers' new, different winning of the New West, but it's under way.

Which is to say, Western literature is entering its mature regionalist phase. Perhaps Harold P. Simonson can help us understand how that process unfolds — and why. In his *Beyond the Frontier: Writers, Western Regionalism and a Sense of Place*, he focuses on a progression. The frontier gave America "a great myth," which "confirmed political democracy, human infinitude and philosophical idealism." The "closed frontier," which he treats "as metaphor" here, "signaled the kind of American tragedy that destroyed illusions on the open frontier and forced the nation to come of age." When that happens — and it may take a while — "a nation, like a person, . . . recognizes that limitation is a fundamental fact of life." So "existentialism" replaces "idealism," and "instead of limitlessness, there is a wall. The tension comes from the illusory prospect of the one and the certitude of the other. Existence in this tension is the heart of tragedy." And here's the clincher:

> But tragedy is not the heart of the matter. The tension . . . may itself lead to a synthesis constituting a new condition — a frontier synthesis manifesting itself in regionalism that conveys a special sense of place. Used this way, the term "regionalism" is not meant merely to suggest a geographical region unique or peculiarly colorful as local literary colorists see it, or as sentimentalists might view it. Nor is regionalism to be interpreted as some imaginative place where a person can escape. Often the West has been seen in such a way. Instead, regionalism is real towns, rivers, mountains and ranches — . . . physical places that one can identify with and connect with inside his own soul. A certain place is thus seen as synonymous with *home*. Home is where tensions are lived out; home is the special place where connections and clarifications occur. In the end home is what brings wholeness and axial centeredness to people, and is therefore perhaps the only resolution any of us can know.[16]

Heady discourse, but it does tell us a good deal about what New Western literature is up to, whether or not its authors have such a reasoned awareness of the synthesis they're effecting.

Simonson discusses a range of literary works that exemplify "the irony of American exploration, whether geographic or spiritual": how booming leads to sticking or how, as he has it, "the striving to get away only brings one back to oneself." *The Adventures of Huckleberry Finn*, Rølvaag's *Giants in the Earth*, and Nathanael West's *The Day of the Locust* grapple with "the tragedy inherent in the closed frontier," the last, published in 1939, about that tragedy turned into "something surrealistic and nightmarish . . . in Southern California, a region inhabited by the totally deluded." Such works of fiction indicate the need for a literature that transcends the concern of Old Western literature with "social mobility (westward movement) and an open, visionary future" and deals with a rootedness allowing knowledge of "a profoundly elementary relationship that redeems tragedy and futuristic nightmare." That is, a literature that concerns itself with a "sense of place [that] restores one's relationship to the land and the community" and variously stories "the universal monomyth . . . of loss and regaining of identity." A literature that Simonson finds exemplified not only in the regionalists he considers in detail — Doig, Welch, and Maclean — but in others he mentions along the way, such as Edward Abbey, Ehrlich, and Theodore Roethke. A literature that, having for the most part passed through the first two stages of regional-literary development (that is, literature as "a written record through the eyes of newcomers" and literature as an imaginative interpretation of such a record), now is coming into the third stage, where *regional* literature becomes regional *literature*, with "an artistic achievement joining artist and place, each bringing life to the other." A literature through which "we find ourselves returning . . . to where we started from," so that "we recognize that the most profound regionalists were the persons who were here long before we arrived with our axes and plows, diaries and journals" — those Native Americans who "knew what it was to live on holy ground . . . and to be in relationship with all that surrounded them."[17] In other words, New Western literature.

No wonder there's been such public sympathy for the Taos people's regaining their sacred Blue Lake or the Sioux people's recovering their sacred Black Hills. We're finally beginning to understand, much thanks to New Western writers, that Dorothy is right when she announces, after awakening in Kansas from the travels of a dream both thrilling and vexing, "There's no place like home." Maybe even Danielle Steel, with her practiced instinct for how to make money out of what's on the public's mind, gets it right at the end of the 1993 movie version of her 1981 romance *Palomino*. There Samantha Taylor, an urban writer who after a spinal injury has taken on the management of a California spread and made it into a dude ranch for disabled children, greets her at-last-come-back-and-no-more-to-roam cowhand lover, Tate Jordan, with the words "Welcome home." Then, strapped in her saddle, she rides beside him off into the sunset, not to move on but to return to the ranch house and make a life with him. Things have changed. At the end of the typical Old

Western story a man says goodbye to a woman and a home. Here she welcomes him to a home and, even in this horsey soap opera or soapy horse opera, all it now means.

In chapter 2 I spoke, intentionally, of the desolation of modern *men* bereft of the Western myth in Larry McMurtry's fiction. I was anticipating something. Let's open it up.

In his foreword to *In a Narrow Grave*, McMurtry allows that the novel is "a superb medium" for "reinventing" a region, an idea he adapts from John Barth. But for himself, he says, the novel is more like "a habitation," and he contrasts it to the essay, which is "a place one visits occasionally, when one is tired of home," a place like "a fine hotel" where "one can stroll about in one's best clothes and ruminate upon all those things one never has time to ruminate upon at home." But there's an irony involved: "What I generally find I am ruminating upon in the essay is home itself, the place where my characters live" — an association, essay-to-home or home-to-essay, that may explain, in part, why home-minded New Western writers have contributed so much to the recent resurgence of the essay as a literary form. And along with the irony goes a confusion very productive for a novelist like McMurtry who evokes place so effectively: "I can never be quite sure whether home is a place or a form: the novel, or Texas. In daily life the two become crucially but vaguely related, and it is difficult to say with precision where place stops supporting fiction and fiction starts embodying place."[18] There's plenty in his remarks to think about in regard to McMurtry's talent for making his characters engagingly real and in regard to "reinventing" a region through fiction as well. You can't get away from myth of some kind, even if it's a myth about mythlessness that embodies a place.

Let me formulate the main point here by way of comments from Jane Nelson on McMurtry's ruminations on ruminations:

> In McMurtry's fiction, two places are embodied: the rural homeplace loved by the cowboy, and the household maintained by a maternal woman. The homeplace has mythic force in McMurtry's conception, but it is also a feature of the past. Without a myth by which to identify themselves, McMurtry's male characters have limited choices: they

> can disappear, like Danny Deck; they can invert the myth to violent and perverted ends, like Hud or Sonny Shanks; or they can learn to accept temporary homes, like Sonny Crawford and Cadillac Jack. In the modern, urban West, McMurtry suggests, women are the powerful characters because they have learned to create homes without the support of a myth.[19]

If you haven't read all of the novels those characters populate, you may find Nelson's catalog slightly opaque; on the other hand, if you've read *Lonesome Dove* or seen the television-miniseries version of it, you can fit its characters, even in a nineteenth-century setting, into Nelson's scheme to an extent. (Clara Allen, for instance, has created a home without relying on the myth, hateful to her, already problematic, that drives otherwise stable—though stubborn, egotistical—Augustus McCrae away from her and on to Montana and his death.) And it may be the case that McMurtry's female characters don't so much live without myth as they live by a myth (or myths) different from the one the male characters have lost. Nelson's comments could trigger other quibbles too, but she's hit something essential: in McMurtry's fictional West the women have the day; they're the stickers.

My point is that McMurtry's strong female characters not only are representative of similar characters in fiction by other New Western writers but also mirror New Western literature more generally—because it is, increasingly, a feminized literature. It's typically a literature somehow about home, the conventional "place" of woman. Just as McMurtry's female characters "create homes without the support of a myth," so are those writers, female or male, creating their "habitations" at least without the support of the traditional Western myth. (Their support, as you probably have already surmised and later will see illustrated, comes from the monomyth of lost and restored identity to which Simonson alluded—a term from the literary critic Northrop Frye.) I wouldn't say that male writers whose work is supported by the standard myth have cashed in their chips any more than I would say that Anglo writers have done so, but there are new players at the table; they are playing new games.

That holds also for New Western literary criticism. As White observes, feminist literary critics are analyzing "the darker West" of abusive men in the works of writers from the 1920s and 1930s like Mari

Sandoz and Agnes Smedley, Laura Ingalls Wilder's "female West" of " 'modern female' virtues" in her Little House books, and Willa Cather's female characters who "form enduring bonds with the land itself." Such "reimagining of the West" involves "critics who consciously seek to re-vision the lives of western women," an act whose "stuff . . . is at once the western past itself and reinterpretations of the earlier imaginings of others."[20] It's hardly coincidental that women, especially women in the WLA, were at the forefront of efforts to establish in 1992 the Association for the Study of Literature and Environment, a fast-growing organization that promotes the exchange of information and ideas concerning natural-history writing, nature poetry, environmental fiction, and the like. Ecocriticism, the criticism of literature from an ecological point of view, is the primary interest of its members. The word *ecology*, at its roots, means "house-study" or "home-story" or the "order" of the "household" (that's a big place in the West) where we live.

Surveying developments in Western women's writing in the mid-1980s, Lou Rodenberger points out trends that have continued unabated. The most obvious, perhaps, are "the emergence of more, often better women writers" and "the *acknowledgement*" of them and "the unique perspective they offer." They are redefining "traditional genres," and their predecessors — neglected artists like Meridel LeSueur or virtually nameless keepers of diaries and journals — are being resurrected and "read in a new way by a new generation." Moreover, "publishing opportunities are greater now than ever before for women," and anthologies of writing by Western women, in several genres, have been pouring out of Western presses. Women writers, whether or not they conceive of themselves as regional (and increasingly they do), thrive in the West and its corollary "artistic freedom not easily found in older, more tightly knit literary establishments."[21] They're taking to the West like horses to open range — not to roam but to find a spacious home. For them the West is less and less a colony or copy of the East and more and more a center, an original place. And to a striking extent they want to strip it of Anglo-male mystification and experience it and write about it differently. Like E.T., they want to get back home.

Fine. Still, the myth business needs a bit more brooding, particularly in relation to this woman business. A collection of critical essays, *Under the Sun: Myth and Realism in Western American Literature*, edited by

Barbara Howard Meldrum, may be of help. In her introduction Meldrum speaks of the persistence of the traditional Western myth, its oddly "realistic status," and questions whether it ever existed beyond "popular fantasies" and whether it matters that it diverges from supposed facts. Whatever the answers to such questions, she counts the myth and its loose associations with "acts of conquest . . . and a cluster of values" (mostly male) as constituting "a weighty legacy for the western writer." That is, he or she has to grapple with it some way or other. So, to use an example from Meldrum, Walter Van Tilburg Clark, in *The Ox-Bow Incident* (1940), wrote a novel based on no specific incident that spurred Western readers to search for and even in several cases to believe they had found, in newspapers or wherever, what he started with. Meldrum explains, quite plausibly, how that happened: "The authenticity [of Clark's story] was 'like history' but was fiction; the reality was mythic, not simply the myth of the West but universal or primordial truth of human character and destiny." Though "universal or primordial" might make for a quibble or two, Meldrum is on to something important: "Western writers do indeed mythologize about their region," whether they "adopt old myths to their regional setting" or "create new myths" or "play one myth against another" (so it's not unusual to find classical myths echoed in the novels of, for instance, Frederick Manfred).[22]

That holds true also when writers are parodying the Western romance or writing anti-Westerns, ironic deflations in the vein of Stephen Crane's 1898 short story "The Bride Comes to Yellow Sky" (where a showdown between Marshal Jack Potter and outlaw Scratchy Wilson comes to nothing because Potter turns up at the scene with his new wife, interestingly enough, and it just don't seem fittin' to Wilson to shoot a married man). Even then, "demythologizing goes hand-in-hand with mythologizing" (Crane, in this example, mythologizes the civilizing effect of women, with their Eastern influences, on the West as much as he demythologizes its domination by men). In other words, as Meldrum puts it, borrowing a phrase from Wright Morris, "The writer with a sun in his belly does not ignore the mythic past, but is not bound by it." Finally, she sums up this slippery situation with a paradox: "authenticity" as only a reflection of "empirical fact" has nothing to do with the imagination's activity; but since "the myths of western literature [do] ring true when they are grounded in empirical fact and transformed into the realities only the imagination can provide," it follows that "myth and realism are ultimately one."[23]

That may not be as deep a paradox as it seems, or it may be becoming less a paradox. In another essay in Meldrum's collection, Max Westbrook discusses the problems of defining exactly what we mean by *myth* and *reality* in Western literature. After some anguishing he suggests that a number of modern works of fiction from several American regions show a pattern of dealing with "myth as truth but losing power and moving toward illusion." More specifically, he interprets Guthrie's *The Big Sky* and Walter Van Tilburg Clark's *The Track of the Cat* as "primarily studies in truth moving toward untruth, or a myth in the process of betrayal."[24] His insight illuminates like a campfire stoked with dry pine.

In this light, then, one major incongruity in *The Big Sky* leaps out: the myth of the mountain man, insofar as it's grounded in fur trading, doesn't fit with the reality of a rapidly diminishing demand for beaver pelts — and an increasing demand for silk — in the hat-making industry. It would be easy to come up with other examples, as Westbrook does. And, of course, it's easy to discern the historical clash between the traditional myth of the wide-open frontier and the more "civilized" space the West has progressively become. The literature that Simonson terms tragic has to do precisely with such a clash. That's Old Western literature, for the most part. What about New Western literature, with its emphasis on feminine place rather than masculine movement? Does it fix the traditional myth in some way — or go beyond it — so that the New Western myth fits reality better?

Madelon Heatherington, another contributor to Meldrum's collection, offers an intriguing diagnosis of the myth problem in much of modern Western literature and adumbrates, perhaps unconsciously, a more "realistic" New Western myth. Since her essay was published in 1985, just before the New Western hog, as Hunter Thompson would say, was really out of the tunnel, it's dated — but in revealing particulars.

Heatherington begins by expressing a concern that shows her tuning in to what's happening with the 1980s West but that the subsequent burgeoning of Western fiction would soon render obsolete: "In recent years, virtually every art form dealing with the American West has become fashionable, profitable, and therefore to some extent respectable —

every art form, that is, except fiction." From her point of view, the fiction is "still regarded as merely 'pulp' trash." And she faults it doubly, for it has "failed to take into account the complexities both of human behavior, actual or fictional, and of the Western's own genre, the romance." Its "arrested development" is manifested especially in the "treatment of women characters," who remain stereotypes both in L'Amour-like popular fiction and, often, in the work of "the most respected of Western writers." But Heatherington isn't hell-bent on launching "an equivalently simplistic revisionist-feminist attack"; her real engagement is with the results of that kind of characterization: "basic dynamics of romance [that] are aborted" and fiction that, by and large, "therefore . . . has never allowed itself to explore and develop its own full potential."[25]

That situation, Heatherington hypothesizes, may be related to what she calls a "schizoid" view of the West as "an uneasy mixture of mythic fantasy and social inertia," a bright land of "Marlboro *macho* where people and things are simpler, cleaner, and wiser than in the East" and "a cultural desert littered with radioactive sheep and half-ton Chevy pickups bearing bumper stickers which vow, 'You can take my gun when you can pry my cold, dead fingers off the trigger.' " Well, a combination of frontier autism and inbred NRA politics wouldn't encourage fully developed literature. Nor would the needs of readers, doubtless male, given to devouring "regional sentimentalism, . . . presumably moving their lips and stroking their Winchesters the while." That's amusing caricature, but, as Heatherington clearly realizes, her hypothesizing doesn't square with the fact that "suddenly Wall Street brokers wear Justin boots, and all of the arts except fiction have acquired a WASP–ethnic cachet."[26]

Nope. Something else has the fiction stalled in 1985, a time when the other arts of the West "have so managed to adapt Western formulas as to have it both ways: they are keeping pace with a more sophisticated (or perhaps a more realistic) apprehension of history and of human beings, but they have also continued drawing on the Western's traditional resources of romance myths." Heatherington finds that true even of some Western-flavored country music — the ironic and parodical turns of David Allen Coe and Jerry Jeff Walker or Loretta Lynn's tough-minded portrayals of women. And she grants exceptions — Tom Robbins's *Even Cowgirls Get the Blues* or *Angle of Repose*, for instance — in early New Western fiction. But most of the fiction is "primarily concerned with the maneuverings of males," with women serving only as "motivators, not actors, important only to the plot." Having men do their John Wayne elliptical struts and women circumscribed to stay out of their way, characterization thus "at the level of Barbie and Ken dolls," Western novels "are self- and reader-affirmative; they reassure the reader that his attitudes are right and just, that he need not bestir himself to question them." The reader, hypnotized by comfortable images, never gets "past the book itself" to "more powerful truths" about the nature of Western romance.[27] That's the stall, the reader's and the fiction's alike.

The "more powerful truths" concern Heatherington much, for a consideration of them may explain the stall more deeply. First of all, the basic romance, articulated in a well-realized Western novel or otherwise, involves a hero enacting an archetypal quest in "an idealized world" and, usually, "a chase of villains by the hero, with civilization — the Princess, the town — as the prize." The hero's job is twofold "deliverance": "to eliminate the savagery [dragon, cattle-baron bully, curse, crooked sheriff, whatever] that has disrupted the community" and made it a sterile wasteland and to restore "the community — however illusorily, however momentarily — " to a fertile paradise. At the highest level, his job "is to give us a glimpse of what we could be if we were better than we are." And in the basic romance women play essential roles, not only as part of the "prize" but also as testers of the hero who offer him preliminary challenges and help him learn "to accept various aspects of himself" before the big showdown with evil; then, after he risks death and emerges victorious, it's a woman as the principle of life itself he embraces.[28]

In the typical traditional Western, on the other hand, that arrangement gets sidetracked and abbreviated, according to Heatherington. Why? Because the hero can't handle the woman thing right. He'll either "fixate on woman as Poison Queen" (this happens with Randle Patrick McMurphy, that con-man cowboy, even in a transmogrified, tradition-inverting Western novel as sophisticated as Ken Kesey's *One Flew over the Cuckoo's Nest*) out of his own Calvinistic sexual self-loathing or see her "as his antithesis, the Princess, an icon" (Heatherington construes Jack Crabb in Thomas Berger's *Little Big Man* as apparently doing this), or deny "that women exist in any significant way at all" (which is what occurs "in most Westerns"). Consequently, the hero winds up self-ignorant, lacking "full romance status," thus not empowered to complete his quest, and so "wastes his regenerative energies in mere adventure for its own sake." In common parlance, he doesn't get the girl in the end and, now a loose cannon, doesn't hang around long. The Lone Ranger rides on — no Princess, no town; no life-goddess, no home. "Sadly," Heatherington argues, "this is what has happened with most fiction about the West, even the best novels."[29] In 1985 things haven't gone much beyond where they were in 1902 in *The Virginian*: Owen Wister's Molly Wood may be the archetypal Princess of the West, but she's still as wooden and purposeless as a drugstore Indian.

So real men in the Western romance don't fall in love and sure as hell don't get married — no bride comes to Yellow Sky. If they do fall in love, they're "removed from the action"; and "a married man figuratively becomes a gelding," a Jack Potter. So what do they do? According to Heatherington, "a 'real' Western man . . . lives, works, and plays alone or with other males, saving his *virtú* and his *preux* for roping calves, shooting scoundrels or strangers, and swatting flies on the bunkhouse wall." His virtue and valiance directed away from the quest, he dwells in an "erotic ignorance" sanctioned by a "taboo against sexuality in any form," a taboo "deeply hidden in most Western fiction beneath the paeans to the charms of rugged individualism and to the moral enlightenment supposedly inherent in an amorphous 'code of the West' derived from nineteenth-century industrialist/expansionist dogma and hell-fire theology." No triumph of fertility over the wasteland here, only "psychosexual stagnation." No "rejuvenation" or "civilization," just James Fenimore Cooper's Natty Bumppo growing restless, maybe "dangerous" in his antsiness, once things begin to look too homey.[30] Charged like a Leyden jar with suppressed sexuality, he doesn't want to settle down: he wants to settle up, saddle up, and split.

Wait. That's not the whole appraisement. After all this psychologizing about the fictional cowboy's "*a*sexual panic" to keep the West "a dry land in more ways than one" and his "being forced to refuse the responsibility of furthering the community's needs" and to withhold "fulfillment" even from himself, Heatherington goes for the punch line: "As a hero, he has been sold short because he has not been allowed to take the one risk that can bring him true salvationary stature: the risk of losing his soul, not to a Princess or a Poison Queen, but to a woman."[31]

Now that's an incentive to check your hoglegs at the sheriff's office and stick around awhile! Rise out of the slough of sexual despond. Give your horse a rest. No more hot lead, just a warm bed. Unless, of course, you feel too nervous, grab your flyswatter, and head for the bunkhouse, a postmodern Scratchy Wilson too incongruous with the situation to cope.

With due apologies to Heatherington for that outbreak (which she nonetheless invites, I think), I have to admit that she beautifully sets the stage for the New Western fiction of the late 1980s and 1990s. Much of it succeeds in developing female characters with startling presence, genuine roles to play, something important to say. The male characters are less and less sold short and are allowed to take the risk of losing their souls to women. The quest, however defined, is pushed toward a completion, however contingent. The romance, becoming more realistic, becomes more like the novel; in that condition it's taken more seriously by literary critics and scholars — by any reader with an appetite for literature that breaks out of its formulas and stereotypes to offer a fresh narrative of the West and its people. And, to complicate the picture, the author and/or narrator is more apt to be a woman than in the past and more apt not to be an Anglo. So is the hero. So is the reader. And, to complicate it more, these generalizations about the changes in Western fiction apply — with adjustments, of course — to Western literature in other genres and forms: poetry, drama, nature writing, travelogues, memoirs, even personalized literary criticism. A great deal of it strives to climb out of stagnation, the mire of the tragic (or pathetic), and give the West a different literary voice — and succeeds in doing so. When it does, it brings the hero home so he or she has a fuller — more self-conscious, more diverse, more maturely expressed, indeed more feminized — experience of learning who and where he or she is than Old Western literature could enact. In many ways New Western writers, in completing the myth of the quest stalled in sterility, transform it into the monomyth of renewed identity. They (re)turn to the West and know it as if for the first time.

Thus you can look back and see the signs of the coming New Western literature in all its abundance. At some point the dime novels, doggerel, melodrama, and the like had to start giving way to better efforts. Enough of Ned Buntline's versions of William Cody, enough of Edward Wheeler's Deadwood Dick in endless titles. Well, almost. The point may be more like a blurred line, and the racist, sexist, homogenized stories aren't all gone. But Willa Cather's *Death Comes for the Archbishop* (1927) and other works of hers promised that Western fiction with a more evocative ethnic and regional texture was possible. So did the late Frank Waters's 1942 novel *The Man Who Killed the Deer*, which may be the classic tale of Anglo-Indian conflict and the search for a cultural home. Still, the 1960s were the years when the literature started really to mutate. Whatever its faults in Heatherington's eyes, Berger's *Little Big Man* (1964) was a different kind of Western novel, experimenting with a whole new perspective on the late-nineteenth-century West. And 1964 was the year Sam Shepard's first play, *Cowboys*, was presented, the first of many plays by the Pulitzer Prize–winning dramatist that performed fragmented, discomfiting transformations on Old Western images and values while still, nostalgically even if obliquely, struggling to retain or revivify them as an apposite heritage. That same year, Ed Dorn's satiric free-verse poetry about the interior West — quasi-epic, bizarrely comic, metaphysical, hallucinatory by turns, intent on a lucid, multicultural sense of place — started appearing in book form with *Hands Up!*, a poetry that may have reached its consummation in *Slinger* (1975), his long poem about ecological and ethnic resistance to the capitalistic takeover of the West.

By 1969 you could find science-fiction Westerns or almost any other refiguring of the Western romance you wanted, a situation epitomized by the publication in that year of Ishmael Reed's *Yellow Back Radio Broke-Down*. That book, by an African American from Tennessee who'd come to California by way of Nebraska, blew the lid off. Kathryn Hume characterizes it concisely: "*Yellow Back Radio Broke-Down* . . . looks at the historical roots of control. The novel reinterprets the cowboy myths of taming the American West as grotesque and perverse cultural rape." Moreover, Reed "challenges Christianity as a form of control . . . , opposing the pope to his Hoodoo protagonist, Loop Garoo, a banished older son of God, cloven-hoofed, but a genuine spiritual power to be reckoned with." Thus, by this construal, "the cultural intolerance derived from Christianity and the contempt for those with less sophisticated technology and therefore less firepower are both important targets in this mock Western." In Hume's perceptive view, Reed and many other writers, Western or otherwise, of the last few decades "would say that their readers are ignorant of true history and believe falsehoods; but Reed does the most to identify publicly accepted myths and rewrite them according to his own truths." His brilliant put-down story of Garoo's liberation of the town of Yellow Back Radio exposes the so-called "taming of the West" as having "little to do with clean, white Marlboro-country suavity and heroism," turning the whole American show on its head in the process: Jefferson and Lincoln are hardly "idealistic and virtuous white fathers"; the outwardly civic-minded city of Washington masks an unpublicized play of powerful negative forces; blacks are the real but suppressed center of human culture; on and on.[32] New Western History with an ethnic vengeance

The book is too rich a mix to analyze at length here, but it's clearly a shake-'em-up precursor to later New Western literature. Like the West itself, as Robert Murray Davis describes it, Reed's novel "is *wild*, not reduced to patterns, not 'occupied' in any of several senses. It is thus a place where, free of the repressions of civilization, the individual can create a new society and, more important for Reed, assume a new identity." And it's wholly appropriate that Davis compares Reed's book, with its "changes on various genres and myths" and its "characteristically postmodern style," to Oakley Hall's remarkable 1985 novel *The Coming of the Kid,* which "programmatically uses something like Joseph Campbell's monomyth [no one owns the word, I guess] — companions, helpers, descents into the underworld, and so on — to show the quest to reclaim the West from those who would exploit and pollute it." The use of that kind of "borrowed pattern" suggests the dead end of modernism to Davis.[33] Maybe so, but to me it suggests also an impulse toward the profound interest in immediate issues of identity and place that haunts more recent Western literature.

After *Yellow Back Radio Broke-Down,* even more fiddling with the Western, besides Stegner's, went on during the 1970s and 1980s — until in a way it seems a wonder that anyone could still hope to live out the traditional Western myth, vicariously or otherwise; could still keep in the mind's eye a vision of the Western past as luminously dreamy as the emulsified image of an autochrome. Abbey's novel *The Monkey Wrench Gang* (1975) and his other fiction and nonfiction express outrage at the megadamage done by that myth gone bonkers in the twentieth century and argue for hard tactics to preserve what's left of the West. Robbins's *Even Cowgirls Get the Blues* (1976) is very much concerned with remythologizing and "regendering" an ecologically saner West. Rob Swigart does a madcap revisioning of the mobile postmodern West in *Little America* (1977), a novel centered on the world's largest truck stop, in Wyoming. Notice in that onrushing herd of texts *The Chickencoop Chinaman* (1972) and other dramatic or fictional works by Frank Chin that rewrite the West in Asian terms, Oakley Hall's later fiction, the novels in Don Coldsmith's Spanish Bit Saga, the nature writing of Barry Lopez and Hope Ryden, and more — and you realize that there's a stampede of this new breed of litterateurs.

In his *Prose and Poetry of the American West*, the most comprehensive, gender-aware, and multicultural anthology of its kind available, James C. Work, perhaps somewhat problematically, divides Western literary history and his book into four parts: the Emergence Period, 1540–1832 (Native American emergence myths, the writings of Meriwether Lewis and William Clark, and the like); the Mythopoeic Period, 1833–1889 (the works of John Wesley Powell, Mark Twain, Bret Harte, and others); the Neomythic Period, 1890–1914 (the works of Thomas Hornsby Ferril, Mari Sandoz, and others — all the way to William Stafford); and the Neowestern Period, 1915–present (the works of Ann Zwinger, Abbey, N. Scott Momaday — up to Jimmy Santiago Baca). Work's term *neowestern* in that scheme covers more chronological territory than my term *New Western*, which covers, in its roughest and most tenuous usage, the years no further back than the early 1960s — and, in its most precise, the years from around 1985 on. But in his introduction to the last part of the book when he speaks about neowestern writers, he's referring usually to more recent ones who fit my time category just fine; and he shares instructive thoughts about the burgeoning of their work in the late part of the Neowestern Period.

Drawing on Gerald D. Nash's historiography, Work rehearses the necessary background — the so-called closing of the frontier, the migration of decamillions of people into the twentieth-century West, then the subsequent anomie, "disjunction" among the cultures involved, and environmental devastation — and arrives at a consequence: the utter difficulty, for contemporary writers acutely aware of what has transpired, of writing about the "West of 'once upon a time.' " Though previously "writers of the West felt free to write about romantic ideals as if these were everyday verities," by now the "ambiguities [that] began springing up like weeds in an overworked field" after World War I have become thick indeed. Living in a region whose conditions mismatch its Old Western image of itself, the writers of "the neo-West" are "caught between heritage and hokum, between history and parody." On top of that, of course, "the neowesterner still has many of the old frontier personality traits," whose less positive aspects don't square with the West's romantic self-image and so provide a model for character development that some readers resist.[34] The horns of the dilemma branch like a wapiti's antlers.

Neowestern writers have dealt with the dilemma in several ways, according to Work. Some, like Louis L'Amour or Jeanne Williams, just say the hell with it and keep cranking the romance machine. Others, like Guthrie, Clark, and Stegner, "breathe new life into the old stereotypes." Still others "resort to writing individualistic poetry and prose, or extremely character-centered fiction, and thereby sidestep the whole mythic question" — a tricky avoidance. And then there are those who "find the forces too strong to ignore and too traditional to modify," for whom influences from the past are so "deeply rooted" that Work calls them "*heritage*, rather than *myth* or *history*." He discovers ready examples of such "heritage-centered writers" in "the Chicano literary movement," mentioning Baca and Rudolfo A. Anaya, author of the classic novel *Bless Me, Ultima* (1972) and, more recently, *Alburquerque* (1992), both concerned with issues of heritage and personal identity.[35] As Work notes, those writers — Baca with his attempt to write Chicano epic poetry, Anaya with his characters' interpretive quests for the past, the ideological dramatists of El Teatro Campesino from 1965 on, and many others — draw upon and continue a heritage four centuries old. A lot of Anglo writers, I'd contend, are doing much the same thing, though their heritage is younger, more eclectic, more confused with popular myth and debatable history. And Native American writers like Momaday, Luci Tapahonso, and Joy Harjo are reaching back much further than Chicanos or Anglos as they engage their heritage. These literary artists may seem to be writing off in all directions at once, but they know where they want to go.

But whatever strategy he or she uses for dealing with the past, "whether coming from a long literary lineage or having newly arrived on the western scene, each writer of the neowestern generation seems to have a conflict of values lurking somewhere behind each story, play, or poem." Thus, to repeat Work's cogent examples, Native American writers "want their literature to preserve the rapidly vanishing traditions of their people, yet they recognize that many of those traditions are archaic"; and nature writers, "if their writing is successful, . . . actually attract more people to the very places they set out to defend." Still, however they come to terms with such conflicts and the ironies they entail, neowestern writers of all genres, Work argues, "continue to be intrigued by one subject — the environment." That surrounding, intertangled, and shaping entirety, material or spiritual, is woven more thoroughly into Western literature than ever before, as are the issues of its future. Neowestern writers challenge the "resource concept" of nature, and many "blame modern western problems on one basic cause: society has lost touch with the earth" — a result that critic John R. Milton, like others, attributes to a "traditional belief in mobility."[36] Neowestern writers are concerned both with the sad or apocalyptic implications of that situation and with recovery from it.

Though those writers have "heard more than one discouraging word" about the natural environment and all the other messes of their world, Work is optimistic that at least some of them "will eventually succeed in struggling through the dilemmas and contradictions, the paradoxical social impulses, the random value and philosophy shifts that have characterized the years since World War I." Borrowing from the wisdom of Frank Waters, he concludes that such success will come not through the usual progress (more vain mobility) but through the evolution of the individual. It's a matter of fulfillment that he sees neowestern writers "finding . . . in three distinct ways: as individual expressive artists, as interpretive ambassadors of their various cultural communities, and — perhaps most important of all — as western people with a true sense of place."[37] Exactly. But those ways aren't always so distinct and in any given New Western writer may be closely interrelated, as may be individual expression, cultural nuances, and environmental consciousness in any given literary work. We've come back to the defining concerns of New Western writers: identity, heritage, place. An overlapping triplet of individual, cultural, and natural Western worlds. Home again, home again.

Once you pick up on this home theme, you begin to notice it everywhere. And I'm hardly alone in stressing the significance of it in New Western literature. Russell Martin, who with Marc Barasch edited the 1984 collection *Writers of the Purple Sage: An Anthology of Recent Western Writing*, remarks in his introduction to the 1992 follow-up collection, *New Writers of the Purple Sage: An Anthology of Contemporary Western Writing*, that an important change in Western writing occurred between the early 1980s and the early 1990s. Martin admits that "the colonial era is still far from over," but, speaking for the people of the New West, especially its writers (and maybe their literary portrayals of Westerners), he argues that "we're beginning to understand that we don't have to be in any sense one-dimensional—those of us who live amid this landscape—whether as awe-shucks kinds of cowboys or land-poor peasants who've never seen Pocatello, let alone Gay Paree, or as grease-stained roustabouts stuck on a God-forsaken rig somewhere out on the edge of the earth." Part of the change, then, is in the Western sense of identity, for "we've proved to ourselves that we can be many things: artists, scientists, ascetics, even." Another part of it, a big part, has to do with the related sense of place, for "it seems certain now that we can fashion as many kinds of homes here as there is vast and varied land in which to set them."[38] When you ponder the diversity of writers represented in Martin's collection—Kittredge, Ehrlich, Anaya, Momaday, almost two dozen—you wake up to how many kinds of homes he really means.

But Martin has more to say about the change and its bearing on the home theme:

> In 1983, back when I wrote the introduction to the first *Writers of the Purple Sage* collection, the interior West appeared to be on the verge of an energy boom of such dramatic proportions that the region was sure to be utterly transformed. And it seemed to me that the new western writers were "chronicling this uneasy shift, the sometimes melancholy slide of one epoch into another." Well, that boom quickly busted, as I and everyone else should have known it would, and I doubt very much now whether we have entered into an era that is entirely different from those that have come before it. . . . It seems instead that what we've undergone is only a kind of welcome maturation, the realization that change is as constant here as the wind, and that people similarly have been lamenting the end of the West for 150 years. . . . And instead of writing stories, novels, and memoirs that bemoan the crashing changes—its filling up with people and the

> shrinking of its space — it appears that the region's writers are paying rather more attention to the issue of home, at once simple and enormously complex, to the questions of why and how we stay anchored here despite that sweep of change.[39]

Things have changed enough, with some changes changing little and some even changing change itself, that New Western writers are finally weary of the tragic phase, of outrage over loss, and are getting "back to basics." In doing so, they're not simply writing the purple sage again: they're really rewriting it in a whole new way.

If you read some of the editorial overviews in *A Literary History of the American West* (1987), you can catch glimpses of the homeward-bound shift in process between 1983 and 1992. William T. Pilkington, writing about the literature of the Southwest, draws attention to one phase of it in discussing the abundant immigration of writers into the geographical and imaginational territory of J. Frank Dobie and Roy Bedichek and points further west — and the recent literary blooming there. Rolando Hinojosa-Smith, Anaya, Momaday, Max Apple, Hillerman — it's a long list. Furthermore, Pilkington notes "the expansion of dramatic activity" and "the astonishing growth in the volume of poetry published in the Southwest."[40] It has become the home of choice for many writers. And Gerald W. Haslam, considering ethnic expression in the West — from the oral poetry of Native Americans presented by A. Grove Day in his study *The Sky Clears* (1968) to the macaronic English-Spanish poetry of Chicano writers like José Montoya and Gary Soto — remarks the extent to which that revisionist literature provides "a more candid view of who did what in the West's development." According to him, "The single most important product of new perspective has been the emergence of significant numbers of gifted, committed authors capable of ignoring stereotypes and projecting their cultural identities and personal realities on the West's dynamic stage."[41] Or read through Haslam's broader look at recent literary trends. There he argues that "western writing has increasingly defined American life" — a corollary to his argument that "American culture is moving West." He discusses "the literary output of women" as "a particularly fecund development," the tremendous increase in regional publishing ventures, the poetry "exploring all sides," the drama surviving way off-Broadway, the writers who are distancing themselves from "the fantasy West" or satirizing it, the "steady growth in concern for nature's fragility" in Western writing. Much of that activity he attributes to an "increased regional sensitivity" in response to which "local writers, local editors, and local readers have reintrenched and reexamined regional roots."[42]

Given that regional shindig of literary homecoming during the late 1980s, it's not surprising that a spate of children's books about the West, many of them hardly the kind of dominantly Euro-American fare of earlier decades, came on the market. Some examples: MaryLou M. Smith's *Grandmother's Adobe Dollhouse* (1984), Steven Kellogg's *Pecos Bill* (1986), Tomie dePaola's *The Legend of the Indian Paintbrush* (1988), Roy Gerrard's *Rosie and the Rustlers* (1989), and Terri Cohlene's *Quillworker: A Cheyenne Legend* (1990). Charming and multiculturally educating literature for future New Westers.

Nor is it surprising that major literary conferences are now being held at practically every crossroads in the West, many of them thematized by topics and issues concerning Western identity, heritage, and place. Two notable ones mounted in the same month (July 1993) were "Returning the Gift: Southwest Native American Voices," a two-day event at the University of Oklahoma, and the "Big Wind Conference: A Gathering of Writers and Rivers," a three-day event at Central Wyoming College that centered on the West and the ways it affects Western writers and readers. And, of course, there are regular annual meetings of the WLA.

Also, it's hardly surprising that Kittredge has written lately of the "death" of a certain kind of Western. Recalling the news on his car radio, while he was headed south across Nevada on Highway 95, of Louis L'Amour's death at eighty from lung cancer, Kittredge mulls over the legacy of the author of a hundred-odd books, repeating much of the mulling he did at that earlier time. He thought of L'Amour's first novel, *Hondo*, published in 1953 and soon made into a *Shane*-like movie staring John Wayne. On his mind's canvas he painted L'Amour as looking like Wayne, recalling the latter as "that old man, perishing of cancer," in *The Shootist*, as contemplative a Western film as had been made by 1976, the year of its release. Kittredge discerns the possibility of elegy in that remembered moment, of course, but he deflates it: "If you had never lived in the American West, you might have felt elegiac, and you imagined the last of the legendary Westerners were dying. I knew better. I grew up on a horseback cattle ranch and I knew a lot of those old hard-eyed bastards. They're not dying out. What was passing was another round of make-believe." He tells of his grandfather finding an issue of the pulp magazine *Ranch Romances* in the bunkhouse when Kittredge was a child: " 'Book people,' my grandfather said. 'Nobody ever lived like that.' " Returning to his drive across Nevada, with this memory in tow, Kittredge speaks of feeling "a kind of two-hearted sadness over the death of Louis L'Amour. He so clearly loved the West and the dreams of the good strong people he found there, and yet he so deeply transmogrified any sense of the real life there that my grandfather might have understood and respected."[43]

Even though most people know that L'Amour's West is chiefly artifice, his sort of artifice has what Kittredge calls a "darker problem" because the story told over and over again is "inhabited by a mythology about power and the social utility of violence, an American version of an ancient dream of warrior righteousness." And it won't fade away. We love the hero "who cuts through the shit," who, like Shane, "straps on his sixguns and solves the problem of Jack Palance." Such "dreaming" leads on, however, to Dirty Harry, Rambo, finally the sort of longing for simplicities that can advocate nuclear solutions to global menaces. It's a "comfortable dream" in a way and not necessarily a bad one — yet dangerous if we don't "keep from forgetting it's fantasy and always was." But that's much to ask; and Kittredge tells of the anger that rang in him on his drive "like the empty buzzing of locusts" as he struggled with the resentment he felt because that dream "has deluded so many of us in the West so long." It deceives about the certainties of a triumph he's at a loss to discover in the gutted-out desolation of Nevada ghost towns, aquifers sucked near dry by irrigated agriculture, tacky towns along the highway that are nothing more than "little . . . clusterings of bars and cafés and brothels." His mulling over remembered mulling leads him to a fever pitch of pissed-off-edness: "That roadside West is like a shabby imitation of our cowboy dreams, a sad compromised place, used and abused, and used again. So many of the people there feel deceived, and with good reason. They believed in promises implicit in the Western, that they had a right to a good life in this place, and it has become clear to them that it was all a major lie. *Take care of your own damned self* [their motto]. Nobody is bullet-proof."[44] So much for L'Amour's land of Winchester heroism that sets things straight. So much for *la dolce vita* in the Great Basin.

But . . . there's a countermovement to this literary legacy come to its last ditch. Kittredge invokes it when, after so much grief, he calls for "another kind of story" that the West needs, one "in which we can see ourselves for what we mostly are, decent people striving to form and continually reform a just society in which we can find some continuity, taking care in the midst of useful and significant lives." Indeed, he's already "finding such storytelling, slowly, in books like [Marilynne Robinson's] *Housekeeping* and *A River Runs Through It*, in the stories and essays and novels of writers like Mary Clearman Blew and Terry Tempest Williams and James Welch and Ivan Doig, Cormac McCarthy and Louise Erdrich and Leslie Silko and James Galvin, and so many others." Kittredge praises that growing body of work as "the flowering of a genuine literature."[45] Poems and plays as well as prose emerging after the Old Western winter of delusion, it's precisely that. A lot of it concerns "housekeeping" one way or another. I think it'll stick longer than a sudden Sonoran spring.

In 1994, reviewing the evolution of Western literature over the previous half-century, Alexander Blackburn spoke confidently of a literary "Western Renaissance." He may have labored unduly "the angst and nihilism so prominent in nonwestern literature" — for instance, "the slick smallness, the self-satisfied emptiness, and the withered humanity which characterizes writing of *The New Yorker* school" — but he was unerring when he proclaimed that the renaissance under way "signals not just the extension, numerically and geographically, of our national literary culture, but its revitalization and transformation."[46]

While one strand of western writing . . . documents what [Northrop] Frye would call a "myth of freedom," one bound up with untrammeled individualism, this is countered . . . by a contrary "myth of concern" which variously stresses the individual ego's submission to the human collective, celebrates both oral traditions and artisan values, and advocates a sensuous participation in the concrete immediacy of place. — Stephen Tatum, "Literature Out-of-Doors"

REWRITERS OF THE PURPLE SAGE, PART 2: A GATHERING

The thicket is gradually thinning, so you can get your bearings better. I'd like to single out some individual blossoms in the recent flowering of New Western literature that Kittredge justly touts. They'll serve to illustrate that literature, particularize its significance, and enhance your list of readables. Let me proceed by genres, dealing chiefly with literature published since 1980, concentrating on works published in the late 1980s and early 1990s. I'll begin with prose fiction.

Mark Siegel, one of the contributors to *A Literary History of the American West* and author of a 1980 book on Tom Robbins, discerns several trends in Western fiction up until the mid-1980s, all of which continue still to one extent or another: anti-heroic characterization, intensifying attention to "the conflict of machine and garden," multicultural broadening, an enlarging search for "ways in which the past and the present might be bridged," more "innovation and experimentation with narrative perspective and time frame," participation in a general "westernization of American literature" in its coming "to deal with a spiritual pioneering for the control of man's self," a questioning about "where we are heading" (and, I'd add, a growing intuition that it's home), increasing interest in magical realism (the heightening of the uncanny in the daily world that Siegel finds well exemplified in Tony Hillerman's detective fiction), and the translation of Western themes and situations into science fiction.[1] Many of the trends may be discerned in other genres as well. No given work of New Western fiction necessarily exhibits them all. But most of them relate, in varying degrees, to an enrichment of characterization in Western fiction — the characters in the place, the place in the characters.

Distinguishing between "the lowercase *w* western" and "the capital *W* Western novel" as he saw them in 1980, John R. Milton derives abundant criteria for contrasting the fiction of, say, Luke Short and Max Brand with that of, say, Wallace Stegner and William Eastlake. For instance, the first "exploits the myths of the frontier" and neglects "the many complexities of the human condition," but the second "is sensitive to human behavior as well as to meaningful qualities of the land." Yet the main difference between the two, which come close to typifying the predominant traits of Old and New Western literature, is in what Milton terms "the realization of character." It "remains a primary task . . . in all significant fiction."[2] Indeed, and New Westers do it much better, on the whole. As in the trial of Claude Dallas, Jr., a "dreamer of the Western dream" accused of the gunfighterlike killing in 1981 of two officers of the Idaho Department of Fish and Game, which Alan Prendergast deftly recounts, so also in New Western fiction: the focus shifts "from the act itself to the personalities involved." While the story unfolds, we watch "on the great screen of the public imagination" how the action goes: "the tempo building as the showdown approaches, the tall dance of death, the arm whipping down, the lightning response, the slower hand twitching in the dust." And yet now "we expect [even] a gunfight to be a revelation of character, and the mystery [of the case] to be a mystery of character."[3]

That's my cue to move on to Hillerman's detective fiction and to suggest, with the help of Jan Roush, that its evolution reflects and capsules that of New Western literature. All of his books are entertaining, but, as Roush persuasively argues, his work — she deems it "a new genre: anthropological mystery" — has developed remarkably since his first book, *The Blessing Way*, in 1970, especially during the 1980s and "primarily through his characters." She sums up the change from 1970 to *Coyote Waits* (1990): "Through the creation of his two main protagonists, Navajo detectives Joe Leaphorn and Jim Chee, and their female counterparts, his art evolves from entertainment to a morally significant statement of a way of life: the establishment of *hózhó* — harmony — for the Navajo people." Thus, in Roush's view, Hillerman's books have gone from being action-oriented stories with plot-driven characters and limited realistic detail to being stories with morally and temperamentally complex characters, less-emphasized action, and more elaborate specification; as an artist, he "has grown from writing romance-as-entertainment into writing novels-that-entertain."[4]

Milton sketches much the same trajectory for the transition from the western to the Western. For Hillerman's fiction, it's cinched in his 1986 mystery *Skinwalkers*. There he finally brings together in one story the two principals who function separately in earlier ones — the older, modernistic Leaphorn in, for instance, *Listening Woman* (1978) and the younger, more traditional Chee (who wants to be a Navajo shaman-singer or *hataałii*) in, for instance, *The Ghostway* (1984). He also creates well-realized female characters — Leaphorn's traditional-Navajo wife, Emma, and Chee's new foil, the lawyer Janet Pete, a far less traditional mixed-blood Navajo. Realistic descriptions of place, complex characters, concern with a fundamental issue of cultural life like *hózhó*, as well as Navajo-like plotting devices (Roush notes "interlocking connections" and "circularity") — all combine to make Hillerman's work after 1986 an exemplification of maturing Western literature.[5] (And this despite the fact that he's an Old Wester at heart, one who occasionally gets ethnic details wrong — though maybe for defensible reasons in terms of his own writerly instincts.)

A lot of the enrichment of Western fiction in the early 1980s had to do with the deepening of characters, especially female characters, in relation to place. Doris Betts's novel *Heading West* (1981) presents a gripping portrait of a kidnapped woman from North Carolina who brutally encounters the contemporary West and yet comes to discover in it, through love, a new home and a new self. Larry McMurtry's novel *The Desert Rose* (1983) is, to my knowledge, unique in its attempt to tell a bittersweet story of a used and abused Las Vegas showgirl with respectable emotional authority. Louise Erdrich's *Love Medicine* (1984), her first novel and one in the line of outstanding contemporary Native American fiction that begins with Scott Momaday's *House Made of Dawn* (1968), rewrites history through an intricate multigenerational, multivocal story of unforgettable male and female characters and their relation to Indian land in the northern West. And Elizabeth Tallent's novel *Museum Pieces* (1985) shares a story, lyrically told, of plucky, independent women and troubled men interconnected through a vividly evoked Southwestern setting, Santa Fe itself a gallery of broken lives seeking wholeness.

By the mid-1980s something definitely different was going on with Western fiction. McMurtry's *Lonesome Dove* came out in 1985, won him a Pulitzer, and absolutely won over the reading public. Reviewers all across the East fell in love with the book. Readers who had never picked up a "Western" before signed on for the drive to Montana and wanted it never to end. A great story seized them, and the story in that book *is* the characters, endearing or repugnant but always singular, not the recitation of the standard myth.

Even Louis L'Amour was up to new tricks in his 1986 novel *Last of the Breed*, which hit the top spot on the *New York Times* hard-cover best-seller list weeks before its official publication date—just at the time when a lot of distracted media-oids thought the Western, except maybe for *Lonesome Dove*, was in hibernation or moribund. Not strictly Western, its story of an American test pilot, part Sioux and Cheyenne, who's captured by Soviet agents and escapes through the Siberian wilderness nonetheless has the feeling, albeit with a few ironic touches, and certain elements of the Western. The principal, Major Joseph Makatozi, may be an Indian constructed largely from L'Amour's own experiences (he taught winter survival while in the army), but his unpredictable adventure is based on painstaking research; and his resourceful quest, following the path of his ancestors across the Bering Strait, pushes not toward vague male freedom but toward his homeland. Reviewers, for a change, praised a book by L'Amour, one declaring him "America's poet lariat."[6] In a critical discussion of the novel, Jane Tompkins (a sophisticated *female* reader of L'Amour, mind you) confesses that she "would rather be out there with Joe Makatozi, listening for telltale sounds, running swiftly down forest paths at night, crouching in the brush while his enemies passed by all unsuspecting, than doing almost anything else."[7] We've come a long way, baby.

After that, the floodgates opened for New Western fiction just as they did for New Western things generally. Elmer Kelton, who had grown up on a West Texas ranch and written westerns for a number of years, broke into the Western with *The Man Who Rode Midnight* (1987). It wasn't his first novel of cowboy life to feature well-realized down-to-earth characters — that was *The Day the Cowboys Quit* (1971) — but it was his best to date; and it won him several awards, including the 1988 Western Heritage Award for Best Western Novel, and hearty kudos from reviewers who hailed him as one of a new generation of Western fiction writers. Then in 1988 came another novel from McMurtry, *Anything for Billy*, a work that virtually every reviewer in the country found beguiling both as an engrossing story about Billy the Kid and as self-conscious metafiction about mythmaking. In 1990 came yet another, *Buffalo Girls* (made into a limp CBS miniseries in 1995), in which McMurtry builds a myth-debunking, ironic history of the Wild West and its sad expiration around his version of Calamity Jane, who does her own recollective reinventing of the past from a woman's point of view.

On into the 1990s, and it's grab your gear, pardner, 'cause all hell's breakin' loose. A woman named Codi Noline returns to her home and her past in Arizona in Barbara Kingsolver's brilliant *Animal Dreams* (1990), a male-marginalizing novel (though Codi learns much from an Apache man) about the mysterious, nurturing relationship of land to its human inhabitants. A gunfighter-turned-lawman named Clay Halser does some housecleaning in the Southwest of the 1860s and 1870s in *Journal of the Gun Years* (1991), a novel that unromantically explores the violence of the Old West and, again, the process of mythmaking — by Richard Matheson, an eclectic writer at last attracted to the possibilities of the Western novel with a difference. The various contemporary narrators of Pam Houston's short stories in *Cowboys Are*

Pam Houston, whose short stories deal with the sexual politics of having cowboys as your weakness. (Photo by Steve Griffin, courtesy of W. W. Norton and Company)

My Weakness (1992) tackle a range of questions about the sexual politics of their entanglements with essentially Old Western men (cowboys, hunters, wild types whom intelligent New Western women are dumb enough to want). The summative irony of the collection may be found in the title story: the narrator, speaking of the "picture in my mind of a tiny ranch," wonders near the end "why I had always imagined my cowboy's truck as it was leaving" and "why I hadn't turned the truck around and painted my cowboy coming home."[8] Frank Copenhaver in Thomas McGuane's novel *Nothing but Blue Skies* (1992) comes to doubt the value of the entrepreneurial greed that has given him the motive for greeting the Montana mornings of his feckless middle age, to see both the unreality of the phoniest aspects of the New West and the cruel geekiness of the remnant Old West, and to believe that he and other Westerners ought to grow up and take care with what's left of their world — the same belief that moved McGuane to write the nature essays in his 1995 book *The Heart of the Land.* And, of course, Abrán González in Anaya's magical-realistic novel *Alburquerque* also digs through issues of identity and environment as he searches for his father and his fragmented heritage in a world stretched between the ceremonial communities in the old northern villages of New Mexico and the ducal dreams of developers intent on turning urban New Mexico into what Abrán's lover, Lucinda, calls "Santa Fantasy."

The Southwest, expectably, recurs often as a setting in New Western fiction. Naturally, it's the setting for most Chicano and Chicana writing. McMurtry's sort-of sequel to *Lonesome Dove, Streets of Laredo* (1993) — in which Woodrow Call, maybe like McMurtry himself, wrestles with the difficulties of age (and *its* sequel, the final Western homecoming) — takes place there. And two extraordinary novels by Cormac McCarthy, *Blood Meridian; or, The Evening Redness in the West* (1985) and *All the Pretty Horses* (1992), are set there, those books chronologically framing a prodigiously productive seven years in New Western fiction and being, to my taste, the most impressive of all of it.

McCarthy was born in New England and grew up in Knoxville, Tennessee. He had several extraordinary novels set in Appalachia to his credit before he moved in the mid-1970s to El Paso, Texas, where he still lives (apparently — he's an elusive person). His arrival in the Southwest entailed an explosively creative encounter of artist and place. Its first fruit was *Blood Meridian*, which reads as if it had been composed through the agency of a sensibility some Western Frankenstein had concocted with traits from Hieronymus Bosch, Edward Abbey, Herman Melville, Flannery O'Connor, William Faulkner, Hunter Thompson, the late Texas novelist and poet R. G. Vliet, and God knows who else. The second fruit was *All the Pretty Horses*, a more restrained performance (and probably the better book) but still packed with astounding verbal fireworks. Like those two other redoubtably talented literary Mc's, McMurtry and McGuane, McCarthy writes prose that leaves you mouth-breathing with awe at the treasure in its net. And, marvelous to relate for the future of Western fiction, *All the Pretty Horses* is but the first volume of his promised Border Trilogy. The second, *The Crossing*, an al-

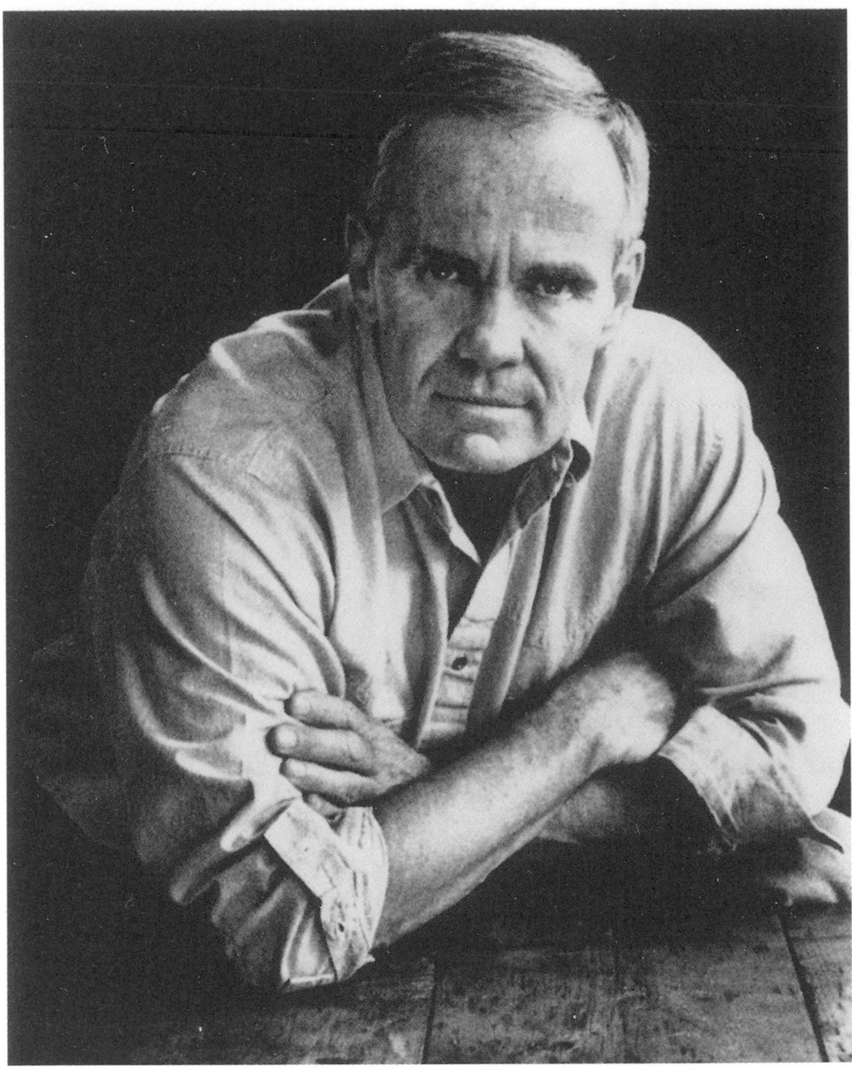

Cormac McCarthy, the William Faulkner of the New West.
(Photo by Marion Ettlinger)

most equally impressive novel, appeared in 1994. The third is in the works.

Wallace Stegner once lamented the fact that no Western writer has been able to create a fictional West with the cogency of the fictional South that Faulkner created in the Yoknapatawpha County of his major novels. McCarthy, having brought his strongly Faulknerian voice west, may be just the one to get the job done. The first national conference dedicated entirely to his work, an unusual honoring of a writer at mid-career, was held at Bellarmine College in Louisville, Kentucky, in October 1993. There's already a critical study of most of his work in print, Vereen M. Bell's *The Achievement of Cormac McCarthy* (1988), which treats him as a Southern writer, and *Southern Quarterly* devoted its summer 1992 issue to critical treatments of his fiction. He's that good. And I suspect that the next conference on him will be held in the West. To give you an idea of why, I'll speak at more length of his two key novels.

As John Lewis Longley, Jr., notes in 1986, "The reviewers in the large national newspapers have been having a terrible time with *Blood Meridian*" — mostly because its violence reaches far beyond what average readers could stand "with their orange juice and corn flakes . . . before rushing off to the commuter train." The story of a teenage boy from Tennessee called "the kid" who in the late 1840s joins up with a motley band of professional scalp-hunters whose mission, assigned by the governor of Chihuahua, Mexico, is to eradicate the Mexican-killing Indians from the chaotic lands of his province, *Blood Meridian* hardly makes for a calm stomach. But Longley's point is that critics need to take the book seriously as a fiercely realistic inversion of the usual Western mythology. It deserves comparison with Joseph Conrad's *Heart of Darkness* (or, I'd suggest, that novella's updated version, Francis Ford Coppola's 1979 film *Apocalypse Now*) as a story of "what happens in a savage wilderness when all restraints are removed." Since the scalp-hunters soon are slaying everyone with dark skin (for the scalps, once dry, all look alike), it's also a story of double genocide. Infanticides abound, as do beheadings and the like (one scene gives you hyper-real awareness of what a skillfully wielded Bowie knife can do). The roaming crazies fight murderously among themselves. The clincher is that the main episodes of this violent tale, as Longley and other careful reviewers and critics remark, are "based on real events" and thus "the major characters are all people who actually existed."[9] McCarthy has written New Western History with a difference, and the difference inheres in his ability to animate historical documents with hallucinatory vividness.

So the corn-flakes commuter has to realize that McCarthy's story, with its desert landscape — itself virtually a character — depicted as being as desolate, indifferent, and empty as the scalp-hunters' hearts, offers no conventional fantasy of the West at all but the actual West as the dystopian confusion of hatred and terror it was when there wasn't a white hat even on the distant horizon. Longley aptly compares the story to the frenzy of slaughter at My Lai, though what it dramatizes is more like a relentless repeating of My Lai–like incidents.[10] But what it's really about beyond that ought to occasion first-class gagging on those corn flakes.

A few reviewers and critics, with some undershooting and overshooting, get pretty close to the target. Geoffrey O'Brien, for instance, readily recognized in 1986 that McCarthy, like New Western writers generally, was up to something otherwise with the Western: "Sam Peckinpah and Sergio Leone appeared to have arrived at its logical dead end, but writers today are taking a fresh look at the genre. . . . Re-inventing the Western means re-inventing America, turning the creation epic upside down to come up with a different end-product: a new Texas, a new Mexico, a new definition of reality." For O'Brien, *Blood Meridian* is not just a realistic novel but "a weird blend of cold-eyed photo-realism and prophetic diction," its "Hardboiled Biblical" prose weaving a Western reduced "to its essential components: landscape and killing." The progressively deeper corruption of the kid, who's backwoods-mean to start out with, and his eventual death, the decimation of the filibusters at McCarthy's rendition of the 1850 Yuma Crossing Massacre on the way, the endless suffering — all come round to an ending that doesn't end since the story "has no more destination than its blood-spattered protagonists, only a relentless forward movement . . . — a process also known as history."[11]

In 1992, in an article on McCarthy's Western fiction, Tom Pilkington, with more retrospect, saw that *Blood Meridian* and *All the Pretty Horses*, the latter historically set exactly a hundred years later than the former, "demonstrate a continuity in our history that time apparently is powerless to erase." The characters in both novels "search out frontiers, those fluid zones of freedom and opportunity, of action and destiny that Americans traditionally have sought," and "what they often find is an actual and metaphysical horror." He thus construes McCarthy as resembling recent "revisionist historians" in challenging "the triumphalist view of American history," though Pilkington advises that "the spin he puts on such contrarian history is not necessarily that of the revisionists." The advice is understandable, given that McCarthy's darkest ideas about conquest are voiced in "arrogant and megalomaniacal monologues" by a philosophizing scalp-hunter named Judge Holden, physically summed up by Pilkington as "an enormous fat man whose hairless body glistens eerily."[12] (The character recalls, inwardly and outwardly, Marlon Brando in *Apocalypse Now*—a depraved Buddha intoxicated with *nada.*)

The basic difference in "spin," I'd say, is that McCarthy isn't just *telling* New Western History: he's *showing* it, realistically textualizing its dredged-up truth, its judgment, in actions and characters tied close to a corollary landscape, which he describes sometimes in overwrought, nightmarish detail. And what he shows is what *Blood Meridian* is really about: the Euro-American frontier mentality gone stark-staring mad. The most typifying and recurrent statements about the scalp-hunters have to do with their riding on, riding through, riding off, riding out, riding away. They're warriors drunk on the violence of clearing the land of life who don't *stay* anywhere, boomers gone too far and still going. They're homeless, morally and existentially, codeless, finally flat evil, motiveless in their cruelty. McCarthy's story concerns the cost of that situation. For all its realism, it finally blurs into allegory because, historically and contemporarily, it's really about, my God, us, at least those of us who are Euro-American males, and what we at our worst did and are still doing to the West. Read thus, it provides an unrelenting warning.

All the Pretty Horses also is a story about homelessness and its consequences. Though it shares some traits with *Blood Meridian* and continues some of its philosophical preoccupations, it differs from it in several ways: tighter narrative structure, less archaically mannered and hence more accessible diction, leaner style, characters that allow the reader closer identification, maybe more hope than despair at the end—and fewer problems for reviewers, especially Eastern ones. Set in West Texas and Mexico in 1949, *All the Pretty Horses* tells the story of John Grady Cole, a sixteen-year-old suddenly cut off from the generations of ranchers that constitute his heritage by his grandfather's recent death, his parents' divorce and departure from the family ranch near San Angelo, and—since he's too young to run it—the sale of the ranch. Thus bereft, he heads south with his friend Lacey Rawlins to seek in Mexico a way of life quickly vanishing in Texas, their horseback journey taking them into as much frontier as can be found in the middle of the twentieth century.

In one long passage concerning John Grady's actions and thoughts after he has left his grandfather's funeral, you encounter a remarkable evocation of the loss, both personal and much larger, that he feels. It's a passage, glorious in its coiling cadences, that exemplifies his obsession with horses and builds toward his full motivation for heading south. It also shows you why McCarthy has received many prestigious grants and awards, including a MacArthur Fellowship and, specifically for the novel in which it appears, the 1992 National Book Award:

> In the evening he saddled his horse and rode out west from the house. The wind was much abated and it was very cold and the sun sat blood red and elliptic under the reefs of bloodred cloud before him. He rode where he would always choose to ride, out where the western fork of the old Comanche road coming down out of the Kiowa country to the north passed through the westernmost section of the ranch and you could see the faint trace of it bearing south over the low prairie that lay between the north and middle forks of the Concho River. At the hour he'd always choose when the shadows were long and the ancient road was shaped before him in the rose and canted light like a dream of the past where the painted ponies and the riders of that lost nation came down out of the north with their faces chalked and their long hair plaited and each armed for war which was their life and the women and children and women with children at their breasts all of them pledged in blood and redeemable in blood only. . . .
>
> He rode with the sun coppering his face and the red wind blowing out of the west. He turned south along the old war trail and he rode out to the crest of a low rise and dismounted and dropped the reins and walked out and stood like a man come to the end of something.[13]

This guy can write a sentence! In fact, if the book has a stylistic flaw, it's in the mismatch between the baroque thought that flows through John Grady's head and the clipped, understated West Texas English that he, like other Anglo characters, speaks.

Be that as it may, John Grady heads south, bearing his loss-filled freedom like a grail. As you might expect, he, Lacey, and a third boy they pick up en route run into troubles galore in Mexico — intercultural misunderstandings, spilled blood, death. "On the surface," as Pilkington notes, "the plot appears a variation on a story that has been told often in western literature. A wandering cowboy and his sidekick ride innocently into hostile territory. There ensue fights against insurmountable odds, the hero's romance with a lovely young señorita, chases on horseback through a harsh but beautiful landscape." But McCarthy has a purpose beyond richly telling a familiar tale of a boy force-bloomed into manhood. In a way he's already done that, in another register, with the kid. He takes John Grady further, for it's clear that, once the young man is back in Texas at the novel's end, he "has fashioned a code to live by" — something the kid hardly achieved. "It is a code," as Pilkington interprets it, "of honor and responsibility — à la Hemingway — that has nothing to do with legality or traditional morality. It is an internal code and has been shaped by hard experience and the hard conditions of an indifferent universe." John Grady may still be externally rootless and seem "like an old man at seventeen" as he wanders the land, obsessively explaining to all listeners his killing of a fellow inmate in a Mexican prison (it was self-defense); but he has carried his quest to a certain point of existential self-knowledge.[14] He's scarcely happy, but he has been compelled to learn something profound and lasting about his accountable relation to a fateful world and will live on differently — even if he didn't get the girl.

If *All the Pretty Horses* has a problem with characterization, it's with the women, all of whom lack full-blown realization — except for, perhaps, the *dueña* Alfonsa, the philosophizing godmother and great-aunt to Alejandra, the señorita who captures the protagonist's heart but is prevented from crossing the ethnic barrier between them and leaving her father's hacienda. And McCarthy is far from adept at describing their lovemaking. He deals wonderfully with the male realm, but I'd feel better about his New Western pedigree if he created women as well as some of his peers can.

Still, McCarthy is an exemplary New Western fictionist, for reasons I've already mentioned but for others as well; two, having to do with *All the Pretty Horses*, are especially notable (and pertinent also to *The Crossing*). In his review of the book, Richard Eder spots one of them when he points out McCarthy's "profound empathy" for Mexican culture and his "sweet skill in portraying it" (though Eder is bothered by the amount of Spanish that McCarthy has woven into the story to achieve credible cultural texture).[15] Kerry Ahearn gets credit for the second reason, in another review of the book, by arguing that "McCarthy seems to be doing what the young Larry McMurtry promised to do:

explore the complex human implications of a time when the old life was passing away in the Southwest, and make us feel that the issue is not merely of the region, or of the past."[16] A tad rough on McMurtry perhaps, but his vision isn't as deep as McCarthy's, which Ahearn, like Pilkington, construes as aligned, finally, with the program of New Western Historians. McCarthy may become the New Westers' Louis L'Amour.

In *The Novel of the American West*, John R. Milton offers a thought-provoking and amusing chart of the differences between Eastern and Western fiction. For instance, the first tends to identify characters in relation to "social environment," the second, in relation to "nature"; the first concerns "frenzy arising out of nothing," the second, "spiritual calm in the midst of fury or disaster."[17] Yet some of the distinctions hold up less well now than they did when Milton constructed the chart for his 1980 study because recent Western fiction, well represented by *All the Pretty Horses*, has become even more "an emergent force on the national literary scene" than Siegel saw it as being in the mid-1980s. And witness here also Ken Kesey's 1994 multicultural novel *Last Go Round*, which its cover labels "A Real Western" (with photographs assembled by Ken Babbs), about the (allegedly) first world-championship rodeo. Though its writers' "concerns and techniques [have] become increasingly nontraditional," Western fiction nonetheless has retained "many of its traditional and regional characteristics"; but it most surely is fulfilling Siegel's prediction that it would "merge to a greater degree with mainstream American literature."[18] That's another kind of coming home. But which is merging with which?

In 1992 HarperCollins published a plump collection of poetry and commentary, *The Rag and Bone Shop of the Heart: Poems for Men*, edited by Robert Bly, James Hillman, and Michael Meade. Its title considerately omitting one telling word in the line that ends William Butler Yeats's poem "The Circus Animals' Desertion" ("In the foul rag-and-bone shop of the heart") from which it derives, the book is yet another of Bly's therapeutic attempts to help men straighten out their inner lives. The oddest thing about the collection is that it includes such a paucity of work by or directly about Western American men. I'm surprised at that, especially since Heatherington, Tompkins, and a wagonload of other self-appointed shrinks have diagnosed them as paradigmatically screwed-up innerly — untalkative, alienated from their feelings, tied in knots about women, half in love with death, whatever. Or maybe they're too negative an example. Or maybe, just maybe, the editors don't associate the West or Western men with poetry very much, even though Bly lives in Minnesota and Meade in Washington. Or Westerners don't write their kind of poetry — expectable Eastern literary snobbishness. Maybe Bly and company are interested only in a few of those poets (with a couple of exceptions, like William Stafford and Theodore Roethke) who are *in* the West but not *of* it. Probably the reasons come down to all of the above.

I don't really care. My point is that the whole scene is changing. There's a multitude of poets in the New West. Some aren't that good. Some are awful. Some are writing and publishing the best poetry anywhere. Blessedly, many lack the effete self-importance of typical Eastern poets. They have a better sense of humor. A lot are men who, mirabile dictu, have complex emotions and articulate them with eloquence. Most, I suspect, are women, whether or not they're widely published. Some write homespun verse. Some write lines as difficult to handle as barbed wire in a high wind. Many are Euro-Americans. Many, more and more all the time, are not. Some of their traditions are ancient; others are more recent, dating back, substantively, no further than, say, the literary salons of Santa Fe in the early part of this century. But whether they're continuing the heritage of Navajo chants, Old Western cowboy ballads, Yvor Winters's plain-style formalist poems, Hispanic *corridos*, even baggy epics of the Plains like Lincoln Phifer's tin-eared self-published 1915 poem *The Dramas of Kansas*, or doing something completely different, the New Western poets, verb-ridin', noun-ropin', adjective-wrestlin', are headed into town. They don't traffic in worn-out lies. A bunch of 'em drink their liquor neat and don't eat fruit for breakfast. They're plannin' to stay awhile.

Speaking of the "order" that poets create through language, William Lockwood, in a survey of recent trends in Western poetry, observes that it "must come as the consequence of a process that involves a sometimes painful reexamination of what is authentic and what is not." He speaks of contemporary poets of the Pacific Northwest, especially Richard Hugo, Vern Rutsala, and John Haines; but his observation holds for New Western poets generally, as does his commending of Haines for "reasserting values that once stressed a gentle and skillful adaptation of man to land." And his distinction, borrowed from the poet William Everson, between "the impulse toward 'participation' " in Western poetry and "the habit of 'discrimination' " in Eastern poetry applies a fortiori to most New Western poetry. Furthermore, that impulse itself has changed in the last few decades in much the same way that the Bay Area poet Thom Gunn has, as Lockwood characterizes him: he has moved from "poems in celebration of action, with their privileging of existential solitude over human contact, . . . toward poems more deeply rooted in place, more fully comprehensive of the complex cultural conditions attached to places, more open to the possibilities of human community."[19]

You can find poems of the latter kind in the work of Texas poets whom Lockwood discusses, like William Barney and Max Westbrook, as you can also in Carolyn Forché's poetry about New Mexico, in which she is able "to quite literally embody the deep, elusive sense of place and of indigenous cultural life that has managed to survive in this area." Keith Wilson, who grew up on a ranch on New Mexico's Staked Plains, has written many poems of that kind, from the mid-1960s on — tough-minded, morally hard-edged writing in which he "seeks to adopt from the attractive indigenous Indian culture of the land a balance between masculine and feminine psychic principles," most notably, for Lockwood, in "The Lake Above Santos" (from *Sketches for a New Mexico Hill Town* [1966]). The poem projects a "sense of place . . . and the presence of the people who inhabited it" with an "imaginative sympathy" and honesty that anticipate both Wilson's later work and the work of many other New Western poets. Finally, to mention one more poet in Lockwood's helpful survey, Richard Shelton, a Tucson poet, has written poems from the early 1970s on that "express a remarkable sense of the 'in-tensity' of place, a moral commitment to act in defense of the region he loves," largely the Sonoran Desert. In "Mexico," from *The Bus to Veracruz* (1978), that sense plays through what Lockwood terms his "authentic longings for rootedness, for release from an increasingly distracting monoculture." His work illustrates a tradition of gifted writers that Lockwood evaluates as "dynamic" and "growing."[20]

Mexican-American poetry began an unprecedented flourishing in the late 1960s with the founding in 1967 of Quinto Sol Publications, a Berkeley-based venture in support of Mexican-American writers that lasted into the early 1970s, when it was succeeded by other houses then eager to publish them. The quest for heritage and home undertaken by Quinto Sol poets, as well as prose writers, continues to preoccupy Chicano and Chicana poets today. As Raymund A. Paredes puts it, that "new generation of authors . . . reaffirmed their ties to Mexico and Latin America and celebrated their aboriginal heritage," and they "appropriated Aztec philosophy and imagery and found particular usefulness in the concept of Aztlán, the ancestral home of the Aztecs thought to be located somewhere here in the American Southwest." Now, *that's* tradition. Scholars doubt the existence of Aztlán; but such doubt, as Paredes argues, has "missed the point," for the importance of the concept lies in its "mythic and symbolic" value, its "providing Mexican-American writers with a powerful sense of 'place' and continuity."[21] Through that sense—and the security of identity it promotes—they have been empowered to write poetry vitally grounded in their region.

That sense didn't die with Quinto Sol but grew stronger. It conspicuously informs the recent work of poets like Francisco X. Alarcón who see behind the Catholic cult of Our Lady of Guadalupe the Aztecs' older worship of their corn goddess—a mother archetype named Coatlalupeh—and who foresee a renaissance of Mesoamerican civilization.

Well, such isn't the standard Anglo brand of Western myth, and it may—I hope not—prove as delusive as that myth or the cities-of-gold stories of Cíbola that piqued Spanish greed in the New World. But it has played a part in building the mood of confidence that has encouraged the writing of Mexican-American poets like Gary Soto, Lorna Dee Cervantes, and Jimmy Santiago Baca. Soto, with his colorful imaginative faculty and his careful control of the poetic line, is perhaps the best of recent Mexican-American poets. He's been prolific, too, since his first book, *The Elements of San Joaquin*, in 1977. Cervantes engages unpleasant issues—violence against women, the ideology of *machismo*, incest—in her *Emplumada* (1981) and *From the Cables of Genocide: Poems on Love and Hunger* (1991). Baca's life history is extraordinary: from abandoned child, juvenile delinquent, convict, and illiterate to novelist, screenwriter, and much-honored poet. Some of his best writing may be found in *Martín and Meditations on the South Valley* (1987), which won an American Book Award in 1988. What you notice in all these poets' work—with its contrasts of hard realities and sensuous fantasy, street violence and domestic peace, hunger and love — is a distinctly self-examining New Western sensibility concerned with immediate issues of land and community that are at once both local and universal.

The same issues pervade recent Native American poetry — though, as we'll observe, in a different way. But whatever their cultural and artistic differences from Mexican-American poets, Western Native American poets since the late 1960s have felt more and more, as Patricia Clark Smith phrases it in her survey of their work between 1968 and 1983, "free to celebrate their heritage proudly." They do so, she reminds us, in a poetry, however much reflecting the authors' Euro-American acculturation, "close to living oral tradition." Native American poets "have grown up . . . in places where secular stories and local gossip — and, in many instances, formal recitals of origin stories, trickster tales, war narratives, and the like — still remain an important part of family and community life." There's frequently an emphasis not just on narrative but, as in the work of Simon Ortiz, an Acoma Pueblo poet, on the teller and his relation to the audience and on "the pleasures and importance of repetition and of 'telling it right.' " There's "respect for the speaking voice" — or maybe *singing* voice is more accurate — to a degree unusual among more print-oriented non-Indian poets. And there's a plentitude of humor, much of it "of a wryly mocking flavor" — remarkably trenchant in the remythologizing work of Sherman Alexie, a Spokane–Coeur d'Alene poet who came to prominence in the early 1990s — and arising from perceptions of "the ironies of Anglo-Indian relations." Some of it comes also from a desire to ridicule, which may have profound purposes of affirmation, or a need to deflate "rigidity and pretentiousness" or "from a consciousness of the complex interrelatedness of things, of the delightfully multiple significance of events."[22]

As an example of poetry that uses the last kind of humor, Smith offers a poem by Geary Hobson, a Cherokee-Chickasaw, from *The Remembered Earth*, Hobson's multigenre 1979 anthology of Native American writing. The poem is uncharacteristic in its brevity — a one-liner makes for a short narrative — and in the length of its subtitle (which is crucial to the poem), but it can serve to keynote at least part of the discussion ahead:

Buffalo Poem #1

(or)

ON HEARING THAT A SMALL HERD OF BUFFALO
HAS "BROKEN LOOSE" AND IS "RUNNING WILD"
AT THE ALBUQUERQUE AIRPORT — SEPTEMBER 26, 1975

— roam on, brothers. . . .[23]

Smith ventures this suggestive commentary: "The poem is a genuine wish for buffalo liberation. It is also a sidelong glance at the parallel histories and interrelatedness of buffalo herds and tribal peoples, and at officialdom's comic consternation when confronted by free-roaming creatures, however mild-tempered and outnumbered those creatures may be; Hobson's buffalo are related in more ways than one to the ghost-dancing Sioux of Wounded Knee." Fair enough. And Hobson's poem and Smith's commentary bear revealing relation to her explaining that dream-vision in American Indian poetry, except when it fails, shouldn't be regarded by the unwary reader as conventionally surrealistic or abstractly symbolic but should be experienced as "reality, not something that stands for it." Dream-vision, as both form and subject, as "reality," may be philosophically difficult for Anglos, but in it inheres the peculiar magical-realistic ability of that poetry, at its most serious, to treat "ordinary objects and beings" as "suddenly invested with extraordinary significance and power."[24] Such reality is both physical and metaphysical, transformative.

Now, Hobson's poem, though hardly dream-visionary in a protracted way, implies at least an instant in which the ordinary transforms into the extraordinary, the daily into the immemorial, for its speaker and for the sensitive listener/reader. But in some contemporary Native American poetry the validity of dream-vision may be questioned by poets acculturated away from their tribal traditions — Smith mentions Momaday in this connection — though, as she further notes, "doubts are likely to end in affirmations." At any rate, the doubleness of mind that causes such questioning turns up in a lot of Indian poetry. Hobson exploits it effectively in playing with the differences between Indian and non-Indian views of the buffalo loose at the airport, just as he, representing many other Indian poets in this regard, effects a view of nature that is "fresh, sophisticated, and highly unsentimental" and yet preserves "the old metaphysical attitudes."[25] That doubleness, in various aspects, historically has been negatively complicating for Indian poets, and their pre–New Western poems say as much. In the New Western era, however, that situation has changed, so that Hobson's poem looks forward more accurately to how doubleness figures in Indian poetry after 1975 than do the angrier poems of cultural alienation that many Native Americans wrote in the 1960s and early 1970s.

Acknowledging that Indians, though still writing poems about "the destruction of nature," have left off "didactic outcries against Anglo earth-rapers" and instead "are finding their strength in subtlety," Smith acknowledges also a change in their attitude toward doubleness: "Growing up with doubled vision — being at once American and American Indian — is another rich theme for these poets, all of whom, whether they like it or not, have been influenced by two cultures, and many of whom are breeds by blood as well. Recent poetry tends less toward flat condemnations and rhetorical rejections of the larger culture, and more toward attempts to come to human terms with this doubled experience." Along with that change, which can involve poetry with an intriguing double voice, comes a very positive effect, one that fosters the desire patiently to educate non-Indians about Indian heritage: the poets' firmer affirmation of "the tribal part of their heritage and its traditional emphases upon sharing, reverence for life, close family and tribal ties, and the ceremonial significance of all human actions, from hunting, cultivating, and eating, to loving, birthing, dreaming, and creating." They frequently express "wistfulness and longing for a fully native past, for older ways they themselves can seldom fully experience."[26]

Chickasaw poet and novelist Linda Hogan, who grew up in a rodeo family, illustrates the complexity of attitude involved here. The speaker in her poem "Heritage," from the late 1970s, declares an alienation:

> From my family I have learned the secrets
> of never having a home.

But the speaker in "Red Clay," another poem from the late 1970s, reassures the listener:

> We are here, the red earth
> passes like light into us
> and stays.

Then in 1991, looking back on such earlier poems, Hogan talks about the treacherous history of Oklahoma's Indian Territory—the story of "places where our uprooted lives have felt broken" and of "an incredible will of survival, how some of us fell through history alive"—and proclaims with both finality and uncertainty that "home is in blood, and I am still on the journey of calling myself home."[27] Increasingly, I think, poets like Hogan understand that their difficult quests for home in a past-haunted present parallel and echo non-Indian New Westers' similar quests.

So there's still frustrating conflict in cultural doubleness, but it tends more and more toward productive reciprocity and reconciliation. You can see conflict aplenty in the work of the Yakima poet George Silverstar, who committed suicide in 1984. You can see it also in the poetry of the Oklahoma-born Muskogee poet Joy Harjo, but she has followed the more typically New Western route toward "acceptance of both heritages" that define her. The consequence is a poetry that, as Stephanie Izarek Smith argues, "preserves her Native American background, while integrating aspects of the mainstream American culture in which she was also raised, to create a unique, poignant voice." That double action of preserving and integrating has proven fruitful also in Harjo's writing of short stories and screenplays, in a career that includes painting, an enduring interest in African-American writers, and, more recently, eclectic musical performances—in all of which she finds connections to her people and their place in the postmodern age. Part feminist, part warrior, she has learned to create a poetry that makes a virtue of doubleness, moves beyond its limitations, and, like the best New Western History, "reflects the truths of being human, our relationships to one another, and our relationship to the physical world we inhabit."[28] Such reflecting abounds in her collection *She Had Some Horses* (1983) or *In Mad Love and War* (1990), a collection that shows her tending away from lyrical form and more toward prose narrative.

Another Native American poet who consistently attempts a positive treatment of doubleness is Luci Tapahonso. Much of her poetry, like

Harjo's, deals with issues of identity and heritage, especially among women, in a bicultural world. Indeed, her work, along with that of poets like Paula Gunn Allen, Hogan, Harjo, and others, makes a good case for Native American women playing the leading role in the development of poetry that engages doubleness productively, forgivingly, hopefully. A deal of Tapahonso's poetry accomplishes the inclusion of mainstream culture almost effortlessly, as in her well-known poem "Hills Brothers Coffee," where, in Patricia Clark Smith's words, "she quietly makes clear how part of Anglo culture like store-bought brand-name brew can be incorporated into the warm heart of Navajo family life." Some of Tapahonso's poetry — like "In 1864," her moving personalized account of the Navajos' tragic forced walk from Dinétah (the Navajos' word for their homeland) to Bosque Redondo in her book *Sáanii Dahataat: The Women Are Singing* (1993) — concerns the dark side of the Anglo-Navajo relationship, but most of her poems, like those of her peers, explore "the possibility of accepting some of what the Anglo world offers, and using it as a means to help preserve spiritual integrity, the possibility of keeping at one's center native values, native places, even though native languages may be lost, and some ways are not recapturable." In Tapahonso's poetry, however, the language isn't lost, for Navajo frames or threads many of her poems, much as Spanish or *caló* (slang) does Mexican-American poetry. Oral history, aspects of Anglo culture, accessibility, an enveloping religiousness, a ubiquitous sense of *hózhó*, a deep connection to tribal landscape and its values, lullabylike cadences, an authoritative and incantatory (and multiply ancestral) voice — all combine to make Tapahonso's understated work wonderfully evoke what Smith, speaking of many recent Native American poems, calls "a heritage still exuberantly alive."[29]

Yes, the women are singing. Not that male Native American poets like Ortiz don't sing well. They do — read Ortiz's generous collection, which includes three earlier books in one volume, *Woven Stone* (1992). But Western Indian women, from Erdrich up north to Harjo down southwest, are singing songs quite different from those of the conventional Anglo-masculine West. They're singing not of conquest and dominance but of openness and balance, not of competition but of cooperation, not of male control but of female nurturance. Earth mothers sharing in the moods of the Navajos' Changing Woman, they are singing softly but

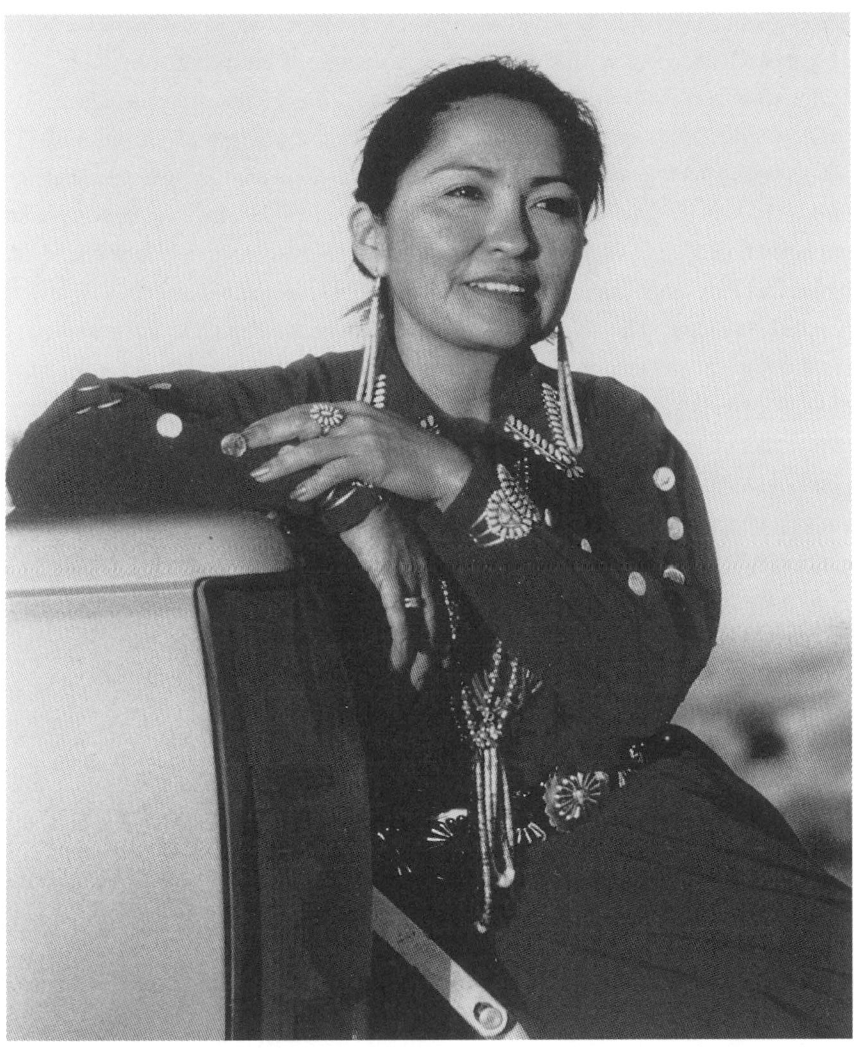

Luci Tapahonso, one of many Native American poets striving to preserve spiritual integrity in a bicultural world. (Photo by Monty Roessel, courtesy of Monty Roessel)

powerfully in counterpoint to what Andrea Millenson Penner, in her study of Tapahonso's poetry, calls "an over-representation of male perspective."[30]

When Harjo sings of mysteriously erotic horses in her visionary poem "She Had Some Horses" (from her collection of the same name) or

Tapahonso sings of how a Navajo child arrives in the world "amid a herd of horses" bringing with them all her heritage of land and time and love, in her poem "Blue Horses Rush In," they sing of horses mighty in unbridled spirit and yet tame, wild and yet very much part of human life.[31] They relate to those horses much as some cowboys of a new generation relate to "unbroken" horses in the corral: with Gandhi-like tenderness rather than John Wayne aggressiveness. No spurs, no bucking. Not breaking but gentling. Not competition between man and beast but a mental meeting. The so-called natural horsemanship that Indians practiced long before the West turned into a rodeo of rugged egos. Adoption of that approach entails "the biggest cultural change on ranches since the automobile," a change that one believer, Dennis Reis, a former rodeo cowboy, says required him "to give myself a 'macho-ectomy.' "[32] Gladly so, apparently. We're in the New West, and that's the world the women are singing.

It's important for Euro-Americans to understand that the world of horses seen anew, even spiritualized, is not new to Native American poets. Quite the contrary, as Patricia Clark Smith stresses:

> Old stories and the presences who move through them are not dead anthropological data; not only do the stories remain meaningful for the values they speak of, they are still quite literally happening, even though names and outer circumstances may be changed in a world of superhighways and fast food chains. Simon Ortiz delights in discovering [the trickster figure] Coyote multitudinously reincarnated, rattling off his slick stories, making deals in barrooms and Greyhound bus stations, fooling and being fooled, and somehow, like the spirit of the peoples he embodies, still beautifully surviving.[33]

Coyote surviving, *real* four-legged coyotes surviving in urban environments, Native Americans still surviving against bad odds: this poetry is about continuance, the survival of heritage, daily survival.

In a 1990 essay, "Poetry as Survival," poet and novelist Jim Harrison records his coming to an understanding — maybe about as clear an understanding as a white male can achieve — of the world modern Native American poetry comes from, portrays, is complexly one with. He begins with a concern about the survival of poetry itself in a greed-oriented sitcom of a nation. He tells of his growing sense during the 1970s that poetry was a lost art in mainstream America and was becoming irrelevant to him as well — until he noticed the enduring vitality of poetry in "cultures less economically sophisticated than our own." Then he had an experience of life-altering magnitude:

> Up until half a dozen years ago I had collected a large library on the Native American, but was unremarkably short on firsthand knowledge — unremarkably and typically, as it is far easier to read about a people than to encounter them. I had been to the Blackfeet Reservation in Browning, Montana. . . . I had also attended the Crow Fair, a massive gathering and celebration in Crow Agency, Montana, with five to seven thousand Native Americans in attendance. This was more than a decade ago, and there were only a few whites present. I watched the dancing for two days and nights, sleeping sporadically on the Custer Battlefield. It was a *spellbinding* experience, one of the few of my life, and there was a deep sense of melancholy that there was nothing in my life that owned this cultural validity except, in a minimal sense, my poetry.[34]

The experience stuck with Harrison. Some years later he visited several reservations, trying always not "to be confused with the anthropologists and spiritual shoppers who drive these people crazy." One day in Canyon del Muerto, a branch of Canyon de Chelly in northeastern Arizona, he had two meetings with Navajos in which he was perceived as some sort of demon — probably because of his "blind left eye, which is foggy and wobbles around with a life of its own." Reminiscing about that day, he realizes that it marked the beginning of "an obsession" with how "these people might clarify why I had spent over forty years wandering around in the natural world. I hoped the two cultures had more to offer each other than their respective demons."[35] They did and do, of course. Apart from whatever else has transpired between the cultures, Harrison learned something about poetry and survival.

The real lesson commenced with Harrison's subsequent immersion in Native American poetry. He read and reread, among other books, Joseph Bruchac's *Songs from This Earth on Turtle's Back: An Anthology of Poetry by American Indian Writers* (1983) and *Harper's Anthology of 20th Century Native American Poetry*, edited by Duane Niatum (1988). He speculates about the neglect, until recently, of Native American writers (they may "represent a ghost that is too utterly painful to be encountered" — and so on), but his strongest concern is with why he's attracted to the work of the poets. One reason is that "you find very little romantic preciousness and almost no self-pity" there. Another, more important one is that "there is a specific immediacy, urgency, and grittiness to the work." It's not Eastern poetry about "Aunt Claudia's doilies": it's poetry that matters. Much of it, he notes, is written by women, much by writers, like Erdrich and Welch, who "are also equally fine novelists." (A lot of Western writers tend to have multigenre talents.) He finds "additional urgency" in the work of mixed-blood poets like Hogan who grapple with their doubleness through striking images. He admires the "rich comic spirit" of Native American poetry that Anglos have not yet fully discovered. Through that learning he discerns the unmistakable signs of "a renaissance in Native American literature similar to that of black writers in the sixties." A most noteworthy sign is the work of Ortiz, with its "absolute emotional credibility married to craft." Though such poetry may be "written in our language but not in our voice," it's nonetheless "the kind of poetry that reaffirms your decision to stay alive." Finally, Harrison observes, "it is indeed ironic that those whom we crushed could help us survive."[36]

How? I'll let Ortiz answer that through some quotations from his poetry. Native American poets help by "talking about how we have been able / to survive insignificance," as he puts it in "The Significance of a Veteran's Day," in a world gone mad with problems. They help by sharing "How Much Coyote Remembered":

O, not too much.
And a whole lot.

Enough.

They help by evoking home while "Leaving America":

It's got red and brown land,
sage, and when it rains,
it smells like piñon
and pretty girls at a Squaw Dance.

And they help by telling the kinds of bits and pieces of stories that the speaker in "I Tell You Now" wanted to tell an Isleta woman on the streets of Albuquerque:

because I do want you to know
and in that way
have you come to know me now.[37]

Native American poets restore faith in the affirmative power of poetry. Certainly they have done that for Harrison, himself a fine poet. And, besides, Ortiz has a poem that's also a dandy recipe for chile stew — it's in *Woven Stone*, along with other truth.

Unlike Indian poets, New Western African-American poets aren't abundant, but you can find some well worth reading — though few from the interior West. A number of historians have documented and clarified the considerable but largely forgotten role played by African Americans in opening the West — as settlers, cowboys, "buffalo soldiers," and so forth. Such history supplies important background for the reading of Western poetry by African Americans (or, for that matter, for hearing blues elements in cowboy ballads). So you might read, say, William L. Katz's thoroughly researched and well-illustrated book *The Black West* in its revised edition (1987) before you enter Langston Hughes's poems about black immigration to the West and related topics, Gwendolyn Brooks's poems about the Midwest, or Ishmael Reed's California-flavored hoodoo-surrealistic poems (the most famous being "I Am a Cowboy in the Boat of Ra"). The Old West didn't prove very fertile ground for African-American poetry, but the New West, with its seeking after historical continuities and deeper ethnic realities, soon may.

Several anthologies effectively represent the development of New Western poetry in general. A good starting point is *Poets West: Contemporary Poems from the Eleven Western States*, edited by Lawrence P. Spingarn (1975), which includes more Californians than most later collections. Then read the 1982 anthology *New Poetry of the American West*, edited by Peter Wild and Frank Graziano. It suffers from not containing poetry by women; but Soto's work is there, as is that of John Haines, Reg Saner, Stafford, and others. The editors carefully distinguish "between writers who exploit the West via superficial celebration of its landscape — who burst into blossom at the sight of a saguaro — and those who genuinely engage with this overwhelming sense of place, who inform their voices with its grandeur." Their book includes only the second kind, poets "dealing with realities" who have moved well beyond the "vapid language" of much traditional Western poetry to cultivate voices as appropriate to their subregions of the West as Robinson Jeffers's was to coastal California in the early part of this century. Each has avoided "romantic misrepresentations" and "earned his voice," as Wild and Graziano phrase it, "by coming up through a West which, in turn, has been rediscovered and reaffirmed by his voice."[38]

Also, numerous anthologies exemplify poetry from a given subregion of the West. A good one is *Desert Wood: An Anthology of Nevada Poets*, edited by Shaun T. Griffin (1991), about as various a compilation as you could wish, with a lot of fresh talent showcased.

There are loads of anthologies of all kinds, many of which address the past neglect of women, Anglo and otherwise, and at least one, *Women Poets of the West: An Anthology, 1850–1950* (1978), edited by Thomas Trusky, that began setting the record straight some years ago. But go directly to the earlier work, the poetry of Janet Lewis and Ann Stanford, as well as work that's more clearly New Western, the poetry of Sandra Alcosser or Elizabeth Dodd. And read the poetry of Linda Hasselstrom, now available bounteously in *Dakota Bones: Collected Poems of Linda Hasselstrom*. Author of splendid prose about her life as a rancher in South Dakota, this Texas-born land-loving woman writes poetry the same way she does ranch work: with unflinching independence of mind, forthrightness, subtle muscularity, careful attention to detail. Consider the last stanza from "The Poet Falls in Love with a Cowboy":

> If I ever see you again, it will be
> from the armchair by my own fire, or some
> motel room, some airport, some other road
> I'll drive, reminding winter that it
> owes me mercy.

Or this whole poem, entitled "Goodbye":

> This frail April day
> we delayed
> as long as we could.
> On the porch stand two clay mugs,
> one orange, one blue; both empty.

Or the second half of "Medicine Rock Rodeo":

> Late in the dusty day, an
> Oglala boy, whiskey-brave, rides a buffalo—
> for thirty feet. While he rolls
> in the dust, the buffalo collects snowfence
> on his horns, scatters the crowd,
> and disappears like smoke into the prairie.
> On the fence or smoking beside the chutes, the men
> squint across the dusty miles
> and wait.[39]

Or "Settlers," an unsentimental look at the West as home. Hasselstrom's is the sort of poetry that prompted George Venn, in a 1990 review of volumes by Anne Pitkin and Lisa Malinowski Steinman, to declare that "the masculine forces that subjugated the frontier have exhausted their passion just as those same forces have nearly exhausted regional resources. Now, feminine energy comes forward with force, insight, and reform." He might well be speaking of many more women across the whole West when he praises Pitkin and Steinman for showing "the means for reinventing the colonial Northwest: honesty, humor, intelligence, compassion. Listen: regeneration can begin."[40]

But, to rein back just a tad, male poets aren't out of the picture yet. Poetry by Brewster Ghiselin, Walter McDonald, or Stafford has been around awhile and has as much to say about the problems of the West and its regeneration as poetry by contemporary women. Furthermore, one of the most talented New Western poets of recent years is a man: Richard Dankleff. In his 1984 volume *Westerns*, his second collection, all the poems concern the nineteenth-century West, most of them focused on—or even in the voices of—diverse specific persons: river trader, bone hauler, missionary, naturalist, pioneer woman, soldier, Kiowa medicine prophet, African-American con man, on and on. It's a gallery of characters rendered in lines informed by historical documents, tightly crafted, tuned to their subjects' rhythms of thought and speech. Dankleff's poems display a broad range of humor—earthy, wry, sardonic—as in these lines from "Posse":

> Their wagon stands
> on the high bank.

Beneath their chopped
hole in the ice
the wretch they poked
is out of sight
till the March thaw,
maybe longer.
"Looks like he's not
a swimming man."
"It beats hanging."[41]

Dankleff handles ballad stanzas deftly in "The Revenge," a cowboy poem about some of John Chisum's fired hands branding his cook. And he convincingly leads the reader to discover with trapper Zenas Leonard a paradise of wild horses in "California."

Dankleff's poems, though not always deep portrayals, offer memorably apt images and smack of authenticity. Also, the endnotes that cite and comment on his sources hold your interest more than most history books. He's one of a number of New Western poets who use historical records to create "voice poems" that dramatically project characters through brief, realistic stories. Jane Candia Coleman does it in *No Roof but Sky: Poetry of the American West* (1990), which features Belle Starr, evangelists, and a host of others, as do I, in a few poems, in my 1993 book *Violence and Grace: Poems About the American West.*

And then, of course, there's cowboy poetry. Though its tradition goes back well over a century, such poetry entered its New Western phase in 1985, the year that saw both a watershed gathering of cowboy poets in Elko, Nevada, in the heart of the intermountain West and the publication of Hal Cannon's *Cowboy Poetry: A Gathering*, a collection, assembled through a monumental amount of fieldwork and editorial sifting, that represents both classic and contemporary cowboy poets and yet will fit easily into the pocket of a duster. The two gatherings of far-flung voices marked and encouraged a ripsnortin' resurgence that gives no indication of abating.

Cannon's succinct introduction to his collection provides thumbnail background. Poems of the kind he has collected — all of which "express an honest spirit which is lean and hard" and move in "a manageable gait"—were first chronicled, along with cowboy songs (many of which were originally poems, sometimes severally authored), by folklorists like N. Howard Thorp and John A. Lomax in the early years of this century, then later, in the middle years, by others. Thus Cannon sees his anthology, complete with annotations for tenderfeet, as "the culmination of this twentieth century interest in cowboy poetry"—a draw that proved to be too quick since he produced another volume, *New Cowboy Poetry: A Contemporary Gathering*, also pocket-size, in 1990. He stresses that the tradition of such poems, "in both the old and new West," involves "the memorized performance." They have been "written to reflect a real voice" (usually of a working cowboy) and, ideally, like any poetry, should be "heard aloud." Though the quality may vary, they're in "a language which reflects light and smell and open places, hard times and soft evenings; a language coded with insiders' words . . . and shared values." Many of the poems are in rhymed couplets or ballad stanzas that recall the work of poets like Robert Service. Finally, Cannon rejoices in the fact that there's a great deal of cowboy poetry in existence, much not published even in rural weeklies but available to anyone looking—or listening—for it in the places where it's composed and performed, the places of "the real life of the cowboy," not in movies but around "the campfire, in the bunkhouse, and on horseback."[42] And, increasingly, at gatherings all over the West (some of which have been replayed on television). A lot of the old-timers have passed on, of course, but their artistic offspring now active on the circuit are numerous indeed; and the circuit includes plenty of gatherings, all with ballooning attendance.

Silver City, New Mexico, hosts an annual July roundup of cowboy poets like Jim "Speedy" Shelton, Baxter Black, and at least a couple of dozen others—verse with good humor, gritty action, vivid imagery of the occupation as well as the ranch-hand-size meals, dancing, and other activities that gatherings include, along with cowboy songs and stories. The Three Rivers Rodeo Association sponsors a gathering of poets and storytellers every March in Farmington, New Mexico. It serves as the kickoff event for the Farmington Pro Rodeo and Western Trade Show and usually attracts an audience of around a thousand to performances of premier poets. The National Cowboy Hall of Fame in Oklahoma City presents the Oklahoma Cowboy Poetry Gathering each April. And every year on Labor Day weekend singer Michael Martin Murphey offers a gathering at his WestFest celebration at the Copper Mountain ski resort in Colorado, featuring Waddie Mitchell, who rivals Black for the title of best-known living cowboy poet. The gatherings occur from Seattle to Muleshoe, Texas, with the gathering at Elko, home of the Western Folklife Center, now held annually every January, being the main event. It had more than 10,000 attenders — cowboys, reporters, tourists, whoever — in 1994.

The poets aren't just cowboys — and, more and more, cowgirls — or ranchers but personalities of a fascinating kind, most of them intent on authenticity. They're heirs to a tradition, itself with variegated roots, that began in the mid-nineteenth century with poets like Eugene Ware and that continued through Allen McCanless and Tim McCoy, the silent-screen star, to the late S. Omar Barker. Mitchell is a true New Western cowboy poet in that he turned to writing poetry only in 1984 after twenty-six years as a professional cowboy and ranch foreman. He has a repertoire of some 200 poems. He performs on television frequently and, like dozens of his colleagues, has his performances out on cassettes, compact discs, and videotapes — mostly without sacrificing, even while ambitiously marketing, the sense of the genuine in his work. Black grew up around livestock near Las Cruces, New Mexico, started writing and sharing his witty poetry while practicing veterinary medicine, then gave up treating ailments in order to poeticize full-time. He has extensive media exposure (like a number of other cowboy and cowgirl poets, he's appeared on television talk shows) and seems to be the only cowboy poet who manages to make a living on rhyme income alone. An even more recent newcomer is Buck Ramsey of Amarillo, Texas, a well-respected poet whose performances are less melodramatic than those of many of his peers. Keep a lookout for Paul Zarzyski too. A past rodeo cowboy with literary training and an intelligent ear, he tells it true and well. As for cowgirl poets, Sue Wallis is exemplary. She's paid her dues in the northern West and has a flair for interpreting her experiences in terms of Nordic mythology — see her chapbook *The Exalted One* (1991). And blessed is any gathering that features a Crow poet named Hank Real Bird or Gwen Petersen, a rancher from Big Timber, Montana, whose repertoire contains limericks as crisp as whip snaps.

New Western "cowperson" poets are coming out of the woodwork these days by the hundreds. Public attention to them includes coverage in the last few years in *People*, *Newsweek*, most of the large-circulation

Cowboy poet Paul Zarzyski reading at the 1994 gathering in Elko, Nevada. (Photo by Sue Rosoff, courtesy of Sue Rosoff)

magazines, even the *Times Literary Supplement*—and Randy Houston has recited his work in a television ad for Western Sizzlin. Some of their poetry is good or better. A portion isn't, and some has the feeling of having been penned by city-slicker nitwits in the workshops of an ill-conceived institute of cowboy poetics. A poem like Black's "The Big High and Lonesome" is prototypically the right stuff. I won't embarrass anyone by citing negative examples, but they aren't rare. And they may present a problem. In a review of Zarzyski's collection *Roughstock Sonnets* (1989), which contains no real sonnets but offers serviceable poetry anyway, Lawrence Clayton argues that the "current popularity of cowboy poetry" will continue only if its typical quality "rises above that of the current mass of imitative material being produced," much of which "is of questionable literary value as orally presented poetry" and in published form "is visually unattractive because it is poorly printed and economically bound."[43] His argument persuades, to be sure; but I think the typical quality of the poetry is getting higher, and there's reason to hope that a number of presses, mostly in the West, will solicit the best of it and put it out competently. (Even so, a bunch of the solid writing may remain hidden in saddlebags.)

My reason for that hope? The well-produced books that recently have been coming out. Consider *Horsing Around: Contemporary Cowboy Humor*, edited by Lawrence Clayton and Kenneth W. Davis (1991). The editors know what they're about in this collection of poetry and prose from Black, Elmer Kelton, and others, which is illustrated with Ace Reid's cartoons and features a useful glossary and bibliography. Or peruse Wallace McRae's work in *"The Cowboy Curmudgeon" and Other Poems* (1992), a book nicely illustrated by Clinton McRae. This much-celebrated poet has been at it awhile, with many live performances and those on the syndicated television program "The West" to his credit, as well as previously published collections of his poetry—at the same time using his nonwriting hand to manage a 30,000-acre cattle ranch near Forsyth, Montana. Or consider *Blood Trails* (1992), a maverick collection by Vietnam veterans and cowboy poets Bill Jones and Rod McQueary, who share a serious-minded double vision of a war zone and the West, of trauma and healing recovery in homeland. Also, consider Cannon and Thomas West's anthology *Buckaroo: Visions and Voices of the American Cowboy* (1993). Winner of a Western Heritage Award, it includes informative editorial apparatus, cowboy poems, a sixteen-track compact disc of the poets in performance, and exquisite watercolors by William Matthews. And, last, to whet your nonpoetic appetite to boot, consider the *Cowboy Poetry Cookbook: Menus and Verse for Western Celebrations* (1992), a fiesta of a book by Cyd McMullen and Anne Wallace McMullen, two Elko sister-in-law ranchers who savvy how to bring people together with hearty and healthy fare.

Good cowboy poetry well published will help keep up its popularity for New and Old Westers alike, but its real success will depend on its power to bring people together through oral performance. Speaking of recent "signs of backlash" against the depersonalized industrialization of the cattle business that has "undercut the intimacies that drew people to country life in the first place," Kittredge notes that "the old desert cow outfits are refitting their horse-drawn chuck wagons" and "going back to some approximation of the old life." They're doing so, he admits, partly "for economic reasons." But also they're "rediscovering reasons for doing the work," which concern wanting "to live in a living world, and work at significant work like raising food, which as a calling is so unlike the alienating efficiency-dream of agribusiness." And such basic desires clearly are related to those that motivate cowboy poetry gatherings, assemblies, at their most honest and essential level, as old as humankind:

> All over the American West cowboys and ranchwomen and farmhands and sheepherders have been gathering to declaim their verse to one another. Such gatherings are heartbreaking in their openness once all the hype and nonsense has slipped aside. Like the other side of that bloody-knuckled coin which is rodeo, these are celebrations of things ranchland people respect and care about most deeply—the land they have chosen to live on, their work, and, right at the center, one another, this companionship.
>
> As the economics of ranching deteriorates, our good people seem driven to open themselves.[44]

I believe he's nailed it. Be thankful that publishers like Gibbs Smith are striving to put out more and better cowboy poetry in print. But the next time you hear a cowboy poem you like, whether it extols "the old life" or laments the end of it, give the author an energetic hand. Even if you're only couch-potatoing the performance on television, join in the community as best you can.

Like Jim Harrison and other spokespersons for the art, the poet Dana Gioia, till of late also a marketing executive, has expressed great worry that poetry in America is becoming an endangered species. In his book *Can Poetry Matter? Essays on Poetry and Culture* (1992) and elsewhere, he has blamed the potential extinction on the academy: workshops that teach students to write shoddy, boring material that has nothing to say to the general public and professors who either neglect poetry or hijack it as grist for the mills of politicized literary criticism that takes no account of its formal beauty. Gioia's accusations are priggish at times, even nasty; but he's put his finger on a problem, and I have sympathy for his position. Also, he's right that poets outside the academy are increasingly more interested in traditional poetic form, in narrative poetry, and in reaching a broader audience. The poetry-performing competitions called slams popular mostly in urban areas around the country, from New York to Taos to the West Coast, are partially a result of such interests, though the events involve only a tentative sense of communal values. The contemporary vogue of storytelling, in the West and nationwide, is a related phenomenon, providing for an oral sharing of experience through crafted language that's far more immediate and engaging than the prefabricated drivel on television most of the time. But surely cowboy poetry gatherings, even if the work isn't wrought to the taste of either a formalist poet like Gioia or an academic literary critic, constitute a genuine possibility for the future vitality of poetry shaped for the ear, colorful in imagery, good-humored in mood, inviting in the stories it has to tell, and relevant to its listeners' world.

In short, cowboy—and cowgirl—poetry matters much to many people. It's *the* public poetry of the New West. It's also changing in some ways. You read and listen to more free-verse stanzas than you used to, a little less maybe of what I once heard described as "tawny grammar," and sometimes you sense a rhetorical attitude more directed *to* than aligned *with* the reader/listener (probably a consequence of a broader audience that takes in enthusiasts who aren't really of the cow world).

In his introduction to *New Cowboy Poetry*, Cannon notes additional changes. He acknowledges that cowboy poetry remains "a stabilizing tradition" and that many of the oldest poems are "still alive in cow camps around the West." But he sees significant differences between "cowboy ballads of the mid-twentieth century," which served to affirm "the occupation from within" and "never punctured the consciousness of people outside the ranching occupation," and post-1985 poetry. Contemporary work "expresses a strong sentiment for place that did not exist in the early verse," a sentiment that he associates with a growing conscientiousness about "stewardship" of the Western environment. Cowgirl poetry treats not only the usual aspects of ranching from a woman's point of view but also "what it means to 'buy into' the dream of cowboy life." Also, "today's poetry is much more personal than the old-time verse," more contemporarily topical, more prone to be panderingly "humorous." (Though it remains, Cannon stresses, "utilitarian — heavy-duty, industrial strength poetry" that's "best used in the natural world where there are starlit skies, the warmth of blazing fires, and sounds and sights of open expanse.")[45]

Such changes tend to irritate people with more old-fashioned ideas about cowboy poetry, whom the advocates of such changes regard as stodgy — so there's a split between Old and New Westers on a few matters here. And you'll discover the usual timeless vices of inflated diction, lines that qualify as no more than doggerel to practically anyone, poets busier with self-promotion than with care for their art, and so on. Still, however, cowboy poetry, at its best, performed in the right context, sustains the Western spirit the way wind holds a hawk aloft.

By and large, Westerners haven't seen fit to write much drama. You could dig around and find old melodramas, like Louisa Medina Hamblin's 1838 play *The Jibbenainosay*, I guess — predictable predecessors to a lot of what would later turn up in B movies and on television. You might even try to piece together a tatterdemalion tradition out of the plays of William Inge, a musical like *Oklahoma!*, Will Rogers's shows, and whatnot. But you would be hard-pressed to find real dramatic activity before about 1960.

I'm not sure why that's so. Maybe because Old Westers were no more given to dramatic dialogue than to verbal intercourse generally. Maybe because the genre requires an urban cultural base to thrive. Maybe because the conventions of its language are inadequate to the traditional Western myth. Or maybe because it entails crowded and closed social spaces full of conflicted chatter that are alien to the optimistic rural Western sensibility but apparently are charming to people of the East, particularly New York, where the theater has enjoyed a long and more or less successful career. Whatever the reasons, drama didn't catch on very well in the West until the early New Western period. Then it began to take off, probably because of urban growth, more migration from and communication with the East, and monocultural monologue yielding to multicultural exchange.

Politics as well had something to do with it. Certainly that was the case with El Teatro Campesino, whose development was spurred by César Chávez's efforts to establish a strong union for exploited California farm workers in the 1960s. The Teatro, founded by playwright, actor, and director Luis Valdez in 1965, and Chávez's *movimiento* entered into a "collaboration [that] proved immediately productive," as Raymund A. Paredes explains:

> For Valdez, the farm workers' cause provided a rich source of dramatic material while Chávez benefited from the fund-raising and polemical skills of the Teatro.
>
> The early performances of the Teatro — and these occurred in every imaginable setting from open fields and flatbed trucks to university auditoriums — were built around a series of *actos*, ten to fifteen minute improvised skits that dramatized the circumstances of the farm workers. Rooted in the traditions of *commedia dell'arte* and Mexican *carpa* presentations [tent shows] and influenced by contemporary agit-prop techniques, the Teatro managed simultaneously to entertain its audiences and prod them toward social awareness and action.[46]

In the next decade or so the Teatro expanded its topics and themes somewhat, reaching a high point with the full-scale production in Los Angeles of Valdez's musical drama *Zoot Suit: A New American Play*, which had a long run in 1978 and 1979. The Teatro, like its dramatic offspring, may not have realized all its promise; but it did participate in and encourage the wide flourishing of Mexican-American literature that continues to the present, and it foregrounded issues of cultural and social conflict and heritage that such literature, mostly in other genres, now explores with increasing subtlety. (For a sample of the kind of work the Teatro presented — minus performance aspects, of course — see *Necessary Theater: Six Plays About the Chicano Experience*, edited by Jorge Huerta [1989]. The collection includes also a couple of plays done by the less well-known Teatro de la Esperanza — though none of the early *actos* of the Teatro Campesino.)

And, of course, Chicano drama, especially Valdez's plays and, later, Carlos Morton's (like *Rancho Hollywood* [1991]), has contributed to the at-large burgeoning of Western drama since 1960, which is associated with the names of New Western dramatists like Sam Shepard, Preston Jones, Frank Chin, Mark Medoff, Velina Hasu Houston, David Henry Hwang, and others. As Mark Busby points out, the burgeoning has occurred through a time of immense cultural change and confusion in America, its events "providing a wealth of subject matter" for dramatists "but requiring a struggle for synthesis." In the West the struggle has been compounded by the "battle . . . against the Broadway clawhold on American theater," a battle gradually turned in favor of the West by "two developments — the growth of powerful regional theaters and the emergence of Off- and Off-Off-Broadway playhouses."[47] Thereby you have some other reasons for the post-1960 takeoff of Western drama — and, in the recognition of its cultural context, at least a partial accounting for the controversial topics, complex themes, innovative structures, and tortuous moods of many New Western plays.

You can experience all that in Shepard's drama, what with characters in his plays from *Cowboys* (1964) to *True West* (1980) acting out the confluences and conflicts between more or less mythical Western values and a fragmented postmodern world. The oversexed Billy the Kid in Michael McClure's play *The Beard* (1965) is a far cry from the Old Western image of him. The anti-heroic characters in plays like Medoff's *When You Comin' Back, Red Ryder?* (1973) or *Doing a Good One for the Red Man: A Red Farce* (1969) are withered, dislocated, ineffectual versions of their mythical forebears. Even a "Texas chic" musical, to borrow a phrase from Busby, like *The Best Little Whorehouse in Texas* (1978), by Larry King and Peter Masterson, speaks strongly of historical distance from the era of *Oklahoma!* and its mid-century innocence. The cultural explorations undertaken by the Native American Theater Ensemble as it toured the country in the 1970s, presenting mostly the plays of the Kiowa-Delaware dramatist Hanay Geiogamah, disappointed any theatergoers looking for a Wild West show instead of demythologizing plays about the harsh history and contemporary plight of Indians. Likewise any who were expecting comfortable Asian stereotypes of Chinese railroad workers in the plays of Chin and Hwang in the 1970s and 1980s.

Though African Americans and women have not typically found the New West to be favorable to fresh dramatic visions, you can, with a little category stretching, include playwrights like Ted Shine and Megan Terry among those creating them. In any case, all of this work, in its grappling with complicated issues, is by "regional artists" to whom, as Busby put it, "contemporary Americans have turned . . . to help make sense of the whirl modern life presents."[48]

A good bit of the whirl has to do with race and gender. Hwang's plays deal with both, and through his work, as Jerry R. Dickey argues, "the Asian-American literary concern has moved beyond a regional experience and now attempts to define a national and international consciousness regarding gender and race relations"—a change New Western Historians would applaud. Nowhere is that more true than in Hwang's *M. Butterfly* (1989), his postmodern redoing of Puccini's opera *Madame Butterfly*, which is "a devastating attack on Western attitudes toward the Orient," attitudes tangled up with questionable concepts of the feminine and the masculine.[49] Issues concerning such concepts chase through Peter Parnell's comedy *Romance Language*, a play first produced in 1983 that counts among its characters almost two dozen well-known figures from nineteenth-century America, including Bloody Knife and Custer. The Denver Center Theater Company's well-toured production (in two versions) of Christopher Sergel's superb 1993 play *Black Elk Speaks*, adapted from John G. Neihardt's 1932 book with the same title, devastatingly relates the winning of the West as experienced by Native Americans. Through an all-Indian cast (even for the roles of whites), the passionate artistry of its language, and heavy doses of irony, the play presents both a sorrowful alternative history of racial confrontation and a vision of a rich past lifeway that still might be recovered, affirmed, multiculturally shared in peace. And *Going to See the Elephant*, a play by Karen Hensel and others that's recently been produced here and there, discredits the popular myths of the pioneer woman. Based on journals written by real pioneer women and set in 1870, it concerns a group of them who get together for a day and a half in a sod house in Kansas while their men are away. What they reveal about their lives and discover about themselves effectively shatters the idol of the meek Madonna of the Prairies and questions other persistent stereotypes.

If such plays help Americans make sense of their world, they do so largely by relating reality to myth and present to past — even if, as in the case of the marginalized characters in Hwang's plays, that involves being "torn between embracing and denying" the past.[50] Two plays from the 1980s neatly epitomize alternate postmodern approaches to treating those relations dramatically: Frank South's *Rattlesnake in a Cooler* (1981) and Medoff's *The Majestic Kid* (1984). By way of concluding my disquisition on drama, I'd like to discuss those two plays briefly, drawing on an insightful comparative study of them by Helen Lojek, who understands what they have to teach New Westers.

Though the theme of both plays is familiar enough, Lojek observes that they "are rarities on the contemporary American stage" not only in that they "deal with the 'myth' and the 'reality' of the American West" but also in that they "face directly what have become central problems for many western writers: what to make of the myth and its relation to reality, and whether literature and life demand choosing one over the other." Both plays concern Easterners who go west fixated by an image of the West as, to use the phrase that Lojek borrows from Archibald MacLeish, an unchanging "country of the mind" — specifically, the mythic West of the cowboy, whose image "retains as apparently unshakable a grip on the American imagination as does that which links the South with Miss Scarlett and Ashley." For the protagonists of both plays the West represents an escape from the overpopulated East and its urban wreckage, "another chance," wide-open opportunity — all the things that make up the West in the music and movies they experienced as children. And "neither pauses" in his flight "to reflect that a myth based on a brief nineteenth-century phenomenon is unlikely to match the twentieth-century reality." Unsurprisingly, neither encounters the world he's looking for, and, as Lojek puts it, "therein lie both tales."[51]

True enough, but it's the differences between the two tales that tell the real tale. The unnamed protagonist from Kentucky of South's *Rattlesnake in a Cooler* is a medical doctor who gives up his family practice, wife, and a life that seems only a routinized path to the grave in order to "light out for the territory, the West, where less is more." He wants to wander "unfettered by women," cowboy-style. He gets a job as a factotum at a dude ranch in Greeley, Colorado. He cultivates a look of authenticity by wearing faded jeans, scuffed boots, and the like. He fetishizes his gun and the therapeutic power of blasting away at critters around the ranch, as if, as Lojek analyzes his conversion, he "has been reading Richard Slotkin's *Regeneration through Violence*." He then goes to Cheyenne with Jim, the wrangler who got him his job, to attend Frontier Days, an annual event that remythologizes the West. He loves it but fails to grasp the fact that such events "are not reality but play." His inflated sense of his own heroism, combined with a Western-mythic "absolute loyalty to his partner," leads him later to kill a New Mexico highway patrolman with a tire iron. The murder leads to his arrest and his winding up in jail, "a rattlesnake in a cooler," where he waits to be hanged and recalls the scenes that make up the play. "Seduced by images of manly independence and rootless lack of confinement," he's finally a self-made Clint Eastwood–like fool who dies for his folly.[52]

The Majestic Kid, Medoff's play, offers a situation parallel to that in South's play, but, as Lojek summarizes their differences, the former "is longer and more complex than South's, the humor is lighter, the conclusion is not bleak but hopeful, the pattern is not ironic but comic."[53] The protagonist, an attorney from the Bronx named Aaron Weiss who's disillusioned about the practice of law in New York, goes to New Mexico with his fellow attorney and childhood friend AJ in order to accomplish real justice by helping the Apaches recover land taken from their tribe. Thus Aaron embraces a better motive than the one that drives the doctor in South's play, but he's just as entranced by myth. Taking on the case, which AJ calls a "last stand," he admits that he came west "because I imagined I could still somehow become who I've wanted to be since I was nine years old, could climb out of the Saturday matinee of my childhood and become at twenty-nine who I was then: The Majestic Kid. Who knew it was possible to help people without hurting other people; a hero who bloodlessly snuffed out injustice wherever it lurked."[54] Aaron is in pursuit of a self concocted out of mythy remembrances of playing cowboys with AJ twenty years before and of a silver-screen hero named the Laredo Kid "who made nine-year-old Aaron think of himself as the Majestic Kid." And part of the play's fun has to do with the continuing presence of the Laredo Kid in Aaron's life, as Lojek makes clear by her description of him: "A rootless, womanless hero who sings love songs to his horse, has a draw like quicksilver, and never deserts a 'saddle partner,' Laredo comes to New Mexico with Aaron. He is a figure of memory and imagination, but one who actually appears onstage, slightly paunchier than he was once, still singing his outdated cowboy songs, bewildered at the world (and the women) of the eighties, but there nonetheless as guide for Aaron."[55]

As you might guess, anyone given to such fantasy projection discovers a West decidedly out of phase with his internal world. The Apaches don't seek a religious reunion with their land: they want it as a site for a resort hotel. They wear polyester clothing and aren't really into tribal dances, preferring the distractions of television instead. And so on. But the crucial difference between Aaron Weiss and South's doctor is that the former recognizes "from the start . . . that Laredo *is* a myth," just as he recognizes more generally "that the myths of his childhood do not match the reality of his adulthood." He, like Laredo, is "bewildered by this New West," but he knows why. And whereas South's doctor sought a womanless rootlessness that Laredo exemplifies, Aaron wants the "family circle," a possibility incarnated in Lisa, a character summed up by Lojek as "a modern woman of the West who sings 'Home on the Range' with new meaning, cooks, ropes, and has a mystical, spiritual sympathy with the land and the people of New Mexico."[56] It's the home theme again, tied up in a bundle with the Western myth, a special sense of place, and a distinctly New Western female presence.

Lojek unwraps that bundle as follows: "The one significant variation between the myth as the doctor absorbs it from Tex Ritter and the myth as Aaron absorbs it from Laredo is the attitude toward the land. Laredo loves the land, and the feel for western geography that Aaron has absorbed from him is reinforced by Lisa. In fact, it is reverence for the land that links past and present in Aaron's perpetual West. . . . No one in *Rattlesnake* demonstrates such awareness of the land." She goes on to observe that such awareness is what distinguishes Milton's *W*estern from the *w*estern and that it marks "Aaron's instinct for adhering to life-affirming rather than to violent elements in the myth." Unlike South's doctor, he doesn't attempt "to shape his life to the myth"; rather, he "preserves only those portions of the myth that match his own priorities" (recall why he went west in the first place). Moreover, his priorities are good ones. His westering wasn't an escape from women, and finally "he wants neither to rescue Lisa [a vague goal having to do with what Laredo believes women are for] nor to be rescued *by* her, but to develop a shared relationship" — then family, community, the whole ball of wax. The uncritically accepted myth, which South rejects as dangerous, drives his doctor over the edge, but Aaron is able to "adapt what is valuable in the myth to guide his life in the New West." Thus adapted, the myth arguably makes him more sane than he was at the beginning of the play — and assures a happy ending. A little like McCarthy's John Grady Cole in his existential faith, Aaron has "the confidence to 'wing it' in a world ungoverned by scriptwriters."[57]

The main difference involved here has to do with how the myth is read — that's Lojek's overall point. One protagonist reads the myth and goes for his gun; the other reads it and goes for the girl — and land and home and hope. One learns the Wild West from it; the other learns the Mild West. Yet another protagonist in another play might learn something else from it. The lesson South teaches is clear enough to anyone fed up with what guns and violence have done to America. What Medoff teaches is subtler but more important, however, for what Aaron, like the audience, "learns from the forces of the New West, . . . though it will modify the lessons of the silver screen myth, will not totally destroy that myth." The trick, then, is to recognize what Aaron comes to recognize: as Lojek puts it, "that myths do not reflect reality," that their purpose is "the embodiment of values and modeling of ideal behavior," and that, because their "pattern lacks the flexibility necessary for modification in response to changing circumstances," attempting "to follow their pattern precisely leads only to disaster." Empowered by that recognition, Aaron " 'rehistoricizes' the myth and is thus able to abandon those portions that do not fit him or the New West, and pursue the values he continues to respect."[58] And that seems as worthwhile a message as any New Western drama, now or in the future, could promulgate.

Then there's New Western nature writing. Whole libraries full of books containing the essays of postmodern heirs to the tradition of John Muir, John Burroughs, Mary Austin, and many others. And more to come. It's a lifetime reading project — but nonetheless an urgent one. So I want to talk about *why* we should read the work of these people before I discuss examples of it.

Something is happening to writing in America, especially in the West, and it's important for a number of reasons, not the least of which is that it involves the enlarging production of fine nonfictional literature whose voices speak to a broad readership of matters both immediate or intimate and global, even cosmic. What's happening is that an increasing number of writers — new and established, popular and academic — are turning to nonfiction, mostly the essay in all its variety, as their genre of choice. A lot of humanists weary of formal theoretical articles now are writing informal essays that deal with experiential particularities. The impersonal mind is yielding to the personal heart, the abstract to the concrete, overwrought poststructuralist puzzles to practical issues. Many writers, again especially in the West, are writing as much nonfiction as fiction — as many memoirs as novels, as many essays as short stories or poems.

The shift seems to parallel — and be connected to — the New Western Historical shift of attention from the West of dream to the West of fact. It seems to parallel likewise the recent general westward movement of literary development in the country: away from the straitjacketed Eastern sensibility and its concern with indoor "frenzy arising out of nothing" and toward the uncorseted Western sensibility and its concern with outdoor encounters with natural expanse. It seems also to have to do with the self's desire to deal with place unevasively — literarily, to be sure, but usually without elaborate fictionalizing apparatus. So recent nonfiction tends to be both personal and about "nature" in some way, and its writers frequently have an urgency in their voices — nowhere more so than in the West.

The beginning of nature writing is a matter of argument that I'll leave to others. Exactly what is or isn't nature writing (is $E=MC^2$?) makes for interesting debate, but I'll leave that also to others — you know it when you see it, I think — though what follows may lend clarity to the issue. There are different kinds of emphases in nature writing — spiritual, economic, political, scientific, aesthetic, what have you — all with somewhat different purposes. It can be very straightforward in what it has to say, or it can deal complexly with both our relation to and separation from the natural environment — and push language to its limits in the process. (It may be the postmodern awareness of excessive separateness from nature that's ultimately motivating so much writing and reading about it.) And then, of course, there's the whole problem of whether a given essay or book is really not so much nature writing as memoir, travelogue, or something else. Blurring abounds.

One of the motives for nature writing is an "ulterior" one. Ann H. Zwinger, who's been doing it for a while, mostly in the West, explains:

"If I can get you to look, you may become curious about what you see, and if you are curious, you will ask questions, and if you ask questions you will get ten more questions for every answer delivered and in the process, by default, will come to be interested, and being interested is just one step from caring, and if you care you will not destroy."[59] (Though you may, of course, seek out what has the writer's attention and thereby, ironically, become a destructive tourist.)

But that motive readily entangles others, a diffusion that Harold Simonson finds common among New Western nature writers: "In recent years Western writers like Edward Abbey, Barry Lopez, Gretel Ehrlich, William Kittredge and Ann Zwinger — to name but five — have extended their nature prose into the social, political, and psychological consequences that occur when modern technology threatens or destroys forests, tundra, canyons, rivers and ancient artifacts." Such writers give their talents, "with urgency and often despair," to describing the effects of soil erosion and pollution, an effort that reaches an extreme in the work of Wendell Berry, who "ruminates on the constant care required to keep a place a home."[60] Glen A. Love observes that "growing concern for, and interest in, the natural world on the part of many of today's readers and writers, diverted from much contemporary fiction by that genre's curiously antirepresentational bias, has emerged in a wealth of important new books and anthologies," and he argues that "many ecologically-conscious readers have apparently turned to nature writing as the clearest and most direct antidote to the presumption of human dominance and control."[61] That extension of the role of nature writing, most notably in the West, often involves its personae — or even the writers themselves, as well as their characters when they write fiction — emerging as types of the "eco-hero."[62]

Literary pitfalls lurk here. The writer can sacrifice art on the altar of politics. The writing can become formulaic or " 'genre driven,' . . . delivering an expected set of responses," as Peter Wild phrases it in a review of C. L. Rawlins's *Sky's Witness: A Year in the Wind River Range* (1992) — a pitfall that he says Rawlins avoids in his Wyoming account, along with another, "the bugaboo of nature writers, the slide into self-absorption."[63] The slide into self-righteousness is yet another possibility, of course, as is irony-deficiency anemia.

So New Western nature writing is a piebald critter, some of it falling prey to such errors, some free of them, much in the middle range. At its best it preserves a careful tension between natural phenomena translated into words and the translator (also present by translation into words). It invites you to identify with the translator, to participate in that balanced relationship, to get reacquainted with those phenomena or to encounter them for the first time through another person's experience — to engage the natural West with fresh senses and sincerely care about it.

Now for examples of writers who do it right and yet show the "distinctiveness" of the contemporary Western nature essay, what Thomas J. Lyon calls "its aura of increased seriousness and urgency as the human population and the technosphere relentlessly expand, wilderness dwindles, and species diversity declines."[64]

In dating the beginning of New Western nature writing, you could certainly go back to around 1960 and find harbingers of it — say, in Loren Eiseley's work or John Graves's 1960 classic *Goodbye to a River*. But probably most Western literary historians would agree that Edward Abbey's *Desert Solitaire: A Season in the Wilderness* (1969) was the shot that started it all. Before he died in 1989, Abbey produced more fine work — as did Eiseley and Graves, for that matter — but that book remains his enduringly popular and most written-about masterpiece. A few years ago I met a guy who always keeps a copy in his pickup and reads it at odd moments of the working day — not an unusual habit, I suspect.

Abbey was a New Western radical ecologist, with a good dose of recalcitrant Old Wester thrown in, a character, sometimes caricature, in his own nonfiction — and fiction — who never strays too far from Jack Burns, the rebel cowboy in a technological world who's the protagonist in his 1956 novel *The Brave Cowboy: An Old Tale in a New Time* (scripted by Dalton Trumbo into the 1962 film *Lonely Are the Brave*, starring Kirk Douglas). More akin to George Washington Hayduke, the beer-guzzling, womanizing saboteur of construction sites in his 1975 novel *The Monkey Wrench Gang* than to conservationists like John Muir or Aldo Leopold, Abbey would wince fiercely at any mention of himself as something as namby-pamby as "a nature writer." Reading *Desert Solitaire*, you can see why — and why he heralded and stimulated a new generation of such writers.

Lyon gives an eloquent inventory of Abbey's differences from your typical mid-century nature writer in this description of his approach (which pertains, more or less directly, to *Desert Solitaire*):

> For Abbey, wilderness experience is a standard by which the aberrations of technological, money-distracted society may be measured incisively. In the canyons of the Southwest ("Abbey Country," as the author once termed it), there is yet a remnant of peace, quiet, and time in which one might make a start toward an examined life. Abbey portrays this wild opportunity cherishingly, in the image-detail that respect for its importance inspires. The distance between the authenticity of wilderness life on the one hand and the abstracted desperation of the mass of men on the other then leads him (as one familiar with the modern nature essay might expect) to a Jeremiah-like vision. This is common enough, perhaps; Abbey, though, surpasses other nature writers by expressing his dismay in sardonic, self- and species-reducing humor, the like of which has not been seen in the West since Mark Twain. The effect of the humor is to democratize and personalize the complaint; Abbey's rapport with the reader is unequalled in the genre. . . .
>
> There are western nature writers with more documentary knowledge of flora and fauna than Abbey, perhaps — his approach to natural history is almost always narrative and experiential — but his mingling of prophetic depth with outrageous exaggeration and satire gives him a unique literary voice, a standing in a wholly separate category from other nature essayists.

Lyon goes on to speak of Abbey's "enlarging the field significantly."[65] No doubt about it. His work passed on to his peers and heirs an activist attitude toward ecology illustrated by his own practice of pulling up survey stakes and more; a unique consciousness of the spiritual romance of the desert (especially, in *Desert Solitaire*, of Arches National Monument in Utah, now infested with mountain bikers in shiny stretch bodysuits); a complex portrayal of what happens, as Ann Ronald puts it, in his "superimposing his sense of the Old West on his vision of the New";[66] and a relentless expression of the need, as the indomitable George Hayduke characteristically puts it, " 'to save the fucking wilderness.' "[67]

As a number of recent studies of *Desert Solitaire* have shown, the meaning of that seemingly casual and journal-like book unfolds through a set of artfully composed and interrelated essays. Like most nature writing, the book is fictionalized in several ways, from its very Abbey-like persona to its spring-to-autumn span condensed from three years of the author's experiences to its patterning of recurrent images.[68] And several qualities indicate differences from earlier nature writing and influence a good deal in its wake: a persona who desires unity with nature and yet is profoundly aware of its separateness, who is worldly and ironic, cynical, and yet "earnest, even pious (in the non-self-righteous sense of the word) toward the overwhelming, soul-filling source of value he finds in non-human nature"; "a certain self-reflexiveness and doubleness" that puts "beautiful, silky prose" cheek by jowl with tricksterly jokes; mixed voices, to be sure; a text driven by the author's self-conscious ego and yet designed "to evoke the otherness of the landscape and the value which inheres in it *as other*."[69] Postmodern maybe, definitely New Western. Abbey still reigns as King of the Eco-Cowboys. Other recent nature writers may be typically more mild-mannered than he, but traces of his influential personality and style, as hard to ignore as a north wind, turn up everywhere.

Wallace Stegner, a less boisterous nature writer than Abbey, better trained literarily, doubtless wiser, has probably had at least as much influence — though largely because of his individual essays, beginning with those collected in *The Sound of Mountain Water* (1969), and not quite because of any one nonfiction book as prominent as *Desert Solitaire*. Still, his *Where the Bluebird Sings to the Lemonade Springs*, a selection of his essays published between 1972 and 1991, not all about nature, may in the long haul give Abbey's classic a good run.

However much influenced — or not — by the work of those two presences and others, like Eiseley, Western nature writing took off in the 1970s like never before. The 1980s were even more fruitful. And the 1990s show every sign of being even more so. If there are dominant concerns in that plethora of writing, they're with the New West as a distinguishable place within a larger order and with the stewardship required to make a home of it, concerns familiar enough to Abbey and Stegner.

Perhaps the most remarkable New Western nature writers of the 1970s are Zwinger, Hope Ryden, and Lopez, especially the last — all still going strong, with much of their work from that decade out in relatively inexpensive paperback editions. Exemplary is Zwinger's *Run, River, Run: A Naturalist's Journey down One of the Great Rivers of the West*

(1975), about the Green River, one of many fragile and threatened natural systems that she explores in this and other books. Or Ryden's scientific but loving investigation of the coyote and its turf, *God's Dog* (1975) — one of several animals, mustangs in two other books, she has studied with accuracy and emotional sympathy. Or Lopez's *Of Wolves and Men* (1978), his attempt to help us, as Lyon has it, "know the wolf as it actually is, with no neurotic hatred, sentimentalism, or anthropomorphic projection," so that "we may know ourselves in a different way, and perhaps begin to make our accommodation" in a world where "disintegration seems to loom."[70]

The theme of accommodation, of the negotiated relationship between humans and their fellow beings, shapes much of the Western nature writing of the 1970s and later, particularly when it deals with endangered species. But the writing isn't always about camping out with coyotes and wolves and eating dehydrated stew. It also can zoom in on the more domestic aspects of that relationship, illuminating the curious connections with wildness it sometimes entails. Lopez's 1978 essay "The Bull Rider" does that in startling fashion:

> What are these, medieval eyes? Up close, under inch-long lashes, they bulge, hair-triggered, the size of cue balls.
>
> Is this what alfalfa has wrought? 1428 lbs. 1701 lbs.
>
> Bulls. A cleated hoof hits the door of a chute with a crack, with the speed of a middleweight's jab. The eyes roll. The head comes up and the wide, wet nose pries between two-by-eight boards. The chute door whines under his lean.
>
> Bulls.
>
> Shit.[71]

That's a long way from the watered-down psalms that New Agers in bodysuits take to be nature writing in the New West. The author of that essay looks straight on.

The best Western nature writers of the 1980s and 1990s exhibit a clear-eyed but increasingly more intricate vision of their subjects. Perhaps less moralizing than their immediate predecessors, they nonetheless offer work with complicated moral significance — indeed, the daunting complexity of environmental issues in the postmodern West as they perceive them seems at times to forestall any possibility of simple moral posturing. To see what I mean, read Linda Hasselstrom's books on ranching in South Dakota, like *Windbreak: A Woman Rancher on the Northern Plains* (1987) or *Land Circle: Writings Collected from the Land* (1991). The latter book, following on her husband's death from cancer, is a dark study but scopic and wise, demonstrating, as Kittredge capsules it in a review, "her utter emotional honesty" in what she says about "a world where you can take it or leave it, but you can always believe she means what she says."[72] She doesn't shy, writes honed prose, and never fails to hold you with sensory nuances, hard-edged reflections, or winding arguments — even if you don't agree with her strictly independent views.

Another nature writer of considerable talent to emerge during the 1980s is Coloradan Reg Saner, whose work during that decade prepared the way for his impressive 1993 book *The Four-cornered Falcon: Essays on the Interior West and the Natural Scene*, an ingeniously unified collection. His approach differs from Hasselstrom's — it's more intellectual, deliberative, bookish even, gentler in voice — but also propels you vibrantly into the Western outdoors (and deep into your head as well). He has an allegoristic ability to lace his stories of nature with human history. The book is framed with a prologue and epilogue woven of crosscut observations and meditations on a marmot in the Rockies and the first-century Roman natural historian Pliny the Elder, who was killed while observing the eruption of Vesuvius.

Saner does something similar also in my favorite essay in the collection, "Technically Sweet," when he interrelates, among other things, the present landscape of New Mexico (mostly the Pajarito Plateau), the making of the first atomic bomb, and the guesswork history of the so-called Anasazi peoples, who disappeared from Frijoles Canyon about 800 hundred years ago. He does that sort of thing with a brisk economy of transition, juxtaposition, suspense, shocking you alternately into thought or memory or wonder. The effects achieved can be very subtle but powerful, as when he imagines the Pliny-like scientists who witnessed the Trinity test in 1945 responding to that event much as the Anasazis or nonhuman animals might: "Each person there is taken by surprise, stunned witless through long, elliptical seconds of animal fear. . . . Only when the skin cringes from appalling heat, only when the fireblind eyes recover, do the scientists' bodies know what their theories feel like."[73] Saner knows profoundly and tells well what their theories (and radioactivity) have done to the West.

Sharman Apt Russell, who moved out of the fast lane and into the Southwest in 1981 and became a kind of Annie Dillard of New Mexico, also knows something about what dangerous ways of thinking have done to the West. In *Songs of the Fluteplayer: Seasons of Life in the Southwest* (1991), she explores them personally in her fragmentary account of her father's death, when she was two years old, in an X-2 rocket plane that crashed in the Mojave Desert. Then she explores them more expansively when she looks at what has happened to the natural and cultural home of the West because of the mental habits that fortify the dark side of the cow world and government bureaucracy in *Kill the Cowboy: A Battle of Mythology in the New West* (1993). There she urges a reinvention of the West in terms of a richer accommodation between inner needs and the outer wild that remains.

Like Russell, Kathleen Norris also is a true New Wester, having moved in the early 1970s from New York City to South Dakota, where she now lives with her husband in the small town of Lemmon, in the northwest part of the state. In her 1993 book *Dakota: A Spiritual Geography* she writes of that move, into a house her grandparents had built in 1923, as "one that took me deep into the meaning of inheritance, as I had to try to fit myself into a complex network of long-established relationships." That acculturation leads her into stories, storytelling, and the lasting oral tradition of both in the Dakotas — among Indians, rural whites, and the Benedictine monastics she comes to befriend. Just as Native Americans "need story to survive" these days, so "we learn our ways of being and reinforce our values by telling tales about each other." Her book consists of such stories — about her stark outback area of the Plains and its life-forms, human and otherwise. The stories betray a special interest in Stegner's stickers, the people who "want to stay," who, like Benedictine monks, make a "commitment to a particular community, a particular place," and are stimulated by it "to develop an inner geography." Such development demands a "countercultural stance in our fast-paced, anything-for-a-buck society," and she finds it common in "other writers of the desert West" who speak of the values in its land, land that has been crucial to her personal growth. From that land left behind by the sea that once covered it, through it, Norris has learned to write beautifully of it as a home both natural and spiritual, as in this passage concerning her trip to another town to teach writing to schoolchildren: "In the schoolyard, a snow angel's wings are torn, caught in grass exposed by the sudden thaw. In the stuffy classroom, a little girl, restless and distracted, probably a bad student, becomes White Buffalo Calf Woman, speaking of a world in which all people are warm in winter and have enough to eat."[74]

Norris's devotion to monasticism isn't to my taste, but it's integral to her treatment of the West as a home. Like other New Western nature writers, monastic or not, she would readily understand the elaborations on the notion of home that Scott Russell Sanders performs in his 1993 collection of essays *Staying Put: Making a Home in a Restless World.* Certainly a nature writer and one who has written about the West, he's not a Westerner — his homing instinct has kept him with his family in the same house in Bloomington, Indiana, since 1974. Still, his sense of the importance of home in the postmodern world is absolutely relevant here. In the preface he outlines the search that his book entails and thereby summarizes much of what New Western nature writing, whatever its other motives, is up to:

> On coming to a new place, my father would take a pinch of dirt, sprinkle it in his palm, sniff it, stir it with a blunt finger, squeeze it, then rake it on his tongue, tasting. When I first saw him do this, I was puzzled. Why eat dirt? "Just trying to figure out where I am," he explained.
>
> This book is my own tasting of the dirt, my effort to find out where I am. It records my attempt to fashion a life that is firmly grounded — in household and community, in knowledge of place, in awareness of nature, and in contact with that source from which all things rise. . . . The search is practical as well as spiritual. Only by understanding where I live can I learn how to live.

Unlike his father, who never "had a settled home" after his childhood, Sanders is a sticker who wishes "to consider the virtue and discipline of staying put" — in a book that "points through my local ground to . . . nature, and through nature to the encompassing order for which we have no adequate name." Thus, in "House and Home," he reminds us that our "local" houses are made from the land's materials, each "only a nest in disguise," each "on loan" from the land that will reclaim it, and "that *home* and *womb* share the holy sound of *om,* which Hindu mystics chant to put themselves in harmony with the ultimate power."[75]

But it's in "Settling Down" that Sanders's search has strongest bearing on the West. "One hundred years after the official closing of the frontier," he observes, "we still have not shaken off the romance of unlimited space." Nonetheless, he proposes that we cease being immigrants driven by such romance and become inhabitants of that space. He acknowledges that "mobility is the rule in human history, rootedness the exception," but he discerns "a way to reconcile our need to rove with our need to settle down." It's suggested to him by Bruce Chatwin's 1987 book *The Songlines*. In that amazing work Chatwin treats the Australian Aborigines' practice of staying in touch with the Dreaming, their "mythic time" of creation, by singing songs as they continually walk, generation after generation, the songlines that crisscross Australia. They thereby sing the geography of their world, renew it, and in turn know it in terms of "the necessities of life" it offers to those who know it. They "wed themselves to one place, and range over it with gratitude and care. . . . Like the rest of nature, they move in circles, walking again and again over sacred ground." They survive because "their mythology" has long ago "come to terms with their ecology"—something that hasn't yet happened in the West, where, as in the rest of America, "we may not have forty years, let alone forty thousand," to make it happen. We must wander like the Aborigines, Sanders argues—in a place. To do that, to help nature and ourselves survive, and more, we need "local knowledge [that] is the grounding for global knowledge."[76] And *that*, exactly, is what New Western nature writers, like New Western Historians, want to shape and share.

So those writers walk their songlines. Utahan Terry Tempest Williams does it in *Refuge: An Unnatural History of Family and Place* (1991) and *An Unspoken Hunger: Stories from the Field* (1994), which sing what a sensuous Mormon has to say about dying, homing, and the renewal of wonder in nature. Richard West does it in Big Bend National Park, Timothy Egan in the Northwest, Charles Bowden in the Southwest, especially in *Desierto: Memories of the Future* (1991), where he has created images of place that, as one reviewer puts it, "achieve the sharpness and clarity of an Ansel Adams print."[77] New Mexican Robert F. Gish does it in *Songs of My Hunter Heart: A Western Kinship* (1992), in part a growing-up book that says more about the changing relationship between man (the gender-specific word is justified here) and nature as the New West redefines the Old than vegetarian New Agers could ever quite grasp. And passels of New Western writers do it in anthologies like *On Nature's Terms: Contemporary Voices*, edited by Lyon and Peter Stine (1992).

Rick Bass is one of the important new wanderers, with books — most notably, perhaps, *Winter: Notes from Montana* (1991) or *The Ninemile Wolves* (1992) — coming out at a staggering rate. He's also a great short-story writer — another multigenre New Wester. He's young and seems to write well as easily as most people whistle. Does it longhand — at first anyway. Studied biology and then geology at Utah State University in Logan because of its proximity to the mountains where Sydney Pollack's *Jeremiah Johnson* was filmed. Now lives with his family in the Yaak Valley in Montana in a cabin. Hunts elk and deer in the autumn. He's a scrapper who's fed up with water pollution, clear-cutting, endangered habitats. He's influenced by Harrison, Abbey, Kittredge, Jeffers, lots of predecessors and peers. Maybe by Stegner most of all.[78]

And we're back to that grand old granddaddy of New Western writers. There's a yuppie-flavored one-liner about dinosaurs that says they died out because they couldn't accessorize. If Stegner were alive to hear it, he might counter that we may die out because we can't stop accessorizing, overstuffing our lives with inessential doodads bought at the cost of a plundered and defiled environment. He would remind us that we inherit culture, Western and otherwise, from our parents but borrow nature, Western and global, from our children. Like all New Western nature writers, he would remind us also that true ecology really is ultimate (good) housekeeping, which we do for only a short spell but must do humbly and carefully. And Stegner does remind us of these things, for his spirit lives on in his work. As I put it in an epitaph I wrote for him on the day he died in 1993,

> You teach even in rest
> the lesson of the West:
> that man does not command
> the household of the land
> but is only a guest.[79]

Now let me rig up a sort of literary catch-pen of New Western writing, some of it as generically mixed or otherwise odd as the horses you'd find in a real catch-pen, and then I'll conclude the chapter with brief thoughts about the future of writing in the New West.

There's some wonderful New Western travel writing, most notably from the late 1980s on. In *Out West: An American Journey* (1987), Dayton Duncan, a New Englander but a New Wester at heart, insightfully relates his postmodern traveling along the route that Lewis and Clark followed in their 1804–1806 quest for the Northwest Passage. I quoted from Ian Frazier's 1989 book *Great Plains* earlier. He's a New Yorker, but he isn't your average traveler: he sees the Great Plains and its people with unclouded eyes, critical intelligence, and generous humor. Two books defined by their routes, like Duncan's, are Thomas R. Vale and Geraldine R. Vale's *Western Images, Western Landscapes: Travels along U.S. 89* (1989) and Kim R. Stafford's *Lochsa Road: A Pilgrim in the West* (1991). Finally, two plump, much-celebrated books by William Least Heat-Moon (pen name of William Trogden, a Missourian) make an intriguing pair when read in sequence: *Blue Highways: A Journey into America* (1983) and *PrairyErth: (A Deep Map)* (1991). Least Heat-Moon is of both English-Irish and Osage descent, so perhaps it's not surprising that the first book stories a sweeping and somewhat European exploration of the country through its backroads whereas the second treats in intricate detail, by a more Native American or even Aboriginal approach, what the author learns by traveling repetitively over a small area, Chase County in the Flint Hills of central Kansas. The first book is a wide map; the second, as its subtitle says, is a deep one. The first book is about mobility, the second about locality. From many places to one, from 1983 to 1991: from Old Western moving-on to New Western homing-in. The first book falls in the tradition of Jack Kerouac's *On the Road* (1957) or John Steinbeck's *Travels with Charley in Search of America* (1961); the second is a road narrative with a difference.

And memoirs. New Westers by now may have more memoirs in print than their contemporaries in any other region of the world. So let me suggest just some combinations that afford variety and the possibility of thought-provoking comparisons and contrasts. First of all, *The Autobiography of a Brown Buffalo* (1972) by Oscar Zeta Acosta, Hunter Thompson's sidekick who figures in Thompson's *Fear and Loathing in Las Vegas* as Dr. Gonzo, a drug-crazed, 300-pound lawyer supposedly of Samoan extraction. Acosta's book is a romp through his *loco* series of careers, cultural alienations, and personal messes as a Chicano in California that makes for interesting comparison with Richard Rodriguez's better-known *Hunger of Memory: The Education of Richard Rodriguez* (1982), another story of confused cultural assimilation and estrangement from tradition and family. Then, for a whole other perspective on the contemporary Mexican-American experience, read *Borderlands/La Frontera: The New Mestiza* (1987), by Gloria Anzaldúa, a Chicana lesbian feminist from Texas who deals with all manner of borders that mark her life. It's a book that has its tragic dimensions but, as is typical of later New Western writing (especially that by women), affords a more positive outlook than the books by Acosta and Rodriguez.

Or juxtapose two books by Montana memoirists of different genders: Ivan Doig's *This House of Sky: Landscapes of a Western Mind* (1978) and Mary Clearman Blew's *All but the Waltz: Essays on a Montana Family* (1991). The two family stories, both impressive narratives of survival, have a good deal in common — even in technique, up to a point — but they diverge poignantly in their portrayals of growing up male and struggling up female in the West.

Doig is the better writer of the two, and his book sits tellingly between two other "sky" books: Guthrie's modern Western novel of 1947, *The Big Sky*, and Kittredge's distinctly postmodern memoir of 1992, *Hole in the Sky*. For one thing, the three books, in chronological sequence, illustrate a characteristic (though hardly all-inclusive) progression in New Western prose from linear fictional narrative to nonlinear nonfictional narrative to a more essayistic and self-consciously polemical nonfiction. The combination may illustrate other progressions as well, but surely the most significant concerns the "sky" business itself. As A. Carl Bredahl, Jr., analyzes *The Big Sky*, it's the story of Boone Caudill's movement from various kinds of "confinement" in Kentucky into "a world in which one could see forever" and subsequently, as the story winds down, into a situation where, for several reasons, the "world closes down on him." *The Big Sky* concerns an effort to break free into openness that fails. In *This House of Sky*, however, as the full title suggests, " 'house,' 'sky,' 'landscapes,' 'western,' and 'mind' integrate to form an image of an imagination seeking its place within a world dominated by land and sky," to make "a story not of breaking free but of discovering and accepting 'place.' "[80] Doig's story isn't of the Western sky turning into a mental prison, which it does in *The Big Sky*, but of mind — and heart — expanding to make it a home. From the tragedy of the mythic Old West to the reconciled acceptance of the actual New West.

Then to Kittredge's sky with a hole in it, a proposition that gives you an uneasy feeling. Early in his book he clues you in on the title, and you know why you have that feeling:

> Up the Skeena River in the cloud-park interior of British Columbia, across the road from the Tsimshian village of Kitwancool and framed by a stand of aspen beside the creek, there is a cluster of cedar totem poles from the early days. . . .
>
> Among them is the house pole called Hole in the Sky. An oval hole cut through the base of the house pole serves as a ceremonial doorway into the long cedar-plank building where the families lived. The hole in this particular pole, as I understand it, was also thought of as "a doorway to heaven," in the literal sense.
>
> The Tsimshians believed that stepping into your house was stepping into a place actually populated by your people, all of them, alive or not — the dead at least to the extent that they were remembered by anyone. It is a lovely notion, the space inside the house connecting to the landscape of communal imagination, the actual space bound together with story and recollection. It is like what I understand as the Latin sense of *familia*, meaning both house and family. . . .
>
> But there is, of course, another kind of hole in the sky, which is the simple emptiness we take as a modernist idea of God. We all know it in our way.

And I can't escape thinking of another kind as well: the so-called ozone hole. No surprise therefore, given Kittredge's double vision of traditional home and heaven and contemporary emptiness, that his stories and recollections are the ones "I learned to tell myself in my most grievous isolations" — nor that they concern the decline of his pioneering family and their vast ranch in the Warner Valley in Oregon, of the hopes of Manifest Destiny, and of the whole Western environment. Still, his book doesn't add up to just holelike negativity about the West. It does involve repudiation of the Old West — most specifically, of his grandfather's "fixation on the accumulation of land and money," which Kittredge comes to see "as a bad idea." But it also involves an acceptance of responsibility for the New West and a view of its living continuities closer to that of the Tsimshians, for Kittredge finds himself "driven to believe in damage control, that we must learn to revere and care for the world and one another if we mean to end up with anything of any value at all." He "can finally acknowledge that I hate the bloodiness" and the moral numbness of the Western past and that "it is time we lay hands on a sustaining mythology," but a shell-shocked hesitancy still haunts his closing thoughts: "I tell my own stories, and I move a little closer toward feeling at home in the incessant world, but I can't imagine where I would want my ashes scattered, not yet."[81] Such notes constitute a New Western chord: a hopeful sound but unresolved.

Along with the reflective remembering of memoirs have come also volume after volume of Western folklore and the like rewritten for New Western readers. Herewith a few titles: Thomas Edward Cheney's *Voices from the Bottom of the Bowl: A Folk History of Teton Valley, Idaho, 1823–1952* (1991); John W. Van Cott's *Utah Place Names* (1990), a book that might well lead you to read George R. Stewart's venerable and fascinating classic, much praised by Stegner, *Names on the Land: A Historical Account of Placenaming in the United States*, fourth edition (1982); and *Plains Folk: A Commonplace of the Great Plains*, edited by Jim Hoy and Tom Isern (1987). Finally, just for fun, there's Roland Sodowsky's *Un-Due West* (1991), a collection of made-up cowboy folklore about the made-up town of Lindisfarne, Texas — humorous though thin after a while, like a "Saturday Night Live" skit that lasts too long.

Literary criticism. In 1990 Stegner wrote the following on that matter: "The West doesn't need to wish for good writers. It has them. It could use a little more confidence in itself, and one way to generate that is to breed up some critics capable, by experience or intuition, of evaluating western literature in the terms of western life. So far, I can't think of a nationally influential critic who reads western writing in the spirit of those who wrote it, and judges them according to their intentions." But, he adds, "such critics will come."[82] Well, they have come, certainly in the form of Stegner himself and at least a few others I've quoted; many more are coming through the draw. Though among their Eastern colleagues some still feel like jackrabbits at a coyote convention, they're emerging strong in a field growing weary of arrogant abstruseness and the excesses of political correctness, becoming more eclectic, interested in personal responses to literature, attentive to its treatment of real-world situations. Our time has been called the age of post-theory. Whatever you call it, it's an age ripe for New Western literary criticism, which shows great concern for the writer's intentions, the reader's reactions, the enjoyment of Western literature as well as the seriousness of the ecological, cultural, and other issues that it stories and discusses. New Western History may be waxing more theoretical, but New Western criticism, like the literature it studies, tends to be as much narrative as discursive and argumentative. It likes essays more than "articles." It's user-friendly.

A short, fast-paced survey of Western literary criticism up to around 1980 may be found in Martin Bucco's *Western American Literary Criticism* (1984). He discusses the work of a number of the critics I've quoted in this and the previous chapter — and many others. Of the more recent critics whose work I've read, two stand out as especially helpful, both, in different ways, essentially personal in approach: Jane Tompkins and Robert Murray Davis.

Tompkins's *West of Everything: The Inner Life of Westerns* has earned her a few shots from some other literary critics and scholars, Eastern and Western alike. The former claim that she's gone intellectually soft in taking a personal approach to minor literature (and film). The latter (mostly males) think that she, a feminist of sorts from Duke University and a Janie-come-lately in their realm, doesn't know what (the culture behind the literature) she's talking about, particularly in her ideas concerning the Western male hero and his problems with sex, silence, violence, and death that have smothered women of the West. I'll admit there's a spate of things wrong with the book (commonplaces disguised as insights, sentimentality, and so on), but I also rate it as gutsy and provocative. Tompkins is honest about the ambivalent feelings Westerns prompt in her, sympathizing with characters even as she judges them harshly, but she's an enthusiast who frequently interprets the genre, along or against its grain, with keen instincts. She's damn sure a nationally influential critic, one who's followed her heart out on a limb. In spite of her mixed assessments, it's almost as if she, as a critic, has found in the Man of the West the "one thing" Curly in *City Slickers* says you have to find, as if she'd asked who else in this treacherous world would be her hero — and made her choice.

Davis's *Playing Cowboys: Low Culture and High Art in the Western* is a horse of a different color. Davis lacks Tompkins's reputation, but he's just as canny a critic. Though he prefaces his book with stories about his background, his father as an embodiment of classic Western-male traits and of the Western myth itself, and about his own turn from more conventional scholarly preoccupations to engage the Western, he's a less personal critic than Tompkins. He puts a lot of humorous and acuminous personal spin on his arguments, but he's quick to leave the "I" behind. Given his ability to deal creatively with a range of Westerns (by writers as different as Owen Wister, Oakley Hall, Richard Brautigan, and various science-fictionists) and his veteran familiarity with the genre, his collection of essays may be better than Tompkins's. My favorite? That's easy: "The Reader as Cowboy: Postmodern Westerns," quintessential work by a New Wester who comprehends the Old.

Like their Eastern counterparts, many Western literary critics wear specialist eyeglasses. Ecocriticism, of course, is warming up rapidly. Ann Ronald's 1982 book *The New West of Edward Abbey*, from which I quoted earlier, is a good example. A more recent one is Scott Slovic's *Seeking Awareness in American Nature Writing: Henry Thoreau, Annie Dillard, Edward Abbey, Wendell Berry, and Barry Lopez* (1992). Though such criticism is attracting a growing number of practitioners interested in privileging the study of literature that dramatizes the interconnections of human life and the natural environment, there remains no small percentage of New Western critics dedicated to other perspectives distinct from — but increasingly seen as related to — that one. Most notable are those of feminist criticism and ethnocriticism. Excellent examples of both, mostly of the former, may be found in Barbara Howard Meldrum's collection *Old West — New West: Centennial Essays* (1993), which contains also an important contribution to New Historicist criticism. Ethnocritics, as you might expect, concern themselves predominantly with Native American literature and its relation to other literatures, reinterpreting and reeducating, like ecocritics and feminist critics, all the way. Arnold Krupat writes some of the best in his book *The Voice in the Margin: Native American Literature and the Canon* (1989) and in his more recent *Ethnocriticism: Ethnography, History, Literature* (1992). So does Lucy Maddox, through her revisionist readings of American classics, in *Removals: Nineteenth-Century American Literature and the Politics of Indian Affairs* (1991). Also, fine ethnocriticism by Louis Owens, Michael Castro, and others has been published by the University of Oklahoma Press in its continuing American Indian Literature and Critical Studies Series, under the general editorship of avant-garde Native American novelist Gerald Vizenor.

So literary criticism is alive and well in the New West. Certainly, as we've seen, its literature is. And the teaching of Western literature thrives. More of it is being read in the schools, at all levels, than ever before. Grade-school students are reading works by and about Native Americans. High-school students who never liked literature are coming round to it in courses with titles like Frontier Literature. College courses in Western literature of all kinds, New and Old, are now offered across the whole country. The number of theses and dissertations on Western literature (especially on nature writing and fiction by Native Americans, Hispanics, and women) and related topics increases each year, as does the membership of the WLA, which seems ever to include more Easterners, to feel less marginalized, to have greater professional self-confidence. Let Muhammad come to the mountains.

In her essay "My Western Roots," Marilynne Robinson, author of *Housekeeping*, observes, as many other New Western novelists might, that "I feel I have found a place in the West for my West, and the legitimation of a lifelong intuition of mine that the spirit of this place is, as spirits go, mysterious, aloof, and rapturously gentle." Having found so much of value there, she, a person who now lives in Massachusetts, shows understandable irritation about Eastern attitudes toward Western culture: "I find that the hardest work in the world — it may in fact be impossible — is to persuade easterners that growing up in the West is not intellectually crippling. On learning that I am from Idaho, people have not infrequently asked, 'Then how were you able to write a book?' "[83] Well, the East has long been a provincial spot, but that's changing. I hear that Larry McMurtry left his sweatshirt printed with the words MINOR REGIONAL NOVELIST behind him in Leesburg, Virginia, around 1970.[84] That's apt, given that he and his New Western peers began about then not just to join the mainstream but to modify its course.

What about the future of New Western literature? Predictions, as the politically incorrect Old Westers' saw has it, are about as reliable as a woman's watch, but I'll venture a few and then let a fellow New Wester have his say on that question.

If rumblings at recent conventions of the Western Writers of America are a good indicator — and I think they are — popular Western novels, like Western films, will enjoy an increasing (and increasingly female and youthful) audience. They will be more thorough in character development, authentic in setting, and credible in story line — and more frank in the portrayal of relationships, sexual and otherwise. More women will write them, and more of them will be about women — keep a lookout for the work of Lenore Carroll, Judy Alter, and their ilk. A lot of those novels, historical or contemporary in setting, will overlap generically with the productions of a growing market in more realistic Western romance. More non-Anglos will try their hands at them. More bookstores will keep their shelves better stocked, not only in literarily thriving Wyoming but even in New York City. The Western dream will still be there within those colorful covers but sobered, tempered, qualified, revised.

In Western literature generally, the home theme — with its emphasis on identity, cultural heritage, the environment, and a sense of place — will become dominant, if it hasn't already, and run robustly through the "ecoliterature" that many critics forecast as the future of New Western writing. Like much of the literature of the Vietnam War, in the wake of which event it has developed, most of that of the West, contemporary in setting, will concern not the now-questionable kind of patriotism that tinged Old Western literature but that of future-shocked people, fractured selves alienated from traditionally significant experiences, seeking wholeness and natural community: the patriotism of people, to paraphrase Abbey, ready to defend their country against their government and all it's tentacled into. The New Western literature of the future will be less and less that of a monocultural fatherland, more and more that of a multicultural motherland.

In his past president's address to the WLA in 1992, James Work spoke of New Western writers as exhibiting "a more comprehensive consciousness" than their predecessors, one that "will seek to re-establish its personal and cultural relationship with all the forms of living nature." For "Western American literature-yet-to-come" he foresaw less interest in "vastness"; writers who "will find inspiration in more limited space" and "see the world more gently"; "more interest in ecology, less . . . in heroic adventures, little attention paid to stories of territorial conquest." Speaking of what's required for literature in "this new, more sensitive West" to bloom with "integrity," he warned that "we must set our wit against pretentiousness." Borrowing from *The Virginian* the notion of the cowboy " 'turning his wolf loose,' having a good time, enjoying satire and practical jokes," Work advocated "turning our Western wolf loose." Near the end of his peroration he returned to that notion and elaborated it into a doughty affirmation of the future of New Western literature: "The wolf is an animal of territory. Our territory is the American West, the largest literary 'region' in the world. The wolf is our Western sense of humor. The wolf is our refusal to become domesticated as a pet breed of some 'higher' and 'more civilized' species of publishers, readers and critics." Finally, addressing an audience well acquainted with the Reverend Doctor McBride in Wister's story, the self-righteous, humorless preacher who condemns the Virginian and his fellow cowboys as "low-minded sinners," Work turned his own wolf loose: "Our wolves haven't been muzzled yet. Our wolves haven't been trained to heel — they haven't been spayed or fixed. And take note of *this*, you who are the Reverend Doctor McBrides of the world: our wolves haven't even had their *shots*."[85]

 I sometimes feel that I am trying to do the impossible in my pictures in not having a chance to work direct but as there are no people such as I paint it's "studio" or nothing. — Frederic Remington, diary, 15 January 1908

There's not only a return to the Western, but in particular to an untold part of American history. — Mario Van Peebles, quoted in Susan Spillman, "Revisionist Westerns, a New Film Frontier"

CROSSED OVER: *UNFORGIVEN* AND OTHER REVISIONS

In spite of corrective forces, for many people Western myths and legends remain, sometimes subtly, often problematically, as durable as a whetstone. Let me illustrate that durability with a story from Nancy Shoemaker, a professor of history at Texas Christian University.

Shoemaker tells of teaching a course in the history of the West at a small college in upstate New York. It dealt with the expectable issues of myth versus reality, Turner versus Limerick, and so on. The students wouldn't buy New Western History, for they "*knew* the frontier was a place of raw opportunity, where individuals flourished and men could prove they were men." All of them, except for two women in the class, named *Young Guns* as their favorite Western movie — "a film about smart-alecky, daredevil young men including Billy the Kid" — and "loved" *Far and Away*, which "glorifies people who cheated their way to good land in the Oklahoma Land Rush." The students were able to see that *Dances with Wolves*, though much praised for its cultural sensitivities, portrays Native Americans in terms of the simplistic "two polar images" that date back at least to Columbus — Pawnees as "brutal savages," Lakotas as "Noble Savages." But they refused "to understand that Indian people are just as complex and varied as white people." They clung to their clichés. The Costner version was theirs as well. Though Shoemaker sanguinely proposes several ways of "demythologizing Indians in history courses" (mainly by having "an Indian presence in the classroom") and otherwise breaking through stereotypes of the West, she obviously found the course discouraging: "Myths about the West seem resistant to knowledge, so I don't make much headway when I try to take the clothes off the emperor of Western history."[1]

Don't be tempted to label Shoemaker's story exaggerated or unusual. I've heard similar stories from other teachers — and concerning not only students in the East. True, more clear-eyed understanding of Western history is possible now than ever before. The knowledge is there. Indeed, though minds, like textbooks and pedagogy, can be slow to change, it's widely shared. But millions of people, in America and abroad, don't really want it. They don't want the West that was. They're in denial, edgily stubborn in their beliefs. They don't want the emperor of Western history stripped naked. They want him decked out like Buffalo Bill. Or Roy Rogers. Or John Wayne. Or Ronald Reagan. Forever.

Who put those clothes on Western history in the first place? Dime-novelists? Boosters? Of course. But the real tailors, from the early nineteenth century on, have been artists in visual media: painters, sculptors, filmmakers, and the like. It's they who have most powerfully formed the global public's images of the West. The images stick like cockleburs to the psyche, especially the American psyche, with its readiness, its deep need, for heroic idealizations and unambiguous ritualized tales of good triumphing over evil. In the United States a lot of people — mostly Anglo males — don't want anyone fiddling with those images, which have to do with who they are or like to think they are. Which brings me to another story.

In recent years numerous regional and national exhibitions of Western art have been organized. The Anschutz Collection of over 500 paintings toured from Denver across the United States and through eight foreign countries, starting in 1974 and ending in 1990, a little after the "Trails Through Time" exhibition got under way for its tour through the interior West. In early 1991 the Brooklyn Museum put together "Albert Bierstadt: Art and Enterprise," which subsequently toured to San Francisco and Washington; and the Smithsonian Institution's National Museum of American Art mounted "The West as America: Reinterpreting Images of the Frontier, 1820–1920," which never made its planned tour to St. Louis and Denver, never got to go west, apparently for financial reasons. In the next few years regional exhibitions were organized by the Buffalo Bill Historical Center ("Discovered Lands, Invented Pasts: Transforming Visions of the American West"), the New York Public Library ("America Moves West: Images of an Expanding Nation"), the Montana Committee for the Humanities ("Their Eyes Tell Everything," a collection of historical photographs of Chippewas and Crees), and other agencies. Many of the exhibitions provoked controversies. Certainly the "Trails" exhibition, with its striking photographs of desolation, ruin, alienation, and revealing absurdities, was intended to do that — though not to the extent finally realized. Sheep swarming over the land like locusts, a car stuck in the mud, a miners' camp littered with tin cans (those objects a miracle of food transportability that helped tie mining dependently to the East): not images designed to inspire Pollyannaism. But of all those exhibitions the one that really stirred the hornets of quarrelsomeness was "The West as America."

The exhibition caused much-celebrated (and not fully anticipated) trouble not just by presenting alternative images of the West, as "Trails" did, but by daring radically to "reinterpret" traditional images, to mess with their meaning as sacred icons of how the West should have been. Many people responded positively, and attendance was high; but many also made Elizabeth Broun, the director of the museum, William H. Truettner, the curator of the exhibition, and collaborating art historians feel about as welcome in Washington as rattlers in a prairie-dog town. In some respects the exhibition wasn't so much an art show as an interpretational showdown, with New Westers and Old Westers going at it from March 15 to July 7, 1991, and afterward.

What was at stake? The 164 paintings, sculptures, photographs, and whatnot that made up the exhibition were annotated with wall texts that interpreted the works as conspiratorial propaganda for Western expansion. Little was said about the aesthetic qualities of the works, nothing about the glory of Manifest Destiny. The subtexts of shame and sham denied, veiled, or avoided by the artists were deconstructively dug out and exposed. George Catlin's paintings of Indians trivialize their subjects. Carl Wimar's 1856 painting *The Attack on an Emigrant Train* portrays them as a barbarous menace, and Theodor Kaufmann's 1867 painting *Westward the Star of Empire* makes them belly-crawling demons — obstacles to civilization in either case. Other paintings "invent" Indians as Noble Savages, already "like us," or betray unconscious fears — of white-Indian miscegenation, for instance, in Irving Couse's erotically and ideologically loaded 1892 painting *The Captive*. Bierstadt's 1867 painting *Emigrants Crossing the Plains* is an idealized depiction designed to persuade Easterners of the sweetness of westering. Frederic Remington's well-known 1903 painting *Fight for the Water Hole* doesn't just represent a last stand against Indians: it's also an industrial-age allegory about opposition to nonwhites immigrating into cities, taking jobs, corrupting the dominant culture. Andrew Joseph Russell's classic 1869 photograph of the golden-spike ceremony *(Dodge and Montague Shake* or *East Meets West)* at Promontory Point, Utah, may record and celebrate the completion of the transcontinental railroad, but it also, in a very cunning way, foregrounds the power of technology and the success of capitalism in the West at the same time that it disclaims the real cost of the project, the sweat and blood of the workers — see if you can find a Chinese face anywhere in the picture. What was at stake was what the West (and America) was (and is) all about.

Some of the reinterpretations were cogent enough. To be sure, icons of the romantic West hide a world of pain, genocide, financial scandal, on and on. But other rereadings wandered off the scale of cogency. Take, for example, Truettner's argument, as the catalog of the exhibition has it, that William Ranney's 1850 painting *The Trapper's Last Shot* portrays a

Frederic Remington, Fight for the Water Hole *(1903): an allegory of xenophobia. (Courtesy of the Museum of Fine Arts, Houston; the Hogg Brothers Collection, gift of Miss Ima Hogg)*

man not so much looking backward from his horse to check for Indians in pursuit as betraying an "anxiety [that] echoed that of a nation overextending itself—rushing westward to conquer and exploit land rather than nurture its productive capacity."[2] At any rate, ridiculous or enlightening, New Western art historians were offering up neither recitations of Western greatness as revealed in art nor a balanced debate among differing positions: they purveyed only a critical negativity, and they didn't smile when they said it. After the show had been open for about a month, many of the wall texts were replaced with less shrill editions in response to harsh public reactions, but the overall tone, with its leftist tendentiousness, was little diluted by that tactic. The harsh reactions continued.

The people reacting included not just a segment of the museum-going public but art critics and op-ed commentators all over the country and, of course, politicians. The exhibition bothered some because it seemed to impose political correctness on an age different from our own. Some found it strident or perverse or Marxist. Others were amused at the im-

Andrew Joseph Russell, Dodge and Montague Shake *or* East Meets West *(1869): foregrounding the profit, forgetting the loss. (Courtesy of the Andrew J. Russell Collection, the Oakland Museum of California History Department)*

plication that the entrepreneurial class in the East was organized enough to conspire systematically with artists in profiting from the West. Ted Stevens, the Republican senator from Alaska, saw the show as another example of Easterners' elitist sneering at the West and grumbled about stopping Smithsonian funding. Daniel J. Boorstin, formerly librarian of Congress, thought it inaccurate and destructive. A stampede of posturing. A good portion of the noise may have had to do with issues concerning the methodology of interpretation, but most of it had to do with the way the exhibition demythologized the rationalizing stories white America likes to tell itself about the positive meaning of Western colonization.

That sort of thing was hardly new in 1991. New Western Historians had been up to it for years by then, and Brian W. Dippie had recently done a revisionist job on George Catlin and other nineteenth-century American artists in *Catlin and His Contemporaries: The Politics of Patronage* (1990). Maybe not quite everybody cared about controversies in

Santa Fe or even Brooklyn, but "The West as America" was put on at the national museum in the nation's capital, for God's sake! And the nation's immortal artworks, through those "panels of text that relied on the writings of the new historians," to borrow Truettner's own words, were displayed as mere "ideological constructions" of artists who "created a fictional West for a nation eager to appropriate its land and resources" — and to justify that appropriation.[3] The museum thus functioned, in Byran J. Wolf's phrasing, "more as a cabinet of curiosities than a repository of culturally consecrated objects" — curiosities that incorporate Barnum-like deceptions rather than objects with "transparent" meaning. It dared to clarify "how much the history of the West is a history of rhetoric," how "the settling of the West blurs with the selling of the West" and "the conquest of native cultures merges with the conquering power of culture itself." It turned visual beauty into "the unpleasantness of a counterintentional way of reading." Like the Bierstadt retrospective at the Brooklyn Museum, which dealt less polemically with "the cash value of ideology," the National Museum's exhibition assembled "the West we have all grown up admiring" and made it a battlefield in "the Critical Wars" of the 1990s.[4] As one result, "The West as America" wound up being what Eric Gibson of the *Washington Times* called "a sort of 'Campfire of the Vanities' — Tom Wolfe's tale of venality and corruption in New York in the 1980s transposed to the 19th century American West."[5] Bottom line: those politico-arty types looked at our favorite images of ourselves as good guys in a simple story and saw nothing but pretty icing impastoed on a dog's breakfast of complicated historical squalidness.

Where did we get the idea that we were the good guys, that the story was simple? Well, from captivity narratives of the seventeenth and later centuries, James Fenimore Cooper's books, dime novels . . . and, most unforgettably, from those visual images. And from later ones on movie and television screens.

The silver screen. A land of dreams — Western from the beginning. A medium, unlike the stage, well matched to the epic scale of the Western myth.

In late summer 1993 newspapers across the country carried an Associated Press story about a tintype in the possession of Ray John de

Aragon of Las Vegas, New Mexico. Passed down from his grandmother, who, according to family history, befriended Billy the Kid, it was alleged to be a seated portrait of the famous outlaw — the only one besides the well-known photograph of him standing homely and slope-shouldered with his rifle. A computer-identification expert attested to its genuineness. As did a physical anthropologist. As did biographer Robert Utley. It soon sold for $50,000.

The issue is ocular proof: does the person photographed look like Billy the Kid? Yep, as far as anyone can tell, largely by comparing the two portraits. Seeing is believing. De Aragon's tintype looks like the real McCoy. But then so does Russell's golden-spike photograph until you detect the mythologizing artifice of it.

The realism, authenticity, factuality, or truth of photographic images is a tricky matter, especially when they begin to move and, later, are further vivified with sound. Seat yourself among the first viewers of the first full-fledged Western, Edwin S. Porter's 1903 film *The Great Train Robbery*, which was produced by Thomas Edison, starred Broncho Billy Anderson and Marie Murray, and ran for ten minutes. It's pioneer work: lengthy and complicated in story line for the time (one year after the publication of *The Virginian*, remember), innovative in its use of close-ups and pan shots. Bandits tie up a telegraph operator, rob a train, get caught. Nothing in the darkness around you distracts your attention from the flickering images. Your eyes are riveted on them: the naturalness of the telegraph office, the dynamism of the train, the louring faces of the bad guys, the danger of their weaponry. It's only a play of light. It's not real, but it *seems* compellingly real. You're in New Jersey. You've never seen the West. For you, the film, this romance of the gun, *is* the West. Almost unerasably.

Such technologized images and their stories have repeated — with variations and refinements, of course — over and over, hypnotizingly, since 1903. The theme of arms and Western men has been sung a lot. Its conventions were locked in early on: heroes were reluctant shooters, but bad guys had itchy trigger fingers and frequently concealed their weapons; heroes never did, and their aim, like their moral sense, was true. Also, myth and reality got weirdly intertangled early on. Story lines were drawn, Richard Slotkin explains, from "a vast literature . . . full of ready-made plots and characters." Yet filmmakers "could also draw on surviving remnants of 'the real thing,' " as he reminds us: "In the first decades of the new century most of the western landscape was unaffected by modernization, and many frontier heroes and villains—Buffalo Bill, Wyatt Earp, the outlaws Henry Starr and Emmett Dalton—were still available to appear on camera. When Thomas H. Ince filmed *Custer's Last Fight* in 1912, many of the participants served as actors and technical advisers."[6] Stories based on stories, conventionalized heroes and villains played by has-been real ones, aging memories influencing the creation of fictional scenes—all, to borrow the title of Slotkin's piece from which I just quoted, "Gunsmoke and Mirrors."

The silent Westerns were as predictable as a bad habit, as Tom Mix and William S. Hart went through their motions again and again. "The 'realism' of these films," of course, as Slotkin notes, "was mostly illusion," what with desert-town settings, "the usual suspects" for characters, black-white haberdashery, chases on horseback, final shoot-outs. But such films were immensely popular and profitable, and soon "a larger, more ambitious sort of western was developed: the historical epic, which celebrated the winning of the West"—epitomized perhaps by John Ford and Ince's 1924 cast-of-thousands work *The Iron Horse*.[7] Then the 1920s roared into the Great Depression. Celebrations of progress were out; gangster films and escapist musicals were in. The Western waned.

Until 1939, when the " 'renaissance of the western' began a 30-year period in which westerns were the most popular form of action picture in theaters and later on television."[8] That renaissance was heralded by Ford's *Stagecoach*, which had it all: Monument Valley scenery, great music, some strong characterization (partly through John Wayne, whom the film made a star), breathtaking climax—and, of course, oversimplified Indians. The period that followed included also the heyday of the radio Western, which had begun some years earlier. Primarily for children until they began competing, ineffectively, with television for the adult audience in the 1950s, radio programs like "The Lone Ranger," which premiered in 1933, "Hoofbeats," and those of singing cowboys like Gene Autry and Roy Rogers were audio dramas of squeaky-clean Western males. Every plot advocated the so-called traditional American values and virtues—though later programs like "Luke Slaughter of Tombstone" tempered such Boy Scout idealism with less resolvable moral quandaries, as did television shows like "The Life and Legend of Wyatt Earp" and the more authentic-feeling "Gunsmoke," both of which premiered in 1955.

But most of that eye-and-ear fare was obedient to expectable formulas and stereotypes. That's as true of Ford's films about making the West safe for attractive young white women without real lives as it is of the "Hopalong Cassidy" television series that began in 1949 as recuts of B Westerns the hero with his anomalous black hat had already starred in. The Westerns in Slotkin's thirty-year period generally showed "little interest in dealing with major historical milestones," as David Daly and Joel Persky observe, but instead were "seemingly concentrated on the romanticization of a few petty criminals and the glorification of certain 'heroes.' " Stock footage was used and reused. The villain almost always had a mustache. Frontier towns got purged of evil by gun-clad Galahads who seldom fitted in well when lawlessness gave way to law, chaos to order. Ford stylized his movies to look like Remington paintings brought to life. What Daly and Persky term "the 'heroes' of the real West," the "farmers and cattle drovers," were neglected, and little attention was paid to "the real adversaries" of the Old West: "loneliness, isolation, and the elements."[9] Native Americans were mostly caricatures, their costumes derived partly from paintings by Catlin and others; all tribes tended to look like Plains Indians — mounted, well feathered, bloodthirsty. The cavalry, which accomplished endless last-minute redemptions, didn't include alcoholics and deserters on inadequate horses whom guerrillalike Indians frequently outfought. Countless thousands of African Americans headed west after the Civil War, worked as cowboys, and so on, but only a handful of films (some with all-black casts) acknowledged that. Women typically stayed out of the way and quietly instantiated the hero's values; if they did otherwise, they usually wound up being tamed shrews or dead ones — unless they were whores, in which case they just kept on doing their thing.

In spite of the enveloping power of myths and their paraphernalia during those thirty years, some directors did attempt to achieve a degree of authenticity. Howard Hawks did in *Red River*. Fred Zinnemann did in his 1952 film *High Noon*, as did George Stevens in 1953 with *Shane*, a film with plenty of psychological credibility. And there were other directors who did, particularly in films later in that period, to which I'll turn shortly. But no such attempt could — or can — bypass the basic situation of film as a medium, a premise that Daly and Persky press: "When critics speak of the 'authenticity' of a particular Western, they are still referring to an illusion. Such films are no more realistic than the ones which show Indians riding in suicidal circles around parked wagon trains." True enough, at the most basic level; but what Daly and Persky say about the audience in that regard strikes me as no longer valid, though it would have been through most of Slotkin's period: "No one really cares when, in *Red River* . . . , Montgomery Clift arrives in Abilene, Kansas, with his herd of cows in 1865, a full two years before the town started shipping cattle east. Such details are superficial. . . . The Western is entertainment and to speak of it in terms of exact, authentic realism is pointless."[10] Daly and Persky generalize too much, because around 1960 the attitude toward those "superficial" details started to change. They began to have a good deal to do with how at least a part — but a growing part — of the viewing public responded to Western movies. The shift of attitude, along with other factors, figured in the slow dawn of New Western filmmaking and then in its up-and-down evolution into 1990s entertainment with a difference.

The period from just after World War II until around 1960 is usually regarded as the golden age of the Western. Ford, Hawks, King, Stevens, and other fine directors of the genre were having their day in the sun. But even in the 1950s something was going on with the old patterns. Apply some hindsight to "Gunsmoke," as Michael T. Marsden and Jack Nachbar do, and you can see it. They note the "increased sense of moral complexity" of the show when it's compared to earlier television Western series. Though they admit that it "made no claims to historical accuracy," they still argue, rightly, that "its sense of realism far surpassed that of *Wyatt Earp*" — and, I'd add, its other competition. Their description of the picture-tube world of "Gunsmoke" and its thirty-minute audience is true to a tee:

> Writer John Meston and producer Norman Macdonnell brought to the television version of *Gunsmoke* a nineteenth-century Dodge City, Kansas, peopled by half-wild buffalo hunters, homesteaders brought to the brink of insanity by the emptiness of the prairie, and men whose only handle on survival was the butt of a six-gun. It was a neu-

> rotic, compulsive world dominated by greed and cruelty, and made livable only by the vulnerable, tiny community of friends headed by U.S. Marshal Matt Dillon, the gimpy, rather stupid deputy Chester Goode, the booze-sipping Doc Adams and the saloon owner–madam, Kitty Russell. It was the ideal show for a 1950s mass audience, brooded over in their own world by the Cold War and by trendy social science and psychology jargon about deviance and the failure to adjust.

The times were achangin', and so was the popular Western, both reflecting and directing cultural moods as it always has (much more than its print counterpart). "Gunsmoke" tapped into the mother lode of late-1950s audience engagement and quickly became "the top-rated program on television, a position it would hold for the rest of the decade." As Marsden and Nachbar point out, the show started "softening its outlook" when it expanded to an hour-long format in 1961; but it commanded amazing popularity "until it finally left the air at the end of the 1974–75 season, as the longest-running and most successful dramatic show in the history of television."[11]

Even though "Gunsmoke" had a more Old Western than New Western feel, it possessed two traits that appealed to the proto–New Westers of its heyday: a measure of realism and, like "Wagon Train" and the other most successful shows of the 1950s, a cast that consisted of an "ensemble" of characters (pictured together on a recently advertised Franklin Mint collector plate) who, to borrow from Marsden and Nachbar again, "functioned as a collective hero in a family or quasi-family structure." What they call "loner-hero shows" didn't last very long. It's the home theme again, psychiatric symptoms in tow, and that theme centered other shows too, like "The Rifleman," "Rawhide," "Bonanza," "The Virginian," "The Big Valley" (with Barbara Stanwyck as matriarch ranchera), and "The High Chaparral," that cranked up from the late 1950s to the late 1960s, with middling or better success and attenuated realism, on the whole. With families more and more gathered around watching the Western families on the tube, realism had to be limited. The latter families may or may not have been "a metaphor for corporate America in which characters become heroic by learning to control individualistic and eccentric behavior for the sake of the prosperity of the ranch," but the former families got tired of Western series in the early

1970s. By 1975 America was suffering from "sheer overexposure" to such series, post-Watergate blues, post-Vietnam "self-doubt," and misgivings about everything and experienced its "first Westernless television season."[12]

Thereafter, whatever television Westerns had to say to Americans about themselves, they didn't want to hear it — not even in the form of the programs of the 1980s that were Western spoofs, like "Gun Shy" and other losers, or in the form of self-consciously New Western series of the early 1990s, like "Harts of the West" and "Angel Falls." Television, as we'll see later, would eventually play a different role in the New Western epoch.

But if the golden age of the Western movie was ending around 1960 while prosperous Western dramatic series on television were being gradually herded to nowhere, still there were interesting changes in Western filmmaking in the offing. They had to do partly with the realism from which television was retreating — defined like all commercial-television shows by the constraints of a small-screen advertising-permeated medium, "Bonanza," for instance, was severely controlled in terms of format and plot and, for good reason, projected the look and timbre of a largely studio-based production. But the changes had to do also with historical accuracy as well as with issues of family, community, identity, place, and heritage that came to preoccupy other New Western art forms. By a twisting path Western film would wind its way, like country music, to the neotraditionalism of the late 1980s and 1990s.

Let's go back for a moment to some other things that were happening in the 1950s and after. Marsden and Nachbar notice the inverse relationship I've already pointed out — that "as Westerns proliferated on television, they began to decline in movie theatres" — but they adduce hard data as well: "In 1950, at least 135 American-made Westerns were released in the United States. By 1956, the number had declined to seventy-eight." The production level sank during the early 1960s until "only about two hundred" were released "in the entire decade from 1965 to 1975." So 1975 was a bad year for Westerns in both media. Indeed, you can see the film industry's decline — and that of the Old West — reflected, surely unconsciously (at first, anyway), in the number of titles that contain the word *last*: *Last of the Comanches* (1952), *The Last Posse* (1953), *The Last Command* (1955, one of the movies about the last stand at the Alamo), *The Last Hunt* (1956), *The Last of the Fast Guns* (1958),

Last Train from Gun Hill (1959), *The Last Sunset* (1961) — and doubtless you could append more. Marsden and Nachbar convincingly attribute the decline to television's "presenting the type of kiddie action Westerns that earlier had been produced as low budget B movies" and simply to "less audience interest," but it was more complicated than those two factors as stated can account for.[13] My list of "lasts" implies other forces at work.

In 1958 Arthur Penn's first film, *The Left-handed Gun*, based on a television play by Gore Vidal, was released. No formula piece, it was a psychoanalytic Western that delved into the tormented nut of Billy the Kid. Then in 1959 came Edward Dmytryk's *Warlock*, based on Oakley Hall's novel of the same name, a gunfighter movie done with exceptional intelligence, maybe less cynical than Henry King's 1950 film *The Gunfighter* — which has a rootless and isolated and mustachioed Gregory Peck waiting for the punk who will do him in — but just as brooding. A protorevisionist Western in which violence leads to deep moral questioning, it includes a scene in which Henry Fonda, as a gunfighter-turned-marshal, does a self-emptying meditation on the vanity of bloodshed that rivals a similar scene with Clint Eastwood in *Unforgiven* in 1992, and it ends with a shotless showdown, weariness with killing, hope for better times.

In 1960 appeared two films that wrestled with the racial issues that a complacent 1950s America was learning hard civil-rights lessons about: *The Unforgiven*, John Huston's exploration of Anglo-Indian relations in 1850s Texas, which gets at some of the issues but delivers a climactic battle instead of negotiated peace, and Ford's *Sergeant Rutledge*, the flashback-structured story, set in 1881, of a black cavalry sergeant's court-martial for rape and murder. Many students of the Western have marked ambiguities and contradictions in Ford's portrayal of the military, particularly in *Fort Apache* (1948), with its curious final scene that uses legend rhetoric to brush aside the terrible consequences of egomaniacal and incompetent leadership the movie depicts, a scene that Max Westbrook labels "the most controversial in Western films," but *Sergeant Rutledge* glosses over nothing.[14] As Daly and Persky argue, "Hollywood's attempts to incorporate black-related themes into traditionally white Western situations were not without difficulty"; the film cinches their argument:

> Sergeant Rutledge's story of racial equality and human dignity is clear evidence that the black presence actually destroys the mythology of the frontier West. John Ford's well-documented romanticized conception of the West either doesn't exist in *Sergeant Rutledge* . . . or it is completely reversed. . . . The confusion which characterizes the military tribunal that sits in judgment on Rutledge suggests that the military has lost control. The film portrays a frontier culture where traditional values seem to no longer have meaning, certainly not a typical Western point of view.[15]

At least it's not typically *Old* Western. Nor are analyses of the gunfighter's psyche, confessional meditations, and so on. All this about the time Dwight Eisenhower, once a military hero, was warning the American people to keep a watchful eye on the military-industrial complex. The emperor of Western history wasn't naked, but his clothes were definitely looking threadbare.

Marsden and Nachbar offer an illuminating perspective on the forces at play here. They note that, despite the slippage in popularity of Westerns during and after the 1950s, "the films themselves have been unusually rich in style and ideological diversity. The classic Western story . . . no longer serves as a constant formulaic model. Instead, the classic Western now provides a basic structure for experimentation within which the old formula is twisted, laughed at, and sometimes bitterly repudiated." Some of those movies, of course, weren't so stylistically rich and ideologically diverse, but many were; and they remain extraordinary works. And many, as Marsden and Nachbar suggest through other critics' observations, relied on psychological theories of pathological behavior (Freudian conflicts in the case of Anthony Mann's 1952 film *The Naked Spur*, for instance, or irrational hatred of Indians in Ford's 1956 film *The Searchers* or his 1964 film *Cheyenne Autumn*) and did indeed involve "formulaic revisions" linked "to immediate historical events."[16]

The reciprocal linkage is obvious enough in any number of politicized John Wayne movies of the Vietnam era in which Rooster Cogburn or Big Jake seemed as ready to don a green beret as a Stetson. Generally, however, it tended to be subtler than that and not to affirm patriarchal values like Wayne's but to question them or turn them on their heads. Richard White argues that "the impact of McCarthyism on Hollywood, a reaction against the conformity demanded by a mass society and a corporate economy, and, later, the countercultural movements of the 1960s and 1970s all found reflection in Westerns such as *The Searchers*, *Shane*, *High Noon*, *The Left-handed Gun*, *Pat Garrell and Billy the Kid*, *One-eyed Jacks*, *Little Big Man*, and numerous others." But he also discerns a shift in how Westerns handled the discords between the individual and society and other oppositions. Thus the classic Westerns, he continues, didn't attempt "to reconcile the contradictions between the premodern virtues of a western hero" and the society he would save, the same one "that threatened those very virtues"; rather, they "flaunted those contradictions." Yet the Westerns in the transition from the 1960s to the 1970s "virtually reversed the old homilies. 'Savagery,' symbolized by outlaws or Indians, now became good, and 'civilization,' symbolized by the town or farmers or the U.S. Cavalry, now became either evil or weak. The defeat of the Indians, the conquest of Billy the Kid, now became the victory of vice over virtue, of oppression over freedom."[17] I'd argue, though, that White's 1960s–1970s shift was already under way in the early 1960s. Its earmarks are clear in *Lonely Are the Brave*, for instance, where Old Wester Jack Burns and his mare, Whiskey, are run over by a truck loaded with bathroom fixtures, as well as in other films of the time, including *Sergeant Rutledge* and, if you read its miseries that way, Huston's *The Misfits* (1961).

But the evolution of New Western cinema didn't proceed just by films with reversed meanings. There were other kinds as well, most of them, whatever their attitude toward it, haunted by nostalgia about the Old West. Marsden and Nachbar group the Westerns of the 1960s and 1970s "into four main categories: traditional Westerns, anti-Westerns, elegiac Westerns, and experimental Westerns."[18] That scheme may be procrustean in some instances, but it's useful to understanding the varietal background for the revisionist works that come after the early-1980s hibernation of the Western. Let's follow Marsden and Nachbar as they offer examples and comments — to which I'll add my own.

Traditional Westerns are easy to spot. They "continued to glorify the white taking of the West," some laboring the point "more strongly than ever, especially the 1970s movies of John Wayne," where he played old farts "who could teach the proven western values to the uninitiated," prime examples being *The Cowboys* (1972) and *Cahill, United States Marshal* (1973). Several of Clint Eastwood's post–spaghetti Westerns—like *High Plains Drifter* (1973), despite its tongue-in-cheek flirting with the mysticism of an "avenging ghost," and even *The Outlaw Josey Wales* (1976), whose former-vigilante hero uncharacteristically settles down again at the end—belong semicomfortably in this category.[19] Membership is relatively low.

Anti-Westerns went against the traditional grain in pretty direct fashion, put a critical eye on "the commonly accepted versions of historical events," and "consciously rejected the heroic components of those events." They portrayed the underside and, "like much activist rhetoric of the 1960s, suggested that the idealist assumptions of the traditional Western formula were naive and masked the racism, violence, and greed of the historical conquest of the West." Include here two movies about the mayhem at the O.K. Corral: *Hour of the Gun* (1967), which pictures that event as "a consequence of a near-psychotic urge for revenge," and *Doc* (1971), which "suggests that the killings were precipitated in part by Earp's political ambition and in part by his repressed homosexual lust for the gunfighter Doc Holliday"—not John Wayne's cup of tea. Include also *Dirty Little Billy* (1972), Michael J. Pollard's portrayal of Billy the Kid as a brain-damaged delinquent nurtured "by a depraved environment," and *Soldier Blue* (1970), a dramatization of the Sand Creek Massacre that appears to symbolize America's involvement in Vietnam. *Little Big Man* (1970) partakes of this subgenre, largely because of its depiction of complexly human Indians and a hubristically deranged Custer. So does Robert Aldrich's 1972 film *Ulzana's Raid*, which manages a creditable job of explaining Apache savagery in terms of tribal beliefs and that of whites in terms of "racism and uncontrolled emotions."[20] Both of those movies are shot through with Vietnam-era antiwar sentiments and demythologizing gestures.

The more you investigate the anti-Western, the more you realize how much the whole Western thing was up for grabs for negative and oblique treatments after 1960. In *There Was a Crooked Man* (1970), Henry Fonda, "who for a generation was a symbol of the integrity of the Western hero, plays a hypocritical prison warden who grabs a bagful of stolen loot and happily runs off to Mexico." In *Hombre* (1967), an ironic remake of Ford's *Stagecoach*, Paul Newman plays an ill-fated mixed-blood Indian loner among various morally rotten stage passengers—no happy ending with John Wayne riding away with his true love in this case. In Sergio Leone's spaghetti Westerns, beginning with *A Fistful of Dollars*

(1964, released in the United States in 1967) and most notably in *Once upon a Time in the West* (1969), where Fonda plays a *really* bad guy in a story lifted from Nicholas Ray's Freudian Western *Johnny Guitar* (1954), you find relentless exaggeration, convolution, parody. In what Marsden and Nachbar summarily call the " 'man with no name' trilogy" (*A Fistful of Dollars, For a Few Dollars More*, and *The Good, the Bad and the Ugly*, the last two also released in the United States in 1967), there's no virtuous hero, only a stranger (Clint Eastwood) with an inflated propensity for gunplay. Conventional style is hyperbolized through "an almost endless number of killings, lush musical background, huge closeups of faces and the melodramatic lengthening of climactic scenes." With that kind of staging, Leone repeatedly presented "protagonists who are stirred into action by personal vendettas or greed for money, thus trivializing Western violence by showing the seedy intentions that lie behind majestic events."[21]

Such movies had a strong influence on later Westerns, finally making the straightfaced traditional Western, especially after John Wayne's death in 1979, a virtual impossibility. Moreover, a lot of other movies could be placed in the anti-Western category: *Welcome to Hard Times* (1967), which has Fonda playing a down-and-out ironic inversion of his heroic role as Wyatt Earp in Ford's 1946 masterpiece *My Darling Clementine*; *Midnight Cowboy* (1969), John Schlesinger's Oscar-winner about a contemporary dim-witted Texas stud wintering in New York City seaminess; Robert Altman's *McCabe and Mrs. Miller* (1971), which thoroughly deglamorizes boom-town bordello life, finally pitting a grubby smalltimer against the brutal mechanics of corporate greed; and more, many of them hardly unalloyed examples, like Sidney Pollack's weak-kneed rip-off of *Lonely Are the Brave*, *The Electric Horseman* (1979).

But to do serious research on the anti-Western, you need to trot down to your local video shop and rent Martin Ritt's 1963 film *Hud*, based on Larry McMurtry's *Horseman, Pass By*, and watch it — for either the first or the *n*th time. It was jarring when it came out, and it remains strong medicine for idealists and romantics. And if you want a devastating experience in double vision, take home also Ford's 1962 film *How the West Was Won*, a beautifully photographed but overweight spectacular that struggles to reanimate the same corpse that *Hud*, with its modern setting, holds a funeral for.

Viewing the two films, you can see dramatically the significance of some distinctions that McMurtry, borrowing from the literary theory of Northrop Frye, makes among Westerns. He argues that "in the fifties the Western began working its way down from the levels of myth and romance toward the ironic level," which it certainly reached in the 1960s. To get there it had to go through the "high mimetic" level (where we find "the hero still superior to other men and to his environment") and the "low mimetic" level (where he no longer is). In McMurtry's exemplification, John Wayne movies are typically high mimetic, as is *Shane*; movies like *The Gunfighter* and *Welcome to Hard Times* are low mimetic. *Little Big Man* is well into the ironic level, as is *Cat Ballou* (1965), a parody in which Lee Marvin plays both a boozed-out gunfighter and a silver-nosed bad guy. *Hud* is low mimetic "though it tends at several points toward the ironic."[22] (Brandon de Wilde looked up to a hero in *Shane*, but in *Hud* he bird-dogs a definitively anti-heroic model.) *How the West Was Won* is high mimetic and pretending to the levels of the romantic and mythic.

Such levels tend to be mixed in any given movie. In John Huston's 1972 film *The Life and Times of Judge Roy Bean*, for instance, low-mimetic realism and plenty of debunking irony are combined but then yield, at the end, to a romantic-mythic wistfulness about the need for heroes. Still, the anti-Western was from the start dominantly a work of the lower registers and exerted its continuing influence because of the New Western Historical mood associated with them. You can feel that mood intensely in *Lonely Are the Brave* but most memorably in *Hud*. There it has to do with a bitter sense of loss at the passing of the Old West that's tangled up with the character Hud himself. As McMurtry puts it, he's "a gunfighter who lacks both guns and opponents" and whose "impulse to violence is turned inward, on himself and his family." Constrained to "waste his force" in meanness, he's "one of the many people whose capacities no longer fit their situations," like "the descendants of trail-hands . . . driving beer trucks in the suburbs of Ft. Worth, Dodge City, Cheyenne and a score of other cities, whose names once held a different kind of promise."[23]

In 1968 McMurtry predicted that "the ironic will yield to the mythic again," and he saw signs of the latter in Leone's films.[24] The tremendous success of his own *Lonesome Dove*, a big-screen story shrunk to fit the tube and its interruption-ripped format, later generally proved his pre-

Martin Ritt's Hud *(1963): a low-memetic anti-Western in which Paul Newman plays a gunfighter whose capacity no longer fits his situation. (Courtesy of Paramount Pictures Corporation)*

diction true, just as it proved that the appetite for Westerns cannot be satisfied only by a low-mimetic and ironic diet. But that diet remained the general rule from the 1960s on. *The Last Picture Show* (another "last" movie), Peter Bogdanovich's 1971 adaptation of another McMurtry novel, fits it, and so does his screen version of its sequel, *Texasville* (1990), along with a bushel of other Westerns with various settings. Given the tendency of post-*Hud* Westerns to deal with the less-than-heroic remnants of and successors to both the golden-age West and the golden age of Western movies, it's not surprising that the anti-Western is in some instances closely related to the elegiac Western.

You can find the roots of that subgenre in preceding movies that carry "suggestions that the individualistic frontier hero has outlived his time" — *Shane*, for example, or *The Gunfighter*.[25] But the elegiac Western, like the anti-Western, begins to burgeon around 1962. *Lonely Are the Brave* and *Hud* both have elegiac elements, but such elements are absolutely essential to two movies released that year: *The Man Who*

Shot Liberty Valance, a late movie by Ford, a director with a reputation for romanticism, and *Ride the High Country*, an early movie by a director building a reputation for realism and iconoclasm, Sam Peckinpah.

In Ford's film the traditional action-oriented and illiterate West of Tom Doniphon (John Wayne) is overtaken by the lawbook-governed and literate West of Ranse Stoddard (James Stewart). Here Ford tinkers endlessly with the standard formulas in order to detail the end of the Wild West. The uncelebrated hero (Wayne), the man who *really* killed Liberty Valance (Lee Marvin), lies in his coffin when the film opens. The girl, Hallie (Vera Miles), doesn't marry him but a lawyer (Stewart) who washes dishes, can't shoot straight, and goes on to become a senator. The film features none of Ford's typical colorful panoramas of Monument Valley: it's done in black and white, most of the scenes interior. The central story is a flashback about a time as irrelevant to the present as the Western past itself (so that one of the journalists hearing from Ranse the truth about Liberty Valance's death tears up his notes and delivers his famous line about the West: "When the legend becomes fact, print the legend"). Ranse and Hallie don't ride off into the sunset but speed by train back to Washington while she ambiguously philosophizes about how the wilderness has changed into a garden, her face full of mourning for a lost way of life, memories of a coffined and forgotten hero who was her first love. In this film rife with reversals, it's finally a courageous woman and not a man who best understands the Old West — and what replaces it. Now, that's downright New Western.

In *Ride the High Country* two aged gunfighter buddies, Gil Westrum (Randolph Scott) and Steve Judd (Joel McCrea), reminisce about the old days and ponder their lives while guarding a gold shipment (which Gil, for a while, wants to heist) and becoming entangled with nuptials in the Coarse Gold mining camp that lead to nasty gun battles, Gil's moral recovery, and Steve's gut-shot death at the very end. With this film and a lesser, previous one, *The Deadly Companions* (1961), Peckinpah began a series of more or less elegiac films — including, most notably, *Major Dundee* (1964) and *The Wild Bunch* (1969) — in which he, as Rita Parks phrases it, "succeeded not in demythologizing but in remythologizing the Western hero." Given the questionable qualities of his protagonists, his fondness for blood-bath scenes, and the like, he does so "in a curious and almost perverse manner." However, Parks notes, "the transformation is perfectly consistent with the audience expectation of the hero (or antihero) that began in the early sixties" and continued to develop thereafter. In line with that expectation, "the present-day legend is existential, sardonic, and disillusioned," and yet "there exists at the core of a Peckinpah hero a certain nobility and beauty that are the essence of the Ford tradition and perhaps even fostered by it."[26] That sums up Gil Westrum, Steve Judd, and their cinematic offspring.

What Parks calls Peckinpah's "older, rugged men"—isolated, male-bonded, disposed to honorable last stands—"are not the stuff of which the traditional hero is made," but they do have residual heroic qualities, riding tall to the ends of their stories. Gil Westrum and Steve Judd, as Parks points out, "share Tom Doniphon's realization of the passing of the West, but like Hallie they face the change with peaceful resignation rather than despair"—though some of Peckinpah's later old geezers don't go so gentle into that good night. The remythologizing of the hero in *Ride the High Country* works partly through the seasonal setting, as Parks observes: "It is the autumn of the old Western man as well as the autumn of the old West, and both—like the autumn—are immortalized in the midst of their dying." The epitome of that man is Pike Bishop (William Holden), leader of the anachronistic outlaw Bunch in *The Wild Bunch*, who in the film's 1914 setting "is a man who knows he is doomed, but a man with a fatalistic panache that makes him determined to play out his hand to the end." Moreover, the maleness of the kind of men who "plan to die" but also "to take many enemies with them" is crucial.[27] Deke Thornton (Robert Ryan), who leads the pursuit of the Bunch (to which he once belonged), makes that vivid when he snaps to his scuzzy crew, "We're after *men*, and I wish to God I was with them." Loyal Old Westers with a vengeance, bound for violent confrontation with a new order.

A sadness trails through the elegiac Western, of course. In *Will Penny* (1968), a story of dispute with rawhiders, perhaps the most realistic treatment of the harshness and loneliness of cowboy life ever put on screen, and in *Death of a Gunfighter* (1969), *Monte Walsh* (1970), *When the Legends Die* (1972), *Junior Bonner* (1972), *The Shootist* (1976), *Tom Horn* (1980)—in these and others, as Marsden and Nachbar infer, "we mourn the loss of the hero. The film message is all too clear—there are no longer men capable of replacing him; there is no longer a West that appreciates him; there is no longer a frontier worth fighting for."[28] Such sadness isn't just personal to the directors or gratuitous, for directors like Ford and Peckinpah, as Parks notes, were speaking "to the concerns of an audience rapidly changing in its entertainment tastes and its social, political and ethical mores." Furthermore, "within the rigid format of the Western," they struggled with "questions that must be asked by anyone at any time" even as they "celebrated the land and the people who ventured and adventured there." They knew "the facts" of Western history but were more concerned with "the meaning of the man — the hero" — for their own time.[29]

So there remains a positive thrust to many elegiac Westerns, something A. Carl Bredahl, Jr., gets at when he emphasizes not the main plot of *Ride the High Country* but the subplot, the romance of Heck Longtree and Elsa Knudson. Read that way, the movie, like other elegiac Westerns, "is not a story of the lost wonder that was the West; it is, rather, one of young people taking the reins of power from an aging generation, discovering the land, and beginning to explore their 'place' within it."[30] The world of two old roving gunfighters succeeded by that of two young people who will discover a home: it's the upbeat transition from the Old West to the New.

One of the most innovative things that happened alongside the elegiac Western was the experimental Western. As a category it may be more blurred than Marsden and Nachbar's other categories, but they define it well enough: "The essential characteristic of experimental Westerns . . . is . . . a fascination with the Western form itself." Since many Westerns, more and more all the time, derive one way or another from other Westerns, it may be hard in some instances to decide what kind of "fascination" is involved — whether it's a matter of imitation, plagiarism, parody, whatever. But Marsden and Nachbar elaborate a qualification that specificizes enough to make the category useful: "Makers of experimental Westerns take a playful attitude toward the genre and manipulate the form to achieve highly personal visions, as well as to extend some of the implications of the earlier films upon which their experiments are based."[31]

As "the most obvious example" of the subgenre, Marsden and Nachbar offer Philip Kaufman's self-consciously stylized 1972 film *The Great Northfield, Minnesota Raid*, in which Robert Duvall masterfully plays a megalomaniacal Jesse James:

Kaufman playfully debunks the older, formulaic movie heroics of the

> James-Younger gang. Jesse's idea for the raid, for example, is actually "conceived" while sitting in an outhouse where he reads notes scribbled by Cole Younger, though he claims the idea has come to him in a religious vision. At the same time, however, Kaufman affirms Western heroism by picturing Cole Younger as genuinely admirable. In yet another reversal of the Western formula, Cole becomes heroic because he foresees and embraces a mechanized twentieth century, an attitude directly opposite those of the outlaw heroes of elegiac Westerns.

Another example is Pollack's *Jeremiah Johnson* (1973), which belongs here because its protagonist, finally more sticker than boomer, "does not obtain his credentials by conquering the wilderness" but earns "his full status as a legendary mountain man . . . only after he has allowed himself to be fully absorbed into the mountains and all their wildness."[32]

You could easily add other films to this category. Michael Crichton's *Westworld* (1973), about an adult fantasy vacation resort where a robot gunslinger (Yul Brynner, in the logical extreme of his earlier steely-eyed Western roles) goes berserk, ought to be included. According to Robert Murray Davis, it's the only movie that uses "the material and values of the Western and science fiction on equal planes." Beyond any doubt, Mel Brooks's *Blazing Saddles* (1974) belongs. A film that Davis compares intriguingly to Robert Sheckley's 1976 science-fiction story "The Neverending Western Movie" (where the author himself enters "a very complicated web of relationships between the West in fiction and the West as fiction"), *Blazing Saddles* has about as much fun with Western formulas as you could wish for. Still *the* most self-conscious postmodern Western film, it finally "bursts the confines of the set and then of the studio and erupts into the world of the audience and then sucks the audience back into that world."[33] Wild as a corncrib rat gone metaphysical. Here, sometimes, the emperor of Western history looks not so much tattered as harlequinlike.

During the 1960s and 1970s many Westerns, however categorized, dealt with timely issues. *The Professionals* (1966), for instance, broke a few clichés about Hispanics. Several films that I haven't mentioned before tried to portray Native Americans more sympathetically and informedly: *Tell Them Willie Boy Is Here* (1969), *A Man Called Horse* (1970), *Chato's Land* (1971), and so on. Several tried to do the same for

African Americans, not always avoiding the "blaxploitation" syndrome: *Buck and the Preacher* (1971), *Take a Hard Ride* (1975), and others. *True Grit* (1969) attempted a certain New Western realism by featuring conventionally heroic John Wayne as fat, thin-haired, eye-patch–wearing, colorfully sottish, and yet stalwart Rooster ("Fill your hand, you son of a bitch!") Cogburn — likewise in a lesser 1975 sequel titled after the protagonist. In 1972 appeared several movies that attempted to do justice to rodeo life, *The Lusty Men* and *J. W. Coop* being the best. The encounter between the horse world of the nineteenth century and the car world of the twentieth (and, by implication, the postindustrial world of the late twentieth) thematized a number of Westerns, *Bite the Bullet* (1975) perhaps most memorably. Practically all of the issues that might interest contemporary viewers were worked into the celluloid — except those concerning the environment and Asians (both still slighted) and women, the last hardly touched by a few misfires, like the bizarre *Hannie Caulder* (1971), in which Raquel Welch plays a much-wronged widow who learns how to shoot and distributes God's plenty of lethal comeuppance.

But something was going wrong. By the late 1970s, the Western, however much some people still hungered for its romanticism or appreciated its realism, clearly was running out of steam even more seriously than it was in the late 1950s. The box-office success of movies like *True Grit* and *Butch Cassidy and the Sundance Kid* proved brief; their sequels and prequels didn't cook. As Marsden and Nachbar note, "the box office popularity of Westerns momentarily revived in 1979" because of public response to *The Electric Horseman*, which moralistically contrasted "the real virtues of cowboys with the phoney glitter of Las Vegas."[34] But the typical fare was sleepy productions like *Comes a Horseman* (1978) and *Goin' South* (1978), and the revival didn't hold. Even well-made films like *Bronco Billy* (1980) and *The Long Riders* (1980) that the reviewers loved or an unusual one like *Windwalker* (1980), a Cheyenne-Crow story, didn't bring much business. The false boom of *Urban Cowboy* (1980) — with John Travolta starring as a mechanical-bull rider — lasted just long enough to lend an air of hope to productions like *Outland* (1981), an okay science-fiction remake of *High Noon* that supports the argument that horse operas were being reborn as space operas in the late 1970s and early 1980s.

The definitive disaster, however, what Marsden and Nachbar call "the near-permanent doom of movie Westerns," happened in 1980 "when Michael Cimino's spectacular dramatization of the Johnson County War, *Heaven's Gate*, was such a dismal flop that United Artists, the studio that produced the film, wrote it off as a forty-million-dollar loss, the largest loss on any picture in the entire history of American movies."[35] The combination of a badly flawed giant of a revisionist movie and a disaffected public made for a knockout punch.

Various theories about the decline that consummated with Cimino's film have been advanced, many having at least partial cogency. Daly and Persky share one, wide in its sweep and as persuasive as any other, in their speculation about the waning popularity of Western myths during the late 1960s and early 1970s: "Perhaps it is as Thomas Schatz suggested in his essay 'The Western,' that the movie Western is an historical narrative 'which served ideologically to enable the audience (i.e., the public) to negotiate a transition from its rural agrarian past and into its urban-industrial (and postindustrial) age.' Once that passage was made, audiences no longer felt quite as drawn to the Western."[36] And thus by 1982 as authentic a Chicano revisionist film as Robert M. Young's *The Ballad of Gregorio Cortez* could be released without eliciting noticeable public reaction.

But a conclusion like Daly and Persky's needs to be placed in historical perspective. Parks, writing about the time the Western was well into its early-1980s nose dive, does that briskly: "The demise of the Western formula has been regularly announced for the past sixty years, yet the critics who have predicted imminent death for the genre have also been forced periodically to review a Western film or television production that pumps new blood into the traditional, hack-weary formula with astonishing results. There seems to be life in the old boy yet." She logically suggests that such predictions "are perhaps patterns in a recurring rhythm indicating a renaissance for the Western in the future." Then she goes on to make, carefully, her own prediction: "If by this time the computer-age superhero has almost had his day and the bewildered audience is ready to return to the simpler things of life, then the man of the land will also return." In addition, if the Western does reflourish, it will do so because "there is something of basic value in the form . . . something that reflects the vitality and stability of recurring themes of ancient myth." Skeptical about any attempt at "rejecting the reality of the present," however troubling its technologized "outer landscape" and its morally confused "inner landscape," she sees no possibility for "withdrawal into the past." Nonetheless, she does see the Western as able to help people "fully live in the present" because — and this warrants her prediction of its return — it addresses their "need to keep in touch with their historical and mythical roots."[37]

Brian Garfield, an experienced scriptwriter of Westerns, maintained in 1982 that "the old-fashioned Western died with Gary Cooper," whose death in 1961 marked the end of a career that included principal roles in films like *The Virginian* (1929) and *The Westerner* (1940) as well as *High Noon*. True enough, by my reckoning. Garfield also maintained, however, that "the new Western [that] was born" afterward was "mindless, heartless," with "neither character nor morality," on and on — in other words, a mistake guaranteed to make the Western movie "dead."[38] Well, I don't agree with all that Old Western condemnation, though it doubtless pertains in some cases. In its early New Western phase, Western filmmaking frequently succeeded in preserving, extending, or even transforming the old-fashioned Western, at times doing all three. The Western movie waned again, but it didn't die. It came back — in the late 1980s, when a good portion of the public grew as weary of urban postindustrial life (civilization become what Edward Abbey called "syphilization") as it had of replays of its rural agrarian past in the mid-1970s, when it longed to get back in touch with its historical and mythical roots. Once more. But with a difference, of course.

In 1984 the Western movie could have won an award for uselessness, but in 1985 the old boy began to stir enough to suggest that he wanted to get out of bed, move around a bit, even get dressed, maybe even strap on the heavy jewelry of his gunbelt, *maybe* even take a ride out over the front range. He might not ever again be the man he was in the 1950s, but he was gettin' it together. He was thinkin' about the old rituals, the classic entertainments, but he was also startin' to think about the rags that still partially clothed the emperor of Western history. He wasn't alone in that regard, as we know.

A 1983 movie, *National Lampoon's Vacation*, a comedy about a middle-class family's trip west from Chicago, had almost enough refigured elements of the genre to be considered not only a Western but nearly as good a Western as the early 1980s produced. Then in 1985 —

the year of the first cowboy poetry gathering in Elko, Nevada, remember — New Western literature and film arrived at a very promising moment of congruence: Larry McMurtry's magnificent novel *Lonesome Dove* was published, and two less-than-magnificent but nonetheless significant films, Clint Eastwood's *Pale Rider* and Lawrence Kasdan's *Silverado*, were released.

McMurtry's novel was a rare bird: a realistic cowboy epic impregnated with mythic overtones, rich characterization, authentic details, big spaces, hang-on-to-yer-hat action — you name it. The book's success led to the 1989 television miniseries based on it and a 1993 miniseries, *Return to Lonesome Dove*, that carried the story further (and in a direction quite different from that of *Streets of Laredo*, McMurtry's own 1993 novelistic sequel, made into a miniseries in 1995) — and even a 1994 heart-lacking mistake titled "Lonesome Dove: The Series." *Lonesome Dove* whetted a neglected appetite and left the public hungering for more.

Pale Rider and *Silverado* weren't box-office bonanzas, but they too elicited response from that appetite. Critical reactions to them sent signals to filmmakers about what would or wouldn't cook in Western films of the future, thereby implicitly forecasting the kind of revisionist Westerns to come.

Eastwood's movie, his first Western since 1976, was praised by Scot Haller in *People* as a "sober effort to resuscitate the genre" but one that winds up with Eastwood playing "a symbol, not a character," and the effort being reduced to "an attempt to revive the Western by fashioning an elegant elegy for it" that yields "*Shane* with skirts."[39] Pauline Kael in the *New Yorker* noted that the movie deals with "family values" and even granted that it "may be an ecologically minded Western" (because of its opposition to hydraulic mining), but she criticized Eastwood because "he never seems to examine the insides of the character" he plays, who comes off as "some spectral combination of Death, Jesus, Billy Jack, and the Terminator."[40]

Silverado didn't fare much better. Richard Corliss in *Time* called it a "Cuisinart western" that "dices, splices, chops, co-opts, hones and clones every oater archetype in just 2 hr. 13 min.," complete with actors "almost none of whom look at home on the range!"[41] David Ansen in *Newsweek* also remarked that the movie seemed "composed of borrowed parts," though he took that quality, along with its being ironic and "purposefully 'inauthentic,'" as aspects of its makeup as "a kind of postmodernist Western." Spelling out the complication behind that assessment, he toyed with a timely question: "How do you make a Western in 1985? . . . Anti-genre movies are now out of fashion, and Kasdan, like Clint Eastwood in 'Pale Rider,' elects to play it straight. Sort of. The sort of is a tone of hip knowingness that underlines the drama, as if the actors are well aware that they are playing out scenes we've all grown up on. It's not satire, but at least one eyebrow remains arched." That "sort of" tone leads to uncertainties of response, so that, for instance, the character Paden, a moody loner played by Kevin Kline, reminds you of Robin Williams and the struggle of a black character (Mal, played by Danny Glover) with "frontier racism" seems less serious than you want to believe Kasdan intended. Nonetheless, Ansen asserted, "the future of the Western may be riding on *Silverado*" (on box-office profit, that is). But the future as he saw it wouldn't deliver anything like "the great Westerns of the past few decades" until a director could "take the audience to a place it's never been." The great Westerns of the future, he argued, would have to be "*inside* jobs" by directors like Peckinpah and Altman "who followed both their gut and their muse" and not "outside" jobs like Kasdan's, which depends too much on "hip professionalism."[42]

That was a tall order, and it would require some time to fill—and then not in numerical abundance. Still, several things were clear from such reactions in 1985. The Western movie was at least a two-step above what it had been. The public may not have packed the theaters to standing room only, but it was interested. A new kind of Western appeared to be desirable and feasible, but directors hadn't scoped it out yet. Whatever else it might be when it emerged, it wouldn't be "anti-genre" or revisionist in quite the previous ways and probably in some sense would have to "play it straight"—though it couldn't possibly escape being self-conscious about its predecessors. It might well keep (maybe ironically, even if nostalgically) part of the old external mythical trappings, but it would need to be realistic in several dimensions. And, of course, it would have to click with the postmodern audience, however much that imperative might conflict with others.

Christopher Cain's *Young Guns* (1988) took a shot at filling the order. Critical response to that Brat Pack story was mixed, but the film's sloppy plotting didn't kill the appeal of its landscapes, action, and the 1980s-style attitudinizing of its characters—which allowed a respectable sequel, *Young Guns II* (1990). But the work that first really made some headway toward filling the order was Simon Wincer's *Lonesome Dove*. The 1989 miniseries, though constrained in a box in the corner of the den and making few concessions to politically correct sensibilities, multiplied and broadened the engaging power of McMurtry's novel incredibly. The old boy was up and about with a vengeance. He was strong again in all those swells of land and sky and music, in the cattle moving across an enormous country, in the precisions of speech and gesture and gear, in the adventures and disasters of the long drive north from the Rio Grande to Montana, in the characters Call, Lorena, Pea Eye, Newt, Jake, Deets, Blue Duck, July, Maggie, Clara, Po Campo, and more—most of all in Gus, the quintessential image of the old boy himself, the Old Wester in roughhewn apotheosis, colorful and at least half-wise, a mortal and morally flawed hero you could care about and even love, Robert Duvall's role of his life.

Hot damn, the Western was back! That was the feeling in the air. Easterners who didn't even believe the West had been mapped yet went for *Lonesome Dove*. Real cowboys did too. In *The Cowboy Life: A Saddlebag Guide for Dudes, Tenderfeet, and Cowpunchers Everywhere*, Michele Morris reports the results of her informal survey to find out which Westerns are best liked by those for whom "tending cattle is the essence of their job description" and who regard most such movies as "horse operas or fairy tales." At the top of the list sits *Lonesome Dove*, "the hands-down favorite."[43] In 1989 such folks probably hadn't seen their world even close to so well attended to on the tube since the old "Rawhide" series—or maybe since the last time they saw, on the tube or in the theater, one of the other movies they picked, among them (twelve total) *Red River* and *Will Penny*. As far as realism is concerned, cowboys may have been revisionists from the git-go; and *Lonesome Dove* passed the test splendidly.

In early 1990, looking back at the handful of noteworthy Westerns released since the mid-1980s, Daly and Persky declared that "the Western myth still retains its power, rooted in American history and world consciousness," and they ventured a prediction more confident than Parks's prior one: "Despite changes in audience taste and interests, there is no reason to believe that the Western will not, like the Phoenix, rise from the ashes, with new meaning and significance for the future."[44] The release that year of Wincer's *Quigley Down Under*, an exquisitely photographed "Western" set in nineteenth-century Australia and dealing to an extent with racial problems, hinted at the validity of their prediction. The movie took another step toward filling Ansen's tall order. But the big-screen event that really got anticipation headed home occurred in late 1990: Kevin Costner's *Dances with Wolves*.

First, the negatives, the things the reviewers pounced on. *Dances with Wolves* unfortunately is vulnerable to Shoemaker's charge of (unintentional) racism. The film is anachronistic in several respects, most obviously in the character of Lieutenant John J. Dunbar (Costner), whose political correctness direly strains the willing suspension of disbelief. Issues are oversimplified, to the point that most of the whites are caricatured as bad guys nearly as much as Indians once were. There's sentimentality here and there. And so on. The film easily invites ridicule.

But the positives, which the reviewers noticed also, impress and explain the film's success. Richard Schickel in *Time* gave Costner credit for doing his cinematographic homework, thought Ford would like the film, and found in its Anglo-Indian role reversal hope that "there is, just possibly, redemption, not only of historical crimes but also of a movie genre lately fallen into decrepitude."[45] Even Kael, though she slammed the film plenty, granted that, however simple the Sioux are made to seem, "it's the sympathy for the Indians that (I think) the audience is responding to," "the Sioux point of view."[46] In *Newsweek* the tall-order man himself, Ansen, praised Costner for "an ambitious revisionist reading of the frontier within an aesthetically conservative form" and for "redressing a century of Hollywood historical bias." He found in the film both "genuine respect for a culture we destroyed" and "a romantic generosity of spirit that one is happy to succumb to." Persuaded by Dunbar's motives for "cultural assimilation" into Sioux tribal life, he found credible how the film's "elegiac 20th-century political consciousness" views an idyll threatened by "implacably advancing white civilization." And he admired Costner's "painterly eye for epic landscapes" and his "almost anthropological appreciation of the Sioux people" (whose representatives in the film consistently speak Lakota).[47]

Whatever its faults, *Dances with Wolves* went on, as they say, to sweep the Academy Awards (no Western had won Best Picture since Wesley Ruggles's 1931 film *Cimarron*, which has dated badly). It announced that a golden age in New Western cinema was under way.

Shortly after *Dances with Wolves* did its sweep, William K. Everson put that announcement in perspective. Noting a growing popular and academic interest in B Westerns during the 1970s and 1980s and television's recent preoccupation with "plugging its own often very ambitious Westerns — such as periodic Louis L'Amour ones — and mini-series," he saw the importance of the movie for the future. He judged it "one of the most ambitious Westerns ever planned or achieved" and found its greatest accomplishment to be in "the faith that it displayed in the Western genre, since at the time of its conception it could hardly have seemed like the box office blockbuster that it ultimately became not just in America but throughout the world." Whatever the swings in critical opinion might mean, the movie, he proclaimed, "has undone much of the damage inflicted on the cause of the epic Western by *Heaven's Gate*." Because of it, he concluded, there was remarkable, if tempered, hope:

> The days of huge cycles of Westerns are clearly gone forever along with the studio system that made them feasible. But the success of *Dances with Wolves* has shown that the public will respond to the genre whenever it is treated with care, respect and integrity, even the kind of lopsided integrity that Costner brought to it. And after all, the best directors of the day — Stanley Kubrick, Bertrand Tavernier, Martin Scorsese, Lindsay Anderson (not an arbitrary selection, merely a cross-sectional one to indicate the possibilities) — have yet to make their first Western.[48]

That's "have *yet* to make," pardner. Wait till Kubrick (my choice) or another of those directors (probably Mike Nichols) tackles Cormac McCarthy's work.

Meanwhile the television people had been making adjustments. In 1985 it was certain that there wouldn't be another time like the late 1950s and early 1960s when an avid viewer could watch Western series fifty-odd hours a week. So, as Everson observed, those people turned their attention to an occasional made-for-television Western, though they tried out new dramatic series every once in a while. But they also got into the Western-documentary-series business — and later, as we'll see, into the country-music business, with all its Western connections. To my mind, the best documentary series of the 1980s were two on PBS: "The West of the Imagination" (1986) and "The West that

Never Was" (1989). The first strived to educate the public about the continual mythic reinterpretation of the West in art forms that, by and large, at least pretended to be representational and intended to promote possibilities from conquest to preservation. William H. Goetzmann and William N. Goetzmann provided a lushly illustrated companion volume, *The West of the Imagination* (1986). The second concerned Hollywood's treatment of the West. Not as insightful as "The West of the Imagination," it nonetheless constructed an informed retrospective and also had a companion volume, Tony Thomas's *The West that Never Was* (1989), which includes stills from, plot summaries of, and critical commentaries on dozens of films.

What William W. Savage, Jr., calls "the 'cowboy underground' " was augmenting its membership in the 1980s, propelled by its "feverish obsessions with the cowboy hero" in various media to the point of an "insistence upon mystical interpretations of cowboy imagery." (In the early 1980s Robert Day, author of *The Last Cattle Drive* [1977], a novel that should be made into a first-rate movie, told me about a group of men in Topeka, Kansas, who regularly met and read aloud from his book, plotting the progress of the narrative and the drive on a Kansas map above the bar in their gathering place.) But the need for Western involvement thereby implied wasn't going to be answered by television series, which generally were as irrelevant to it as "the cowboy establishment" was distant from the mysticism of the underground obsessives.[49] Television was simply proving to be an inadequate medium for the kind of film that *Dances with Wolves* exemplified, the kind that the New Western public, including cowboys and their underground interpreters, wanted.

How so? There are several problems with the tube in that regard. Let's turn to Parks, who does a thorough job of singling them out. First, what she calls the "auteur function" is suppressed because the writer and director of a television series can bring no controlling vision to bear on their work — everything gets decided ahead of time by the marketing yuppies. Also, of course, the ups and downs of action must be coordinated to accommodate incessant commercial breaks. And character enrichment is severely constrained, for "in a Western series the hero cannot risk change" — that unrealistically stable personality ensures "audience loyalty" (though " 'guest' characters" can change). Furthermore, a curious "schizophrenia" is entailed: "The story line of each weekly show must be believable yet provide fantasy and escape." In other words, the stuff spun by "the electronic mythmaker" of the series isn't totally what the serious New Wester has in mind.[50]

But there's an overarching problem with the tube as a medium for the Western. It's related to the preceding ones and has to do with the difference between a Western series experienced on a television screen and a full-blown Western movie experienced on a two-story wide screen in a theater. The tube works okay for documentaries, but it can't begin to match the movie theater for the panoramic visual scale and encompassing sound required to express the production values of a state-of-the-art Western. Parks explains the difference in McLuhanesque terminology: "The scaling-down process that takes place in the television Western . . . turns the bold colors and vibrance of the epic form into the leisurely pastels of the pastoral mode. Drama becomes soap opera." It's a difference that correlates with the distinction between film as a medium that "lends itself to free form" (even in a conservative genre) and television as one that "tells its story in a much more mannered fashion."[51]

Such a difference may be offset to a degree by the fact that New Westers are more pastoral in temperament than Old Westers. The former may need "the warming nostalgia of the pastoral" as much as they need "the vigor and fire of the epic," but television is losing the battle of the screens, partly, I'd suggest, because Western filmmakers are able to incorporate elements of the pastoral mode into their work better than the television people are able to incorporate elements of epic form into theirs. Stay tuned. Whatever time will tell, I'm not surprised, any more than Parks, that "the Western television hero" has ridden off "wearily into the sunset." Also, I believe, with her, that television, in dealing with Westerniana, "should capitalize upon its ability to complement rather than compete with Western literature and films."[52] Television seems to be doing that more and more — by presenting cool-mood documentaries, miniseries, country-music videos, imaginative cartoons, and so on. It does that also by generously re-presenting Western films and thus serving, if not to stage them properly, at least to keep the archives open to a Western-hungry public.

Maybe some lessons were learned in the early 1990s. For instance, Ric Burns's 1992 PBS–aired documentary *The Donner Party* (a contribution to "The American Experience" series), with its New Western

Historical approach to demythologizing one of the best known and grisliest blunders in Western history, made exemplary successful use of the power of television to educate. So did Discovery's 1993 miniseries "How the West Was Lost." And so did the 1993 and 1994 A&E series "The Real West," which synopsized the range of overlapping New Western attitudes by forthrightly acknowledging and yet wistfully regretting the patterns of change in the West, debunking its myths and yet celebrating its romance — a doubleness of vision that apprehended truth but still imagined it might somehow be otherwise.

Other kinds of presentations that clicked: the 1993 CBS miniseries *Return to Lonesome Dove* (a crassly commercial project that illustrated the creative bankruptcy of most of the television industry but panned out better than I thought it would), ABC's parodical Saturday-morning cartoon show "Wild West C.O.W.-Boys of Moo Mesa," weekly shows like ABC's "Countdown at the Neon Armadillo" and NBC's "America's New Country," PBS's "Austin City Limits," the Disney Channel's "Adventures of the Old West" series, and even (credit where credit's due) the CBS series "Dr. Quinn, Medicine Woman" (by reason of its laudable violation of stereotypes).

Presentations variously at odds with the postmodern role of the medium that didn't click: the CBS series "Harts of the West" (an Easterners-in-the-West sitcom as much as anything else) and "Walker, Texas Ranger" (karate goes cowboy), the FOX series "The Adventures of Brisco County, Jr." (watered-down *Blazing Saddles*), the Family Network's reruns of "Bonanza" (nostalgia for dead people), and NBC's made-for-television film *Bonanza: The Return* (despite the predictable use of Ben Johnson to hint at Old Western authenticity, nothing more than a nostalgic assembling, sort of à la *The Big Chill*, of the progeny of the dead people in "Bonanza").

And a little something probably was learned by both the television and the movie industries from Jerry Jameson's 1992 film *Gunsmoke: To the Last Man*, yet another "last" movie, the third postseries attempt since 1987 to resuscitate the Matt Dillon legacy. But there was no Dodge City community in that drama of Arizona range war and no contemporary relevance. It felt as tired as aged Bill Cody must have in the waning days of his Wild West show, when he needed help to mount up, listlessly rode around the ring only a time or two, and then collapsed from the exertion. Wrinkled James Arness looked like a mummy. Times had changed. Old Western tube shows wouldn't translate into New Western movies.

After *Dances with Wolves* there was still some market viability for the video library of the old "Rawhide" series, but a lot of people were buying documentary videos about Native Americans, too. Something happened between *Lonesome Dove* and its sequel. *Return to Lonesome Dove* was much more multiculturally conscious, concerned not with just movement north (with a herd of mustangs this time) but with the establishment of a new home in Montana. It proposed the possibility that the surviving characters might make a lasting family and community of a kind. Simply put, it was more late New Western in orientation and flavor. So was media mogul Ted Turner's unprecedented series "The Native Americans: Behind the Legends, Beyond the Myths," which premiered on TNT at the end of 1993 with the made-for-television film *Geronimo* and went on to include other dramatic films, like *Lakota Woman: Siege at Wounded Knee*, and a TBS documentary miniseries—accompanied by, of course, the ultimate coffee-table book, *The Native Americans: An Illustrated History* (1993)—as well as a CNN series on contemporary Indian issues. Though you might well criticize Turner, whatever his motives, for his efforts to buy up the scenic land of the interior West, his series surely was sympathetic to Native Americans. Both the films, co-produced by Kiowa-Delaware dramatist Hanay Geiogamah, and the documentaries were hardly designed to make Euro-Americans comfortable about their ancestors, who were roundly demonized. Politically correct to a fault.

Turner's series may not have achieved the balanced picture desirable for a truly multicultural revision of history—such pictures are hard to come by in an age of more zeal to expose ideologies than care in interrelating them—but it commendably redressed wrongs and provoked thoughtfulness germane to the postmodern world. *Geronimo*, for instance, was an imperfect film in several ways (it had Apaches speaking beige English throughout, suffered from stiff acting, and so on); still, it triumphed in being the first film ever funded by a major movie company to have a Native American (Joseph Runningfox) in the title role—and one realistically heroized at that. In addition, it combated stereotypes by portraying the Apaches as people with a deep sense of family, community, and place—with a rich heritage of relation to a specific environment — who understandably reacted with violence toward those Mexicans and Americans who perpetrated violent crimes against them. The film strived to break the spell of delusions not only about the Apaches, traditionally characterized and caricatured as among the most vicious enemies of Euro-American civilization, but, by extension, about all other Indians as well. Such reappraisal and demythologizing, in *Geronimo* and in succeeding productions, patently were intended to spur viewership thinking about present-day issues concerning the loss of cultural heritage and social identity, the dissolution of the family, all manner of dislocations and disrespect, the genocide and shortsighted idiocy involved in destroying rain forests, and like matters.

In the wake of *Dances with Wolves*, filmmakers of the early 1990s moved ahead of the television industry in bringing to the public Western productions with a different taste. Released in late 1991, Gus Van Sant's *My Own Private Idaho*, thematically similar to his 1989 film *Drugstore Cowboy*, offered itself as a sort of twisted contemporary Western about male prostitutes in the urban Northwest. It was a brilliant but incoherent mixture of Shakespearean variations, skid-row imagery, and ironic Western allusions. If the film did nothing else, it prophesied that the 1990s Western was going to be a new kind of ride. But anyone who'd seen a film by Ridley Scott earlier in 1991 already knew that, for *Thelma & Louise* was a ride that turned the Western upside down, inside out, every which way but loose.

In her book *The Cowgirl Companion: Big Skies, Buckaroos, Honky Tonks, Lonesome Blues, and Other Glories of the True West*, Gail Gilchriest provides background helpful to understanding the impact of that tale of contemporary desperadas. She briefly surveys the history of women's roles in Western cinema. With few exceptions (Dale Evans in Roy's flicks, for instance, or Barbara Stanwyck in *Annie Oakley*, Joan Crawford in *Johnny Guitar*, Jane Fonda in *Cat Ballou*) those roles, right on through the 1980s, cast women as little more than "scenery." But then something happened: "When the western finally slipped back into theaters, the recipe had changed. Academy Award winner *Dances with Wolves* worked as a sort of reverse western, in which the Indians played the good guys. The comedy *City Slickers* centered around touchy-feely men exploring their more emotional sides during a cattle drive, and it did gangbuster business at the box office. . . . Modern moviegoers seemed to be shopping for something new and different." They found what they were shopping for — and maybe more than they bargained for — when Western movies, as Gilchriest puts it, "got a shot of estrogen." *Thelma & Louise* was indeed "something new and different," and, just as it "cleared away the goopy makeup from the cowgirl image," it also cleared the way for future explorations of women's roles in the Western.[53]

The neglect of women in the Western dates back to early Western fiction, which was written partly in opposition to "domestic" fiction by women and almost exclusively stressed the idealized deeds of men. By 1991 that long practice had been much poked at but not yet downright scorned. *Thelma & Louise* took care of that, revising the Western as never before. It wasn't ever going to be the same again — whatever "same" meant by then. Like the emperor of Western history, the old boy himself now was nearly naked and would have to find some *real* new clothes. The suppressed female side of the Western had broken free — with hell to pay. But the full meaning of that freedom was, like Thelma and Louise at the end of the movie, left hanging.

Let's slip the video of *Thelma & Louise* into the VCR and have another look. Scott, who had previously directed the science-fiction quasi-Westerns *Alien* (1979) and *Blade Runner* (1982), knew how to tell Western stories in a different way — though *Thelma & Louise* has discernable ancestors in earlier Western car-chase movies, like *Vanishing Point* (1971), or movies about independent women moving on (usually west), like *Alice Doesn't Live Here Anymore* (1975). It also extends some of the conventions of what I call the vacation-from-hell movie, which category includes films with Western elements from *Deliverance* (1972) through *National Lampoon's Vacation* (1983) to *City Slickers* (1991), but it differs from them in two respects: the protagonists are women, and their experience leads not to their reintegration into society (or even escape into the legendary sanctuary of Mexico) but to their deaths (the latter respect making them more like the male-buddy protagonists of *Butch Cassidy and the Sundance Kid* than the male trio of *City Slickers*). It might well be termed a vacation-from-hell movie as anti-Western, and it invites substantial reevaluation of the Western myth.

There's no mistaking that anti-Western thrust (the protagonists at one point even ease their car through — against the grain of — a cattle drive), and the movie occasioned a flood of exultation (mostly from women), complaints (mostly from men), and controversies. Callie Khouri, who wrote the screenplay for Panavision, has expressed some surprise at all the noise, arguing that "this is an adventure film. It's a film about women outlaws. People should just relax." But the film's "adventure" involves no shortage of meaning of a disturbing sort, particularly for men. Khouri herself says as much in registering her annoyance at critics who objected to the film's portrayal of women because, as she puts it, "they don't really want to see women operating outside the boundaries that are prescribed for them, misbehaving and enjoying themselves."[54] The source of that disturbance lies precisely in the fact that Thelma and Louise are *women* outlaws, women who not only run away from their conventional claustrophobic social roles but who also, when their vacation turns to hell and heads west, enjoy their misbehaving and seek the audience's respect for doing so.

Thelma & Louise disturbs because it goes beyond what's prescribed, what has been, literally, "written before." As Khouri says, "I wanted to write something that had never been on the screen before."[55] The resultant gender-reversed story thus exceeds and inverts (and, at times, parodies) not only the culturally but the cinematically prescribed as well. It violates especially the prescribed genre of the Western, largely by transgressing its number-one traditional *pro*scription: that the heroic figures, outlaws or otherwise, shouldn't be women.

Thelma and Louise's hell begins when what started as a getaway to a cabin in the Ozark mountains takes a dark turn at a lounge aptly named the Silver Bullet. Louise (Susan Sarandon), her mind embroiled with some past rape experience of her own, angrily shoots to death, in this gunfight at the Not–O.K. Corral, a foul-mouthed man named Harlan who had pinned Thelma (Geena Davis) to a car and nearly succeeded in raping her. By using the power of the pistol/phallus ("borrowed" by Thelma from her husband), she heads herself and her companion down a trail that will end with a plunge into the Grand Canyon, all the armed and technologized policing power of the male world in a posse behind them allowing no alternative for these Western Stampin' Anti-Barbies who have tasted the openness and wildness of the West on their own terms.

Indeed, wildness is a crucial theme in the movie. It's what Louise initiates Thelma into. For a good part of their journey through the Wild

West, they drink Wild Turkey. After Thelma robs a grocery store, she stands up in the westbound Thunderbird and rejoices explicitly in her "calling" being "the call of the wild." Against the backdrop of his gasoline truck in flaming ruins, the trucker whose obscene pestering the two pistol-packin' Calamity Janes have avenged screams the summating accusation that they're "bitches from hell," women, their anger at insensitive men turned to destructive delight, gone wild beyond all help.

But such Western wildness, whatever its positive effects on Thelma and Louise, inevitably leads to a terrible reckoning for their sins against the male world (whose presence, constantly symbolized by heavy-handed phallic imagery, like that of omnipresent trucks and then cacti, they never evade). When the reckoning does come and can't be undone even by the pleading of the one morally decent man in the story, detective Hal Slocumbe (Harvey Keitel), it's reminiscent, as the Thunderbird floats into a freeze-frame above the Grand Canyon, of a scene (to which Jane Tompkins has directed my attention) in J. Frank Dobie's *The Mustangs*, the story of a stallion named Starface, unknown, I suspect, to either Khouri or Scott.[56] The mustang has been raiding ranches for mares for some time, so irritated ranchers hire four cowboys with stout horses to kill him. They chase him for several days and at last trap him in a canyon whose level leads only to a high bluff above the Cimarron River:

> As the leading rider emerged to the level, he saw Starface make his last dash. He was headed for the open end of the bench. At the brink he gathered his feet as if to vault the Cimarron itself, and then, without halting a second, he sprang into space. For a flash of time, without tumbling, he remained stretched out, terror in his streaming mane and tail, the madness of ultimate defiance in his eyes. With him it was truly "Give me Liberty or give me Death."[57]

Thus it is truly also with Thelma and Louise. Though the stakes are higher for these wild women (like mustangs, maybe like Indians pursued by cavalry — but at last, jewelry and lipstick left behind, with their bandannas and gritty sunburns the colors of Scott's Ford-esque, encircling Southwestern landscape itself, more like mythically cursed cowboys-gone-bad), they resemble the three amigos in *City Slickers* to the extent that for them there's no going back to the trapped consciousness in which they lived earlier. The stakes are so high that they choose the sisterhood of death over life without the freedom from disappointing (or worse) men, brief and criminal though it may at last be, that they have won. The alternative would be only a more severe (and more literal) imprisonment by men than they had once endured.

In *Thelma & Louise*, then, we don't have men fleeing Huck Finn's female-dominated "sivilization," as in the traditional Western, but women fleeing male-dominated "Civilization," if you will, a system that seems closed inwardly and outwardly for them. Throughout the film it's Louise who's most like the traditional Western hero, harboring a secret past, as tightly self-contained as Gary Cooper's characters. At first she's the one in charge — and wise enough to know, as she laconically (and indirectly) tells Thelma in the desert night, that they're moving toward "nothin' " — but even before Thelma understands that something has, as she puts it, "crossed over" in her (Thelma), that she has entered her own inner outland, Thelma takes charge in a different way. Yet by the end both women have "crossed over" a great deal. The extent is summarized by the snapshot blowing out of the backseat as they "spring into space," that portrait of "sivilized" innocence taken only days in the past.

With *Thelma & Louise* the Western itself "crossed over" — into no-man's-land. Its protagonists undo the classical formulation of the ethos that says it's acceptable, even sanctioned, for the American male to move in retreat from "sivilization" but women are supposed to *be* "sivilization" and not dispute or try to assume the prerogatives of power and flight (or be depicted as doing so). Thelma and Louise cross the system. Finally, their fate seems to affirm as much as it questions male privilege. Issues remain moot, to be dealt with by critics, scholars, and further Westerns. Not the least of the issues concerns the extent to which the film stories a frustrated and diverted quest for place and identity — the protagonists at first wanted only a cabin in the mountains, natural room of their own. *Thelma & Louise* might well be read as a parable about the unresolved tensions between Old and New West.

There was a lot of crossing over in 1991, a watershed year of revision. Garth Brooks did some resinging of the West on his album *Ropin' the Wind* (listen to "Against the Grain," "Shameless," and "In Lonesome Dove" again). "The West as America," with its reseeing, struck. *City Slickers* explored the feminity of men. *Thelma & Louise* explored the masculinity of women. And, among other things that happened, a less-recognized film, Lou Antonio's *The Last Prostitute*, was released. It's ostensibly a tale of two boys coming of age under the tutelage of a horse-farming ex-prostitute, but it winds up being about a man physically saving a Hispanic woman at the same time that she saves him from becoming an "old coot" — that is, a hardened Old Wester. Each such revision questioned numerous Western notions but especially those concerning gender.

Such looking from the other side for new meaning, maybe new wisdom, through Western film continued, as it continues still. In 1992 even a shallow movie about California baby boomers gone gloomy, Lawrence Kasdan's *Grand Canyon*, employed *the* image of Western natural beauty and immensity, the Grand Canyon itself, as a metaphor for human insignificance under the aspect of eternity, one that counterpoints Los Angeles as a metaphor for all the anxieties, poverty, and chaos of postmodern urban life. But the big revisionist happening in Western filmmaking that year was Clint Eastwood's *Unforgiven*.

In that movie Eastwood finally created a character with an interior life that's shared with the audience. Iron John opened up and made an intelligent movie-of-ideas classic that was nominated for nine Oscars and won four, including Best Picture. The exploration of Western violence and its deeper consequences was hardly new in 1992 (I've mentioned previous movies that undertook it to some extent, and note Owen Wister's description of remorse and emotional confusion after the hanging of the cattle rustlers in *The Virginian*), but such exploration had never been done with so much darkness, eloquence, intricacy, and persuasive provocativeness. Those qualities aren't hard to account for.

First, of course, there's the realization of the principal, William Munny (Eastwood), a reformed gunslinger and widower single-parenting his children on a Kansas hog farm who returns to his old ways in order to collect the reward for avenging the mutilation of a prostitute (who dared to remark the small size of a cowboy's penis) in Big Whiskey, Wyoming — at what you gather must be the worst little whorehouse there. Eastwood makes shrewd use of this character to question the icons of his own past roles. Munny is no squint-eyed young killing machine but an ironic autumnal extrapolation of that sort of character, full of guilty hauntings, rueful degradations. And other characters contribute to his development and make their own statements: Ned Logan

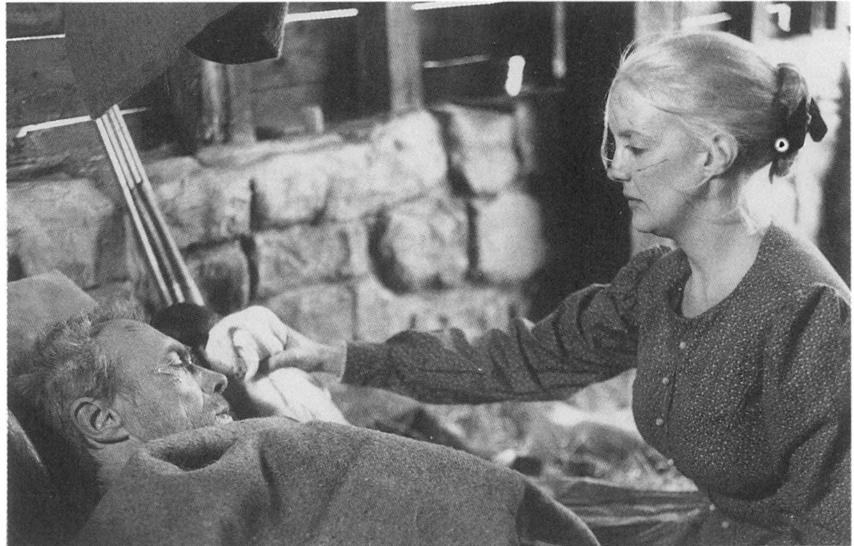

William Munny is comforted by the woman (played by Anna Thompson) he has come to avenge in Clint Eastwood's Unforgiven *(1992), a bleak and reflexive vision of violence.*

(Morgan Freeman), his saddle mate in crime, also called out of retirement from gunfighting by the unheroic lure of reward money (the rhyme with "Munny" is surely no accident); the vindictive whores, who aren't on camera much but have strong debunking power whether they are or not; Gene Hackman as Little Bill Daggett, a demythologizing and demythologized lawman more sadistic than Karl Malden's similar character in Marlon Brando's 1961 film *One-eyed Jacks*, whose meanness repels the craven citizens of Big Whiskey as much as it does the viewers; even Munny's dead wife, whom we never see but whose reforming influence still mightily affects his psychology. A terrific supporting cast indeed, including Richard Harris as English Bob, a philosophizing bounty hunter, and Saul Rubinek as W. W. Beauchamp, his dime-novelist biographer and mythmaker.

When you stir that cast into David Webb *(Blade Runner)* Peoples's tight screenplay and Jack N. Green's gorgeous brooding photography, you get, among other things, a major elegiac anti-Western about several kinds of unforgive(n)ness and the bloody cost of settling grudges through violence. And you get it at exactly the time when most of the American public had had a bellyful of drive-by shootings, suicidal nuts mowing down innocents with assault rifles, and NRA sanctimoniousness about the right to bear arms. Eastwood's bleak and reflexive vision of violence begetting violence displays John Wayne's world over the edge, burned out in nervous vengefulness, cruelty, alcoholic blur, cadaverous nothingness. It comes down harder on the old mythiness built with legend, rumor, and journalistic balderdash than *The Man Who Shot Liberty Valance* could have dreamed three decades before, and it makes Ron Howard's *Far and Away*, another 1992 Western of sorts, look like a lamb-eyed fairy-tale of sweetness and light. In stronger words, the film does an autopsy on the Man with No Name and damn near guts the Western myth, at least in some of its aspects. Eastwood's New Western change-of-heart values invert clichés, reverse expectations, and ironize unflinchingly. Munny may revert fully to his former ways toward the end, but any avenging heroism is profoundly qualified, even contradicted, by the tenacious undertaste of the horrible truth of killing. If you cheer him, you do so with an uncomfortable lump in your throat. He saves the town for people, controlling women and weak men, who may not be worth the grief.

Unforgiven carries a valedictory inscription to Sergio Leone and Don Siegel, both of whom directed Eastwood in many earlier films. So his film is both a tribute to those directors and their films and a good-bye, a homage to the Old West and a hello to the New and, hopefully, to more Westerns of a new breed. Murky as the film is in many ways, it works for that kind of balance, riskily at times, throughout. It's naturalistic but also Calvinistically allegorical. It both affirms and undercuts the myths it deals with. It's a traditional Western laden with postmodern judgments. The third reward-seeker, the Schofield Kid (Jaimz Woolvett), is a Billy Bonney parody, too nearsighted and squeamish to be dependably deadly. Munny's flintiness seesaws with his misgivings (as Scott Rosenberg phrased it in his review for the *San Francisco Examiner*, " 'Go ahead, make my day' gives way to 'Go ahead, make me doubt' " — repeatedly), just as his masculine firepower wrestles with the angel of his feminine conscience or his existential wobbliness is countered by Ned's practicality.[58] The glory of the lone gunslinger meets its match when Ned asks the womanless Munny if he masturbates. And, again, when the film turns Peckinpah toward the end, it does so after considerable sobering meditation on brutality and mortality. Even the last calm frame, back in

Kansas, is a component of a to-and-fro polemic about fundamental Western values.

Given the broad culture's adjustive logics, it's probably not surprising that *Unforgiven* itself was balanced not only by *Far and Away* but also by another 1992 sort-of Western, set later historically, *A River Runs Through It*, which offers almost as much mystified gentleness as *Unforgiven* offers in the way of demystified violence. At any rate, by late 1992 it was obvious that *Unforgiven* had stimulated the appetite for Westerns, already well aroused by *Dances with Wolves*, to a whole other level. Video stores were doing a land-office business in renting and selling Westerns like *Conagher*, *Lonesome Dove*, even a fortieth-anniversary gift edition of *High Noon*. The New Western thing by then was exploding in fashion, food, music, dance, everywhere you looked. Western scripts became hot properties. Some critics were saying nay, but dozens of films were in the planning stage, many in production. Screenwriters, directors, and actors, like New Western writers generally, were conceiving engrossing characters and unpredictable plots. Like New Western Historians, they were interested in telling what was untold. Walter Hill was set to direct a film about Geronimo that would attempt a fuller portrait of a man simplified and demonized in previous treatments. Mario Van Peebles was making *Posse*, a revisionist look at African Americans in the West. In the wake of *Thelma & Louise*, several Westerns about women were baking. And others — movies about Davy Crockett, Wild Bill Hickok, you name it. The lid was off Pandora's box, and filmmakers were thinking about big spaces, issues of place and culture and gender, ways to redefine the genre for a new generation.

Released in May 1993, *Posse* is a revealing case in point. In many respects it's a conventional action-based Western, a remake of *High Plains Drifter* with Van Peebles playing the steely-eyed Eastwood part and greedy Ku Klux Klan types playing the bad guys who terrorize the town, here the Southwestern settlement of Freemanville. No study of the morality and psychology of violence like *Unforgiven*, it's basically about racial vindication. Though the movie has comic moments and the media had some fun with it (phrases like "Ride 'em, cow bro" turned up), there's no doubt that Van Peebles wanted to put some serious contemporary spin (complete with a rap mood) on a traditional genre. He was out to rectify the record on the history of black people in the West, to give a sense — not just through the outlaw posse but also through the populace of Freemanville — of the lives a million-odd African Americans lived in the Old West as cowboys, lawmen, saloonkeepers, and whatnot (women as well as men).

Van Peebles did his research and talked it up, and *Posse* opened the public to learning about neglected or suppressed black heroes and villains of the West: Bill Pickett, a star of rodeo and early Western films who claimed that he invented bulldogging and who, after a picture mix-up, is now featured in the U.S. Postal Service's new Legends of the West stamp series; Mary Fields, also known as Stagecoach Mary, a legendized mail carrier; Cherokee Bill, an outrageous outlaw whose premature death on the gallows didn't ensure mythical immortality; and others. The movie retrieved a heritage that had been largely lost by the prolonged whitewashing of Western history and demonstrated that the West was no stranger to racist attitudes toward African Americans. Also, Van Peebles self-consciously suggested continuities in the history of African Americans in the West and in Western films by framing *Posse* with the riveting presence of Woody Strode, surely the finest black Western star ever; by cameoing Isaac Hayes, Robert Hooks, and others; and by montaging scenes involving blacks in earlier Westerns during the final credits. Unlike most Westerns that feature black roles, *Posse* foregrounded issues of race. Sales of books about blacks in the West picked up. By early 1995 the television viewership was uniquely prepared for CBS's miniseries *Children of the Dust*, a well-acted and fairly realistic saga, based on Clancy Carlile's carefully researched novel of the same name, about African Americans' conflicts with the Klan during the first land run into Oklahoma Territory in 1889.

Posse and its predecessor untold-tale Westerns responded to and stimulated a growing public interest in what Slotkin calls "the dark side of the western, the dark side of American cultural myth — the side that sees violence as essential to progress and to the vindication of one's moral character, that sees a massive (but miraculously precise and selective) shoot-out as a viable solution to almost any given problem; the side that divides the world along lines of race and culture and dehumanizes those on the other side of the border by identifying them as savages and outlaws." Moreover, he's quick to stress, such films suggest that "the western can be more than a device for reinforcing a mythology of violence and division," that, quite the contrary, "because it is so closely identified with American history, . . . [it] provides superb opportunities for artists to reexamine our past and reimagine our myths." That hopeful vision leads him to venture a cautious prophecy: "Perhaps the best westerns of all are waiting to be made."[59]

That was the mood in mid-1993, and it hasn't had a downswing yet. Telling the untold has proven to be the magical approach for Western filmmaking at the end of the twentieth century. It's an approach attuned to contemporary awareness of issues of multiculturality and gender—but then, to cite film critic James Ryan, "the western has always tended to synchronize with the national hoofbeat." Writing in the wake of *Posse*, Ryan astutely recognized, however, that such "revisionism doesn't necessarily translate into historical accuracy." Since even the best Westerns of the past had played "fast and loose with facts," he was concerned with how Westerns of the 1990s were doing—and would do—in reconciling the demands for accuracy and authenticity with those for entertainment and political correctness. He speculated that "in the wake of *Dances with Wolves* . . . it may not be possible to make a movie dealing with American Indians that's both p.c. *and* historically accurate." And he pertinently quoted Walter Hill, who was then directing his big-screen *Geronimo: An American Legend*, which was released in late 1993 just after TNT's *Geronimo* was aired: " 'I certainly don't believe we are making a movie that would stand scrutiny as an exact historical rendering,' admits Hill. 'But this is going to be a humanizing depiction of Geronimo. You'll see his side of the story as well.' "[60]

You do see Geronimo's side of the story in Hill's film, which has Wes Studi in the title role, as you do in the TNT version—though more fragmentarily and obliquely in the former, with less didacticism and less attention to daily tribal life. Both versions have historical inaccuracies or inauthenticities; both certainly soft-pedal Apache atrocities. Still, there's one really significant difference, besides that of the media, between the two movies: though both sympathize with Geronimo and his people, Hill's movie doesn't demonize all whites, makes the Apaches a tad nastier, and, on the whole, offers a more balanced presentation of White-Eye and Indian sides of the story. That seems more politically correct to me, even though he neglects women entirely. But Hill's attempt to represent all viewpoints and keep the mutual respect between enemies flowing has a price too: the movie feels more ideologically wishy-washy than all-embracing. Such a result was probably worth risking in order to strive for balance, but it leaves the old-fashioned Western fan with no one to root for — which, I suspect, is partly why Hill made the battle scenes so dynamic, for they entertain in their gory way whether or not you can calculate who the good and bad guys are.

Each *Geronimo* has serious limitations. If the best qualities of each had been combined in one historically careful film, it might have been a true artistic landmark — and without insulting the muse of the marketplace. Besides, many New Westers may well be prepared to root for something besides the triumph of one violent force over another — that is, New Western film may be in for some changes of the sort that James Work prophesied for New Western literature. Whatever else may be said about the Geronimo movies — as well as about, among others, *Dances with Wolves* and Michael Apted's *Thunderheart* (1992), a solid thriller about a part-Sioux FBI agent who discovers his heritage while investigating a murder on a South Dakota reservation — Native Americans have been nothing short of delighted to see themselves more fully and sympathetically portrayed. Not always entirely as they might wish, maybe, but at least by Indian actors.

However difficult the job of juggling the demands now on the genre, "there are still," as Ryan put it in mid-1993, "western tales to tell — stories of people mostly ignored in the earlier films, minorities and women. And ironically, they are who now hold the reins to the genre's future." Enough more of what he called "neo-westerns" were then in production or being planned for him to say that with confidence — Hill's *Geronimo* and Joel Silver's *Buffalo Soldiers*, for example, as well as a host of Westerns about women, from John Duigan's *Outlaws* to Jonathan Kaplan's *Bad Girls* to Gus Van Sant's film version of Tom Robbins's *Even Cowgirls Get the Blues*.[61] And more recent releases appear to bear Ryan out. Tommy Lee Jones's 1995 TNT movie *The Good Old Boys*, for instance, has credible roles for women as advocates of settling rather than roaming — in an unadorned story, based on Elmer Kelton's 1978 novel of the same name set in 1906 West Texas, almost perfect for the medium. Nonetheless, you could offer qualifications: white-male tales retold (George P. Cosmatos's *Tombstone* and so on) remain a go, and movies about Asians in the West are scant.

The home theme prevalent in New Western literature turns up here too, as we've seen, in various issues of place and community — telling the traditionally untold entails neotraditional tales. That seems particularly true, with a twist, of 1990s Westerns about women, something Ryan was getting at when he noticed that "in place of the lone, avenging gunfighter, all of the contemporary female westerns feature a group of cast-off women banding together in proto-NOW style to right an injustice." To borrow from Ryan, the *neo-* part has to do with, among other things, the fact that such banding "mirrors nineties society, where women have organized to challenge the male-dominated power structure," the *traditional* part with, likewise, "an acknowledgment that, as [*Outlaws*-producer Denise] Di Novi admits, 'the audience isn't ready for a female Clint Eastwood.' "[62] Well, it still may not be, but it's plenty ready, after *Thelma & Louise*, for movies about *non*-lone desperadas — and the more cowgirl-like, the better.

Indeed, Joseph Hooper argues, "the culture has gone cowgirl-crazy," and he offers the recent "spate of rough-tough western-women flicks" as primary evidence. But this ain't just the old Dale Evans business. Though she's hardly forgotten, there's something weirder afoot:

> While soul-searching boomers rent *City Slickers* and ponder cattle drives, a different impulse has taken hold in the urban subculture. Those with the energy and inclination for experiment make fashion out of gender play, pushing at the distinctions that still remain about what constitutes masculine or feminine behavior. Lesbian is chic; gays are heroic, beleaguered; drag is a political act.
>
> And so it is the cowgirl of all the unassuming cultural types who finds herself at the intersection of the Old West and the new androgyny. For more than a century the cowgirl has nimbly mastered "a man's job" in the land of rugged individualism, but it's only lately that Hollywood has elevated her from perennial sidekick to the Star of the West.

For Hooper, Van Sant's *Even Cowgirls Get the Blues*, with antipatriarchal, polymorphously sexual women riding herd on whooping cranes (you've got ecological issues tangled in here too) and a sound track by k. d. lang and Ben Mink, is "the most outrageous installment of the cowgirl-mystique-in-progress." The mystique isn't a new phenomenon, however, but a longtime one in terms of which we can see the cowgirl "as the seed of a fantasy that drifted through the decades until it took root in our more egalitarian society." Now it has rooted to the point that "Hollywood is betting the ranch, or some percentage of it, that the cowgirl will emerge as a new feminine ideal for the '90s — Wonder Woman with a little cow dung on her boots." Probably Gilchriest and others who have explored the cowgirl in contemporary culture would agree with Hooper's contention that you can sell such an image because "there are so few historical role models available to women who are heroic *and* sexy."[63]

Hooper talks about variations on this image in Hollywood history — the cowgirl as dominatrix (Marlene Dietrich in *Destry Rides Again* [1939], say) or as "superfem sex goddess in the saddle" (Marilyn Monroe in *The Misfits*) — but it's clear to him that the reborn cowgirl stands "for strong women and a rough-and-tumble sense of fairness between the sexes." It's the feminization of the West, in a way scarcely anticipated by Henry Nash Smith's *Virgin Land*, once again. And there's a pronounced tendency toward New Western peacemaking, tolerance, and balanced synthesis in Hooper's vision of it, especially in a time when there are fewer and fewer actual cattle-working women and a transformed ideal is needed: "After she's done the work of the physical world, the cowgirl passes into the symbolic one, shouldering the burden of values, new ones like gender equality and old ones — community, nature, open spaces — that the culture has discarded and then decided it is famished for."[64] Sound familiar?

Such themes continue to recur in New Western cinema and probably will indefinitely though the telling of the untold will, of course, frequently entail unfamiliar perspectives and emphases. TBS's not wholly satisfactory recent documentary miniseries "The Untold West" may have given some indication of what's yet to come as the show's historians, writers, actors, and cowboy poets dealt with neglected — or avoided — other sides of the West: Billy the Kid's origin (as Henry McCarty) in the Irish slums of New York, Jesse James as a kind of outlaw Elvis, sexuality in the Old West, and so on. At least three movies released in 1993 suggest that there's still wisdom in expecting the unexpected: in Geoff Murphy's made-for-cable *Blind Side* a psychotic blackmailer rigs himself up in gunfighter regalia and gets electrocuted in a hot tub, pistols blazing away in the suburban night; in Mike Newell's *Into the West* two Dublin kids steal a horse and ride into their own Western-movie fantasy of living as desperados; and in Maggie Greenwald's *The Ballad of Little Jo* an Eastern woman travels west, doesn't band together with other women but does disguise herself as a male settler, acquires the usual masculine skills, and shares her bed with an Asian man. And, if that's not New Western enough, I understand that at least one "borscht Western" has been filmed in post–cold-war Russia — complete with an international cast (including "Indians" from Mongolia and Kyrgyzstan), an antiracist story, and an ecological message or two.

So it goes, with the Western projector cranking up a storm in 1994 and beyond, no end in sight. *Tombstone* (made by a director who knows the Western though not the West but featuring great Leone-type close-ups, analysis of the cost of bloodiness, Val Kilmer as an unforgettable ambiguously gendered Doc Holliday, and the final historical perspective of Tom Mix crying at Wyatt Earp's funeral in 1929). *8 Seconds* (fairly realistic, about the short life of champion bull rider Lane Frost, the subject also of Garth Brooks's hit "The Dance"). Comedies like *The Cowboy Way*, *City Slickers II: The Legend of Curly's Gold*, *Lightning Jack*, and *Maverick*. More dramatic works like *Wyatt Earp*, *Legends of the Fall*, *Wild Bill*, and *The Quick and the Dead*. On and on. It's no surprise that the business of training actors to ride horses is improving geometrically.

Though the Western arts now thrive in resonance, with the continuing development of each tending to promote that of others, such hasn't always been the case. Sometimes they've been out of phase with each other. So it was with Western film and television in relation to the other Western visual arts in the 1960s and 1970s: the first headed down while the second headed up. Later they got together on the upswing.

A useful, if perverse, starting point for a brief discussion of the other visual arts in the New West is an opinion expressed by a New York City art dealer, Ivan Karp, in 1982. Speaking of art markets outside his usual Eastern territory, Karp praised a few but reserved his energy for the condemnation of places like Houston and Dallas. Though he complimented them on "splendid new museums replete with funds for all purposes," he dismissed them from further consideration because "the galleries and the collecting public are largely involved in something known as 'Western' art, which has nothing to do with our culture."[65] Apparently Karp (apt name) thought Western art still looked mostly like Russells and Remingtons endlessly redone. The situation was much more complicated than that, of course, as was the growing market for Western art that Karp failed to foresee. But he was right about one thing:

many people — in Houston and Dallas, out in the boondocks, and elsewhere — were "involved in something known as 'Western' art" in 1982. More are now, and what they were and are involved in has a great deal of significance for "our culture."

As Karp's view suggests, the main misconceptions about modern and contemporary Western art, less and less widely cherished, are these: that it's dominantly narrative and escapist; that, with the exception of Georgia O'Keeffe (who may well be the mother of the artistic New West, the progenitrix of its feminized landscapes), it counts none of the great figures of twentieth-century American art among its practitioners; that it's "merely" regional; and that it's aesthetically naïve, unaffected by the main artistic movements of the last hundred years. There's certainly a strong strain of narrative and escapist art, much of it dismal stuff, about the romantic West, but there's also much artwork that rejects the idealization of the West and depicts it realistically, satirically, makes the iconic ironic, or otherwise re-presents the West not as some retarded Eden but as a complex, multifaceted region. The artists who have shaped those diverse responses to the West, artists in turn shaped by the West, include, besides O'Keeffe, many of the best-known figures in twentieth-century American art: Max Ernst, Edward Hopper, Jackson Pollock, Milton Avery, Marsden Hartley, Richard Diebenkorn, Fritz Scholder, Andy Warhol, Roy Lichtenstein, Wayne Thiebaud, and more. The work of such artists is hardly regional in any narrow sense: it relates to the region variegatedly, but its play of meanings is more global. Doubtless that's true of, say, Ansel Adams's photographs, but it's true also of the work of painters who have treated the West in styles that, according to Patricia Janis Broder's 1984 inventory, "can be described as Impressionist, Post-Impressionist, Fauvist, Cubist, Futurist, Synchronist, Expressionist, Structuralist, Precisionist, and Surrealist, and, during the past three decades, as Abstract Expressionist, Pop, and Photo-Realist."[66] And God-knows-what-else-ist — in all manner of media, too.

Such artworks, Broder argues, "do not belong to a special category isolated from the evolution of mainstream American art," though until around the mid-1970s "modern paintings of Western subjects by mainstream artists were dismissed as atypical of the artists . . . and were rarely considered part of the aesthetic heritage of the American West." Over the next decade, however, " 'Western' galleries [had] begun to feature modern art, collectors [had] begun to broaden their interests, and museum curators [had] begun to retrieve from the obscurity of their storerooms scenes of the West by major twentieth-century figures." Furthermore, that revolution occurred without overthrowing the narrative art of the Old West, with its documentary tradition that fused "objective reality and cultural myth."[67] Indeed, such art still has remarkable appeal and practitioners whose representational style holds its own among a slew of alternatives. But the stylistic experiments of mainstream artists contributed manifoldly to the development of those alternatives, which continue to be applied in reinterpreting a West far more complex than earlier artists like Thomas Eakins or William M. Harnett knew.

As you might suspect, American Indian modernists and postmodernists, particularly those whose nontraditional (nonritual, nonceremonial) and individualized styles engage political issues, are avid reinterpreters — though almost all Indian art deals, one way or another, with traditional cultural identity. R. C. Gorman, surely the best known of recent Indian artists, is exemplary here only to a degree, for, though his exuberant celebrations of the Navajo treat an ancient heritage in a contemporary way, he sees himself as a painter's painter with little interest in identity politics. More typical, perhaps, are artists who in the 1960s and later turned to peyote visions as a way to express both tribal identification and ancestral spirituality — artists like Al Momaday (Kiowa), Jerry Ingram (Choctaw), and Rance Hood (Comanche). Hood's haunting *Peyote Song* (1973) well exemplifies such work. Or consider the abstract-expressionist work of Scholder, a mixed-blood Luiseño, which painfully sketches the psychological tensions of contemporary Indians lost in a transitional zone between their own cultural heritage and a mainstream world that stereotypes them. Look hard at his *Indian with Beer Can* (1969), *Super Indian No. 2* (1972), and *Sunset Indian* (1980) and see the cost of limbo. Or study the work of T. C. Cannon, a Kiowa-Caddo artist and Scholder's most successful protégé, who died young in 1978 but not before, as Broder eulogizes him, he "quickly established his own artistic identity using a blend of Abstract Expressionism and Pop Art to expose the dilemma of people stranded between two cultures."[68] A veteran of the Vietnam War, he also quickly shifted from boldly militant political statements to more satirically flavored ones — as evidenced by his *When It's Peach Pickin' Time in Georgia, It's Apple Pickin' Time at the B.I.A.* (1971), then *Village with Bomb* (1972) and later paintings.

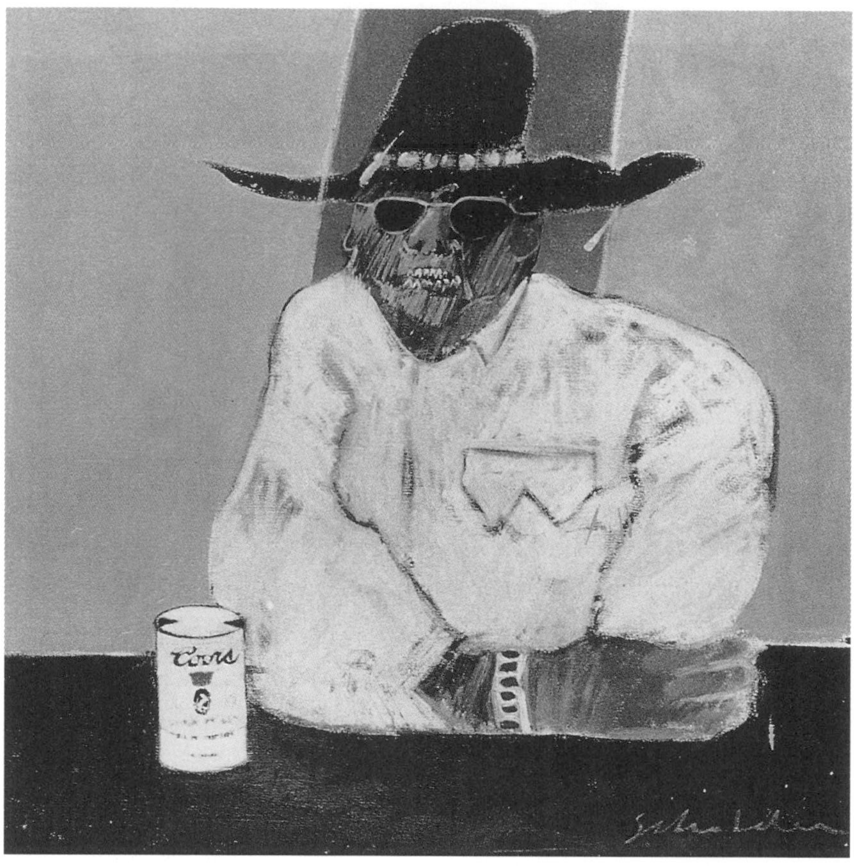

Fritz Scholder, Indian with Beer Can *(1969): the cost of cultural limbo. (Courtesy of Fritz Scholder)*

If the early New Western period of Indian art, the 1960s and 1970s, was one of "social commitment and ethnic consciousness," then the more recent period has been one of enlarging "critical sanction and popular success," to use Broder's phrases. Though it's true that the latter situation has been exploited by artists of a kind she labels "the *nouveau* Native American, a painter who only recently has discovered an Indian identity," it's also true that since the early 1980s many Native American artists with a secure sense of ancestry have enjoyed burgeoning and well-deserved appreciation — artists like Kevin Red Star (Crow), who reinterprets Hollywood Indians, and Jaune Quick-to-See Smith (Flathead-Shoshone-French Cree), who elaborates contemporary iconography in the ledger-painting style of the Plains Indians, and Joe Baker

Joe Baker, Chief Thunderfoot Takes a Dip *(1982): satirizing the absurdity of Western stereotypes. (Courtesy of the artist)*

(mixed-blood Delaware), who paints "cultural satire depicting the absurdity of stereotypes in the West." Baker, a resident of Phoenix, serves as a particularly apt example here because his vision is distinctly post-1970s, taking as its subject "the affluent West of Hollywood and Scottsdale, where the swimming pool is as much a basic symbol as the cactus"—thus his portrait of a swimming dog, feathered headdress left poolside, entitled *Chief Thunderfoot Takes a Dip* (1982). He's a kitschy "romantic and a humorist, . . . delighted by a culture in which fantasy is a part of everyday life."[69]

Baker's work shares in the renaissance of Native American art since 1962, when the Institute of American Indian Arts (IAIA) was founded in Santa Fe, an organization that succeeded the Santa Fe Indian School. The latter had encouraged artistic practice in terms of traditional culture, but, as Goetzmann and Goetzmann note in *The West of the Imagination,* "there was a dearth of nourishing artistic influences" and no "supportive tribal context in which the more traditional art forms had evolved." That situation resulted in "a kind of stasis and sterility . . .

against which a later generation of American Indian artists vigorously rebelled." The IAIA, with support from the Rockefeller Foundation, played a crucial part in the success of that rebellion, for it was established "in the political context of a pan-Indianism which . . . ultimately created the wider sphere of interaction and exchange of ideas that made possible the vital Indian art of today." Its teachers, Scholder especially, "awakened Indian painters to their potential role in the broader context of American art."[70] With the founding of the IAIA, everything changed: Indian art began an evolution entangled with countercultural politics and lifestyles, pop art, ethnic consciousness, cultural reinterpretation, and an aesthetic eclecticism that embraced previously denounced representational realism along with other stylistic possibilities.

Yet however self-conscious that art may be about its nontraditional roots, particularly in the case of realism, it continues ever more richly to express the Native American view of the West and its history. That's as true of Cannon's ironic portraits as it is of the work of Scholder, Baker, and others. Though such artists explore the meaning of being Indian in the postmodern world with understandable seriousness, there's abundant humor to their work. Observing that "humor has become an increasingly dominant mode for contemporary Indian artists," Goetzmann and Goetzmann speculate that it may be "in reaction to the weighty self-importance which has characterized much of the work of their predecessors in Western art." They offer Harry Fonseca's television-cartoonlike images as extreme examples, but you can easily find it elsewhere. Typically, it's combined with an IAIA "sophistication" that shows Indian art as "a product of its troubled and creative times in which Native Americans have sought to reject even the positive stereotypes placed upon them by whites, and to search for their own identity in the melange of cultures, symbols and styles at their disposal."[71]

Much the same could be said of contemporary Hispanic-American mural art, which reinterprets both Mexican history and immigrant experiences, or of the fiberglass statues of Luis Jimenez. The latter are "glitzy, powerful," presented, for Goetzmann and Goetzmann, as "true reinterpretations of our Western heritage." *Progress II* (1977), for example, portrays a cowboy mounted on an almost toylike vaulting blue horse who has lassoed a majestically lunging longhorn *cow*, udder abulge — a piece that "satirizes the whole Wild West tradition of Rem-

Stan Herd, Portrait of Saginaw Grant *(1988), carved and mowed in wheat stubble on a farm north of Lawrence, Kansas. (Photo by Jon Blumb, courtesy of Jon Blumb)*

ington and Russell." Through such work Jimenez articulates "a deconstructive vision of the Old West."[72] And he's not alone.

Broder as well as Goetzmann and Goetzmann appropriately stress the endurance of the representational-realist tradition in New Western art. For all its unclassifiability O'Keeffe's work is part of it, as are the earth sculptures of artists like Michael Heizer and Walter de Maria and the crop art, with whole fields serving as canvases, of Stan Herd. There's a documentary impulse in Western art that can't be nullified. It's certainly alive and well among the members of the Cowboy Artists of America. You can see it in David Hockney's touristic images of the West, John Fincher's still lifes of sometimes ironic heroic-looking cowboy paraphernalia, Woody Gwyn's images of landscapes invaded by highways and other man-made structures, Marci Haynes Scott's watercolors of rodeo action, Donna Howell-Sickles's paintings of cowgirls, on and on.

And, of course, you readily discern the tradition and its impulse in the work of contemporary Western photographers, many of them women.

Richard Misrach's aerial photograph, taken in 1986, of a bus and craters at the Bravo 20 bombing range: the West reduced to lunar rubble. (Courtesy of Richard Misrach and Johns Hopkins University Press. From Bravo 20: The Bombing of the American West *[Johns Hopkins University Press, 1990])*

Wanda Hammerbeck has done some astounding landscape studies that dramatize both the vastness and the fragility of the West. Sharon Stewart's vivid images of environmental toxicity in Texas ought to cause any industrial apologist to clear his throat. Robert Dawson's photographic investigations of the problems of Western aridity, technological plundering, and pollution make for even stronger medicine. He's adept at both direct and wry visual statements that don't fade quickly — see his work in *A River Too Far: The Past and Future of the Arid West*, edited by Joseph Finkhouse and Mark Crawford (1991). Another tough-minded revisionist is Richard Misrach, whose *Bravo 20: The Bombing of the American West* (1990) illustrates the results of U.S. Navy bombing on public land in Nevada and even proposes educational tours along "Devastation Drive" and "Boardwalk of the Bombs." Such work parallels that of realists in other media in its insistence on depicting a West ignored by romantics.

Though numerous New Western artists adhere to a representational aesthetic and thereby, as Broder puts it, "are discovering a wealth of subject matter that has given a new vitality to contemporary Western art," others certainly go in other directions. It's "a time of renaissance for the art of the American West," and the mood of critical tolerance, at least in the region, has encouraged positive outcomes: artists in general "are free to paint the West without criticism of their choice of subject or style," and Native American artists "are making a major contribution to America's cultural heritage," many of them synthesizing "the techniques and aesthetic ideals of modern art with the stylistic traditions and symbols of their indigenous art." Moreover, according to Broder, "the reappraisal of representational art and the acceptance of images of the nonidealized West have resulted not only in a renewed interest in historic Western art but in a reevaluation of the work of artists who painted Western subjects throughout the twentieth century."[73] Western artistic individualism, after several cycles of fashion-governed production, has returned with a vengeance.

If you want an idea of the extent to which that's true, peruse *The New West*, the catalog for the 1986 exhibition of the same name at the Colorado Springs Fine Arts Center that showcased the work of twenty-five artists from the Rocky Mountain states and Texas. Among those represented are Baker, Fincher, Gwyn, Jimenez, and Scholder. About a third are women — like Deborah Butterfield, who does Giacometti-like sculptures of horses; Fran Metzger, whose representational pastels explore the relationship between the self and the enormity of natural space; and Genevieve Reckling, whose sensuous oils spring from her love affair with the sharp light and intense colors of the Southwest. And note the work from photographer Gus Foster, mixed-media artist Suzanne Klotz-Reilly, painter Earl Linderman, ceramist Nancy Lovendahl, and others. Very individualized, all over the map in media, styles, techniques, subjects.

But the New Western artists — and most of their peers, from the most promising new IAIA graduate or apprentice with a master sculptor like Allan Houser to even some Old Wester who's taken up carving kitsch cowboys — have things in common, too. In his introduction to *The New West*, Charles A. Guerin, curator at the Colorado Springs Fine Arts Center, rounds them up. These artists have bucked the notion that they have to go to New York to make their mark, voting against "the benefits of that close association to the art market curators and collectors" as well as "against the quality of life in a big city and the pressures to conform." Thus they "have placed the integrity of their work above all other concerns." Eschewing the congestion, distractions, crime, and

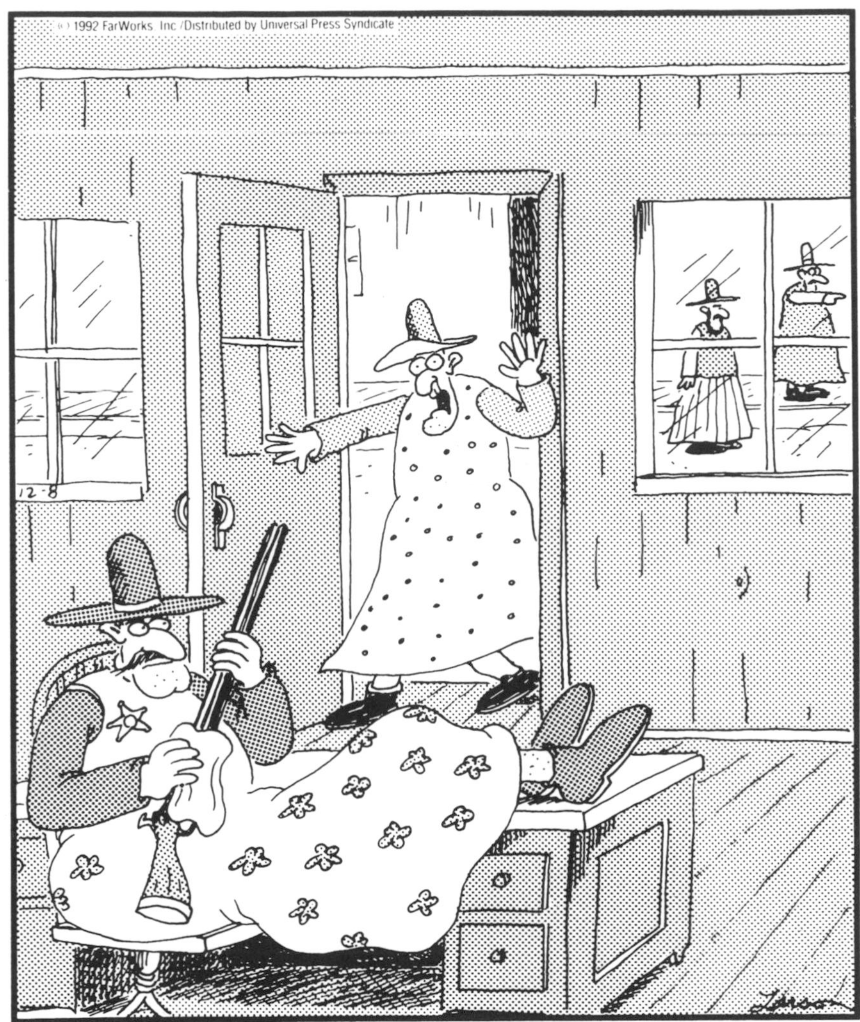

"Sheriff! Ben Wiggins is ridin' into town, and he's wearin' that same little chiffon number that he wore when he shot Jake Sutton!"

The feminization of the West, Larson-style. (Courtesy of Universal Press Syndicate. The Far Side© 1992 Farworks, Inc. *Distributed by* Universal Press Syndicate. *Reprinted with permission. All rights reserved)* "outrageous cost of adequate studio space" in major cities, "they are either transplanted urbanites who have come here searching for tranquility, beauty and a more humane lifestyle, or they are natives . . . in favor of living and working in the quiet isolation of an environment which allows them time to work from within." That environment figures in art that "graphically expresses some close relationship to either the land or the culture." In any case, it "has an effect on them all," largely through an unpressured energy that "manifests itself with a sense of clarity uncommon in contemporary art." The artists of the New West are lovingly engaged in work that is "truly unique, vital," and that "sells itself."[74]

So be it, still. Take that, Ivan Karp!

And last here but hardly least among New Western revisionist artists, there's Gary Larson. The millions of people who every day, before his retirement from newspaper cartooning in 1994, spent a brief and humorously profitable time in the syndicated world of "The Far Side" or now flip through his anthologies probably don't think of this reclusive Washingtonian genius as that sort of artist, but in a remarkable percentage of his cartoons that's exactly what he is. His Western-theme work features absurd variations on Hollywood clichés, odd twists of perspective on race and gender, New Western send-ups of Old Western sentiments and myths and legends, and other quirky turns — vegetable gunslingers, cow poets, centaur rodeos, God knows what. He must love the West to have such fun with it. Also he must be something of a cowboy, for he has the cowboy's sense of humor — terse, ironic, understated — as he looks at things from a different side.

 And here's to putting "WESTERN" back with the word "COUNTRY."

— Michael Martin Murphey, liner notes, *Cowboy Songs*

GARTH AND FRIENDS: RESINGING THE WEST, DANCING TO THE COWBOY BEAT

It's a cold night in January 1992. CBS prepares to air a Michael Jackson special, an event expected to gather the eyes and ears of most of the known cabled and antennaed world. Tens of millions of channel changers click away. But wait. What the—? What's going on? Yuppie television executives wince as the half-digested food in their stomachs gets a superfluous dose of acid. People out there in medialand are tuning in to the wrong network. You can almost hear the VHF equivalent of Ross Perot's giant sucking sound. It's crossover time. They're switching to some hat act on NBC. There go the ratings. Plop, plop. Fizz, fizz. May as well see what the competition is up to.

Plenty. Hang on, tinhorns. This ain't no show about an overgrown kid tryin' to look like Diana Ross while he moonwalks against some street-gang backdrop. You're in Dallas, Texas, at the Reunion Arena. The house is packed to the gills. The New West is about to detonate with music. *This Is Garth Brooks.*

And Garth walks out on the stage, pumping his fists in the air. He's all over the place. The audience goes wild. You can tell he's *on*. He's got the power like nobody since Elvis, who was himself something of a country singer. The winter is warming up. Narrow-crowned black cowboy hat with a dip at the rear. Western shirt in blue and black, with white piping. Black jeans skintight on football-player thighs, stacked just right over black roper-style boots. Applause hits him in waves, every woman leading the cheer. He shouts, "Hello, Texas!" The arena roars. He strums his dark acoustic guitar and gets after it with "Not Counting You."

Then comes "Rodeo," with Garth putting extra stress on the word *Texas* when it occurs. Now the audience is *really* with him, singing along seriously. He wiggles a forefinger at a woman near the shore in that sea of excited faces. The song has a big deep beat you can dance to in the dream called rodeo that Garth spins with magical control, gesture by gesture, moment by moment.

This Tulsa-born boy knows how to execute. Roses are handed up to him, and he plants kisses in return. He's an exhibitionist, an attention-grabbing homegrown charismatic. He stretches himself. He takes chances. He gives it everything he's got. Kick-ass rhythms and raw musical dynamics all tangled up with sex. He locks informally with the audience, but his shirt is buttoned up to the throat. He's a perfectionist who's able to let it all hang out. He's a hick with Wall Street business sense. He's quick-success rich. He's a private man who wants everyone to be happy. He's focused. He's dreaming of Hollywood. He's nuts. He's competitive. He's generous. He's quiet off-stage. He's politically liberal, mostly. He's a bag of intriguing contradictions.

When "The Thunder Rolls" begins, with light-and-smoke effects worthy of Kiss (with which group he later would perform), you realize what a good band rides with Garth — Stillwater, named after the town that harbors his alma mater, Oklahoma State University. Unbelievable bass. Crisp drumming. He sings the version of the song with the vindictive, murderous ending that country channels refuse to play and wins the heart of every woman any man ever abused.

Garth goes philosophical with "The River." He's still driven by a high-school kind of passion. He sings like he writes: from the heart. He's still a George Strait wanna-be. Cut his teeth on Dan Fogelberg, James Taylor, the Eagles, hypershowy groups. He does "Much Too Young (To Feel This Damn Old)" and salutes Chris LeDoux. What Garth has been up to since the early 1980s clicks here and now like never before. His energy loop with the audience surges with lightninglike amperage. New country propelled into an epic dimension.

Then into "Papa Loved Mama." Gritty messed-up-marriage country violence done tongue-in-cheek. Garth and Stillwater pull out all the stops, the beat driving with the heavy momentum of an eighteen-wheeler. He's hopping up the steps to the top of the stage, slapping cymbals with the neck of his guitar. At the end the whole audience is on its feet.

Garth takes off his guitar, walks about sensitively, as he croons "If Tomorrow Never Comes." The camera watches the faces of women in the audience. They adore him. Just as he did when he played local bars in college, he gives his audience what it wants. Eclectic material. So then he belts out "Shameless," still without guitar, with all the vocal wrenching of a man out of control in love. He opens his arms out like a crucifix.

Next he does "Friends in Low Places," the audience singing and clapping along in proletarian sympathy. For a while you hear only Betsy Smittle's bass behind him. Garth scurries around like a gerbil. At last he licks his thumb, and he and James Garver smash their guitars together into flinders of wood and dangling strings. He hands what's left of his to a boy in the audience.

The lights go down. A solemn rapture fills the arena, thousands of folk holding up flaming cigarette lighters, those small fires like stars as Garth, near tears, sings "The Dance." He's flying as high as God.

But then he cuts loose with "You May Be Right," turning into a wrangler Mick Jagger. He swings from a cable, does a hunched Chuck Berry guitar skip, throws mineral water all over the stage. Leaves the scene for a bit. Returns, looking totally zany. And, God almighty, picks up a spotlight and sweeps its beam slowly across the audience, all those entranced faces becoming part of the closing spectacle. Then, suddenly, he's gone. An amazing, one-of-a-kind concert.

Good night, Texas.

Meanwhile, back at the past—how did things come round to such a happening? We know many of the reasons by now, of course, but to answer that question more fully we need to investigate the history behind the recent florescence of country music, particularly in terms of its Western elements and aspects.

People were singing songs out there in rural America long before anyone spoke of country or Western or cowboy or whatever music with self-consciousness about its category. But modern *country* music, as a more or less distinct type, was born, in the words of music journalist Jimmy Guterman, "on front porches and in dance halls in rural communities of the mid and late '20s." And he observes that though "conventional wisdom for half a century has stated that the early ballads of country music were a direct descendant of Anglo-Scot-Irish folk music, . . . the influence of European styles was dwarfed by the impact of blues and other African-American forms."[1] (It's not just coincidental that Brooks gesturally quoted Chuck Berry—the man who invented rock 'n' roll put considerable Western and country seasoning in his music.) However much "conventional wisdom" and its prejudices wanted to suppress that impact, open-minded research shows that modern country music not only began in the 1920s but began with both the Carter Family and a great black musician named Jimmie Rodgers.

Those two acts, as Guterman summarizes it, created the "music and personae" that "still define the limits of hard country." The descendants of the original Carter Family (including June Carter, who's married to imperishable Johnny Cash and sings in his band) still play, and "its spiritual descendants control the country music establishment to this day." Carter Family music was a mixture—gospel, folk, string-band, Celtic—much concerned "with, er, family values," as Guterman puts it in the post-Bush age. Jimmie Rodgers, who "fancied himself as much a bluesman as a hillbilly singer," died at the age of thirty-six, but his spiritual descendants didn't. He "invented whole strains of blues and country" that still live on. In fact, the immortality of both the Carter Family and Rodgers began to be ensured at the same recording session in August 1927 in Bristol, Tennessee. According to Guterman, "Johnny Cash calls this recording date 'the single most important event in the history of country music,' and he isn't exaggerating." How so? Because it "was the first time that hillbilly culture collided with Northeastern-urban aesthetic and production values, and it was full of musical and cultural innovations." As we'll see, analogous collisions and innovations have figured in the rise of Garth Brooks and friends; but in both 1927 and the late 1980s the takeoff occurred because of the extraordinary production of music that a lot of people wanted to hear. In both cases the music was done by artists who were "singing about real life, rather than just love songs, for a mass audience."[2]

What about the Western part of what everybody used to call country-and-Western music? Another music journalist, Colin Escott, offers a useful distinction:

> In popular histories, "country and western" is described as an amalgam of the hillbilly tradition (Roy Acuff and several guys named Hank) and western music (Roy Rogers, Gene Autry, and several guys named Tex). But in truth, hillbilly music absorbed elements of pop and R&B to become "country and western" while western music atrophied. One would have pronounced it dead but for the fact that there were always a few guys on little labels keeping the spirit alive, a spirit that revolved around the notion of gentlemen cowherders singing to their charges under the big, big sky.

Escott's "truth" isn't the whole story, of course, but it's sufficient to account for the precariousness of a musical marriage that never really occurred — and to explain, for instance, a major difference in style between "the regionality in the hillbilly voice" and the "straight" timbre of the Western voice. In many ways the difference between country music and Western music now is the same as it was around 1933 when "the quintessential western group," a vocal trio called the Sons of the Pioneers, was formed.[3]

Roy Rogers was responsible for that forming, along with Tim Spencer and Bob Nolan, the latter of whom "wrote some genre-defining songs with an outsider's sense of wonder, like 'Tumbling Tumbleweeds,' 'Way Out There,' and the odd, surreal 'Cool Water.' " In 1934 the group, then a quintet, was recording its "prairie romanticism."[4] And the rest, as they say, is history.

But there's a little more to that history and to the history of the country-Western relationship that needs to be told. In his 1979 book *The Cowboy Hero*, William W. Savage, Jr., devotes a chapter to "The Cowboy of Record" that begins with a consideration of cowboy as, in the words he borrows from country singer Bobby Bare, "an attitude" rather than "an occupation." He takes "the widespread affectation of cowboy dress" and the like as "the physical manifestations of that attitude" and "contemporary popular music" as "an index of its psychology and a measure of its prevalence." Though the music carries on the tradition of the cowboy hero, it nonetheless "presents a complex series of images of the cowboy that is a radical departure from traditional imagery."[5] Savage discusses the images in detail, along the way sharing information and insights crucially relevant to my historical investigation.

"The historical cowboy had quite a bit to do with music," Savage notes, though typically he wasn't much of a vocalist. But he amused himself and his fellow riders, and he "soothed the cattle at night and made them less inclined to stampede." Through such efforts "he created a substantial body of music," a portion of which was later collected, studied by scholars of folk music, and published. Thus in the early twentieth century cowboy songs entered popular culture: "They were featured in the radio and stage performances of hillbilly musicians in the 1920s, and by the 1930s the 'singing cowboy' was a mainstay of popular entertainment. Otto Gray, who began performing with his band, the Oklahoma Cowboys, in 1923, is said to have been the first." Moreover, many country musicians of that era "embraced the cowboy as a personal model because, according to Dorothy Horstman, 'the cowboy image — the tailored shirt, bright colors, ten-gallon hat and high-heeled boots — was more appealing to the country singer than the costume of the mountaineer or farmer.' " Now here's something interesting: the notion that the country-Western connection first involved a marriage not of two kinds of music but of country music and Western style. It seems to offer an accurate account of what occurred back then — and of what is still the case. Certainly Savage, after examining the imagery at Nashville's Grand Ole Opry and on country-music television shows of the late 1970s, finds "Horstman's suggestion . . . confirmed."[6] Exceptions, such as on the comedy program "Hee Haw," were and are for comic effect.

After the "wedding" — that "of country music and the cowboy image" — came the invention, "to add some interest to the talkies," of the singing-cowboy movie hero, a role filled first by Ken Maynard and later by, among others, Rogers and Autry and, less successfully, the young John Wayne. That hero and "his B-film vehicle," as Savage puts it, "expired in the 1950s" (though you can get them back now on long-playing videos); but by that time "the cowboy image was firmly fixed in

American popular music, and the musical genre that had once been labeled 'hillbilly' had become known as 'country and western.' " There's another connection Savage points out, however, that hints at the more deeply mixed nature of the marriage: "Country music had formally acquired its western flavor in the 1930s and 1940s partly because of the crooning of cinematic cowboys, but the union received most of its impetus from the performance of white string bands in the rural Southwest" — the Oklahoma Cowboys, Bob Wills's Texas Playboys, and similar groups whose members "wore cowboy costumes and played sophisticated renditions of an admixture of traditional cowboy tunes, Negro blues music, and popular songs known variously as 'southwestern swing,' 'Okie jazz,' and, finally, 'western swing,' by which term it is identified today." And Savage observes that the garish costumes characteristic of Nashville country-and-Western music weren't worn "in lesser musical centers like Austin" where "the cowboy image, though just as popular, is more subdued."[7] The same distinction holds today between old-guard country artists, like Porter Wagoner, who still go for the sequined-and-embroidered look, and young-country artists, like Brooks and many others, who sport simpler, more "Western" Western outfits.

Savage delves into other interrelationships entailing cowboy imagery, country music, crossover phenomena (of the kind that have powerfully excited the music industry in recent years — country songs that top the pop charts, rock songs that turn out to have country appeal, and the like), and schizophrenic groups like the Charlie Daniels Band that "dress in cowboy garb and sing songs suggestive of western themes" and yet remain essentially Southern.[8] But most pertinent here is his survey of cowboy imagery in the lyrics of four generations of cowboy songs.

First-generation songs were the traditional ones of the historical cowboy, many of which recently have been revived by Michael Martin Murphey, Riders in the Sky, and others. Such songs frankly encoded the cowboy's way of life, his values, his likes ("women who could manage to be simultaneously feminine and rugged," for example) and dislikes ("stingy persons," for example), his "zest for life" and philosophy about its hard spots.[9]

Second-generation songs were largely of the singing-cowboy type fittingly associated with the B films of the 1930s and 1940s. They didn't concern "riding drag," and they toned down the directness, sexual and otherwise, of first-generation songs. Blatantly commercial, many "dealt with themes of romantic love," and their moods were "alternately maudlin, saccharine, or hopeful." From Rogers's "That Palomino Pal o' Mine" to Autry's "South of the Border" to the Sons of the Pioneers' "Empty Saddles," the titles alone suggested a Western never-never land, "evoking flights of fancy that have not yet ended."[10]

Then things changed. Third-generation songs, which Savage classifies as those that came out between World War II and the Vietnam War, showed all the signs of belonging to a time when "history had done damage to innocence" and would do more. Autry warned immigrants "to love America or leave it" in "Don't Bite the Hand That's Feeding You," and "patriotic gore" defined songs by artists like Elton Britt, Cowboy Copas, and Montana Slim. More songs emphasized "shoot-'em-up aspects of western history" and "cowboy killers" as Tex Ritter cut the theme for *High Noon* and Marty Robbins narrated the violence of killing in "El Paso," "Big Iron," and "Running Gun." The cowboy, in Savage's words, "lost some substance." As is appropriate for a killer, he became "less thoughtful and more active." There's a clear progression here: "The insights of the first generation and the illusions of the second all faded before the violence of the third," which, with its bloody realism, "led naturally to the 1970s and the themes of the fourth generation."[11]

Unfolding along with the rise of New Western History, the evolution of a more reflective Western literature, and the decline of Western cinema, the themes of fourth-generation cowboy songs were typically less concerned with physical violence but were, in Savage's opinion, "even more disturbing, inasmuch as they portrayed the utter psychological debasement of the cowboy image." That "utter" may push his case into overstatement — or may not, given the evidence he summons up. Still, it might be more accurate to say, with his own phrase, that fourth-generation songs embody the confusions of "conflicting images" as much as they portray "utter psychological debasement." Consider, in that regard, his critique of a Roy Rogers song from the mid-1970s, "Hoppy, Gene and Me." It's "a nostalgic song concerning the influence of Western films on the character development of a couple of generations of American males," one done by a man who apparently never stopped believing in the "moral import" of such films: "Here is the performer who never escaped — outgrew? — his best role; but Rogers's circumstances, including his failure to grasp the difference between history and entertainment, may be our fault and our responsibility. So says the cowboy music of the fourth generation." And therefore Savage finds pertinent a 1975 rock song from the Amazing Rhythm Aces, "King of the Cowboys":

> The lyrics describe childhood and the movie cowboy hero from the perspective of a young adult who, realizing that the world created by the B western was a false one, nevertheless recognizes that the cowboy hero taught him how to be a man. In the process of growing up, the youngster effectively trapped the hero and held him in his mind, presumably as an ideal; now, suddenly, the adult becomes aware that the hero is an old man who, having served his purpose, must be set free from "a life he doesn't need." However much one might wish otherwise, it is at last necessary to "say goodbye to the King of the Cowboys" and attend to the problems of adulthood.[12]

Happy trails.

Of course, however, fourth-generation music, with its conflicting images, has more twists than that, according to Savage: "On the one hand, the music merely acknowledges the status accorded the cowboy as a fixture of popular culture. . . . But, on the other hand, the music redefines the cowboy in contexts purely contemporary and suggests that there are better things to be — if one has the choice." By this cultural double action "the cowboy becomes, through his music, a new social type on the American landscape. He remains a hero, but for the reason that he endures a life without spectacle, a life that is led in dives and low haunts but is otherwise unexceptional." Savage exemplifies this tangle with Waylon Jennings's 1976 recording of "My Heroes Have Always Been Cowboys," which he terms "a peculiar blend of nostalgia and pessimism." In it "the adult confesses an early addiction to movie cowboys and a childhood desire to emulate them" but also recognizes that cowboys are loners and drifters headed for a sad end — yet decides to emulate them anyway and so becomes another hero who "dreams his dreams but can never quite catch up with them." Savage sees a more obvious version of such complication in Ed Bruce's 1976 release "Mamas, Don't Let Your Babies Grow Up to Be Cowboys," in which the cowboy "is an antisocial fellow," self-centered, mobile, misunderstood, excessively proud, and so on. He's not so much an "individual" as "an insensitive sociopath." And — one more twist — "he is a hero because of it, for

Bruce's song is a paean to this neo-cowboy, a paean in the negative mode."[13]

And other twists came into play. Performers like David Allen ("Take This Job and Shove It") Coe, Willie Nelson, and Jennings styled themselves as "country-music 'outlaws' " (by dint of their avoiding Nashville). They looked like cowboys, and they added "a strange mixture of themes" to fourth-generation music, singing "of lives spent on the road or in honky-tonks." They also took the violence of third-generation music a step further with the likes of Coe's belligerence on stage and Nelson's much-lauded 1975 album *Red Headed Stranger*, whose songs are chapters in the "ghastly story" of a cowboy who shoots to death his unfaithful woman, her lover, and another woman and then, unpunished, settles down and lives to enjoy his old age.[14]

Such images of the cowboy, on stage and in songs, however conflicted, held and still hold appeal because they present a figure who's "his own man"—a constant through all four generations of cowboy music. Savage elaborates:

> Whatever he is, he knows that he is better than we are, and we know it, too. He is at only his own mercy, while we of the industrial, bureaucratic, computerized twentieth century are at everybody else's. That is enough, it seems, to make him a worthy hero. . . . Indeed, his musical commemorations make it possible to say that in the hiatus of the 1970s, when detectives private and otherwise replaced the cowboy as a television staple and hasty critics rejoiced over the decline of western movies, cowboy imagery thrived in song and was thereby saved for better days.[15]

Better days were coming, of course, and with them the rise of what I'd call, extending Savage's scheme, the fifth generation of cowboy music. But before we get into that, we need to explore some changes in the larger world of country music during the period of Savage's fourth generation and thereafter.

More conflicting images. Or, as George H. Lewis puts it, broadening the perspective on country music of the 1970s and 1980s, more "duellin' values"—all manner of conflicts and tensions and contradictions running through the "three minute word-movies" (singer-songwriter John Hartford's term for country songs) of the period. From their beginning, those word-movies, often with a confessional tone, have concerned and reflected "the everyday trials, troubles, hopes, fears, and dreams of their audience," sometimes so intimately as to be a "way of life." As Lewis notes, "Over time, their lyrical content seems surprisingly steady, revolving in general around the topics of home and family, patriotism, work, love, liquor, and the passing of the good old days." Since the 1950s, however, such topics have become increasingly complicated by the tensions of social and economic changes, including "migration from rural to urban settings" and "shifting lifestyles." Lewis adduces analytical evidence that by around 1970 the "core country music listeners" were urban white adults with rural roots who had achieved the expectable job-family-home situation but were patently discontent with all of it.[16] They sound a bit like New Westers. Some of them already were, of course.

After 1970 such tensions only intensified, so that, looking back two decades later, Lewis remarks how, when examining closely the "core values that are expressed in country music, one is immediately struck with the inconsistencies, conflicts and, in some cases, contradictions among them." You find unquestioning patriotism cheek by jowl with bitterness toward American institutions, "concerns for individual expression and freedom" along with "yearnings for the security and dependence of a stable family life," political conservatism served up with economic liberalism, and "the glorification of illicit sex" just across the road from "the yearning for a stable, loving marriage" — duellin' values indeed. And, in Lewis's view, it's the duels that "give the song its sharpness of purpose, its interpretive power, its cultural cutting edge." Duellin'-values songs "seem to engage their audience more thoroughly, to be talked and thought about more, than do pieces that more statically reflect cultural harmony."[17] Culturally troubled times give rise to more interesting music, particularly if the music, like country, deals with the basics.

The duels that Lewis describes aren't all so new, of course, but in recent years they've become more gnarly, intense, and widespread. Their sardonic thrusts and parries weave through songs like Dolly Parton's "In the Good Old Days, When Times Were Bad." And the ironies of the rural-urban duel turn up plentifully as "musical reaction to what are seen as the problems of impersonality and strangeness of urban life as contrasted with the past rural simplicity of home continues into the late 1980s to be a theme in country music, even though," as Lewis grimly puts it, "the rural-urban transformation of the country is nearly complete." In that regard, Dwight Yoakam's breakthrough 1984 song "Guitars, Cadillacs, Etc." (the "Etc." was later dropped) is perhaps Lewis's most compelling example, though others aren't hard to come by. Dealing with the home theme mostly by indirection, it consists of a word-movie about Los Angeles "in which the singer is carved by the sharp knives of urban culture into a new man — soulless, but better able to survive the modern urban environment because of this."[18] The song also tells us, however, that in the "lonely, lonely streets that I call home" there's something besides guitars and Cadillacs "that keeps me hanging on": it's "hillbilly music." There's another possibility for "home," but there's doubt that the singer "can find my mind now" and "just leave."[19]

If "social change" produced that kind of alienation, it produced as well "an audience far larger than the original subculture." The "explosion of popularity of country music," as Lewis terms it, began its rising curve in the early 1970s, hit a peak in the early 1980s (which "coincided with the conservative, even reactionary climate of the country"), took a dip in the mid-1980s, and then again headed up — and up and up. In the early 1980s traditional country music seemed doomed to turn into "slicked down, easy listening 'urban cowboy' music." Refried dreams. That situation stirred up feelings of difference parallel to those sometimes between New and Old Westers, and so you had a sound edging toward country Muzak opposed by an old guard in an "I Was Country When Country Wasn't Cool" mood. Thus, as that urban-cowboy music, much of it restricted to "safe" or "pious patriotic" subjects, continued to be produced and performed, in a kind of debasement perhaps more "utter" than that Savage discusses, the opposition — George Jones, Merle Haggard, Loretta Lynn, and others — kept "traditional themes and songs" alive. As a result, when "country music sales dropped off in the mid-1980s and the larger middle-of-the-road audience turned elsewhere for its entertainment, there began a revival of traditional forms and themes in country music." That is, once the crossover audience crossed back over, the field was cleared for the old sound to reassert itself — but in a new way. What happened then was "neo-traditional music" that both "looks to the themes of the past, the common core of concerns that has always existed in country music, and attempts to update these concerns," with their "conflicts and contradictions" in tow, "making them fresh and relevant for the contemporary country audience."[20] With Ricky Skaggs, Reba McEntire, George Strait, and others going stellar in the mid-1980s and performers like Yoakam anxious to do so, that audience was about to expand again, this time taking in enough crossover strays to form a King Ranch–size herd.

Actually, country music had been tinkering with achieving more freshness and relevance for quite a while by the late 1980s, especially in its treatment of what Lewis terms "interpersonal relationships." Much of his discussion refers to country songs with Western elements — from Marty Robbins's "El Paso" to Townes Van Zandt's "lyrically ambiguous" buddy song "Pancho and Lefty" to rodeo-theme songs like Dan Seals's "All that Glitters" — and they contain tensions, conflicts, and contradictions galore that bear on contemporary interpersonal dilemmas. For instance, Billy Joe Shafer's "Willie the Wandering Gypsy and Me," which made a hit for Waylon Jennings, has to do with a man who wants "to follow the rodeo" but "is caught between the expectations and responsibilities of family and those of the free roaming buddy system" that has its origins in "the days when the west was wild." And Lewis notes that many cowboy songs of the last few decades, like trucker or even railroad songs, "celebrate life on the road, but usually include a yearning for the settled life as a subtext." Subtexts abound also in songs that grapple with women "acting like the 'honky tonk angel,' or like 'momma,' " and they intertwine their way through the increasing number of songs of the 1970s and, especially, the 1980s written and sung by women that dramatize a range of feminist issues. From the 1970s on, as Lewis observes, "country songs concerning traditional male-female role relationships were increasingly overlayed with comment, reaction and critique."[21] Indeed, such subtexts have more and more become "supertexts" as they've been incorporated into music by Dolly Parton, Emmylou Harris, Patty Loveless, K. T. Oslin, Suzy Bogguss, and others. It's the kind of disillusioning transgression that made for a better fit between country music and its expanding and better-educated audience in the late 1980s, an audience with a yearning for tradition as well as an awareness of the nontraditional complexities of the postmodern age.

In any case, country music turned a corner in the mid-1980s. Though you encounter disagreements about which factors contributed most to the turn or were most indicative of what was to come, students of the genre tend to concur in emphasizing the importance of the neotraditionalist impulse and certain Western elements associated with it. For instance, in a 1986 issue of the *Journal of Country Music*, Bill C. Malone cautiously saw significance in the degree of "recognition given to the young traditionalists" when the Country Music Association (CMA) bestowed its industry-voted awards in October 1985, naming Reba McEntire as Female Vocalist of the Year, George Strait as Male Vocalist of the Year, and Ricky Skaggs as Entertainer of the Year. Malone was cheered "to know that there still is life, vitality, and appeal in the tradition-based styles," and he descried a clear suggestion in the pattern of the awards: "that there is still a large, and generally unsatisfied, market for hard country styles, and that the voting membership of the CMA . . . has responded to this public mood." Fair enough. However, the top award recipients not only showed "a healthy consciousness and knowledge of roots" but also were able to "effectively combine older and modern traits in a commercially winning way." For at least two of the three performers, that way entailed strong Western appeal: Strait's "cowboy persona" and ability to "project the sound and ambience of the Texas dancehall circuit" and former barrel racer McEntire's presence as a representative of "the small-town rodeo world of the Southwest."[22]

With a longer retrospective view, Gary Graff in a 1993 syndicated piece argued, as other critics also have, that Randy Travis's 1986 album *Storms of Life* marked "the beginning of the new era" in country music and the end of the watered-down, wide-audience music of the " 'Urban Cowboy' period." For Graff that album ushered in "the so-called New Traditionalist movement," which was "led by Travis . . . and other country singers whose music had a familiar twang, but was muscled up by improved production techniques" — so that "country no longer sounded like music for dusty wagon trails but had a modern energy and sheen." Also, Graff observed, "Travis' emergence . . . coincided with country's foray into the video realm with the Nashville Network [TNN] and other stations." Furthermore, Travis and performers like Clint Black and Ricky Van Shelton were good ambassadors in the neotraditionalist world because "they attracted young fans to country, but their music bowed to traditional conventions and therefore didn't alienate older listeners." There was more sexiness to the music and to the performances, particularly those of tight-jeans types like Yoakam, who was given to "Elvis-like hip-swiveling on-stage."[23] You got that as an erotic bonus to the hillbilly twang and Western clothing.

Still, there was some displacement of old-country performers — a trend that would continue — and those "dusty wagon trails" dismissed by Graff weren't out of the picture by a long shot as new country gathered its increasingly larger audience. By 1987 the Escape Club was singing about "heading for the nineties, living in the wild, wild west" — in a song to whose "beat that we like best" Western-dressed boot-scooters would soon do the electric slide.[24]

In 1988 a Canadian business pundit, John Parikhal, once a student of media guru Marshall McLuhan and a researcher of trends in country music, assessed the scene. Parikhal had predicted the nostalgic rise of neotraditionalism after the mid-1980s country-music slump, and now he offered observations about that music's situation in Reagan's America, along with guidelines for marketing it and more predictions. Among them, as reported by country-music writer Jack Hurst, were these: "Rock and roll is now 'stale,' with only a few vital stars, several of whom . . . are sounding themes that are basically country"; "country music will have to lose the remaining vestiges of the hayseed image" in order to appeal to "the huge Baby Boom Generation in the 35–54 age bracket," most of whose members are college-educated; the public is overloaded with "information and entertainment" and has a growing appetite for "reality and 'truth' " that can be addressed by music with a "longstanding preoccupation with real life"; a progressively more rootless America will have "an increasing longing for music that returns listeners to scenes from the less-complicated past, to . . . the less-selfish values that are the stock-in-trade of country songwriters"; there will be "another explosion of country music into the pop market," made possible by stars who "are totally new and fresh to everybody in America except the country audience"; and the " 'most interesting' new star in terms of potential appeal" is Yoakam, "the nasal-twanging neotraditionalist who combines a James Dean demeanor with a highly educated intelligence."[25] Parikhal didn't foresee Brooks, who emerged with his *Garth Brooks* album in 1989, but Yoakam has become an amply bright star. Though Parikhal didn't address the distinctly Western elements and aspects of what was happening and would happen, on the

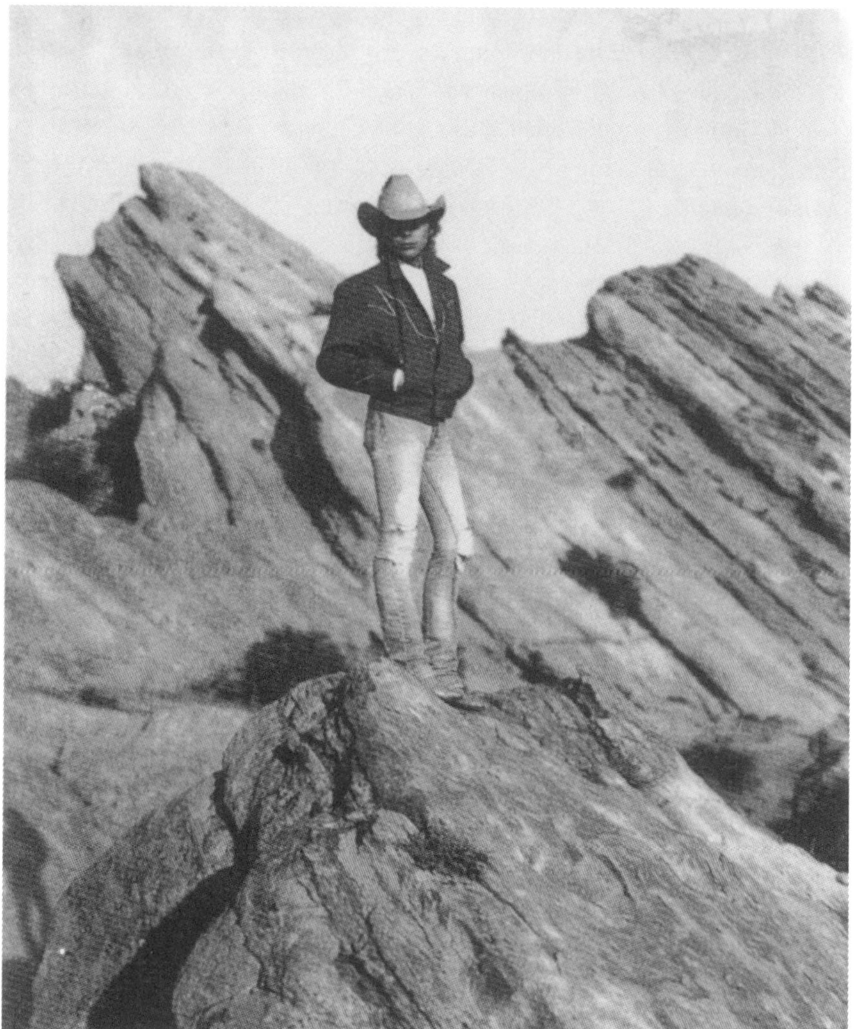

Dwight Yoakam, " 'most interesting' new star" in 1988. (Photo by Peter Darley Miller, courtesy of Reprise Records)

whole he deserves credit for the accuracy of his observations, advice, and prophecies.

By 1990 not only had the country thing expanded: the Western connection had enriched tremendously. Sixteen CMA nominations that year were for four hat acts whose music, appearance, and/or performance style had a decidedly more young-country, New Western and less old-

Nashville feel to them: Black, Alan Jackson, Strait, and Brooks. By 1991 *Billboard* ratings indicated that an unprecedented number of people were tuned in to country-music radio and its "real-life" songs for unreal lives. By 1992, the year of Brooks's television special, there were nightclubs all over, for instance, Chicago that featured live country music, Western fashion shows, free instruction in the Texas two-step and other dances, barbecue buffets, rodeo-sweetheart pageants, you name it. A place called Elbo Room sponsored a gun-juggling contest and staged a saloon brawl as special events in a series of country-Western hoedowns. Even people in New York City, weary with hip-hop and rap, were sneaking into country music through the back door. Western wear was a spring theme in Macy's windows. The Cowgirl Hall of Fame, the Rodeo Bar, and similar music-dance venues were flourishing.

In 1992 the young and largely wholesome sound of country had turned into a multibillion-dollar industry of a different order, and its listenership well exceeded that of Top 40 music. In December ABC put on "Best of Country '92: Countdown at the Neon Armadillo," featuring a horde of stars from Brooks to Bogguss as well as a gratuitous gaggle of tank-topped dancers. Countdowns of country hits were more accurate in 1992 and thereafter thanks to the new SoundScan system whose unprecedented precision in calculating retail sales of recorded music had revealed for the first time the extent of the country feeding frenzy. TNN was profiting mightily from the frenzy, and its corporate cousin Country Music Television launched never-off-the-air programming in Europe and the United Kingdom.

By 1993 anyone could inventory what Strait, McEntire, and company had wrought by opening doors for others during the past decade, and it was just those two, along with Randy Owen, who served as hosts of the 1993 Academy of Country Music (ACM) Awards show. Garthomania remained in full swing. Country music flavored the sound tracks of numerous movies, a trend that grew stronger after Tammy Wynette and Lyle Lovett songs were featured in *The Crying Game* in 1992 and continued with movies like *8 Seconds*. And 1993 saw Toby Keith's first single, "Should've Been a Cowboy," become a hit as the exemplary expression of a fundamental New Western sentiment. Some of the best new-country artists contributed renditions to *Common Thread: The Songs of the Eagles*, a consummate album that saluted the country-rock background of contemporary neotraditional music and raised money for the Walden

Woods Project in order to save a parcel of the natural realm that such music, in its best moments, cherishes and celebrates. At the end of 1993 even Boston had two country radio stations.

By 1994 . . . well, the pattern was obvious enough. The CMA claimed that 42 percent of American adults listened to country radio, and TNN boasted 50 million subscribers. By then you didn't have to watch TNN's "Music City Tonight" or PBS's "Country Connection" to know which way the wind was blowing. As one of Alan Jackson's 1994 hits announced, "The whole world's gone country."

Together with the rise of neotraditionalism in country music and the general revival of interest in the West that began in the mid-1980s, there came a gradual revision in the image of the cowboy. It may have begun in 1980 with *Urban Cowboy*, for that movie ends with the undoing of a debauched, cruelhearted prison-rodeo rider who's almost a parody of the debased cowboy delineated in Savage's fourth-generation songs and with the discovery (or recovery) by the young urban-cowboy protagonist of moral selfhood and more viable manhood than he had tried to fabricate out of honky-tonk machismo. That is, to oversimplify, it ends with the delayed and, for the time being, tentative triumph of the traditional straight-shootin' cowboy over the post-Vietnam dissolute cowboy. The triumph can be read, of course, as one that resolves a battle within the protagonist himself—and maybe, up to a point, within American culture. In any case, the good-guy image didn't get lost after 1980 and, really, never had been before that: it was just being, in Savage's words, "saved for better [in some sense] days."

Those days arrived with neotraditionalism, which effected a cyclical return of tradition that, like the returning West with which it was to a great extent identified, entrained differences. Just as neotraditional country music restored traditional values, attitudes, and styles but contemporized them, so too did it, along with other forces in the culture, restore the traditional cowboy but also contemporized him. The resultant fifth-generation figure may not be all simple good guy — indeed, he may at times be very complicated, conflicted — but he's usually far more positively attractive than his fourth-generation predecessor. But whatever contemporizing such restorations necessitate, they appear, like the rampant public acquisition of things Western and country, to illustrate the significance of the impulse to restore as Susan Stewart discusses it in her book *On Longing: Narratives of the Miniature, the Gigantic, the Souvenir, the Collection*. In terms of her insightful argument, restoration (accompanied by — beware — what she calls its "false promise" of authenticity) "can be seen as a response to an unsatisfactory set of present conditions" that generates "a conservative idealization of the past," a "context of origin" that's essentially "imaginary" and "whose chief subject is a projection of . . . childhood," a childhood both personal and (here, nationally) historical.[26] That dissection pushes toward the abstruse; but the more you ponder it, the more it's as applicable here as a canteen on a cattle drive.

Though you can ferret out earlier hints at the thoroughgoing restoration of the cowboy in country music, it happens most dramatically in the late 1980s — and paradigmatically in the 1988 song "Cowboy Bill," which Brooks recorded on his 1989 debut album. That song — placed, interestingly, after "Much Too Young (to Feel This Damn Old)," which portrays a burned-out rodeo cowboy who recalls the fourth-generation image prominent a decade before — tells, through an adult's memory, of a retired Texas Ranger named Cowboy Bill. The old man, a sort of more aged Augustus McCrae, would enchant "us kids" with stories of his adventures on the *bandido*-ridden border. Though "to all of us kids Cowboy Bill was a hero," the grown-ups warned them to "keep your distance" from him and his "lies." But after the kids find him dead, surrounded by mementos of his former days and "clutchin' a badge that said Texas Ranger," the grown-ups change their tune: "Well now they're all sayin' Cowboy Bill was a hero / Just as true as his blue Texas skies."[27] Cowboy Bill himself may be gone at the end of the song, but it announces the return of the cowboy as a positive image, one not unrelated to that dismissed by the Amazing Rhythm Aces in 1975. The dangerous tales of the imaginary suddenly have the feel of memories of the authentic, and we're ready to saddle up — again.

Variations on this fifth-generation image of the cowboy, some presenting him more ambivalently than others, are scattered through Brooks's subsequent albums. The songs don't all treat literal cowboys, tenders of cattle, any more than "Cowboy Bill" or lots of other so-called cowboy songs do; but they do concern figures identified in the popular mind with cowboyness. Thus *No Fences* (1990) offers "Wild Horses" (about a bronc rider who can't stay home) and "Wolves" (which reflects on the demise, at the hands of bankers, of ranches fallen on hard times). *Ropin' the Wind* (1991) has "Rodeo" (about another hard-to-hold rodeo cowboy — like the last one, not a fourth-generation debauchee, just a guy devoted to the arena) and "In Lonesome Dove" (about how a stout woman copes and doesn't cope with the murder of her Texas Ranger husband). *The Chase* (1992) contains one, a fine one, "Night Rider's Lament" (which reflects on the craziness of the cowboy lifeway, concluding that living under the open sky is less crazy than living as most people do). *In Pieces* (1993) also, unless you count the up-tempo truck-sex song "Ain't Going Down ('til the Sun Comes Up)" as partly about rodeo, contains only one, but it too is a dandy: "The Cowboy Song" (about the trying world of the actual, as opposed to the cinematic, cowboy, who's nonetheless "chasin' what he really loves"). And so on.

"The Cowboy Song" doesn't fit well on that last album, but Brooks, who's done numerous rodeo performances, remains very loyal to his cowboy fans, whose songs he knows how to sing. As Charles Hirshberg, quoting Brooks, notes in his 1992 cover story on him for *Life*, "Though not really a cowboy, Brooks is proud to wear the hat. . . . 'I owe those cowboys. They were with me when no one else cared about me, and, good Lord willin', they'll be with me when everyone else forgets.' "[28] That loyalty accounts in part for his contributing to singer-songwriter Chris LeDoux's 1992 album *Whatcha Gonna Do with a Cowboy* and for Brooks's veneration and promotion of LeDoux, whose twenty-odd previous albums (from American Cowboy Songs) of rodeo songs, cowboy and Western classics, and Western country songs that many a cowboy had played in his pickup were reissued in 1991 by Liberty Records (now Capitol), Brooks's label — another step in the New Western restoration of the cowboy.

But Brooks's affiliations with the fifth-generation image of the cowboy involve more than that laudable loyalty — though it's a chief component. You might be tempted to see a man who apparently prefers to wear a sweat suit and baseball cap off-stage as just another of many singers who dress on-stage like actors playing cowboys, but there's more to notice. In many ways Brooks, as a person and as a performer, is the exemplar of the fifth-generation cowboy figure, the quintessential male New Wester. He's a multiple winner of the ACM Entertainer of the Year Award, complete with Lewis's duellin' values. In spite of at least one (well-publicized) sexual indiscretion on the road and his international aspirations (in recognition of his global impact, the ACM honored him with the Jim Reeves Memorial Award in 1995), Brooks presents himself as a home-themer who's fanatically devoted to wife and family. In general, his values are at once as basic as those enshrined in the first-generation cowboy's code of the West and as idealized as those touted by second-generation cinematic types: honesty, friendliness, willingness to help those in need, tolerance of human differences, piety — the whole kit and caboodle. Third-generation violence and fourth-generation debasement aren't absent from Brooks's music, but they're definitely diminished topics there — as they are in his life. Though some people judge him to be too willing to please everyone, he's a solider role model by a country mile than Waylon Jennings or Kenny Rogers or, for that matter, the latest one-shot rapper.

Brooks's exemplification is, of course, more complicated than a simple emulation of the traditional cowboy. His obsession with sex turns up in his music, performances, and interviews. Such frankness may recall first-generation cowboy music, but it also suggests conflicts with his home-and-family values. He prizes authenticity, but his concerts entail elaborate theatrical artifice that other performers have picked up on — especially his awesome show in the Texas Stadium in 1994, which NBC broadcast as "This Is Garth Brooks Too!" While he's good ol' dependable Garth, he also has a streak of unpredictability that keeps his fellow performers on their toes. He may have a conservative sensibility in some respects, but in others he's politically as opened-up as his music. In his 1992 song "We Shall Be Free," most memorably in the video version that the ACM honored as Best Video of the Year in 1994, and otherwise, he's declared his liberal position on a spectrum of issues, setting himself against racial prejudice, religious intolerance, suppression of free speech, homophobia, an economy that ignores poverty, and ecological indifference.

Doubtless it's taken courage for Brooks to speak out in that fashion, given the tenacious conservatism prevalent in the country-music industry and among country radio stations and fans. He's not "pure country," and his habit of not rendering closed-minded pat morals in his songs has put off some people. On the other hand, it's hardly hurt his overall popularity. Brooks has trained market acumen, but deft advertising alone doesn't sell tens of millions of albums. Besides, much of his music — "American Honky-Tonk Bar Association" or "Friends in Low Places," for example — has enough social bandwidth to make mossbacks feel included. Indeed, he appeals to people all over the map, a lot of them just normal folks out there across the country (and the world, especially Europe) who never listened to popular music until he struck.

Brooks's success has been variously explained. He respects his audience and keeps his concert prices low. He's an ordinary person but blessed with charisma. He violated the orthodox clichés of country music and freshened it up in a new honky-tonk, pop-folk, driving-rock fusion of styles. Many of his songs wrestle with perplexities of memory and emotion that resonate deeply in confused postmodern lives. His combination of gentlemanliness and earthy sex greatly appeals to women, who after all account for the bulk of country-music sales. His opposition to spousal abuse and his support of the Future Farmers of America and other worthwhile causes have won him many friends and awards. He was reared by country musicians who encouraged his artistic ambitions. Children love him and he them.

All of those points have explanatory power, and several of them relate to my argument that Brooks is the principal living icon of the New West, a dynamic one who's helped manifoldly to make country music more Western and to restore the cowboy to positive stature, who's encouraged his listeners to be their own men and women, to live by an updated code of the West, and to take the world's problems but not themselves seriously. And there's some Old Wester in him too — that's part of his neotraditionalism. Or you might consider him a man with a country soul, a rock-'n'-roll heart, and a New Western mind. What he means is difficult to pin down. Like New Westering itself, he's still in process. At any rate, his example has inspired plenty of other country-music performers.

To get a flash of revealing perspective on the meaning of Brooks as a vital pop-culture icon, let's go back to another of his television appearances. This time it's not on a cold night in January but on a hot night in August. In 1993. On NBC, not CBS. It's the night of August 30, of David Letterman's first "Late Show" on CBS, of the so-called battle of the late shows. But a spate of people aren't watching Letterman because NBC is smart enough to have Brooks on the "Tonight Show." Brooks, whose *In Pieces* will be released the next day, does a couple of songs. Before the show is finished, host Jay Leno dons a cowboy hat. Guest Luke Perry, who in 1994 would star in *8 Seconds*, has one too. Brooks, Leno, and Perry wind

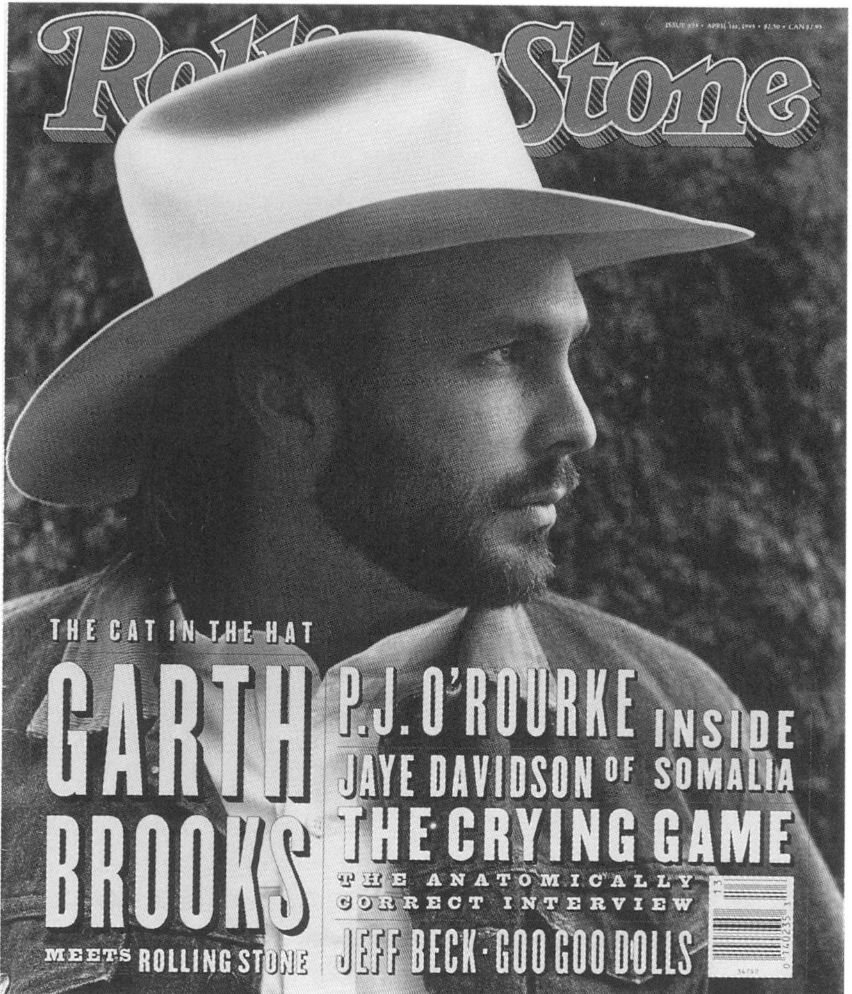

Garth Brooks: a fifth-generation cowboy, the principal living icon of the New West. (Photo by Kurt Markus, courtesy of Straight Arrow Publishers, Inc. From Rolling Stone, *April 1, 1993. By Straight Arrow Publishers, Inc., 1993. All rights reserved. Reprinted by permission)*

up sitting in a row, cowboy-hatted. The hat mood takes over. And it's clear that the three ain't bein' just country: they're bein' *Western.*

When I was a child, my parents refused to let me listen to the country music that was available on radio in my hometown of Lebanon, Missouri, just an hour and a half northeast of Branson, Missouri, which recently has become the new Mecca of country. I was warned that it was music for trailer-park poor white trash, degenerate hicks, and such. (No surprise then, I guess, that my first heartthrob was a country-music wanna-be who went on to a career at the Ozark Opry at the Lake of the Ozarks and later performed on occasion at the Grand Ole Opry in Nashville.) My parents were typical "respectable" Americans of their generation in their attitude toward such music and its fans.

That was in the 1950s. Now country music — most of it anyway, for some of it remains what a friend calls "blue-collar-squalor music for stupid people" — has crossed over, as certainly as Thelma did, into something different. Its singers and fans also are different. Now, as I've heard countless DJs assure me, it's okay to say you listen to country music. More radio stations are dedicated to it than to any other kind of music. And they don't offer much in the way of news: they're promulgating not the unrealities of postmodern chaos but the realities of the music itself, realities detailed even more in the videos that have been crucial to its ascendancy. It's about home, but it's also about passion — not music for people, as the title of one of Brooks's 1993 hits has it, "Standing Outside the Fire." Music with common human dimensions, it delves into classic tears-in-my-beer situations, but it frequently has a neotraditional puritanism to it as well. The lines chime as always, but there's more off-rhyme than in the old days. It's less self-serious music, more self-conscious, as songs like George Jones's 1993 tongue-in-cheek "High-Tech Redneck" illustrate. It's nostalgic and sentimental, but it can explore hard-edged issues. In the hyperelectronic age it's acoustic guitars playing simple rhythms anyone can move to. Whatever else it may be, much of it is as New Western as Brooks's Oklahoma accent or the gaudy Bonnardi-style cowgirl gowns and cowboy tuxedos at your local bridal salon.

Writing for *Forbes* in 1992, Lisa Gubernick and Peter Newcomb were quick to pick up on that quality when they keynoted their investigation of the country-music market (in its third boom, the first coming with Johnny Cash in the late 1960s, the second, of course, in the wake of *Urban Cowboy*) with a phrase from James Bowen. Bowen, whose Liberty Records was then distributing Brooks's music, characterized him as "Led Zeppelin meets Roy Rogers."[29] Simultaneously, Priscilla Painton, writing for *Time*, realized that baby boomers, the same heritage-hungry people who were into Western memorabilia and clothing, had "found a cast of artists . . . very much like themselves." The artists were doing music for grown-ups who looked like them and who found themselves hanging out at "country music clubs, where cowboy wannabes pull up in Hondas to dance the Slappin' Leather, the Tush Push or the Texas two-step."[30] The music was nourishing them in their flight from urban madness, their attempt to hold their lives together, their embrace of New Western values like down-to-earth amiability and naturalness.

In the early 1990s a lot of country-music pundits talked about cowboy chic, Stetsons as symbols of sincerity, and the like. But people with heads for business may have had a better fix on the extent to which the hybridizations of neotraditional country music involved the quest for the New West. They understood the backlash against rap and all that, but they also understood, as Susan Holly wrote in *Nation's Business*, that country music was "spreading its Western accent" and that it was repeating a "down-home message" that "people are internalizing" in their "longing for a simpler, more bucolic time." The boom, in her view, was "about more than a change in America's listening habits. . . . For the thousands of new cowboys out there, this is about life."[31]

On the other hand, people perhaps too close to the industry have misunderstood the presence of the West in recent country music. For instance, when Allen St. John, a contributing writer for *Schwann Spectrum*, explored the state of the boom in spring 1993, he accurately recognized the appeal of Brooks's songs about domestic situations; but he was off the mark when he asserted that Brooks's "ballads celebrating . . . the open range are played light, with Brooks well aware of the museum pieces they've become." St. John classified "Night Rider's Lament" as "a touchy-feelie ballad that should have been on the soundtrack for *City Slickers*." So much for in-depth analysis. Maybe those songs are "museum pieces" in a way, but their appeal goes well beyond that. He ignored, among other things, the implications of his own observation that the boom was based not only on "unprecedented crossover sales" but also on the continuing interest of "country's core audience — older folks in the South and West."[32] And there's a final twist: about the time St. John was writing off the West in Brooks's music, Schwann Publications was moving the offices of its editorial staff from Boston to Santa Fe, where most of its other offices were already located.

Thus, though contemporary country music and Western music are distinct in some respects, they are increasingly blurred together in others. Sushil K. Dulai, surveying the career of Randy Travis, draws on his experiential authority in her discussion of the distinction involved:

> "It's funny," Travis notes. "You look back over the years, and there used to be no difference. It was country-and-Western, and that was it. . . . As years have gone on, there's been a change, and now there's a difference between what's called 'country' music and what's considered 'Western.' " Western songs tend to deal with the daily lives of working cowboys, and are almost invariably written by someone who lives that life. The lyrics often are first written as poetry, and the tunes are tempered by acoustic instruments.

True enough — up to a point. The persuasiveness of the man some regard as the single-handed beginning of neotraditional country music, especially when your mind's ear picks up his North Carolina drawl in the sentences above, is unmistakable. Still, this man also grew up raising cattle, has a horse farm outside Nashville (whose stock includes a stallion descended from Trigger), loves Western movies, collects guns, is something of a quick-draw artist, and recorded the Western-music sound track for the 1994 made-for-television movie *Wind in the Wire*. The singer Nashville once declared "too country" has a lot of New Wester in him, even if you can't tell it from most of his music.[33]

But you *can* hear the West, more all the time, in no small amount of country music. In numerous Willie Nelson songs, as CBS's celebration of his sixtieth birthday in May 1993 prolifically demonstrated. In the Western-soul, sagebrush-blues, cowboy-rock, rodeo-pop sound of champion ex-bronc-rider LeDoux. In the Texas sound of Lyle Lovett or of performers like poet-musician Jimmie Dale Gilmore and Tracy Byrd, whose beat synchronizes with the music of Townes Van Zandt and other exponents of that blend of folk, country, blues, rock, God knows what else. In Billy Dean's 1992 hit "Billy the Kid," in which the singer's nostalgia for the innocence of his six-gun childhood hints at a nostalgia for the relative innocence of the real Billy the Kid's own time. In the Western-swing feel, recalling Bob Wills, that runs through Shelby Lynne's 1993 album *Temptation*. In the McMurtry-esque songs of Kevin Welch, particularly on the album that he and his band the Overtones cut in 1992, *Western Beat*. And, of course, elsewhere.

The sound of the West turns up more frequently in the work of male musicians than in that of their female counterparts, though there's no shortage of Western spirit in either case. Furthermore, just as the cowboy attitude in country music has changed with the evolution of the fifth-generation image, so has the cowgirl attitude in that music changed in the feminist age. The latter attitude has two main facets, soft and hard, that have developed through two different — but precariously related — traditions. The soft-facet tradition probably begins with Patsy Montana's Southwest-flavored "I Want to Be a Cowboy's Sweetheart," a 1935 song that Gail Gilchriest proclaims "the first country hit by a woman," a song of the kind that Dale Evans later would sing. The hard-facet tradition arguably begins with Kitty Wells and her 1952 hit "It Wasn't God Who Made Honky Tonk Angels," a shocker at the time, "an 'answer song,' which defended the woman disparaged in an early Hank Thompson hit, 'The Wild Side of Life,' " and prepared the way for Patsy Cline and her no-holds-barred musical offspring.[34]

It's difficult to find a contemporary singer who purely exemplifies the soft-facet tradition (though there are cousins around in the form of unliberated buckle-bunnies [rodeo groupies] and some of the bimbos in boots who make a living as the giggling sidekicks of male country-music DJs), but you can easily find one who's close to a pure — and intensified — example of the hard-facet tradition. Mary-Chapin Carpenter, with a degree from Brown University, fills the bill pretty well. In her torch-and-twang phase, Cline descendant k.d. lang certainly did, her cross-dressing vegetarian lesbianism unnerving a lot of DJs and fans. And Carlene Carter, another member of the legendary family, does when singing numbers in the vein of her 1990 hit "I Fell in Love," which Painton characterizes as "Sylvia Plath at the honky-tonk."[35]

What you're most likely to find, however, is female performers who combine the two traditions of attitude variously — and, again, precariously. Gilchriest discerns such a combination in a musical group called the Dixie Chicks: the members "harbor a healthy respect for the prairie nightingales who came before" and "titled their first album 'Thank Heavens for Dale Evans,' " but they're also tough-minded enough to project a total image that "mixes Dale-Evans glamour with Thelma-and-Louise grit." You encounter that combination, with differing ratios of soft and hard constituents, in contemporary female performers who are glamorous, sexy, and yet also, to use Gilchriest's epithets, "smart, literate, and sometimes topical."[36] More of those duellin' values, and you can hear their interplay palpably in the give-and-take between the texts

Suzy Bogguss as pictured for her Aces album (1991): a rodeo Cinderella with subtexts. (Photo by Peter Darley Miller, courtesy of Capitol Nashville. ℗ 1992 Capitol Nashville)

and subtexts of songs by McEntire, Carpenter, Loveless, Pam Tillis, Trisha Yearwood, Bogguss (especially in her 1993 hit "Hey Cinderella"), and others. Sung in ever-kinkier but family-values-oriented Nashville even by men impersonating such stars, country music—like the film, literature, historiography, and ecology of the New West—is getting feminized. And well it might, for the women in country music have had a rough row to hoe through long-established resistance to their success.

There's no little irony in the fact that the feminine-tough, vulnerable-topical combination represents the classical cowboy ideal of womanhood. Within limits. New Westers show more tolerance for and understanding of gender differences than any previous generation, and they strive for enlightened balances in relationships. Much contemporary country music reflects that new dispensation. But the precariousness abides, so you don't have to look far for a New Wester with an Old Western streak who's irritated about McEntire's support of gun control or edgy about Kathy Mattea's leadership (along with Carpenter, Mark Chestnutt, and many others) in country music's joining the battle against AIDS and K. T. Oslin's view of marriage on her 1993 album *Songs from an Aging Sex Bomb*. Some of the guys wonder what's happening to their Western girls, their shit-kicker redneck women, those images that Keith, Vince Gill, and others conjure for them. Well, if they get their feelings askew over excesses of topicality, they may be detecting the possibility of significant *im*balances, the kind suggested by Connie Schultz Gard when she praises "these country-music boys" for "forever asking if you're going to forgive them for being such swamp sludge"—that is, men who spend too much time drinking, loving, and living in their pickup trucks.[37] If country music is, as it's been called, soul music for white people, then a lot of it now sung—and written—by women is certainly soul music for white women with a New Western cowgirl attitude.

And "white" highlights a curious and troubling datum about country music: almost all of it is written, performed, and listened to by white people, with whose Caucasian world it's dominantly concerned. You may properly complain that these days Nashville carpetbaggers are signing up anybody who can hold a guitar, but they aren't contracting many nonwhites. You can adduce historical reasons for that situation, of course. Nonwhites have seldom been invited into country music, and Charley Pride, to my recollection, is the only nonwhite performer of it who's been decently honored by the industry—most notably by the ACM Pioneer Award in 1994. Also, country music that's insultingly racist is still produced and consumed. Tim McGraw's 1993 single "Indian Outlaw," for instance, however Western in theme, is an appalling babble of stereotypes, but it enjoyed ample airplay. When John Parikhal was asked in 1988 "if country music can do anything to try to appeal to the increasing black, Hispanic and Asian audiences in the United States," he replied with "a blunt yes: 'Don't have all white people singing it.' "[38]

White people continue to do most of the singing in a land where there's no shortage of white people who believe that country music was born full-blown from the head of Hank Williams, the still untoppled king of the genre. Doubtless you could cite examples of black country-blues

Tish Hinojosa as pictured for her Culture Swing *album (1992): adumbrating a fresh hybrid genre of Western country music. (Photo by Alan Pogue, courtesy of Rounder Records)*

artists as a weak opposing argument, and I've heard a little reggae country on the radio and even witnessed what appeared to be cowboy rap on the Black Entertainment channel. But if there's any immediate hope for multiculturalizing country music — and this doesn't pertain much to African or Asian Americans, as far as I know — it's to be found in the West, specifically in Texas, more specifically in the environs of Austin, Nashville's Western counterpart.

I began to ponder that possibility in 1987 when Linda Ronstadt's *Canciones de Mi Padre* came out. Then in 1989, when Tish Hinojosa's *Homeland* was released, I got more intrigued. In the next few years several of her earlier albums were reissued by Watermelon Records in

Austin, followed by a splendid new one in 1992, *Culture Swing*, from Rounder, and I was convinced. Here was an excellent Chicana singer-songwriter from San Antonio who discovered her voice at fifteen and spent, in her words, "a young adulthood carving a path through folk music, to honky-tonks in my own adopted Northern New Mexico, to Nashville, and back to Texas again."[39] There she hit the jackpot with her limpid instrument, singing an original blend of hillbilly, folk, and cowboy songs in either Spanish or English, Tex-Mex or maybe Mex-Tex songs that struck me as adumbrating a fresh hybrid genre, Anglo-Hispanic Western country music. Time will tell how well such music, which tends to be topical and politicized, will fare, but keep an ear on her and on musical peers of hers like David Rodriguez and Santiago Jimenez, Jr. Also, listen to *Ricky Lynn Gregg* (1993), the first big album of country rock by another singer-songwriter from Texas, a mixed-blood Cherokee of the title's name. And look for a string of albums from Lakota singer Steven Emery. Native American country music too may have a trail into the future.

Just as there are differences inside the country-music world—intergenerational, intercultural, and so on—there are, of course, enduring differences, subtle or not, between country music and Western music. Both are involved in resinging the West, and performers like Chestnutt, Travis on *Wind in the Wire*, and team-roper Strait represent significant bridges between the two. Nonetheless, each has evolved through traditions that, in many respects, remain distinct, as Escott and others have made clear. That's perhaps ironic, given the extent to which Western elements and aspects have contributed to the recent country-music boom, suggesting the possibility of a country-Western reunification of a whole other order. And such an order may indeed be forthcoming, but it hasn't arrived quite yet. However you analyze it, "Ghost Riders in the Sky" is a Western, not a country, song; and its tradition is a lot more alive than celestial spooks, for that tradition has been restored along with the cowboy. Unsurprisingly, it consists largely of his music.

Here's another way to talk about how Western music differs from country, an oversimplified one that also suggests their potential for complementarity: Western music tends to be positive about its subjects;

country music, as the joke goes, is usually positive only if you play it backward — then you get your kids back, your wife back, your pickup back.

Here's yet another, related way, also maybe not entirely accurate but cogent, offered by Michele Morris, who, observing that country-Western music "has always been long on country and short on western," explains that "probably that's because Nashville happens to be east of the Mississippi." Observing further that "most cowboys in Nashville are the rhinestone variety," she elaborates:

> How can you tell a country singer from a cowboy singer? It's not easy. . . . But if you listen to the words, you can spot the cowboy every time.
>
> Country singers are far from their country roots. Many of their songs are about the three Ds: drinking, divorce, and depression. Cowboy singers, on the other hand, stay close to the land they love. Their lyrics tell tales of the three Rs: riding, roping, and rodeo. Instead of singing about the mock heroism of truck drivers, they celebrate the quiet courage of early-day trail drivers.

Those differences mesh with others that Morris at least implies. Cowboy songs, even if partly occasioned by boredom in open spaces, reveal a staunch sense of interactive relationship with them, whereas country songs usually seem bound to the more claustrophobic world of domestic tribulations and honky-tonk compensations. "Classic cowboy songs tell stories, rich in detail, of the cowboy's daily work and life," whereas typical country songs, being less rooted, tell less particularized, less immediately engaged stories.[40] Cowboy songs thus tend to have more verses than country songs.

Morris shares additional helpful distinctions or qualifications to boot: not all cowboy songs are of the "Whoopi Ti Yi Yo" variety, and cowboy singers aren't much into the yodeling that cinematic cowboys once thought charming. Also, she helpfully names the names of the paramount contemporary Western singers who "have a musical voice and cowboy soul": Red Steagall, Don Edwards, Michael Martin Murphey ("the evangelist of western music," who's "responsible for convincing Warner Records to put out a new label, Warner Western, that features all three, along with the Sons of the San Joaquin, a California trio," and others), LeDoux, Strait, and Ian Tyson ("a folk singer" — once half of the popular Canadian duo Ian & Sylvia — "turned rancher turned cowboy singer") — all of whom are both "exploring their roots and reinventing cowboy music."[41] Since I've already mentioned LeDoux and Strait, I'd like to discuss briefly those other New Western exploring-reinventing singers.

Cowboy songs at their best stake out a territory somewhere between the gorgeous musicality of Yoakam's "A Thousand Miles from Nowhere" (a "country" song that's puredee Western in mood, almost abstractly so, on his 1993 album *This Time*) and the cow-world narrative specificity of a poem with musical backdrop of the kind that Waddie Mitchell performs on his album *Buckaroo Poet* (1993). The instrumentation is important — but hardly more than the voice and what it tells. The middle-ground balance is well illustrated by Steagall's album *Born to This Land* (1993), which Huck Talbot summarily describes in a review focusing on the "authenticity" of recent Western music: "Red Steagall's sound is the dry, dusty sound of the West Texas plains. It's the songs and poetry of the harsh life on the open range of mesquite and longhorns. The waltzes and ballads contrast with the imagery of tough living." A dancer's perfect blend that results in "an unmistakable beauty."[42]

You encounter that blend — and the sense of authenticity it requires — also in Don Edwards's superbly convincing songs, though a darker tone intrudes here and there. As Escott observes, Edwards "sounds like a rough-hewn Marty Robbins, with a grit in his delivery" — a quality readily apparent on his *Songs of the Trail* (1992) and *Goin' Back to Texas* (1993). And he does his homework too, the liner notes on the former album explicitly "citing which dying cowboy said what to whom." What Escott calls the "tapestry" of that album presents a moving "series of cameos of cowboy life from disparate sources" that's consistent in its interweaving but winds up on the final track, "The Campfire Has Gone Out," in a doubt-ridden corner of New Western consciousness: "It acknowledges that western music is a paean to lost values, and states indirectly that the cowboy value system can't begin to address the intractable litany of problems that beset us."[43] Such songs may evoke the Old West, but their trail leads to both more and less than the contingent comforts of nostalgia — a spot harder than a banker's heart.

But that's not the case if you're headed into Murphey's Marlboro country. Warner Western's wonder boy, he sings (and writes) songs that most fully incarnate the spirit the company seeks to preserve and promote. He's no fan of hillbilly music and knows where he's located on the Yoakam-Mitchell spectrum. If Brooks is *the* New Western country singer, then Murphey has to be *the* New Western Western singer. Of his handful of successful albums, *Cowboy Songs* (1990) and *Cowboy Songs III: Rhymes of the Renegades* (1993) are perhaps the best.

Cowboy Songs includes a copious selection of classics like "Red River Valley" and "Home on the Range," a couple of movie-cowboy songs, and songs written by Murphey, Chick Rains, Tyson, and others. Both history and fun run through the songs (and the liner notes), and Murphey's rendition of "The Streets of Laredo" (also known as "The Cowboy's Lament") — surely, with its centuries-old Irish tune and archetypal cowboy-gone-wrong story, the paradigmatic cowboy song — bears the Western soul into sublime sorrow.

Cowboy Songs III also is something of a musical history lesson, complete with elaborate notes. Ballads about the bad abound: Billy the Kid, Jesse James, Frank James (in a duet with Hal Ketchum), Cole Younger, Belle Starr (in a duet with Bill Miller), and more — even the outlaw horse is represented in "Strawberry Roan" (in a duet with LeDoux). Of the several duets on the album, my hands-down favorite is "Big Iron," which Murphey sings along with the electronically isolated voice of the late Marty Robbins, who made this definitive duel-under-the-Arizona-sun song famous decades ago. Also included is Murphey's own lighthearted, wound-up boot-stomper "The Wild West Is Gonna Get Wilder," which rounds up all manner of legendary Western outlaws and heroes, cowboys, cowgirls, buckle bunnies, and wanna-bes at a contemporary dance hall, finally regaling us with great fiddling and a medley of Western tunes.

But whatever he's singing about, on a recording or at one of his WestFest blowouts or at the Sagebrush Inn in Taos during ski season, Murphey's music is part and parcel of his broader effort to educate the public about the West, Old and New, and its art and culture. In his reliance on what he calls "infotainment," he seems to many people like a New Western Buffalo Bill, a more enlightened and maybe less self-serving avatar of that ancestral showman. Thus Julie L. Semrau argues that he "emphatically echoes Buffalo Bill Cody [when] saying, 'We have to entertain people, make 'em smile and have 'em fall in love with the beauty

Michael Martin Murphey: a New Western Buffalo Bill. (Photo by Melissa Gross, courtesy of Yippy-Yi-Yea*)*

of the West. If they see the beauty in it, then they're going to support it.' "[44] And if you can't see that beauty through his music, your ears are as blind as a rattler in August.

Among the regular performers at Murphey's WestFest are the Sons of the San Joaquin, whose guest voices you can hear on *Cowboy Songs*. With harmonies as smooth as expensive whiskey, they come off as exactly what Escott says they are, "the Sons of the Pioneers made new again," maybe with too much dependence on the predecessor sound of that group and its devotion to songs from Western films.[45] Still, on albums like *A Cowboy Has to Sing* (1992) and *Songs of the Silver Screen* (1993), they do the songs right, with an informed sense of their tradition that's attractive to both young New Westers and older fans of the Sons of the Pioneers in their heyday. Indeed, the appeal of such music, like the desire to scoot a boot or eat barbecue, is scarcely confined to any one generation.

Ian Tyson might be termed Canada's Murphey, except that the epithet doesn't suggest the extent of his popularity in the United States. He has cut a number of albums since he seriously took up ranching (an occupation, side by side with rodeoing, that he grew up with) in Alberta, in addition to singing and songwriting, after the mid-1970s. The albums include the well-received *And Stood There Amazed* (1993), but the one that seems destined to become a classic is *Cowboyography* (1987). It has secured his reputation as, in Talbot's words, "one of the artists most responsible for resurrecting Western sensibilities in contemporary music," one who "has re-invented a unique sound in Western country and folk."[46] The album includes cowboy songs, certainly, but others create what Escott calls a "broadened . . . scope" for them. And Escott notes further factors that account for the success of the album and Tyson's music generally: "His music is contemporary, not simply rooted in a misty-eyed longing to roll back 90 years of history. . . . Tyson [has] found something that's uniquely western rather than Canadian (as if the subcontinent were divided vertically rather than horizontally) and he communicates honestly and intently on every level." What Escott says of the "uniquely western" clicks for anyone who knows anything about Tyson's part of Canada (where Calgary annually hosts a sprawling rodeo); if the music of *Cowboyography* has a "sustained magic," then the essence of it is a quality that ought to be labled New Western.[47]

A singer whom Morris doesn't mention but who also fits significantly into the recent Western-music flurry is Tom Russell. His music, like Tyson's, is contemporary, and that on his *Cowboy Real* (1992) derives from a combination, as Escott nails it, of "his western background" and "his love of cowboy and Tex-Mex border lore." Such music is, for Escott, easier to categorize than Russell's earlier recorded work and thus may save him from being "so marginalized." The point here isn't just that the music is good but also that it's Western and thereby has the same "core appeal" that "the producers of the film *City Slickers* latched onto," an appeal that's in part "a symptom of the current wave of disillusionment" and in part the expectable correlate of "an attempt to discover a new set of values from what is imagined to be a shared communal heritage on the range."[48]

In spite of the strength of that appeal, however, Escott predicts that "it'll still be an uphill battle trying to sell this music to country radio." But you do hear more of it on country stations these days, and he hints at the possibility that their "rigid formatting" might open up to Western music, just as Warner did in producing Murphey and friends and in promising to produce "new music from veteran Red Steagall and Native American Bill Miller" and "to include Hispanic western music." Even if those stations remain stubborn, it's not unreasonable, "if Warner succeeds" (and I believe it will), to "look for Capitol Western, RCA Western, PolyGram Western, MCA Western, and yes, Sony Western."[49]

There are other signs that a revolution may be imminent. Membership in the Western Music Association (WMA), formed in 1989, is on the rise. TNN has become more interested in Western music — witness the network's special in September 1993, "The Music of the Wild West," which used Old Tucson as the setting for songs intertwined with late-nineteenth-century history. Also, there's more such music available to children. See, among other possibilities, *The Book of Kids Songs 2: Another Holler-Along Handbook* (1988), by Nancy Cassidy and John Cassidy, which is packaged with a cassette and contains a number of Western tunes. And, of course, the humorous Western-music group Riders in the Sky is enjoying a popularity bonanza, with over a dozen albums out, concerts on the road, frequent appearances on "Austin City Limits" and other television shows, the "Riders Radio Theater" series on National Public Radio, and a 1992 book from Gibbs Smith that shares in print the group's weird Western world of close harmony, dramas of odd and corny characters, and fifth-generation philosophy of the Cowboy Way (which plugs white-hat values and opposes sundry postmodern villainies).

But if the Western-music revolution starts to seem slow in coming, get ahold of some CDs, cassettes, or even LPs of Robbins, Autry, Ritter, the Texas Tornados, and — well, you know who they are. A lot of plump collections of vintage stuff are out, not the least of which is *Old-Time Cowboy Songs*, a 1988 anthology, edited by Hal Cannon, of more than fifty songs, most composed between 1880 and 1930, with cassette. Or go buy Emmylou Harris's 1994 album *Songs of the West.* But the revolution will arrive whether you listen — and learn to sing, maybe all over again — or not.

And if you can't sing, then dance.

And if you think dancin' to the Western beat ain't the thing to do, then you've missed Snoopy two-steppin' (slow, slow, quick, quick) while stone-footed Charlie Brown looks on. And you must have passed up the halftime celebration at the 1994 Super Bowl in Atlanta (the Dallas Cowboys and Buffalo Bills again), an event that boasted more viewers internationally than any other anything ever broadcast on television: during "Rockin' Country Sunday" some 2,000 Western-dressed dancers flooded the portable stage and playing field and scooted their boots to the live sound of performers Clint Black, Tanya Tucker, the Judds, and Travis Tritt while the stadium audience went bonkers.

But that's a bunch of pale abstractions compared to actual dancing, which is better exercise — and friendlier — than skipping through the neighborhood with dumbbells in your hands or shuffling your legs back and forth on a walking machine. If you don't know how, you can rent or buy instructional videos. Or someone at a dance club can teach you.

Still, let your fringe hang straight just a spell while I talk briefly about the when, why, who, where, what, and how of this New Western epiphenomenon.

First, the *when.* The growth trajectory of what more and more people now call country-*Western* dancing rises a little more sharply than those for the music and general interest in Westerniana and lags somewhat behind them — the support system of sound, clothing, and cultural atmosphere had to be functioning before the dance craze could occur. But all the trajectories were in unison once the 1990s got under way. Though I've heard the contention that the clubs are simply descendants of discos (and many are converted discos) and that the dances, especially line dancing in its hundreds of variations, are simply disco dances with a rustic syncopation, I can't buy it much. There's little nostalgia for the dull 1970s involved. Regardless of the urban settings of a lot of the clubs, their whole purpose is to offer an alternative to the urban ambience of discos. Though the clientele consists partly of people who are fed up with discos, singles bars, and the like, it includes also a different crowd of people who may not have danced since the 1950s, if ever before. A different attitude is displayed. And line dancing itself, maybe postmodern in its partnerlessness, appears to derive more from floor-hogging dances like the Latin American conga than it does from any of the leisure-suited twitching of the mid-1970s. And so on. Any culturologist who's intrigued by the fact that the star of *Saturday Night Fever* and the star of *Urban Cowboy* are the same person, an icon suggesting that the present craze amounts to nothing more than a synthesis that some call country disco, had better emote his or her theorizing through a smile.

The *why* of the dance craze has to do with many of the New Western impulses I've already discussed: a desire to get back to rural basics, an interest in casual colorfulness, a need to identify with cowboy heritage, and the like — impulses that in their more precious versions send Old Westers into conniptions. It may be true to an extent that, as conventional wisdom has it, real cowboys don't do line dancing (and don't like its reliance on recorded music or its militaristic coordination), but a spate of wanna-bes sure do. One reason is that both singles and couples can join in on the dips, bumps, hitches, kicks, and turns, adding their own nuances. Another may be, as Guy Garcia submits, that "with its emphasis on old-fashioned manners and clean fun, the country line is square dancing for the '90s, the perfect pastime for the chummy, cuddly, slightly corny Clinton years," a trend that "was already gathering steam when Billy Ray Cyrus's 1992 hit *Achy Breaky Heart* spawned a line dance called the Achy Breaky." Garcia quotes enthusiasts on the absence of drugs, fights, and even alcohol at typical clubs. Some neopuritanism may perfume these reborn honky-tonks, but don't be fooled: there's a full dose of good old-fashioned passion at work in all those whirling skirts and tight jeans, some of which move (Garcia claims, though I've never seen it) "to cuts by M. C. Hammer and Madonna," maybe other sexual compulsives.[50]

Nobody should be surprised to find at the clubs something of what the female protagonist in Elizabeth Tallent's short story "Why I Love Country Music" finds at a place called the Line Camp:

> The cowboys, leaning against the left-hand wall as you go in, look you over with the barest movement of the eye, the eyelid not even contracting, the pupil dark through the haze of cigarette smoke, the

> mouth downcurved, the silent shifting of the pelvis against the wall by which one signals a distant quickening of erotic possibility. The band is playing "Whiskey River." My white buckskin cowboy boots — I painted the roses myself, tracing the petals from a library book — earn me a measure of serious consideration, the row of Levi-shaded pelvises against the wall swiveling slightly (they can swagger standing still, for these are the highest of their art, O men) as I go by.[51]

She soon dances, with the one she came with, finally more intimately in a more intimate place, an old mine. The clubs aren't just about Disney dancing. They're about men and women who like to move to music and watch and feel each other doing so — as Garth and friends understand well enough. And even if the dancers don't use illegal drugs and carry weaponry, some of them might want a smoke or a real drink every now and then.

Who are those dancers? They're a democratic group in regard to age, so you see young people pumped up wet-rawhide tight with hormones as well as old folks smiling at the chance to shake a hoof one more time. You see rednecks, white-collar yuppies, real cowboys with Tallented pelvises, drop-dead-gorgeous cowgirls with their phone numbers tooled into their belts, beer bellies, fallen butts, couples, singles, few people with two left feet. They dress Western, in some cases with extraordinary individuality. But this isn't a multicultural scene: it's mostly white people dancing to white people's music. Still, that exclusionary situation may be changing, slowly, just as it is in the country-music industry.

Where are those dancers? At the clubs, by and large. No coastal vogue that hicks are gradual to pick up on but a heartland happening that's spread from the center outward, these clubs as thick as prickly pears along the San Miguel Creek, maybe with names that recall song titles, have interiors as Western as the exteriors in country-music videos: pine-paneled walls, beer signs (for Clint Black Lite, say), mounted buffalo heads, lariats, photographs of Western landscapes and personalities, wagon wheels, pool tables, Winchester cartridge boxes, maybe a stuffed "jackalope" — paraphernalia aplenty, replete with a mechanical bull and a *big* ol' stretch of wood. Like the Beaumont Club in Kansas City, Toolie's Country in Phoenix, Mama's Country Showcase in Atlanta, or the Crazy Horse Saloon in Santa Ana, California — or Billy Bob's in Fort Worth, at two acres of enclosed space the hugest of all (so

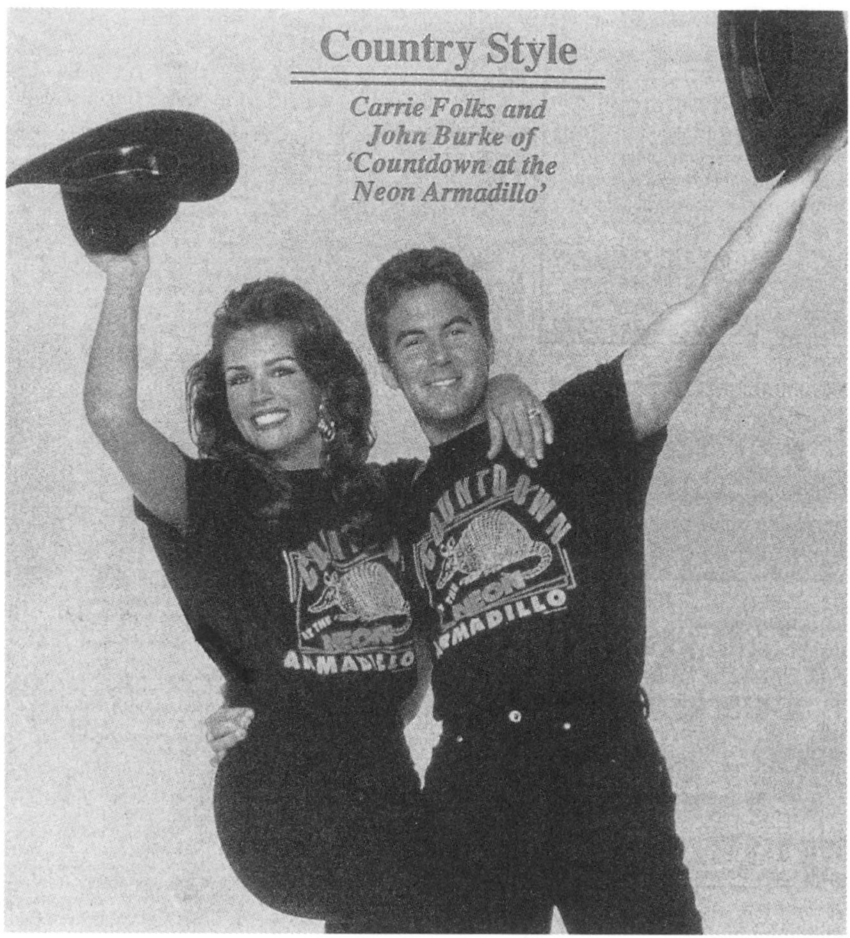

ABC's "Countdown at the Neon Armadillo" debuted as a weekly series in September 1993, at first emphasizing the music, then, increasingly, the dancers. (Courtesy of Print Marketing Concepts)

far), a converted open-air cattle barn at the historic local stockyards that the ACM voted Country Nightclub of the Year not long ago and that has been featured in several movies (including Bobby Roth's 1988 *Baja Oklahoma*) and in its own television series, "Billy Bob's Country Countdown." Scooters swarm on television shows like TNN's "Club Dance." Well, wherever those places are, they aren't drive-by locations: they're *destinations* — where the long-necks are cold, the stories short and sweet, the floors busy.

What do the dancers do there? The pony swing, the horseshoe, the

Pam Sosa and Don Doyle shake a hoof at the New Country Tavern in Olathe, Kansas. (Photo by David Pulliam, courtesy of the Kansas City Star*)*

cowboy hustle, the tush push, the slappin' leather, more and more new dances all the time to the tunes of Brooks, Loveless, Brooks & Dunn, Carpenter, Diamond Rio, Yoakam, on and on. Invent your own new rhythmic maneuvers.

Which brings me to the *how* part. There are dos and don'ts, some hard and fast, some subject to change with fashion. Men should wear (stacked) jeans (Levis look sexier, leaner, and more athletic in line, but Wranglers let you move better — as rodeo riders know), never overalls or polyester outfits. Women ought to go for some frills but not a Minnie Pearl getup. Dance clubs aren't haylofts in Arkansas. Broomstick skirts twirl well on the turns, which fringe too can accentuate. Women who come in full skirts — mid-calf length, to cover the boot tops, or mid-thigh length — announce their willingness to dance. There's nothing wrong with cold-shoulder and off-the-shoulder tops, either. Let your partner have a good look at you. And it's fine for men to get flashy, as long as they don't sport gold chains. They should wear Western shirts (cotton, silk, or satin) a size too large to emphasize their shoulders and let them reach over their heads easily and buckles that won't act shy. T-shirts don't make it, really, for men or women. Matching his-her outfits are viable but may overstate the politics of possessiveness. Women need to think about their undergarments, given the skirt-lifting effect of twirls. Men should never sport baseball-style caps, backward or otherwise, and women worried about "hat hair" should leave their head covers in the closet. And tuck your wrist wear away — or a fervent grasp will tear it off — though boot bracelets or chokers are okay.

Also, don't forget terpsichorean style. In that regard, here are a few tips from Patsy Swayze, mother of Patrick (himself no mean dancer) and the woman whom René E. Riley (against whose advice I checked my own) classifies as the leading expert on country-Western dancing: "Make the dance and the music become one. . . . Don't dance the same step at the same time in every dance. Be individual. Don't be a show-off, but make certain moves stand out. Develop your own style. . . . Dance it the way you feel it."[52]

It's time to warm some wood. Back to back and buckle to buckle.

And the cowboy beat goes on and on and on and on.

I live not in myself, but I become
Portion of that around me; and to me
High mountains are a feeling, but the hum
Of human cities torture. — Lord Byron, *Childe Harold's Pilgrimage*

I ask your indulgence if I sometimes speak in terms of my personal experience, feelings, and values. . . . In doing so, I shall be trying to define myself as well as my native region. — Wallace Stegner, "Living Dry"

THE NEW WEST: A SENSE OF PLACE

Now saddle up for more literal New Westering, an excursion that entails brief visits to selected places. Not a comprehensive trip, just a traveling west across meridians to representative spots that, for me, vividly illustrate the New West. Some are Old Western sites with New Western spin on them. Some are emblematically New Western. Some may be as much bad news as good, admonishing us about the postmodern consumption of the West, revealing the loss as well as the profit from tourism and development. All have something to say about the New West, about moving through or to it, about exploring a still strange land as well as searching for a familiar home. But, to borrow from T. S. Eliot's poem "The Love Song of J. Alfred Prufrock," before we "go and make our visit," we need to ask, against the urging of the poem's speaker, "What is it?" We need some cold-light-of-day analysis of New Westering.

First, let me return to Susan Stewart's *On Longing*. Just as she cautions about "the false promise of restoration," so too she passes on sobering reflections concerning the "other side" of restoration, "separation," in "the uses of the souvenir." According to her, the souvenir, a token of remembrance of having been somewhere, is invested with meaning through nostalgia, a "process of . . . reconstruction" whereby "the present is denied and the past takes on an authenticity of being, an authenticity which, ironically, it can achieve only through narrative" — stories, in other words. Nostalgia is a paradoxical emotion, what she calls "a sadness without an object, a sadness which creates a longing that of necessity is inauthentic because it does not take part in lived experience." Nostalgia yearns for a past that's "always absent," and it "wears a distinctly utopian face, a face that turns toward a future-past," an imaginative "re-union" of "nature and culture" in, ironically, "a utopia where authenticity suffuses both word and world." And here's the crux of the relations among nostalgia, authenticity, and the souvenir:

> The double function of the souvenir is to authenticate a past or otherwise remote experience and, at the same time, to discredit the present. The present is either too impersonal, too looming, or too alienating compared to the intimate and direct experience of contact which the souvenir has as its referent. This referent is authenticity. . . . The nostalgia of the souvenir plays in the distance between the present and an imagined, prelapsarian experience, experience as it might be "directly lived." The location of authenticity becomes whatever is distant to the present time and space; hence we can see the souvenir as attached to the antique and exotic.

Furthermore, the antique "always bears the burden of nostalgia" for a particular kind of "experience impossibly distant in time: the experience of the family, the village, the firsthand community." It's also "linked to . . . the pastoral" and not infrequently promotes an "aestheticization of rural life."[1]

Now, clearly, those reflections illuminate the delusions that may be tangled in attempts at restoring the Golden West by personally collecting it, preserving it in museums, and so on — or in wishing for a utopian New Western future. Also, they gloss tellingly the motivations for visiting, revisiting, or moving to the West, for trying to construct the past "from a set of presently existing pieces." In terms of such motivations, "the function of the tour is the estrangement of objects — to make what is visible, what is surface, reveal a profound interiority." Writing about travel, by that logic, "functions to miniaturize and interiorize those distanced experiences which remain outside contemporary lived relations," much as souvenirs "allow the tourist to appropriate, consume, and thereby 'tame' the cultural other."[2] Of course, if you move *to* the West, rather than just through it, without overcoming such estrangement and distance, then you will remain as alienated *in* an interior world as you are alienated *from* whatever exterior world you yearn to flee.

This is subtle stuff but important as a warning to anyone unself-consciously determined to experience the New West. It's a kind of warning echoed by Stephen Tatum, who's analyzed the ideology specific to the West much more than Stewart. In a 1989 study "of the catalogues published by the (at least until recently) highly successful Banana Republic Travel and Safari Clothing Company," which have Western wear among their eclectic offerings, he discusses "the connection between adventure and shopping." Both involve "pursuing and eventually acquiring some remarkable object of desire poised tantalizingly on or beyond the horizon" by which "we hope to ensure that the future will become in reality what we only dream of in the present." Both are motivated by a drive "to supply something that is lacking, to correct a problem occurring at 'home.' " Focusing on traveling, Tatum elaborates: "Traveling for pleasure locates the 'real' in another place and time, somewhere beyond the familiar boundaries of everyday existence. . . . A *true* safari will somehow put one in confrontation with an authentic existence — authentic not only in the sense of 'real' or 'genuine' but also in the sense of a *substantial* ground of being." Traveling, as he nutshells it, "constitutes a quest for a sacrament which will restore the values of intensity and excitement to a world grown grey."[3] Though it's not his direct intention, he could easily be writing about New Westering as both geographical and mental traveling in quest of such a restoration.

But wait. There's more. Tatum comes even closer to, as it were, home when he argues that "the whole syndrome of adventure — experiencing life as an authentic adventure, writing and reading about such adventures, and wearing clothing marketed with the myth of adventure — illuminates the particular alienation characteristic of a particular society." What New Wester isn't out to escape the alienating jumble of present society through his or her Western lifestyle, reading, and such? What one doesn't seek "a Cinderella-like transfiguration of the self through the consumption of 'adventure' " in Western forms? What one doesn't rely on the power of Western clothing "to foster the ability . . . to imagine oneself as a character from an adventure novel, even when performing the prosaic tasks of everyday life"? Or go west "to retrieve a sense of what an authentic existence would look and feel like"? Or want the West to "become made over into a Home" and thus, unlike a catalog, more than "symbolically triumph over the discontinuous nature of postmodern experience"?[4]

Tatum's point isn't that there's something flat wrong with "the whole syndrome of adventure" but that it lodges detrimental possibilities. The commodification of adventure can "deflect attention" from the hard realities of the world that call for deliberative action. Searching for adventure, especially as a "private redemption," can "weaken the sense of historicity," and with "the draining out of historicity" comes "the substitution of the image" — a reversion, perhaps, to a private version of Old Western History. Adventure as Tatum treats it is necessarily part of "the 'popular,' " which he, paralleling Stewart, says "can be characterized as a bourgeois production which appropriates the images and values from proletarian and ethnic Others so as to construe 'safe' narratives or iconographies of such alternative or residual cultures' existence."[5] To tell stories or make pictures that trivialize cowboys and Indians, turning their respective cultures into toys, for instance, with the result that the West is never really reached — because of the intervention of distance mediated by such stories, pictures, preconceptions.

Nonetheless, as we have seen, that mediation has governed attitudes toward the West all along. Most critically, it has defined how immigrants to the region have perceived and used it as a place, as what Leonard

Lutwack in *The Role of Place in Literature* calls "inhabitable space," a kind of space that he explores at length, through its history and literary representation, in his book.[6] Appropriately, the American West constitutes one of his main concerns.

As Lutwack formulates it, "The relation of people to land is finally a product of the interaction of three factors: the basic physical nature of the environment, the preconceptions with which it is approached by its inhabitants, and the changes man makes in it." The preconceptions merit Lutwack's sustained interest, particularly in his discussion of the imagery of America in its national literature, a discussion that, implicitly or explicitly, pertains mostly to the West. That is to say, the way European settlers conceived America is generally repeated in the way Eastern settlers conceived the West—an aspect of the West-as-America paradigm, which itself recaps the typical pattern of European conquest. In both cases the invaded wilderness in its pristine vastness was seen as a domain to be converted "into a copy" of the settlers' places of origin or to be plundered for what it could yield and then left behind. In both cases the land promised "the renewal of individual, family, and society," and the "abstract, unlocalized ideal" of such a renewal "was more important than the actual place in which it was to be realized." Immigrants into the West, like those into the New World, "were thus forced to conceive of" it "before experiencing it." Once there, "they continued to hold onto their preconceptions, which duly found their way into the 'official' ideology spread by mass education, political oratory, and advertising." In the case of the West, as in the case of the New World, the preconceptions were animated—much as they still too frequently are—by "vague expectations . . . attached to the three principal images of the New World [or the West] as a garden, a wilderness, and a place of treasure." Eden, wilderness, Eldorado. "Each ideal," according to Lutwack, "prompted a different treatment of the land: the garden wanted cultivation, the wilderness taming, the place of treasure quick consumption. Each was basically opposed to the others: the garden encroaches on the wilderness, the wilderness in time reclaims the garden, and Eldorado ever extends its domain over the garden for its produce and over the wilderness for its timber, furs, ore, and oil." And the economic implications of these yet-nurtured ideals remain poignant as Jeffersonian agrarianism has turned into agribusiness, "romantic primitivism" into return-to-nature tourism on a grand scale, and "folk capitalism" into ecologically unconscionable extraction, industrialism, and real-estate development.[7]

The three ideals may be "abstract" and "unlocalized," but their consequences for the West have been and are concrete and local enough. Thus the Spanish quest for the abstract gold of some nonspecific Eldorado is followed by gold rushes, silver mining, drilling for oil, timber harvesting, on and on. Such exhaustive extractions create "abandoned places," with "the abandoned mining town," which Lutwack terms "the symbolical end-product of American Eldorado," serving as "the prototype of other money-making places that have outlived their promise." American literature and history are shot through with stories of how, "in the Eldoradan use of land, both land and the people engaged in its exploitation are wasted or reduced to some infernal condition." Moreover, the "millennial hopes in the form of an agrarian society" — which survive "even today in America's last frontier, Alaska" — have fared no better. "The garden image faltered," as Lutwack puts it, "because it had not taken account of American geography, the character of American settlers, and the economics of agriculture," all of which "turned farming . . . into big business, successful farmers into entrepreneurs, and unsuccessful farmers into farm labor or city dwellers." The myth of the garden didn't foresee the extent to which pastoral fantasies would lead to competition with the cattle industry, to the disappointments of suburbia or the "deep disillusionment" occasioned by dust bowls and other disasters, at last to an age when "the possibility of 'westering' in the old style is but a sentimental dream, for there is no more land to settle on." And gradually "the wilderness image" — maybe "more dominant" than the other two "in an over-civilized time, when the revival of primitive experience seems desirable" — has encouraged such passions for travel and recreation that they, ironically, "now must be added to extractive industries as rabid consumers of wilderness."[8] How long before the West has not only ghost towns and ghost farms (and ghost ranches) but ghost wilds as well?

Tourism seems out to devour the little that's left of anything like the real West. It's not surprising that Native Americana figure in the business of providing "primitive experience," for "the Indian is the white man's link with the wilderness spirit" (a recognition that helps us understand the neglect of African Americans in Western narratives —

they have an "association with agriculture" rather than with adventure). In the West, as elsewhere, massive tourism is partly a consequence of postmodern placelessness, a condition in which "being in motion is an alternative for staying put in a disagreeable place." But that motion nonetheless operates to fulfill a "need for engaging places," especially "the few unique places that are still to be found," as Lutwack explains:

> The passion for tourism is the attempt of people to acquire a commodity in short supply, unspoiled and truly distinguished places. And truly distinguished places, for many people, are those that are associated with a supposed golden past in distant lands. Catering to these needs is a lucrative business in a world becoming more and more uniform in appearance. . . . Ironically, tourism itself destroys the very places it seeks out. . . . When notable places cannot be made available, they may be faked.

So you get the Acropolis "perishing . . . from excessive use," Cancun overbuilt with accommodations to the degree that it's all hotels, and another Western theme park (witness Disney World's latest annexed attraction) or restored frontier town — though, as Lutwack notes, speaking of Marcel Proust and his literary quest for the past, "the re-creation of places is essential" if we want "to recapture the past" and all that it can mean.[9]

Still, despite the destruction stimulated by the now profoundly ironic ideals and images of Eldorado, Eden, and wilderness, there may be hope. Lutwack speculates that in the future "the sense of failure and guilt may possibly do more to strengthen ties with the land than the pride of achievement. The old images of the land no longer apply, but new expectations, more reasonable than the old, may be forming from their ruins." Like numerous New Westers, he applauds the development, which he sees beginning in literature earlier than in science, of "a new sensibility to environment in preparation for a time that appears now to be the start of the age of ecology." You can't go back to Eden, he temperately argues, "but respect for earth's remaining beauty and for the health of its soil, air, and water may be revived out of the heritage of the past and refined with the new knowledge of earth sciences." That project, he predicts in his 1984 book, "will be a service for literature to perform in the immediate future."[10] As we learned earlier, no literature is trying harder to perform that service than the recent literature of the

West, most notably its nature writing, because no literature is more alert to the problems attendant on its region's old images and to the urgent need to engender new ones "more reasonable than the old."

There's no avoiding images, their mediation of the relations between humankind and environment. However we categorize them — literary, historical, philosophical, economic — we're stuck with them as essential to human consciousness. Be that as it may, the new images of the West, though jockeying in their evolving variousness, at a minimum share a common motivation: to represent the region more fully and accurately on its own terms.

A. Carl Bredahl, Jr., like Lutwack, recognizes the limitations of the old images, the need for new ones, and the role of literature in providing them:

> The land-based economies of the Great Plains, in contrast to the commercial economies of the East, grew out of lives dependent upon the land and subject to its whims and characteristics. Confronting an environment of extravagant size, weather, and configuration, the western imagination had finally to discard assumptions of imposing self and enclosing landscape, efforts that in the West met inevitably with disaster. . . . Farmers and ranchers ultimately had to ask what the land would tolerate. What therefore developed in the place of the effort to impose and reshape was the perception of the need to realign assumptions about an individual's relation to the land. Much western writing is the story of that realignment.

That story may occur more extensively and pressingly in recent Western literature, but it's been around awhile. In *Roughing It* (1872), for instance, Mark Twain tells a version of it in discerning "that his western experience tested traditionally held assumptions" and in his less humorous presentation of "more troubling thoughts on the discrepancies between dream and reality." And many other writers have portrayed how pioneers transported to the West ideas and values that, in Bredahl's view, encouraged a vain effort to encompass and control Western space and left them "cheated, diseased, and disillusioned."[11]

If some Western writers, like Twain, have an analytical fix on the limitations of old images and the need for new ones, there are also writers whose works dramatically instantiate touristic attitudes shaped by either habituated assumptions or a fresh attentiveness. Classic examples, for Bredahl, are Francis Parkman, who wrote a well-known account, *The Oregon Trail*, of his 1846 trip west to study Indians, and Lewis Garrard, Parkman's junior by five years, who wrote *Wah-to-yah and the Taos Trail*, an account of his 1846 trip west, one inspired not by any desire to "study" the West but by a need to really experience it.

When Parkman, a New Englander and something of a misanthrope just graduated from Harvard Law School, departed from St. Louis in spring 1846, he was infused with an "initial commitment to 'curiosity and amusement.'" Bredahl admits that "to a certain extent that seems a valid approach, for the narrator comes to appreciate, even love, aspects of the land and its inhabitants. But the overarching imagination in *The Oregon Trail* linguistically encloses itself from involvement with the physical experience." The narrator sees "through romantic lenses," idealizes "in terms comfortable to the eastern mind," and — though "Parkman's book is wonderfully rich in detail and experience" — illustrates "the enclosed stance of an individual who came West in order to reinforce eastern superiority."[12] One of *those* guys, in other words.

Garrard, on the other hand, wasn't so distanced from the people in the West he met and, by and large, liked. Born in Cincinnati, he "brought attitudes of mind from the then western state of Ohio, attitudes of openness and receptivity to the physical environment." Having read John C. Frémont's account of his 1842–1843 tour through the Rocky Mountains, he was "drawn by the excitement of the West." Thus, whereas "Parkman's judgmental response allows the reader to maintain the comfort of intellectual distance, . . . Garrard's narrative . . . conveys the experience of a strikingly new world." It's a picture painted by an individual whose "mind had been stretched."[13] Through his narrator, Garrard, in spite of deprivations and even danger at the hands of Indians, emerges as a person who, though he might be judged naïve, knows the West more as it actually is than a control freak like Parkman could ever imagine.

In the spirit of Garrard, then, let me proceed, maybe from time to time invoking a small measure of a more Parkman-like studiousness if it seems appropriate.

In the summers of 1983 and 1985, as well as in February of the latter year, Dayton Duncan, a New Englander, traveled in a Volkswagen camper from St. Louis west along the route of Meriwether

Lewis and William Clark to the mouth of the Columbia River and back again. In *Out West: An American Journey*, he tells the story of what's actually "three separate journeys: Lewis and Clark's in 1804–1806, mine in 1983 and 1985, and the American West's during the years in between." His purpose was "to compare what they encountered so many years ago with what I saw and experienced." He pursued it with a "sense of urgency" not unlike that revealed in Lewis and Clark's prolific journals and with worry that "by the time of the expedition's bicentennial in the year 2004" the trail he describes in his book "may be vastly different . . . and another way of life — the life of small-town, agricultural America as we know it — may have vanished."[14]

At the beginning of his account, Duncan writes of his eastern approach to St. Louis on the interstate. There's a traffic jam, giving him time to consult his map for the spot where Lewis and Clark began their trip and to reflect: "The route I plan to take — and the spirit in which it is followed — will be the same as theirs. Nearly everything else will be vastly different." His concern, therefore, "is not the Northwest Passage," Jefferson's great water-based hope for commerce with the Pacific Ocean as well as other goals, "but the passage of time." When Duncan does find the spot, "at the mouth of the Wood River in Illinois," no one is about but some taciturn fishermen. After that anticlimax he drives south to where he can contemplate the 630-foot Gateway Arch on the other side of the Mississippi, an engineering marvel conceived by its designer, Eero Saarinen, "as a spectacular 'Gateway to the West.' " The view from East St. Louis sticks in Duncan's mind:

> The Arch frames the skyscrapers of St. Louis, a gleaming city on the hill bathed in twilight colors. East St. Louis itself — with its vacant industrial buildings, high crime, high unemployment, ghetto-like homes, and palpable feeling of desperation — tells me that some of the promises [of westering America] have been broken. . . . The rainbow is pretty, but made of stainless steel. The pot of gold is not in East St. Louis. It is across the Mississippi River, through the rainbow Arch, and somewhere out West.

Thus does he recall the millennial hope invested in a West in which he would have many memorable and educating experiences, but after them, back at the Gateway Arch, he would conclude that "the myth industry is the only one that has always boomed and never gone bust."[15]

During the 1993 spring-to-fall sesquicentennial celebration of the opening of the Oregon Trail, thousands of people walked, rode horses, or endured the jolting and pitching of wagons for at least a portion of a re-created journey from Independence, Missouri, just east of Kansas City, through Kansas, Nebraska, Wyoming, and Idaho to northwestern Oregon. Following a trail marked by the countless graves of less successful ancestors, exhibits, and festivals, those would-be pioneers got a taste of what overland travel was like for the 875 men, women, and children who in April and May 1843 headed for the Willamette River Valley, "the land of milk and honey." They were out for "reliving history" through "rugged authenticity," as one reporter put it.[16]

But those folks couldn't have gained more insight into the hardships of a journey repeated, before the transcontinental railroad, by half a million people than I did from one anecdote. It was related to me in fall 1993 by James J. Fisher, who earlier that year had done a series of stories on the Oregon Trail for the *Kansas City Star.* The essence was a conclusion reached by Pete Peters, a man from Roscoe, Nebraska, who has long collected old bottles on the Oregon Trail: most of them once contained liquor.

Many people believe that St. Joseph, Missouri, an hour north of Independence, is a sensible place to begin a tour of the Old West. There are several museums, including one that's part of the Pony Express National Memorial, which commemorates the town as the starting point of the horse-borne-mail route to Sacramento, California, and had a grand opening in April 1993 that drew 5,000 visitors. Jesse James's home is one of the museums, and inside you can see a hole in the wall supposedly made by the bullet that passed through James's head after leaving the barrel of Robert Ford's Smith & Wesson. The gun, after elaborate authentication, sold later that April for $165,000.

Whatever your sightseeing activities in Missouri, if you follow the Oregon Trail west from Independence, through Lawrence, Kansas, and on toward Topeka, you'll find that it splits into two routes at the edge of Shawnee County, five or six miles east of Topeka. The two routes pass through the northern and southern extremities of the city and reunite in the northwestern part of the county. Between the two, a little over halfway through the split portion, lies the Kansas Museum of History. A wealth of Midwesterniana is housed there, from prehistoric Indian artifacts to nineteenth-century clothing and weaponry. Outside, near the entrance, tourists gape at Lumen Martin Winter's monumental piece *The Great White Buffalo*:

> Before them thunders a sculpture, tons of white
> marble barely holding an Indian who rides
> close beside this great rare creature, the blunt end
> of his spear just touching it, as horse and man —
> heads, mane and hair, thrown back alike — know the same
> moment of spirit, mouths open wide to the sky.[17]

If you take Highway 75 north out of Topeka, you can get to Lincoln, Nebraska, in less than three hours. There you will find, at the University of Nebraska, the Center for Great Plains Studies. Founded in 1976, it promotes fuller understanding of the Great Plains through annual symposia, impressive collections of Western art and writing, two journals and other publications, and teaching and research programs. Like its sister centers at Emporia State University in Kansas and the University of Regina in Saskatchewan, Canada, it's dedicated to helping people learn, in Carolyn J. Mooney's phrasing, "to respect the all-important weather, the deep-rooted sense of community, the isolation, and the subtle beauty of the land" and "to develop . . . 'the plains eye' " for natural detail. And the indifferent summon up an expectable attitude: "As for all those drivers tearing down Interstate 80 bound for more conspicuous destinations: Maybe, some Plains lovers here suggest, it's best they just keep driving."[18] But in the age of the New West, thanks partly to the work of the center, more and more of those drivers slow down, pull off, and look.

If you follow Interstate 70 west from Topeka, you can reach Abilene in about an hour and a half. There you can visit Old Abilene, a reconstructed version of the first cattle boomtown, at the end of the Chisholm Trail. It consists of buildings that are relocated and rebuilt originals from the town's heyday (the years from 1867 to 1872, when several million head of cattle were shipped, very profitably, east on the Kansas Pacific Railroad) or replicas that serviceably duplicate originals: the log church, the school, the jail, the Merchant's Hotel, the Alamo Saloon (which Wild Bill Hickok made his headquarters when he was called in to clean up the cowboy anarchy), and so on. Cancan girls will bounce their cans and gunfighters shoot their guns for you. Also, you can buy souvenirs and ponder their psychocultural vibrations.

For a change of pace from Old Western reconstruction to New Western constructive thinking, take Interstate 70 west half an hour to Salina. Just southeast of town, on the banks of the Smoky Hill River, you'll encounter the Land Institute. Established by innovative agronomist Wes Jackson in the mid-1970s, it's dedicated to research into sustainable agriculture. Jackson wants to free agriculture from the destructive practices that homogenize farming and encourage dependence on bureaucratic government. Appalled at the results of an industrialized agriculture that has tried relentlessly to fulfill a Jeffersonian ideal in a dry region, he promotes "a second settling of West," one that would get it right this time by husbanding the natural rather than the monetary economy. The function of his institute is to help Westerners be what he calls "homecomers." He wants them to face their mistakes and "get native"—his rendition of the home theme, articulated at length in his book *Becoming Native to This Place* (1994). Like Wendell Berry, he believes they don't yet know what they've done because they don't know what they've undone.[19]

As science writer Rex Buchanan puts it, Jackson "wants to reinvent agriculture by mimicking the prairie, by mixing perennial prairie grasses and flowers that can be harvested like so much wheat or corn." That sort of "polyculture" doesn't require the annual planting that most conventional crops do, so soil erosion can be minimized; and its diversity works to "keep down weeds, disease, and pests, and thus negate the need for pesticides and herbicides."[20] The Land Institute, which opens each spring with a Prairie Festival, thus strives to create a Western agriculture for the future based on nature's own agriculture of the past. Wilderness is hard to mimic, but Jackson is a resolute man: he may redo what's been undone — with help from his friends.

Some of Jackson's friends may be found in the Flint Hills of Chase County in a little town two hours southeast of Salina and just off Interstate 35.

A few dozen people live in Matfield Green, Kansas, which once had a population of 160. Jackson is out to revitalize the place. Yet another Western recipient of a generous MacArthur Fellowship, he and several partners have purchased a number of buildings in the town, which they hope to make into a model community "that recognizes the cost of its consumption" — not in dollars but in the real terms of natural resources. Quoting Jackson, Buchanan captures the implications of their project:

> He wants to talk about ways to go back to small towns. . . . "Right now, college offers upward mobility," he says. "It ought to offer homecoming, teach people how to dig in, live within our means. . . ."
>
> Jackson says the problem with Matfield Green, as with much of Western society, is largely one of rational economics. Walking along one of Matfield Green's dusty streets, Jackson sums it up.
>
> "Economics is what drives us. . . . Places like Matfield Green have become marginalized because they are not economic. Yet we all know that the things that count the most, we can't count. . . . We're not talking about mere nostalgia (for small towns). We're talking about resettling the countryside with a different set of assumptions than the first time, when we thought the resources were endless."[21]

That's not Old Western squinting through blinders: that's wraparound New Western *seeing*.

If you hang around Matfield Green awhile, you'll doubtless hear about other New Western goings-on — at a nearby 6,000-acre ranch run by a woman named Jane Koger, a handful of hands, a vet, and a changing roster of guests. Guests? Well, yes, but this ain't your ordinary dude ranch. Writing of the place she's nicknamed "the Estrogen Ranch," Gail Gilchriest explains:

> Remember Curly, the Jack Palance character in *City Slickers*? Well, Jane Koger plays that part in real life, except she's not nearly so tough-talking or scraggly-looking, and her dudes are always women.
>
> On the Homestead Ranch in the Flint Hills of Kansas, Jane offers paying female guests a chance to play cowgirl. Through a program called "Prairie Women Adventures [and Retreat]," gals of all ages can help deliver calves in February and March. Or they can schedule their vacations to coincide with castration time in May. Some sporty city slickers sign up for the Flint Hills rodeo in June. What pavement-dwelling nine-to-fiver wouldn't want to spend a sabbatical in the wide-open spaces?[22]

Sisters to women studying ranch management at Texas Christian University or taking the University of Utah's continuing-education course called "Women Wranglers' Roundup" (which features roping, herding, singing — the whole schmear), these female-bonding cowgirls don't get the blues much. They're too occupied. And beef eating nationally is on the rise — witness the recent prodigious proliferation of Lone Star Steakhouse restaurants.

Koger ain't your ordinary ranchera, either. She goes to Broadway shows a lot, and she doesn't eat beef all that much, really. She's into raising cattle organically and helping women learn about the natural environment and their own capabilities — activities that those she calls the good ol' boys have direly neglected. Her underlying philosophy seems to be this: if you want to feminize the West more, it wouldn't hurt to Westernize more women more.

If you leave Matfield Green, get back on Interstate 35, and roll south for an hour, you'll be in Wichita, where plenty of Western amusements are available. For instance, you can visit the Old Cowtown Museum or eat comfort food and experience nineteenth-century melodramas at the Empire House Restaurant and Theatre, complete with a sing-along. Or, maybe best of all, you can go to the flagship Sheplers store, which Gilchriest aptly dubs "a cornucopia of boots and hats and saddles" that is "to western wear what Bergdorf Goodman is to haute couture." With its "heady scent of wood and leather," it smells "the way a ranch might smell if it was air-conditioned and dung-free." It's a "retail

Ponderosa" that "makes a fashion-conscious cowpoke who ambles in think she's gone to her final reward."[23] Well, it does that to male cowpokes too.

Then, with your new Sheplers duds on, tool down to Oklahoma through territory that in September 1993 celebrated the centennial of the Cherokee Strip Land Rush with a pageant in Arkansas City, Kansas, a chili cook-off and theatrical production about the rush in Kiowa, Kansas, and other such events. Head east over to the Tallgrass Prairie Preserve, a 36,600-acre tract north of Pawhuska where the Nature Conservancy is trying to re-create and maintain a small piece of the ecosystem, complete with bison, that was the Great Plains before the cross-continental land rush occurred. Or slip out to Yukon, west of Oklahoma City, and visit Garth Brooks's boyhood purlieus, checking out a memorable Chisholm Trail mural downtown while you're at it.

And by all means don't miss the National Cowboy Hall of Fame and Western Heritage Center in Oklahoma City, the city that, incidentally, hosts the annual Red Earth Festival, a signal recognition of Native American cultures. Now you're in cowboy country. Outside, walk the Trail of Great Cow Ponies, pausing at the graves of Tornado, the damnedest rodeo bull of all time, and Five Minutes to Midnight, *the* bucking bronc of that same chronological stretch. Inside, step into a gold mine, sod house, or livery stable in a special gallery called The West of Yesterday. Study the memorabilia in the Rodeo Hall of Fame or the Western Performers Hall of Fame. Pick up some books on the West. Stroll through the Joe Grandee Museum of the Frontier West. View more historic and contemporary Western art than you thought could be hoarded in one place. And check out the John Wayne Gallery. There you'll find a superfluity of the Duke's saddles, kachina dolls, guns, and whatnot, including the Winchester he carried in many of his movies. An elegy for Wayne's world.

And while you're in the area, more or less, grab Interstate 35 on down to Forth Worth and visit the historic stockyards and Billy Bob's. You'll find a passel of cowboys and cowgirls at the latter but no cows, except maybe a few for atmosphere, at the former. People there still deal in cattle, though, around a million head a year. It's all done by catalogs, satellite television, and telephone bidding. Fort Worth may have been the starting point of the Great American Cattle Drive of 1995, a symbolic six-month trek that took two dozen cowboys, hundreds of outriders, and a herd of longhorns to Miles City, Montana, but it ain't down-country Old West anymore: it's uptown New West.

Now let your map eye zip up the 98th meridian from Fort Worth, and you'll come back to Salina, from where you can continue west on Interstate 70 for less than an hour to a turnoff north that'll take you to Lucas, Kansas. And there, on a perfectly normal-looking small-town residential street, you'll find a spectacle called the Garden of Eden. It consists of the conglomerated artistic works of the dotage of one S. P. Dinsmoor. But the place isn't very peaceful. "In fact," as Jane Stern and Michael Stern describe it in their *Way Out West*, "it is a parcel of fuming chaos in the form of concrete and limestone statues that depict such bloody tales as Cain slaying Abel, the crucifixion of the working class, and warfare between the U.S. cavalry and Native Americans." That chaos contains also a mausoleum in which you can view, through a window in his coffin, the moldering remains of Dinsmoor, "the man who created this environment (to educate mankind) between 1905 and 1933."[24]

That chaos may be a parable about the West as the Garden of Eden—or just another story of the Western mind at the end of its tether. Not the first such story in these parts, where settlers galore wandered off their mental reservations. Nor the last.

And if you want some real perspective on the West, haul on out to Hays, Kansas, and visit the Sternberg Museum at Fort Hays State University. History there is archaeological history, natural history, geological history—deep retrospect on the *old* Old West. When sea creatures swam above the plains.

Let's not forget that sobering perspective, but let's not linger in it too long, either. So head south again. Go to Dodge City, one of many towns along the Santa Fe Trail, which stretches—or once did—

from Boonville and (Old) Franklin, Missouri, to its namesake in New Mexico. Plenty used to happen in Dodge as it grew from outpost to center for traders and buffalo hunters to cut-loose cattle town and railroad hub. Home for a time to famous and ambiguous lawmen like Bat Masterson and Wyatt Earp, it once had the reputation of being the wildest site on the frontier. Now it's a magnet for tourists worldwide.

Something of that 1870s Dodge is preserved in the Boot Hill Museum and the reconstructed Front Street, which features the Long Branch Saloon (with a painting of a topless woman, *Cowboy's Dream*), that adjoins it — and a bunch more, enough to tell you that those Old Westers didn't meditate on the long view frequently. And when you venture outside town and look at what's amazingly left of the Santa Fe Trail even over a century after it was closed, you begin to comprehend the momentum and perseverance of the commercialism that opened the trail and drove Dodge and other towns along it into mercantile frenzies. As you study that worn, abandoned route, tireless prairie wind pushing at your inconsequential flesh, you may have a haiku-length moment like this:

Just west of Dodge,
old ruts there still
suffice to judge
the trader's will.

Increasingly, the people now along the trail trade almost as much in heritage as they do in goods — maybe more. You can think about that as you follow the trail, approximately, by highway on out to its end. Take the northern, mountain branch through Raton Pass, and stop at the St. James Hotel in Cimarron, New Mexico, where half the notorious personages of the Wild West stayed and now have expensive suites named after them. Check out the bullet holes in the dining-room ceiling; if you're foolish enough, stay up late for a glimpse of a ghost that's supposed to haunt the environs — many Old Western hotels lay claim to ghosts.

Or take the southern branch, the Cimarron Cutoff, being sure to pull in at the Eklund Hotel in Clayton, New Mexico, for the best Western chuck this side of cowboy heaven.

But beware: traveling through southwestern Kansas, you're apt to get many a whiff of the excremental nightmare of feedlots that the cattle industry is now dependent upon.

Of course, before you reach Clayton and as long as you're in the vicinity, you could drop down to Dalhart, Texas. There you doubtless still could have an experience much like the one that Larry McMurtry had during a trip he took around the Lone Star State back in the 1960s. Near the end, since he was about to leave Texas for Dodge City, he wanted "to perform some *acte symbolistique* to give the drive coherence, tie the present to the past." He did:

> I stopped at a cafe in Dalhart and ordered a chicken fried steak. Only a rank degenerate would drive 1,500 miles across Texas without eating a chicken fried steak. . . .
>
> The waitress was a thin, sad-eyed woman with hands that looked like she had used them to twist barbed-wire all her life. She set the steak in front of me and went wearily back to the counter to get a bottle of ketchup. The meat looked like a piece of old wood that had had perhaps one coat of white paint in the thirties and then had had that sanded off by thirty years of Panhandle sandstorms.
>
> "Here," the waitress said, setting the ketchup bottle down. "I hope that steak's done enough. There ain't nothin' like steak when you're hungry, is there, son?"
>
> "No ma'am, there ain't," I said.[25]

Pure Texas. Some things in the West don't change any faster than a glacier slides, including an almost mystically positive view of beef.

McMurtry's experience concerns matters of a sort that are treated and appreciated in fiction, essays, poetry, lore, song, and academic discourse during the annual National Cowboy Symposium and Celebration, sponsored by the Ranching Heritage Center, in Lubbock, Texas, about three hours south of Dalhart. You can get a chicken-fried steak there too — fixed the same way it was three decades and more ago.

If you want to take the Cimarron Cutoff to Santa Fe, you'll be retracing it by driving west on Highway 56 and then south on Interstate 25. That'll take you to a few interesting places on the way. But you can go easily to Cimarron instead. Then, whether you've come in from the north or south, you might change your itinerary and approach the City Different by a more intimately picturesque route, through Taos.

However threatened by boutiquery, the swarming of artists and

Taos Pueblo: nearly a thousand years of tradition. (Photo by Mike Roberts, courtesy of Scenic Art)

spiritual kooks and tourists, and the multiplying enterprises of developers, Taos and the highway-circled land north of it remain a curiously magical place. D. H. Lawrence and other famous sensibilities who "discovered" it in the early twentieth century were hardly the first to do so. New Agers will be hardly the last. If you want some grasp of the antiquity and — I hope — durability of the area's qualities, visit Taos Pueblo. Preferably in the early morning, when most tourists haven't yet left their beds.

And now we're there, standing in the plaza of an adobe village with nearly a thousand years of tradition. The July sun shines as clear as the Rio Pueblo water flowing right behind us. Though I've been here before, I protectively fold myself in Parkman's intellectual distance. I walk about as if I'm in a museum. A woman stokes the fire in an *horno*. Calm smell of cedar smoke. What has changed in all the centuries these people have inhabited their stories of mud and straw, the stories they tell?

I kneel beside the small river, that cool flow descending from the Taos' sacred Blue Lake high in the mountains. I lift a pebble out. I pocket it — not just to help me remember (that's what *souvenir* means in French) but to help me fill a hole in myself, a lack. Then comes a sudden unease: by this act I, like other Anglos, am a thief of time, stealing someone else's heritage.

I brood on the matter now and again during the day's further activities of eating, shopping, sightseeing in and around Taos. That evening the Taos Pueblo Powwow is in progress. In the Sangre de Cristo twilight, my three-year-old daughter and I join in the carnival of color of an intertribal dance. Among hundreds of brightly dressed Indians, Indian wanna-bes and other eccentrics, self-conscious cowboys and cowgirls, I move step by slow step through continual chanting and drumming, circling back through memories, toward something. . . .

I remember Custer's horse, Comanche, stuffed and displayed in glass in the Natural History Museum at the University of Kansas in Lawrence — an emblem of my ancestors' ambiguous, at best, relations with Native Americans. I remember my uncle Bill's 26,000-acre ranch near San Angelo, Texas, where, at the age of six, I tagged along with an old Mexican hand named Miguel who seemed as dark, wise, and other to me as an Indian. I remember powwows in Lawrence, at Haskell Indian Nations University: Kiowa, Navajo, Potawatomi, Cheyenne, tribe after tribe proudly displaying traditions, heritages, cultures more ancient and indwellingly vital than any I felt connected to. What Wallace Stegner has said of the Mormons' influence on him, I would say of those Native American celebrants' influence on me: "Their obsession with their history . . . eventually made me aware of growing up entirely *without* history, and set me on the trail to find or construct some for myself."[26]

My youth wasn't migratory like Stegner's, but it nonetheless didn't provide me with a thorough knowledge of who I was, where I came from, where I still am. Some family stories I listened to too late, the usual boring history courses in school, a religious affiliation that always struck me as arbitrary — that was about it. The kind of predicament of placelessness, both historical and contemporary, that motivates a lot of New Westering, I suspect. In any case, it was the experience of several powwows, more than anything else, that set me on my trail to find or construct some history for myself. Maybe I hadn't been without history so much as I just hadn't been encouraged to notice that it, in part at least, was there, within me, all along.

When the drumming and chanting cease and my daughter and I are returning to our seats, I realize that I've achieved what I was working on during the dance: an almost absolute clarity of rededication to my quest for the West and my place in it. Also, by here and now dancing at a powwow, which I've never done before, I've accomplished a more Garrard-like engagement with that quest, closed some distance. Maybe I've shared in an event significant for my daughter, who's already trying to figure out where she fits in the ever-shifting scheme of things post-modern and futuristic. And I understand better the life of a bizarre relative in my wife's family, her great-great-grandfather, an Ohioan, born Scotch-Irish, who immigrated to frontier Kansas and Oklahoma. As a child, he played with Indian children, wore Indian clothing, then grew his hair shoulder-length. Till the day he died — through his varied career as marshal, buffalo-bone peddler, poet known as the Pilgrim Bard, who knows what else — he apparently never stopped believing and living the romance of being a mixed-blood Indian.

Let's rodeo!

You can find more to do in Santa Fe than even God can keep track of. But we're going to the Rodeo de Santa Fe, whether or not we get anything else done. By the luck of the calendar, it's on the same July weekend as the powwow. So let's take in what's rightly called, Hispanic roots (and competitors) and all, the sport of the West. The Professional Rodeo Cowboys Association (PRCA) sanctions about 800 rodeos each year in twelve geographical regions defined by the association's circuit system, but surely this one, the sun just now slipping down behind the Jémez Mountains, has one of the most beautiful settings.

Some Santa Feans claim the first rodeo happened here. That would be difficult to prove. There are counterclaims, and conventional history says the first organized rodeo was in Prescott, Arizona, in 1888. Whatever such contentions, one thing about rodeo that's true is that it doesn't require any particular locale. Small or large, PRCA–sanctioned or not, in an arena or on a ranch, whether in Florida or Oregon or New Mexico, rodeo is itself a place, its own place, definitely a Western place.

The most obvious thing you notice about rodeo, in timed events or judged events, from the first bareback bronc ride to the last bull ride, is that it's dominated by an Old Western ethos — even in a place as densely New Western as Santa Fe. The sequence of events is nearly invariant from one rodeo to the next, though odd ones, like wild-cow milking or chuck-wagon racing, are sometimes tossed in. That bullfighter clown out there, a walking congeries of scars, has the same function — to protect cowboys in the dirt — and expresses the same bumpkinish humor in all rodeos. The announcers obey the same rigorous protocols about what they can and can't say, about the jokes they crack. With typical Western taciturnity and by the tact of the rodeo code, they don't say much about the cowboys' victories or defeats—and damn little about their injuries. Such practices have been in force awhile. Even the cowboys' names seem to hold to tradition: Payne, Shane, Monty, Brad. So do the cowgirls' names. You hear a lot of names like Bo, Regina, and Kelly, maybe Lamita or Annesa. And though there are cowgirl rodeos—and gay rodeos, for that matter—maybe more all the time since the sport's popularity is gaining ground along with feminism, women in so-called regular rodeo since the late 1930s, even champion Charmayne Rodman (now James-Rodman), can compete in only one event (besides, sometimes, breakaway roping): barrel racing. In line with the traditional Western combination of chivalry and condescension toward women, it's typically called "ladies' " barrel racing.

On the other hand, you may pick up on contemporary aspects. Like cowboys who ride tough but have been trained in clinics instead of on ranches (or even in high-school or college competitions), have bachelor degrees, and are articulate enough to handle interviews well during television coverage. Like animals being assigned by a computerized draw. Or like greater SPCA-inspired public-relations efforts concerning the care of "animal athletes," which have long been tended to, usually, better than most of the public understands—because of their value as investments (since their owners share in the winnings), if for no other reason, like PRCA rules or common humaneness. But, despite such innovations, rodeo still emphasizes the traditional.

Watch these cowboys, not only in the arena but around the chutes, out by their traveling rigs, in the local bars. The purses may be bigger than ever—well over a dozen rodeo champions, including Rodman and Ty Murray, have cleared a million dollars by now—but not that much has changed since the so-called golden age of rodeo back in the 1950s, 1960s, and 1970s. Steer wrestlers still leap off their horses like danseurs. Competitors still haul their horses in trailers, wear about the same style of boots (lots of ropers), chew Skoal long cut—forget all the hullabaloo about mouth cancer. A rodeo cowboy still never takes off his hat till he's ready to bed down—unless a rank animal removes it for him. When these guys grow old, they'll still have reunions, sit around fires, eat grilled meat, swap tales about long-gone horses or bulldoggers or women, and refuse to admit they've gotten soft.

Out in the arena saddle-bronc riding remains the classic event because of its pivotal association with ranching, and you still can lose a bushel of points for letting your free hand touch the animal or equipment during a ride. Also, your spur strokes still have to be high on the horse's neck if you want to do any good riding broncs bareback. Flank straps are still used to encourage hard bucks and high jumps. Headers and heelers in team roping still employ ropes made of natural materials. Chute bosses still hold strict sway over their realm. Riders are still addicted to danger.

But the tensest event, always the last, is bull riding. The bulls still have names like Savage, Anthrax, Bodacious, Toy Boy. Eight seconds of fear-shot madness, with a fierce rate of injury. As in other judged riding events, the two judges can each award up to 25 points each to rider and animal, but I know of only one 100-point bull ride: Wade Leslie on Wolfman Skoal at the Wild Rogue Pro Rodeo in Central Point, Oregon, in 1991. So there's another bit of yield in a stubborn tradition, I guess.

And there may be some subtler changes in rodeo, despite resistance to them, as a consequence of its popularity and television coverage like that of ESPN's roving "Wrangler World of Rodeo" or TNN's broadcast of the Mesquite Championship Rodeo.

In any case, if you want a sense of the difference between rodeo during the first three quarters of the twentieth century and rodeo now, rent a 1990 video entitled *Guts & Glory: Legends of Rodeo* — from Cabin Fever Entertainment. It's a documentary with abundant action footage and insightful conversation about the mental game of the sport with four greats: Casey Tibbs, Jim Shoulders, Roy Cooper, and Larry Mahan. Shoulders, who's now into beer advertisements, and Mahan, who's into selling shirts and boots, supply especially instructive stories and comments. Or, better yet, visit the ProRodeo Hall of Fame and Museum of the American Cowboy in Colorado Springs, which city serves as home also for Westworld Travel & Tours, an outfit that packages trips to tournaments like the Calgary Exhibition and Stampede and the National Finals Rodeo in Las Vegas. (The latter, hosted by Vegas since 1985, now attracts around 200,000 fans each year.)

Otherwise, if you want the lowdown on what's transpiring here, turn to Elizabeth Atwood Lawrence's book *Rodeo: An Anthropologist Looks at the Wild and the Tame*. She explores rodeo as "more a way of life than a way to make a living," one that's "identified as 'Western' by Americans, and . . . as 'American' by the rest of the world" — a world whose

Bull riding: eight seconds of fear-shot madness. (Photo by James Svoboda, Jr., courtesy of James Svoboda, Jr.)

International Rodeo Association sanctions hundreds of rodeos outside the PRCA's bailiwick. Mostly she delves into how rodeo, which is "the direct outgrowth of the cattle industry" and "serves to reflect and preserve that heritage" of experience, "is used by the ranching society—and by the population which shares that ethos—as a ritual event to express, affirm, and perpetuate its values, attitudes, and way of life." Her approach is interpretive and compares aspects of the tame and the wild, "themes from the pastoral life of the cowboy, past and present," that rodeo "exaggerates" and "makes . . . explicit through patterned performances."[27] She wants to know what rodeo means culturally.

Lawrence's analysis yields a bumper crop of conclusions, all provocative. Her overarching conclusion is that "rodeo, like the duties of the working cowboys from which it was derived, deals with the relationships between men and animals, both domesticated and undomesticated, and on a deeper level with the human relation to the land — the wilderness and the wild." That conclusion in turn correlates with other, more specific conclusions: "Rodeo embodies the frontier spirit as manifested through the aggressive and exploitative conquest of the West, and deals with . . . the reordering of nature according to the dictates of this ethos. It supports the value of subjugating nature, and reenacts the 'taming' process whereby the wild is brought under control."[28]

That sounds like the traditional Old Western male enterprise, of course, and largely is. So it's hardly surprising to Lawrence that rodeo thoroughly stresses conquering maleness, "the force of 'culture' reaching out to dominate 'nature' " (animals, wilderness, women too), even in the symbolism of the cowboy hat: "The big hat, with its phallic shape emphasized by the crease in the crown, and the width provided by the brim, gives powerful expression to the aggressive sexuality of the rodeo man, creating as it does an image of him as a larger, taller, and more impressive figure." Cowgirl hats, on the other hand, she notes, "are quite different, with the sides of the brim ordinarily rolled up, making the whole hat narrower. Their usual bright or pastel colors, too, make them appear less substantial than the cowboys' hats of white, tan, black, or brown." Well, you could go on in that vein, pointing out, as Lawrence doesn't, the female-genital symbolism of cowgirls' rolled and narrow hats or, as she does, the symbolic function of the trophy buckle as "perhaps the modernday analogue of a 'cod-piece.' " Or you could take a cue from her and speculate further about the meaning of one of the well-known ads (its image also on the box top) for Nocona boots that shows a rattlesnake, the iconic essence of dangerous Western wildness (nature), with its jaws gaping "under the impact of the cowboy boot" (culture — or nature already turned into culture) on its neck, its body twined about the boot, a large knife held in a rugged hand descending toward its head, a sturdy ring on the ring finger of that hand that reads "LET'S RODEO."[29]

This recent poster by L. D. Burke III lends credence to Elizabeth Atwood Lawrence's analysis of the sexuality of the rodeo man's hat. (Courtesy of L. D. Burke III)

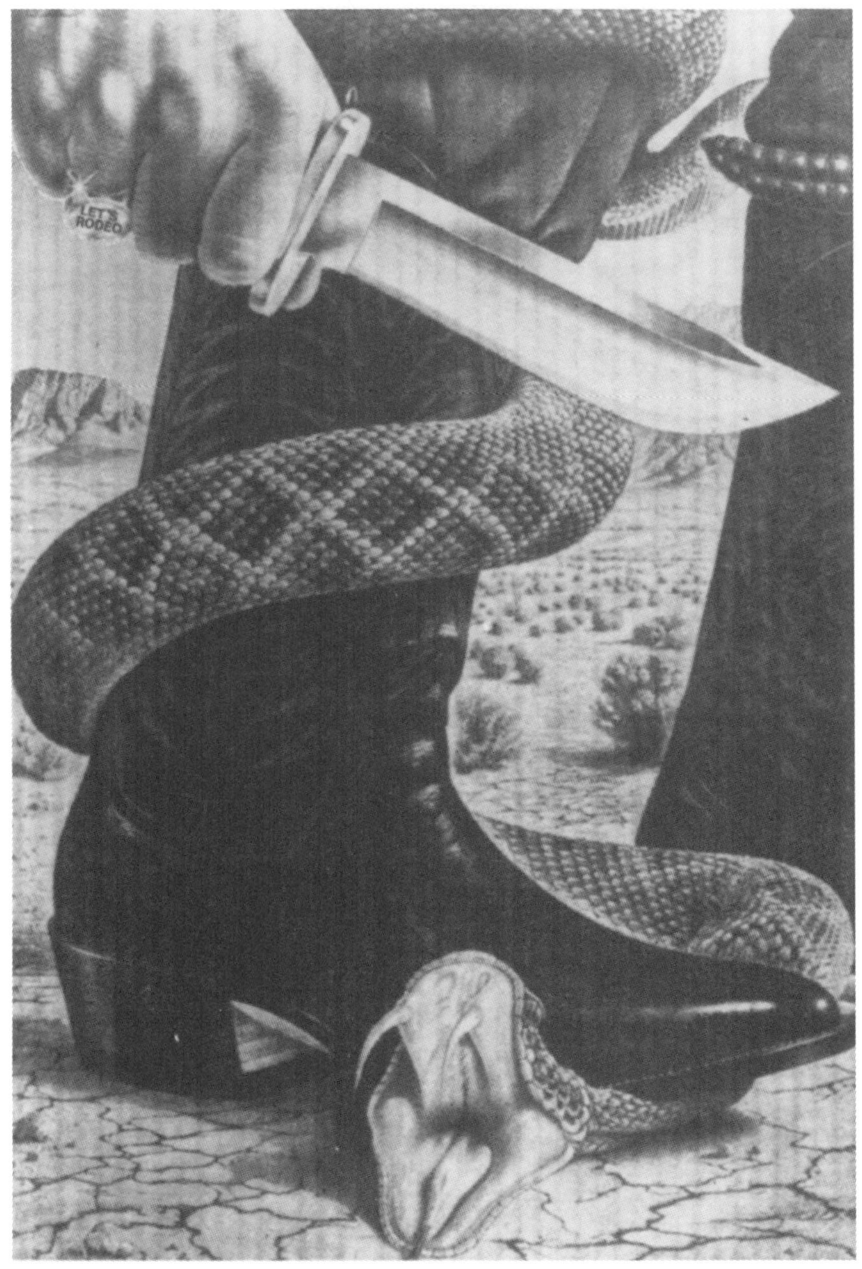

Culture conquering nature. (Courtesy of the Nocona Boot Company)

And so on. The symbols of male power, control, and order are everywhere at the place called rodeo.

But such symbols entangle the same ambivalences and contradictions that recur in Western history. Rodeo society is nomadic, wild in its way, but nonetheless promotes the conquest and taming of wildness (thus, it's not unusual to see novelty acts with horses and other animals in human clothing). Contestants represent the settling of the land but don't want to settle down — marriage is almost always derided in the rhetoric of rodeo. They're patriotic and sometimes born-again-Christian believers in the homeland who don't like domestication. They like their animals rank, but the whole purpose of riding is to prevail over rankness. They savor risk and unpredictability, but their own behaviors and standards — from the way they talk to the way they wear their hair (short, under the brimmed privacy of a black Resistol, maybe with a trophy-like hawk feather in the band) — are subject to "considerable [socially] inward conformity" and "uniformity." They're loners obedient to a group (through the rodeo code, PRCA rules, and so on), people of the country who, oddly, promote relatively urban values. For them, "women are associated with animals" and yet are to be protected systematically from the profane roughness of the male world, "are supposed to be feminine," with fingernails intact. At the same time, rodeo cowboys are wary of "the 'good woman' " because of her power to weaken their untamed strength, not untypically preferring "the 'bad' woman" who won't question their nomadism. Also, of course, they relate themselves, centaur-like, to animals and women to children (by apron strings). Like many Old Western ranchers, they, as Lawrence puts it, "seem to identify with the wild which they seek to destroy."[30] As in country music, there are among such oppositions tensions and conflicts aplenty.

It's illuminating in this connection to contrast male–WASP rodeos with those held by Native Americans (historically, splendid horse handlers). In the latter case you find an identification with nature grounded in "great respect and awe." As a result, Indian rodeo tends to have ranker animals, crazier rides, more reveling in the animals' power, less worry about control and its ambivalences — at least from the point of view of whites as Lawrence typifies it, whites for whom Indians in their loved and hated otherness "have generally retained their wild image."[31]

Quite a ravel. Quintessentially Western as a mustang — and yet not uncharacteristic, in principle, of other herder-oriented cultures, as

Lawrence repeatedly reminds us. That ravel doubtless will change, simplifying in some ways and complexifying in others, as the Old West increasingly yields to the New. There may be more Indian rodeos, more gay rodeos, more women's rodeos (along with more women ranchers), more who-knows-what kinds of rodeos in the multicultural, multigendered New West. Maybe fewer rodeos of any kind, eventually. But one thing is as clear as Santa Fe evening air: the future of rodeo will be a telling index of the future of the West. And — whoa! D'yew see that cowboy's mount pitch him into that gate? Damn! Let's rodeo!

Now I'm on Interstate 25 again, headed south to Las Cruces, then west on Interstate 10 to Tucson. On the way I dip down to Tombstone. Once one of the most violent silver-mining boomtowns in these arid parts, it's now, as one billboard proclaims, "The TOWN too TOUGH to DIE," a place of Western romance and at least quasi-history. Travelers galore mosey around the O.K. Corral, grinning at shiny lifesize figures of Doc Holliday, Earps, and Clantons frozen in face-off; view an electronic diorama; or watch a staged gunfight and cheer in half a dozen different languages.

Onward to Tucson. I arrive late in the day, haunted by saguaros standing like sentinels in semidarkness. After a night's sleep, the city and I awake:

> Bronze haze hangs over apartments, hotels,
> motels, duplexes, condominiums.
> The well-heeled breakfast by their swimming pools,
> and four dozen golf courses get a douse
> of off-peak water. Old Tucson prepares
> for tourists to gape at Hollywood streets.
> Fighters from Davis-Monthan slice the sky.[32]

Yet, if you sweep those dour meditations aside and get your Garrard mind-set rigged up, there are things to throw yourself into. Eat brunch at the Casa Molina. Check out Old Tucson — what the hell. Or take a glorious hike through Sabino Canyon. Or go take a walk on the weird side and schedule yourself to star in your own Western movie at Earl Wettstein's operation out at the Wild Horse Ranch, where John Wayne himself used to stay during film projects. It's the Original Cowboy Movie

The West as movie studio: stuntmen perform a gunfight for onlookers at Old Tucson. (Courtesy of Old Tucson Studios, Tucson, Arizona)

Fantasy Camp. The staff will cast you appropriately, costume you, make you up, rehearse you, and let you realize your role on a scaled-down set that makes you look truly Western-heroic in stature. A double does the stunts. And you return to Poughkeepsie with ten minutes' worth of videotaped personal Western legend in your hand. Forget the dude ranches and epicurean pack trips, because *this* is playin' cowboys.

According to some recent poll, gambling has now surpassed baseball as the national pastime. That's not unexpected, given the chancy state of postmodern America, with its lottery frenzies from coast to coast and its still unsquelched dreams of boundless individual wealth. In the West, of course, gambling, of one kind or another, has been the national pastime for several centuries. An appetite for taking risks defined the temperament of yesterday's mountain man or settler as much as it does that of today's rodeo cowboy or Midwesterner bound for Las Vegas — our next stop, a day's loping drive northwest of Tucson.

Las Vegas is a New Western Historian's worst nightmare, a strange romantic overgrowth to wax hypercritical or even apoplectic about. A city of magicians, casino-hotels as theme parks, it's ahistorical pseudo-reality freed from time (there are no clocks in casinos), any myth you want, Western or otherwise, without a sense of its origin and meaning. The Aladdin with its country shows. Circus Circus with its circuses for the masses. The Excalibur with its medieval pageantry. The Luxor with its gargantuan sphinx. Or Caesars Palace, that computerized plastic ancient Rome, where a woman who works as a "princess" tells me that she qualified for her job by being a princess before, at another equally unreal, sealed-off land of neon lotuses where nobody talks about where the electricity comes from. As an advertisement for a saloon cum steak house named Wild Bills boldly announces, "WE'RE CHANGING THE FACE OF THE WEST!"[33] Indeed.

If losangelization is taking over the Pacific shore of the subcontinent, then lasvegasation is after the Reno–Las Vegas corridor, the fastest-growing part of the nation's fastest-growing state. Already, among its other depredations, drying up farms in northern Nevada by theft of water, it may be after the entire interior West. It's myth gone wacko in technologized spectacle — like the artificial volcano at the Mirage or the jungle "paradise" of the Tropicana. Lasvegasation is what happens when the American dream in its virulent Western strain loses track of American fact. That was true in diamonds in 1971 when Hunter S. Thompson offered his diagnosis in *Fear and Loathing in Las Vegas: A Savage Journey to the Heart of the American Dream*, the definitive gonzo-journalistic opus by a man who has since proven to be perhaps the most oddball New Wester of all. Now it's true in spades, a situation that Kirk Robertson anticipates in his *Driving to Vegas: New and Selected Poems, 1969–87* (1989). As I overheard a cabby saying to his crestfallen fares boarding for their spin to the airport, "God didn't make this place. God made what was here before. Man made this. Hell isn't somewhere else. Hell is here."

Las Vegas is about what it's been about since it was invented by Bugsy Siegel and his gangster buddies: gambling, especially slot machines, thousands upon thousands of them arranged in casino after casino, everywhere you turn. There's no end of hype about "family" vacations here, and kids certainly can find fancy amusements. But the place, despite that home-theme travesty, operates for adults. Which is to say, it's about what the West has been about for most of its invaders since Coronado: the mother lode, the windfall win, the golden opportunity.

Everyone here, like Jay Gatsby in *The Great Gatsby*, functions in "the service of a vast, vulgar, and meretricious beauty"—the perfect terminology for this Gomorrah of monstrous architecture rising on alluvium.[34] The people who come to Vegas in herds have what Wallace Stegner in *Angle of Repose* calls "the incurable Western disease," the blind hope of finding the Big Rock Candy Mountain, of getting something wonderful for nothing.[35] Rags to riches, riches to rags. And remember that the mythical and sartorially magnificent hero of Fitzgerald's 1925 novel was a Westerner (or at least an upper-Midwesterner, from North Dakota) and that the narrator, Nick Carraway—like all the principal characters, from the same region—finally heads back west, "back ceaselessly into the past," in flight from the decadent East.[36] Irony upon irony.

So the dream of Gatsby's beauty lives on, indeed thrives, as more vulgar development is planned and undertaken in Vegas, further down the shrinking Colorado River, and through adjacent parts. In the elevators at the Tropicana, "The Island of Las Vegas," an inveigling recorded voice speaks ceaselessly of "where winners play and players win." Time will tell, as it always does for risk-takers.

If you travel quite a ways northwest from Vegas, you get to Reno, Lake Tahoe, and the place where the Donners and their companions took too big a risk (wrong route for the time of year) and wound up in more literal cannibalism than goes on in Nevada's gambling cities. Not far from there is the "Bonanza"-based Ponderosa Ranch, where you can eat a Hossburger. But if you go just a handful of miles in that direction from Vegas and then turn southwest, all the glitz of Glitter Gulch recedes; and you enter Kyle Canyon. Immemorial mountains slope upward on either side of the road, their strata folded in synclines and anticlines—a layer cake shuffled and spread out like a deck of cards by the demon of geological faulting. Time hasn't stopped here, but it's slow in these ecotones (varieties of sage, then juniper and Joshua trees, then yellow and ponderosa pines). Here you can't help but be aware that you're on the edge of the Great Basin, a giant slab of cheese that broke along two north-south lines when stupendous stresses tried to bend it.

From a high spot on Mount Charleston, through tens of miles of haze, I make out the peak of Yucca Mountain in the suffocating mid-afternoon sun. Intervening playas stretch toward a testing ground where over 800 thermonuclear bombs have been detonated deep, more or less, in the earth. David Weide, a seasoned geologist from the University of Nevada at Las Vegas, dryly tells me that the atmospheric fireworks from such tests are sensational, even from sixty miles away, and that the prevailing winds carry any leaked dust off into Utah — not to worry.

The federal government may decide to store nuclear waste under that mountain in the distance. Politics aside, the arguments are pretty sound, Weide avers, though there are questions about how watertight the storage facility would be. However you fret over it, the risk is academic compared to the possible peril from the myriad house-size melted radioactive wads hidden underground in the vertical range of a water table that someday might, conceivably, with a change of climate, rise dramatically. But such megaproblems are the kind that New Westers must face. They're also the kind that Old Westers don't grasp, can't even imagine, really — till invisible deadliness begins mysteriously to disappear too many of the friends they used to meet for serious drinking and manhood's oblivious rituals.

Since it isn't that far, let's just drive on across to the West Coast and visit the most losangelized city in the country, Los Angeles itself. Forget about earthquakes. Forget about the state's economic and other disasters. After a little browsing through Worn Out West, Kowboyz, or any of a score of other such clothing stores that have opened in the wake of the recent slew of Western films, we're headed straight for Denim & Diamonds.

Whether they're just practicing their kicks, thrusts, dips, spins, and all manner of individualized moves or doing full-tilt hour-after-hour footwork, the main patrons are almost always posing. They're "attitude cowboys," because, as Aaron Latham explains, "it's their attitude that makes them cowboys. Always dancing harder. Always trying harder. Always taking the hurts harder. These attitude cowboys ride a range that exists — that throbs! — but only in their own minds." And they're good at that attitude, so much so that, when they're into their low grinds on the elevated dance floor, "cowgirls sometimes come up and stick dollar bills into their Wranglers." Latham understands that this Southern California New Western chic is "about style," but he understands also that Denim & Diamonds and "other like-minded places" are, as Gilley's was in *Urban Cowboy*, "all about 'lookin' for love.' "[37]

But that lookin' involves more than just libidinal drive. Latham mentions one patron who "generally changes in his car in the garage at work," shedding "his tasseled loafers for cowboy boots" and the rest of his costume. Moreover, the exercise of "true grit" on the floor can send cowboys out to their cars for multiple shirt changes in the course of an evening. Such hurried "Clark Kent–like transformations" and such commitment, over and over, suggest that the regulars have some other need that is being met here. Latham nails it: "Most of them are first-name friendly. . . . They take off their big-city suspicions and fears — and there is a lot to be afraid of in this well-armed, gang-ridden metropolis — and they put on small-town trust and openness. . . . Denim & Diamonds . . . has become their hometown, and they return to it every night."[38]

Posing and sexual intrigue, to be sure. But also men and women searching for — and finding, as best they can — something down-to-earth, simple, whole. The regulars, like their counterparts at hundreds of other like-minded places across the country, are lookin' for a home inside themselves, inside the club, inside the West.

You didn't have to go south back there in Hays, Kansas. You might have gone north and driven up to Custer, South Dakota, and then visited Wounded Knee, where the U.S. Cavalry massacred Lakotas in 1890 — though there's little to mark the spot. While in the Black Hills, you could have seen the prodigious in-process sculpted-granite monument to Crazy Horse, the Native American answer, at last, to the arrogance of Mount Rushmore. Ian Frazier describes it as "the one place on the plains where I saw lots of Indians smiling."[39] Or you might have driven up to Deadwood to observe how gambling has metamorphosed that classic Old Western town into a New Western hub.

Or you could have stayed on Interstate 70 and traveled on through Denver, where the Center for the New West conducts research on economic and technological policies as they affect the American West, and then up to Cheyenne, Wyoming. From there an afternoon on Interstate 80 gets you to Rock Springs, Wyoming. And there, if you've made your summer plans right, you can attend the annual Our West Institute organized by Western Wyoming Community College. It's a week-long program that immerses people from all over the country in presentations, field trips, and camaraderie concerning the West. Challenging stereotypes, the program helps participants appreciate the West — its history, environment, and culture — realistically.

Continue northward, by a long roundabout route, and you'll eventually reach Cody, Wyoming, a rodeo town if there ever was one, its founder duly memorialized by the Buffalo Bill Historical Center. There, wandering through the complex of museums that exhibit Western art, Cody memorabilia, Plains Indian artifacts, and the firearms of the West, you may have an experience like the one Jane Tompkins had when she visited in 1988. In her account she finds the center an institution largely opposed to stereotypes, self-conscious about the relativity of interpretations, educational "in the best sense of the term." Maybe almost too educational. She's troubled by the sadism in Remington's paintings and statues, their "aestheticization of violent life." She probes the rodeolike paradoxes in how Cody both hunted and worked to preserve buffalo, in how men like Remington and Roosevelt, however destructive, needed the West "to reanimate their own lives." Tompkins personalizes and contemporizes the meaning of the Historical Center, its artworks and taxidermy and bones, as "a kind of charnel house that houses images of living things that have passed away but whose life force still lingers around their remains and so passes itself on to us." The place "caters" to an urge that Stewart and Tatum well understand: "the urge to absorb the life of another into one's own life." Contemplating Cody and other human predators of the historical West, she concludes that "our visit is only a safer form of the same enterprise as theirs."[40]

The artifacts of the Plains Indians speak to Tompkins of a culture "made entirely from animals," "all bloodshed and killing, an unending cycle." The exhibit of guns she finds "too technical," and she rejects their violence, especially when genocidal, that continues. Still, what she says of the Buffalo Bill Museum proper seems to pertain to her experience of the whole Historical Center: it's "a wonderful array of textures, colors, shapes, sizes, forms. . . . For a moment you can pretend you're a cowboy, too; it's a museum where fantasy can take over. For a while."[41] Only for a while.

Leaving the Historical Center, you too may be "full of moral outrage" at how it "did not repudiate the carnage that had taken place in the nineteenth century" but, instead, "celebrated it." And yet later, after you have learned more, you may discover why Tompkins "came to love Buffalo Bill." Here are some excerpts from her explanation, which is at once Old and New Western in its pertinence:

A color-lithographic poster, circa 1900: Buffalo Bill "in the guise of a redeemer." (Courtesy of the Buffalo Bill Historical Center, Cody, Wyoming)

> Why is he still so appealing, even now, when we've lost, supposedly, all the illusions that once supported his popularity? There's a poster for one of his shows when he was traveling in France that gives a clue. . . . The poster consists of a huge buffalo galloping across the plains, and against the buffalo's hump . . . is a cutout circle that shows the head of Buffalo Bill, white-mustachioed and bearded now, in his famous hat, and beneath, in large red letters, are the words "Je viens."
>
> *Je viens* ("I am coming") are the words of a savior. The announcement is an annunciation. Buffalo Bill . . . comes in the guise of a redeemer, of someone who will . . . lift us above our lives, out of the daily grind, into something larger than we are.

He comes to "that part of ourselves . . . that got left behind," the part that got suppressed "out of existence" during childhood, and he "promises that that part of the self can live again." He brought for us what he still brings: "the West itself" and all it means. "He not only represented it, he *was* it," as Tompkins sums him up, seeing him in her mind's eye resplendently performing his feats before audiences—countless millions in the aggregate — now long dead, that original promoter of rodeo riding "his watersmooth silver stallion at full gallop." He came, as he still comes, "to show people that what they had only imagined was really true. The West really did exist."[42]

Thus Tompkins finds in Buffalo Bill a "deeper legacy," which has to do with him as "a person who inspired other people. What they saw in him was an aspect of themselves." And it wasn't — and isn't — the aspect that grows indignant and alienated but a more Garrard-like aspect: "It really doesn't matter whether Cody was as great as people thought him or not, because what they were responding to when he rode into the arena . . . was something intangible, not the man himself, but a possible way of being." And that way of being in "an inward territory" or "a Wild West of the psyche" is, I take it, what the Historical Center is really about.[43] Cowboy up. Forgive the West, and get on with it.

From Cody it's just a trot up across the border and into southern Montana. There, at a camp on Davis Creek, you can undergo a ten-day campaign as a member of the Upper Stillwater Cavalry, the brainchild of one R. L. Curtin, an outfitter and Western-history aficionado. You wear the authentic gear, carry a .45-70 Sharps carbine, care for your mount, clean out stables, ride on maneuvers — the whole shebang, all in preparation for your participating in the annual reenactment of Custer's Last Stand as part of Little Bighorn Days.

And remember, while you're singing out under that big sky before taps is sounded, that Montana, which now has caught many a New Wester's interest, could be the *West's* last stand. Unless. Unless.

Unless we, as tourists and inhabitants of the West, recognize what's at stake and assume an intelligent preservationist stance. If we don't, something like what's happened to California will indeed soon happen to the interior West. Nobody understands the threat better than Raye C. Ringholz. A journalist from Park City, Utah, with a sharp eye for patterns of environmental degradation, she portrays in *Little Town Blues: Voices from the Changing West* "a kind of living history of the growth that is changing the American West today — a growth spawned by floundering mining and agricultural economies turning to tourism as a salvation, and manifested in progressive urbanization of once-rural communities and commercialization of the outdoors." In general, that "growth" proceeds thus:

> If there's a mountain to hike or ski, redrock backcountry to explore, a waterway to play on, or a desert oasis to green into a golf course, it's being developed by entrepreneurs with hordes of tourists and recreationers hard on their heels. Within a few short years, the immigrants follow and authentic mining camps, rustic cow towns, pioneer farming communities — historic signatures of the American West — succumb to cosmetic changes that leave them little resemblance to their original selves. Even worse, they all start to look alike.[44]

It's happening from Santa Fe and Taos to Telluride, Colorado, to Sun Valley, Idaho, to wherever. Many of the changes go beyond being only "cosmetic" as values clash, lifestyles shift gears, the rich move in, prices rocket up for locals, delicate ecologies become condominiums and Wal-Marts, and heritage gets plowed under or Disneyized.

In Ringholz's informed view, "the mold seems set" in most of the places subjected to "resortification" of this kind — "unless it can be broken." The bulk of her 1992 book is based on detailed investigation of the stages of "evolution" of three representative towns: Moab, Utah (which "appears to be on the cusp of change"); Sedona, Arizona (where "change is readily apparent" but a "vision of the future" may help keep "retirees, artists, and New Agers" under control); and Jackson Hole, Wyoming (where "the transformation from rough-and-tumble western town to glitzy new resort is almost complete") — all more altered by now. Clearly, the mold is doing its work. New Westers themselves are the problem, for "Americans are departing big cities in droves, each seeking a piece of paradise in the rapidly shrinking frontiers." But there are signs of hope because Ringholz, like others, discerns "a new mentality evolving as a concern for the environment encourages a philosophy of planned, well-considered growth."[45] That is, New Westers are also the solution, the best one we have.

And don't think about turning New Norther to escape all this. Those chilly zones are next on the entrepreneurs' list.

 Thus the West lives on, even today, in the hearts of most Americans. Now we have only to ask, as we move toward the year 2000: What new myths will the West engender? — William H. Goetzmann and William N. Goetzmann, *The West of the Imagination*

CONCLUSION

STAYING PUT: THE FUTURE OF THE NEW WEST

Grand conclusions that are also true are as scarce as bird shit in a cuckoo clock. They aren't appropriate in the postmodern age, maybe, anyway. Besides that, the Western story has become too variegated for them to apply well. Contradictions proliferate, of necessity, in much that I've observed about the New West, and many appear unresolvable. The reality of the New West consists of numerous realities, some newer than others, some hard-nosed, some dreamy — with no shortage of conflicts among them. I sympathize with Boone Caudill's mountain-man reluctance to grapple conclusively with knotty issues: they're to be avoided because usually "the mind dug into [such] a thing and got itself tired and cranky and then had to back out the same hole it had gone in."[1]

Nevertheless, I owe you a roundup and a few last shots before I depart — not backward, I hope. And I hope also that what I have to say deals as much as possible with, to borrow words from the poet Wallace Stevens, "the full flower of the actual, not the California fruit of the ideal."[2]

It's not difficult to inventory threats to a West already ravaged by mistakes. Shortsighted use and pollution of water endangers virtually every Western river from the Rio Grande and Pecos on up and out. There are fools who kill grizzlies in Wyoming only in order to sell their gallbladders to Asians apparently in dire need of expensive aphrodisiacs. There are others who kill Rocky Mountain sheep only in order to turn a profit from the horns. From all indications, such poaching has been on the increase in recent years. Of course, New Westers themselves, by virtue of sheer numbers as well as sometimes desperate or less-than-enlightened motives, pose no small threat.

In a 1993 issue of *Time* that was focused on the Rockies, Montanan William Kittredge addressed this last situation:

> Look down the two-lane highway, past the beauties of the Sawtooth Mountains and the swales along the Salmon River, over Lost Trail Pass into the Bitterroot Valley, across the Clark Fork of the Columbia and past the Mission Mountains and Flathead Lake and Glacier Park to the blue Canadian Rockies. It's all sort of glorious. And it's a bumper-to-bumper raceway — Jeeps and Winnebagos and Harleys, Californians and Canadians, illicit drug vendors on holiday, fly-fishing nuts who saw *A River Runs Through It*. Who knows? Some of them are tourists, but many are coming to stay. They've sold a house in some suburb; they're bringing what money they've got; and they're intent on buying in, souls on the run.

This still-enlarging invasion by "latecomers" has uncomfortable consequences: taxes go up; farmers go broke; and locals "end up in the servant business, employed as motel clerks and hunting guides." But what really disturbed Kittredge was what he perceived as the typical motive: a desire not so much for natural beauty and cheap land as for "safety" and "sanctuary" after "our old America fantasy — a New World and social justice all around — has gone seriously defunct." People motivated more to find "a hideout" than to establish a responsible communal way of life may not, he implied, become the best citizens of the New West.[3] Indeed, many such people haven't yet, and some of them never will. That's the down side of the home theme: the wrong kind of homing, what Hispanics would call a false *querencia*.

Kittredge addressed also another kind of threat, that which environmentalists represent to logging, mining, and ranching. It's the kind of threat that, "if you value the integrity of the natural world, is a good thing."[4] Sure enough. But one result of environmental concern — and a rat's nest of politicking as well — is that Congress continues to haggle intermittently over proposals to increase public-land grazing fees for ranchers. Many people in the cattle industry feel that higher fees would mark the beginning of the end of what's left of anything like traditional ranching in the West. If so, then the fees would mark a similar fate for the cowboy. Or would they?

Since the last of the large-scale cattle drives in the late nineteenth century, the cowboy, in one reincarnation or another, has repeatedly faced beginnings of his end, as we've seen. The doomsayers meditating on what they perceive as liberal Eastern do-gooders' ideas about grazing fees now, even in a time of his resurgence as a popular image, divine his more decisive termination. So, in a way, does James McMurtry, Larry McMurtry's son, in the cynical musical stories he tells on his albums like *Too Long in the Wasteland* (1989) and *Candyland* (1992) — thus the fate of the child who took a "vertical ride" back in chapter 1. Doubtless the stupendous popularity of Robert James Waller's 1992 novel *The Bridges of Madison County* had to do partly with the way the male principal, Robert Kincaid, convincingly played by Clint Eastwood in the 1995 film version, fancies himself "as one of the last cowboys," an evolutionary cul-de-sac in an overtechnologized world.[5]

Still, Waller himself went on to publish another sort of cowboy novel, *Border Music*, in 1995 and even continues to dress like a cowboy, more so since he recently moved from Iowa to a ranch near Alpine, Texas. There's some cowboy yet in the grazing-fees doomsayers, perhaps in James McMurtry too. Rumors of the cowboy's impending death may be greatly exaggerated. William W. Savage, Jr., noted in 1979 that " 'last cowboys' are in vogue." They were well before then, and they are again. Lastness heightens the romance of the cowboy image. Certainly, there are fewer and fewer real cowboys, but the image, the idea, of the cowboy refuses to die — if for no other reason than that, in Savage's words, "America has too few heroes to risk discarding any." The cowboy's survival, through veneration or merchandising, is more complicated than that, as we know; but "he is available to those who want him, and many do."[6] Watching the finale of Alan Myerson's 1973 film *Steelyard Blues* decades from now, whatever sort of New Westers are around will still cheer when the zany fantasist named Eagle (Peter Boyle), who imagines himself something like Marlon Brando in *One-eyed Jacks*, brings a string of saddled horses to carry his beleaguered friends to a better place.

Real cowboys too are hanging on, "even though," as Western scholar Lawrence Clayton puts it, "they continue to adapt to change."[7] Well, maybe *because* they do. Maybe also because they have a sense of humor, for what folklorist Ernestine Sewell Linck says of pioneering women surely holds for contemporary cowboys (and cowgirls) as well: "She who laughs, lasts."[8] But, real or otherwise, the cowboy survives and will survive mostly because he's what novelist Clay Reynolds calls "the quintessential American hero." Whatever he once was, he's now "newer, shinier, bolder, braver. He is the knight-errant, a living symbol of independence and common sense." He, like his original era, is "a state of mind," and he "lives in a land no more definable than Camelot." Thus it may be true that "the American cowboy belongs to a once and future time," but it's also true that "all who celebrate his image truly are celebrating something stronger than nostalgia, they are seeking a validation for the values that they have been taught are positive and constant."[9]

But there's another thing about the cowboy that must be borne in mind, and it has to do with exactly the "future time" of the New West. Admitting to being more New Wester than Old, Reynolds gets at it when he discusses two range-worn, scraggly cowboys he encountered in a Pizza Hut in Vernon, Texas, some years ago:

> The Shortys and Slims and thousands of other working cowboys on the modern American range may be automatically following a pattern of behavior and dress that was established a century ago.... But they are for-real cowboys, and as such, it matters very little whether they are parodies of a by-gone age and mythical icon.... I may still wear my boots, drive my pickup, and "Howdy" and "Haw-yew" my way around my home town when I visit, but unless I and other urban cowboys seek to understand something of the lives and work of people such as Shorty and Slim, of the deeper meanings underlying their attitudes, values and codes, we can never come close to knowing what it means to forge our own codes and face the future and be comfortable with ourselves and satisfied with our heritage.[10]

That is to say, if the future of the New West is to be more than shallow style, New Westers have not only to understand Shorty and Slim better but also to construct new codes on the basis of that understanding — a matter of adopting a tradition and then adapting it. It's neotraditionalism, once again, and that involves creating a revised, updated, enlarged, and corrected edition of the dominant ideal of the Western lifeway.

Many New Westers — most visibly those who are historians, nature writers, filmmakers, and so on but less noticeable people as well — seem to fathom this principle and are intent on enacting it. Interestingly enough, a lot of them engaged the West about when the Soviet Union collapsed and Americans stopped worrying about the red menace, stopped defining themselves in terms of it, took a hard look at their own cultural and natural resources, and began thinking differently about what they wanted to be. That was also when people who had read *Rolling Stone* in the 1970s and *Money* in the 1980s bought subscriptions to *Consumer Reports*, when narcissism and moralism met each other on their respectively falling and rising curves. It was when a fair portion of baby boomers started getting fed up with Madonna and Donald Trump and feeling more kinship with Dale Evans and Roy or even Will Rogers (witness the success of the Tony-winning Broadway musical *The Will Rogers Follies* in the early 1990s). In other words, countless Americans in need of a sanguine attitude toward the future have recently been returning to the Western past to find a blueprint, whatever its faults, that they can modify.

As a consequence, Western accessorizing, dude-ranching, and so on are gradually giving way to genuine attitude-building. People are reclaiming ideas that once had faded to almost irrelevant memories. Those who've had it with ecological screw-ups are trying to learn the veteran working cowboy's patience with nature or the Native American's religious respect for it. Those who "live in a world that seems impersonal, computerized, mechanized, out of control," are embracing a "cowboy culture [that] is personal, romantic, and old-fashioned," according to Michael Stern, coauthor, with Jane Stern, of *Way Out West*. They find in the West, he argues, "a great relief — in every sense of the word, including the moral sense. Because if there's one thing true about the West, it's that there has always been associated with it a code of honor. In researching this book, a lot of people told us that this was the most important aspect of the West for them — this sense of being an honorable human being, which the mythic cowboy always was." The myth supporting that cowboy, Stern stresses, "is a very real thing" for those people, and they seem to believe, with him, that, "whether it's true or not, it's something we as a nation ought to really treasure and hold on to."[11] And they are coming to comprehend that, at its best, "the Western mythos," conservative in the root sense of the word, is, as Robert Murray Davis sums it up, "not about power, which you impose on others, but about strength, which you find in yourself."[12] New Westers are learning through such heritage what they're worth, taking the measure of themselves.

The more New Westers explore that heritage, the richer and more various it becomes. It concerns how a cowboy faces death with grace, but it concerns also the sanctity of Indian burial grounds, many of which have been plundered by scientists or thieves. It concerns Native American, Asian-American, and African-American as well as Caucasian concepts of honor. It concerns "second languages" that must be preserved. It concerns a great deal more than all the Western knockoffs available to the gullible. It certainly concerns women as much as it concerns men. That augmenting heritage concerns a future that will preserve and emphasize some of its aspects while challenging or transforming others.

Inevitably, I think, the New Western vision of the West and of being in the West will become more androgynous. Indeed, that shift is already well upon us. Stegner saw it coming decades ago. The historically dominant male way of doing things has fouled up too frequently and now is yielding to more balanced ways. *Playboy* contributor Cynthia Heimel may not be a New Wester and may overstate the case in one of her "Women" columns, but she makes clear the mandate for a thoroughgoing shift from a boomer to a sticker philosophy: "Much of what defines masculinity is now useless. Fighting is out, wars are bad. There's nothing left to conquer besides outer space, which we can't afford to do. We no longer have to protect ourselves from wild animals, we have to protect wild animals from us. No more cutting down trees. Even tilling the land has become problematic." Therefore, she concludes, "the skills needed today are feminine: getting along, sharing, nurturing those weaker and needier than ourselves, communicating, empathizing."[13] She's talking about getting rid of guns and such — or at least about an end to the use of penetrating instruments for purposes long championed by many an Old Wester. She's talking about changes in the roles of Western men and women that may seem drastic to traditionalists, but in fact a lot of what's in the offing involves not so much revising or even rejecting traditions as it does emphasizing neglected traditions. Or inventing new ones that complement or supplement the old ones.

The complicated interplay of traditions that constitutes the New West promises to become more complicated in the future. Foresight may be assisted by thinking of it in terms of what Sharman Apt Russell, in the subtitle of her 1993 book *Kill the Cowboy*, calls *A Battle of Mythology in the New West.* The "battle" she describes is, in many ways, between the Old West and the New though it encompasses more than just two conflicting mythologies or traditions. It has to do primarily with issues of land use and wildlife preservation, and she tries to achieve a balanced representation of differing viewpoints on those issues and even to reconcile them by arguments that lead finally — since she, like Richard Slotkin, believes in the alterability of myths — to a myth of her own making.

Russell's struggle with those issues is both sophisticated and down-to-earth, tender and tough-minded. What with ancestors who homesteaded in the Southwest, rancher relatives (including "the requisite great-aunt who got married on horseback"), growing up in growth-crazed Phoenix, and a home in the Mimbres Valley in New Mexico, she knows whereof she speaks. She begins with the cowboy:

> There are those who would argue that we need the cowboy now more than ever. . . . As our last frontier urbanizes, we need the psychic ballast of people who make their livelihood directly from soil, grass, and water. We need people who understand, rather more than the rest of us, that our society . . . depends on a base of natural resources. We need dreams.
>
> Thirty years ago, that might have been a concluding sentence.
>
> Today there is much more to say about the cowboy. Dreams, as we discover again and again, are half seduction. And the cowboy, the seductive cowboy, has a dark side.

She evidences that side with several cold-eyed observations: that "over 70 percent of the West is grazed"; that the "job" of the cowboy, who believes that "you can't eat scenery," "is to transform the wild West into something that resembles, prosaically, a feedlot"; and that wildlife therefore is nothing more or less than "competition" and "must be destroyed."[14]

The history of foraging implicated here has resulted in rangeland whose "health . . . is unclear." Half is "severely degraded," some is in good shape, some hasn't been assessed. Perennial native grasses, much munched since cattle were first driven north out of grass-poor Texas, have been badly overgrazed, superseded by annual weeds and shrubs like cheatgrass and mesquite (the latter, as I noted earlier, now being overharvested). "The new plants are less efficient in anchoring topsoil and leave the ground vulnerable to trampling hooves and erosion," Russell explains, and the decline in the variety of plant species carries with it a decline in the variety of wildlife. Trampled and eroded soil doesn't absorb rainwater well, so flooding increases. And on and on — leading to ubiquitous questions about grazing practices, especially from people who "want not the Marlboro man but what he stands in front of," which is largely "that half of the West that belongs to the American public." What's at stake in the battle, an old one now more intense, is "a lot of land."[15] Furthermore, there's no ready resolution in sight.

"Despite the growing polarization," however, Russell believes "that an opportunity exists to find common ground, in all senses of that phrase." The opportunity inheres in viewing the land not as a "commodity" that people fight over but as a "community" of life. It's a way of seeing that Russell at least takes steps toward developing as she explores the common desires of both ranchers and environmentalists, not only for healthy land but also for "new myths" to promote keeping it healthy. Such myths, innovative and yet recalling the oldest wisdom of sound ecology, would be more inclusive than the conventional Western myths, proposing new roles for men *and* women, country folk *and* city folk, whites *and* nonwhites, cattle *and* wildlife, ranch *and* park. Also, the new myths wouldn't forget the cowboy, couldn't, shouldn't, can't, as Russell explains:

> My own concerns are not entirely academic. My five-year-old son has identified himself as a cowboy ever since he could ride a rocking horse. . . . He believes that one day he will ride a larger horse, wear a six-shooter, and chase cows.
>
> The bitter antagonism between environmentalists and ranchers is striking because in many ways they share the same needs and the same values. They are both seeking connection. They are both seeking ways to enter the landscape.

> If there were no cowboys, my son would have to invent them.
> Connection. Invention. Reinvention.
> This may be the real work of the West.[16]

But that work may call for a different kind of cowboy.

A different kind of cowboy? Yes. Russell suggests that he and much else different will be required in the New West of the future. She investigates a host of Westerners' diverse ideas and perspectives — political, scientific, religious, you name it — till she comes up with "my own image." It's "syncretic," but she bases it on a description in an essay by John Fowles of a mythical and variously manifested "green man," adding a feminist twist:

> Let's call her the green woman, an elusive dryad hidden in our hardened modern selves. A powerful green force. A generous spirit.
>
> Let's call her the green woman, and let's call her out. Let's call her out in every cowboy and rancher, Christian and non-Christian, Navajo and Nez Perce, Anglo and Hispanic and black, ecologist and environmentalist, in the city and in the country, in homosexuals and heterosexuals . . . in all of us who live here and make this our home. . . .
>
> Let's see what she has to say about the West.[17]

Isn't this invocation of the ultimate cowgirl and her mythical trappings a bit New Age and starry-eyed? Well, of course, but it's also rightminded. If we read Russell's epilogue, following on the heels of the text above, as giving voice to what the green woman has to say, which surely we're invited to do, then that cowgirl gives useful advice. It concerns how we can "become better visitors" and "find better ways of being at home" — not just in the West but "on the earth." Much of it is in the form of a sort of New Wester's credo that we might take as a springboard for more thought, maybe action as well. Here are some excerpts:

> There is no blanket solution. . . . We must decide these things place by place. . . .
>
> I believe in wilderness and large expanses of wildlife habitat because wilderness and wildlife have an intrinsic right to exist. Moreover, we need them. . . .
>
> I believe that cattle should be slowly and honorably phased out of most wilderness areas, wildlife refuges, and national monuments. . . .

I believe that we need the cowboy. We need every root and roothair.

I believe in a biodiversity of myth.

Remembrance is an acknowledgment of the past, of all that was good and all that was bad.

Repentance is a transformation lured by the vision of what the future could be.[18]

And I believe that we need the green woman. I believe that she can help us shape a future for the West that will hold more than just ostrich ranches and other travesties of the past.

The problems that confront the green woman aren't, of course, all caused by cattle ranchers. Ringholz, Kittredge, Stegner, and others have eloquently described and analyzed a spectrum of messes awaiting her attention. There are promising good-luck stories in the contemporary West — durum-wheat farmers offsetting economic woes by getting into pasta production, say, or the Oglala Sioux, like dozens of other tribes, countering poverty with very profitable casinos. There are, however, endless unpromising bad-luck stories as well. And what's promised or not either way can be treacherously uncertain or ironic. But the whole problem-riddled future of the West, whatever your perspective, comes down to issues that concern the natural environment.

Nobody knows that bottom line with finer clarity than Jim Robbins. More occupied with the hard-ball political, economic, and ideological realities of the New West than Russell, he investigates, in his *Last Refuge: The Environmental Showdown in Yellowstone and the American West*, a cornucopia of litigious enigmas that challenge the green woman in all of us. An Easterner now living in Helena, Montana, he begins the book with an account of his reporting, for the *New York Times*, on unbridled wildfires in Yellowstone National Park and ends it with a cautious note of hope. In between, he tells how the West has changed in this century, what problems its changing has occasioned, and what might be done about them.

Robbins's version, in summary, runs as follows. The Old West was "the West in which nature was battled and forced to give up a living," but "the New West, the urban West, the West of tourism and adventure and national parks," relates to nature far less fearfully and combatively, with a view of it that's "a luxury." In the Old West "the lands that fell into the public domain were considered worthless," but in the New West "the open spaces . . . are fast becoming invaluable." So there's "a protracted land war" over all those millions of acres. The contest "between New West and Old" isn't just about land, though: it's "about two different ways of seeing the world, and about a new kind of vision that seeks a middle ground that might preserve the best of both."[19]

Robbins covers considerable geographical territory in dramatizing his story, but he centers it on the Yellowstone ecosystem because that site "works well as a paradigm for the American West." It's big. There are disagreements over the rights of wolves. The area surrounding the park proper is peopled in a pattern typical of the West, with "large tracts of empty land with small or medium-sized settlements." Employment in the settlements is typically Western. Yellowstone has a status as "a 'visionshed,' a place where mystery and adventure and beauty are stored like the water the mountains harbor."[20] As the name seems to imply, it represents all the golden treasure of the West, physical and spiritual, that too many people want—and they want, in one sense or another, as the Eagles' song goes, to "take it to the limit one more time."

In portraying the showdown of the New West and the Old, Robbins wrestles constantly with an overarching question: "What should the 'western experience' be?" It's not a simple question. New Western "marketing of charm and myth and landscape" makes money that "is welcome," but it turns out that tourism and second-home development can "eat the scenery" just as surely as mining or logging can. Tourism is no longer "a clean industry," not with so many tourists who don't leave. Robbins, recalling Kittredge, elaborates:

> A few who set down roots are fine, but it seems that more and more are staying, and many people are finding themselves strangers in their own town. . . .
>
> In some communities, the influx of refugees has, for some, taken on nightmarish proportions. Many people who work for a living . . . have found that they can't afford to stay in the town their grandfather or father may have come and settled. The town is now full of "swells" that have turned the local drugstore into a Ralph Lauren factory outlet, the local cafe into a fern bar, the coffee shop into a cappuccino

> bar. . . . In many ways the West really was an egalitarian place. Now many "natives" are finding two distinct classes in the hometown, with themselves the "lower" class. (Ironically, it mirrors the treatment accorded those who lived on the land before the white men came.)

So Old Westers play Indians as New Westers play invading whites. And, by a further irony, "many of the people coming to the West are fleeing from California, the place that was built on its unparalleled quality of life." *That* part of the West is choked by "unmitigated gridlock" in several dimensions, and nature there "has disappeared beneath pavement."[21]

Consequently, Californians seek out organizations like the Greener Pastures Institute, "which, for a fee, helps people who are fed up with the urbanization of California find a new life in some small- or medium-sized town elsewhere" — mostly in Western states. The vast majority of those people are white. Along with a racism that's kinder and gentler than that of the Old West, they bring "the electronic cottage," the usual yuppie gadgetry through which they can carry on etherealized business from remote locations. The "refuge and redemption" they seek has a mythy feel to it, but it also "has elements of truth." In Santa Fe, for instance, they find "a city whose scale serves humans, rather than having humans serve the city." Still, there are also realtors on the make, proselytizing geeks into ear coning or Sufi mysticism, and so on — as well as angry locals trying to solve the problems of divided neighborhoods, Native American cultures devolving into curio boutiques, and building that strains the municipal water system. In Santa Fe and places like it, the refugees threaten to destroy the very "character," "regional identity," and, especially, natural environment that configure the myth they're responding to. As settlers, they, like their predecessors, bring too much of their old world inappropriately into the new. As tourists, they insist that the West pander to their fantasies, so Western towns "become something they're not."[22]

Nonetheless, however "aspenized" Santa Fe or Jackson or Sun Valley or even Aspen itself gets, a high percentage of the refugees who move in to stay don't stay very long.[23] There's heavy turnover. The home theme sours. Many stickers don't stick it out longer than a year or two. They can't find a job. They miss the urban scene. Or, as a Santa Fe realtor explained to me, they get bored with clear starlight and slow living.

Somehow reality doesn't fit dream, so they try another place. Such coming and going makes for local smirks and profits, but it doesn't lessen the impact of invasion on cultural and natural environments.

Implicated in aspenization are Western laws, most of which were passed when expansionist zeal was in its prime. They were designed to promote population growth in the West, not to control it. Historically, they have nurtured laissez-faire development. So they ill prepare the West to limit the consequences of a process that Jack Lessinger explores in his 1991 book *Penturbia: Where Real Estate Will Boom After the Crash of Suburbia* and that Robbins nicely synopsizes:

> His theory, based on census data from 1790 to the present, is that there have been four great migrations in American history, the last one being from urban to suburban areas. The fifth migration, he says, is just getting under way: a migration from urban and suburban America to penturbia — rural places fifty to one hundred and fifty miles beyond suburbia. . . . It is a fundamental, back-to-the-land movement, Lessinger says, a deep yearning for the basics of life. A movement away from a consumer society to an ecologically conscious society, a rejection of urban and suburban America with its pollution and crime and depersonalization.[24]

New Westering accounts for most of this surging population transit, but, however understandable and laudable it may be, there are few laws on the books to mediate its attendant disruptions.

What's to be done? You can't just hide the West. New laws need to be passed, obviously. Compromises need to be made. Most important, attitudes need to change in several respects. Robbins discerns signs that they are starting to. The Greater Yellowstone Coalition (GYC) "is looking for ways of preserving . . . social, economic and biological diversity." Its project for establishing sound ecological practices, Yellowstone Tomorrow, "does not seek to ban logging or ranching or mining, or to turn the area into wilderness or a bigger park; instead, it seeks to integrate humans into the ecosystem. It hopes to bring New West and Old West together in a way that ensures a future for both." The GYC, like Russell and others, advocates sustainability. Robbins believes that, if it works in Yellowstone, the GYC's "integrated approach as a new way of doing business can be applied anywhere in the West, or the world."[25]

That way involves "living on the interest . . . and not on the principal," and Robbins applauds its being applied elsewhere — by the Sonoran Institute near Tucson, for example, or by Wes Jackson's Land Institute. Numerous Western eco-organizations are redrawing maps to make ecological rather than geometric sense of their territories, rethinking water management, encouraging careful small-scale logging that leaves biological diversity intact, ranching that grazes land less intensively, and farming that takes "nature as a partner." They're lobbying for laws that will minimize the environmental damage of mining and moderate the impact of tourism and make cities like Phoenix "*a part of* the desert instead of *apart from* it."[26] They're supporting projects to restore as well as preserve what they can of nature inherently protean and much meddled with.

But along with the revolutionary fervor comes "a counterrevolution" of conservatives, Old Western in temper, fed up to the teeth "with people making a living by attacking them and claiming their whole way of life is dead wrong." It's backed by groups like People for the West! and the National Cattlemen's Association. With corporate support, they're as committed to "a holy war" as deep-ecology groups like Earth First!, "with both sides believing their vision of nature and God is the true celestial design." The conflict isn't just "a political debate," and Robbins is convinced that the Old Westers "will not go gently into what they see as the dark night of change."[27]

Robbins is convinced also, however, that "the New West is in the ascendancy" and "the Old West is outgunned." The Clinton-Gore administration early on made halting headway toward an ecologically healthier New West. Particular administrations aside, a lot of moneyed and politically powerful urbanites "have a stake in the West in the form of public lands, and they are moving to claim the benefits of ownership as never before." But the real opposition that the Old West faces, politics (and religion) aside, is informed common sense with a long view: "The weight of scientific and economic arguments lies with those who want to change the West. There is no such thing as a free lunch, but there are lunch bills deferred or passed on to someone else. That is what scientists and economists say is happening, as taxpayers and future generations get stuck with the bill for scientifically unsound methods of resource extraction." So the free-lunch era may be coming to a close, inevitably and not without conflicts, though Robbins expresses hope that the conflicts can be resolved multilaterally. He believes that "ranchers, loggers and miners . . . need to make their peace with a new kind of West, even take advantage of it."[28] Like Stegner, he finds it difficult to be pessimistic about the West.

The region, Robbins argues, "is a land of 'lasts,' " of life and lifeways "that have vanished from much of America, and are threatened in the West." In the conflicts there what's "at risk, in a word, is diversity. Cultural, biological and economic diversity."[29] Old Westers, I'd argue, are part of that diversity and ultimately stand to win by its preservation and by the more difficult task, as Buffalo Commons advocates and restoration biologists well know, of its rebuilding. Besides, any ecologist will tell you that, other things being equal, a high-variety system has a better chance of surviving than a low-variety one.

Still, though, the question lingers: how will the game turn out? Maybe the destruction of the West already has gone too far or soon will. New Western Historian Donald Worster has researched Western environmental problems at length in the final decades of this century. Though his trenchant criticisms of government bureaucracies like the Bureau of Land Management (for creating more problems than they've solved) and his wise, if radical, proposals for reform (like implementing the idea, borrowed from John Wesley Powell, that the West be bioregionally reorganized into 150-odd commonwealths based on watershed basins) have met with insufficient response, he remains optimistic. Furthermore, despite the consequent complications, he finds much virtue in the return of urban people to the land, which only about 2 or 3 percent of the United States population now inhabit. The reasons for his optimism are worth sharing.

In his 1992 book *Under Western Skies: Nature and History in the American West*, Worster muses on Bill McKibben's 1989 book *The End of Nature*, its "melancholy title" implying all manner of mescal nightmares: "Its author . . . is deeply worried. . . . We have conquered nature, McKibben laments, and worse, we have utterly destroyed what we have conquered. . . . Everything that exists on the earth has become, in some measure, a human artifact, reflecting back our own flawed human nature." Worster, however, is unpersuaded by McKibben's apocalyptic argument: "Of course, we have much reason to worry about the ecological havoc we are causing and feel guilty about it. . . . But have we seen the 'end of nature'? Is this planet now nothing but an extension of human culture? No, not at all; that is a victory we could never win. Or perhaps I should say that is a crime we are incapable of committing." Worster not only finds McKibben's argument philosophically implausible but also is heartened by signs, particularly in the West, that a new countercon-quest awareness is taking hold: "Today, the West has become a very urban place, indeed it is the most urbanized part of the United States in terms of where most of its people live. Yet for all that, Westerners may be more aware today of the significance of nature and of its role in their lives than they were fifty or a hundred years ago when they were down on the farm. So it is all over the earth." Recognizing that new awareness, remembering how much of nature hasn't been — and maybe can't be — ruined, and also acknowledging that the West's "odd fantasy of a pristine, inviolate, edenic wilderness . . . was, after all, never adequate to the reality of the natural world as we found it," Worster offers this conclusion: "If nature were ever truly at an end, then we would be finished. It is not, however, and we are not."[30]

So, to paraphrase a line from one of the late William Stafford's poems, it's not true that wherever you go in the West is Bing Crosby's ranch. It hasn't all been turned into gasoline fumes, stuffed wildcats, Las Vegas, and housing tracts.[31] Not yet. Maybe not for a long time. Maybe never. The West wasn't meant to be merely a plunderable treasure trove for government-underwritten mining companies, a butte for in-line mountain skaters, a junkyard for the military, or an irrigated sward where the rich can play golf (a game invented for the humid turf of Scotland). Both Westerners, with their appetite for nonhuman openness, and Easterners, with theirs for human enclosure, are coming to realize the value of Western nature on its own terms. They seem to be proving out evolutionary biologist Edward O. Wilson's biophilia hypothesis, which he first presented in his 1984 book *Biophilia*, that humans have a genetically based emotional need to affiliate with the rest of the living world.

There's also something more than such emotional need involved here. Reg Saner articulates it with his usual eloquence. Noting that "the etymological opposite of *religion* is *negligence*, just as the etymological root of *pollution* is *power*," he meditates on the human habits that have damaged the West: "The question every victim asks of its destroyer is 'Why?' The answer varies endlessly yet is always the same, 'Because I can.' Pollution: a display of power. Negligence: disregard of what's sacred; refusal to connect one thing with another." Saner's etymology is only half right—since he has the derivation of *pollution* wrong: it's from the Latin *polluere*, "to befoul"—but his moral construal is dead on, as is his subsequent assertion of the magnitude and religious meaning of the real power, far exceeding human contrivance, of the West: "Our grand Western spaces are . . . an empty plenitude. On the thoughtful person they confer depths beyond any *thing* humans can ever put there. The middle of nowhere is a power, a moving unity of spirit in us, one that habitation can only break up, never enhance. In such a midst, we've our best chance of sensing what this world is, and ourselves."[32]

The present of the New West is a border between the past and the future. Its story, which I've been telling throughout this book, is therefore a "border story," a kind that, in its spatial version, as A. Carl Bredahl, Jr., reminds us, is "the most common story in western writing." The border therein—temporal, for my purpose here—"becomes . . . a place of transition rather than demarcation," a "new frontier [that] describes . . . an area of continual opening."[33] The history of the American West sometimes seems long, but in fact it's pretty short. In various respects, many of its inhabitants, characters in this postmodern border story, are still immigrants. They're much less confident than their ancestors about how to handle the future. By this time the region betrays a hair-trigger nervousness about any sort of "new frontier." And the role of its problematic and seductive past continues to be ambiguous. You can't try to retain that past whole hog in the changing present, much as the protagonist in Rebecca Brown's short story "Annie" tries to keep a surrealistically resurrected Annie Oakley in the contemporary world, without painful results.[34]

So the relation of past to future and future to past in this border story is complicated. Our understanding of it might be enhanced, as David Daly and Joel Persky suggest in *The West and the Western*, by invoking media theorist Marshall McLuhan's notion that "we are 'marching backward into the future' and view life as if through a 'rear-view mirror.' " They elaborate:

> These two facets of the McLuhan catechism are key to the discussion of the public's love affair with the West. For McLuhan, the present and the future are mere reflections of the past. We live in the past, creatively and unconsciously, and judge the present, while predicting the future, by it. For McLuhan, then, our current fascination with and love of the American West would be no surprise. The fact that people who live in Manhattan are wearing cowboy shirts, boots, and hats would be no surprise to McLuhan. The fact that cowboy bars and country and Western music are more popular today than they have ever been would be no surprise to McLuhan. McLuhan would tell us that we are merely looking at life through a "rear-view mirror," and we like what we see in it.[35]

That way of moving into the future, though commonplace enough, isn't indefinitely viable. That is, it works for past times as pastimes, as McLuhan might have said when he was still strutting the earth and preaching his catechism. But New Westers profoundly concerned about the West, its cultural and natural heritage, may well be learning the importance of the opposite approach, that of the Kesh people in Ursula K. Le Guin's 1985 "cross-genre 'novel' " *Always Coming Home*. Those fictional people, "patterned after several groups of Native Americans who inhabited the Pacific Coast," according to Mary Catherine Harper, abide by the principle of going backward while looking forward. What Harper says of Le Guin's text pertains also to the world of the Kesh and surely has relevance for the New West as well: "Because the text goes backward into the past for its philosophy of living close to the land and then projects itself into the future, the past and future are able to converge. The past way is realized and the future benefits."[36] That's how the most sentient New Westers are "always coming home." They know, as Richard White puts it, that their "imagined West [has already] not only reshaped a historical past, but also cast a future partially in its own image."[37] They're going back into the future.

Still the Grand Canyon is there. So are the Rockies and the Sierra Nevada, the Great Basin, the Columbia River, and the Great Plains. The West remains grand and great. The land that Daniel Webster once condemned as useless now has become the most desirable of all. The people once regarded, despite their heroic stories, as the preterite jakes and zanies of American history may be becoming, in spite of their troubles, the elect. As the end of the twentieth century nears, countless New Westers are intent on an almost millenarian ghost-dancing back of the Western lifeway, traditional but transformed.

While soothsayers of sundry stripes prophesy cataclysms for the year 2000, New Westers typically foresee the possibilities for a better world — at least in the interior West. Such foresight can entail inflated or deluded expectations, for the West has served as the screen on which all sorts of weightless and unanchored dreams of new identity and old authenticity have been projected. Old Western hope has been disappointed time and time again. But New Western hope, with its fuller comprehension of the region and sensible skepticism, may be vindicated. Read the first publication of the University of Colorado's Center of the American West, *A Society to Match the Scenery: Personal Visions of the Future of the American West*, edited by Gary Holthaus, Patricia Nelson Limerick, Charles F. Wilkinson, and Eve Stryker Munson (1991). The collection is somewhat a hodgepodge of voices not infrequently at odds with one another, and yet most imply that there's a vigorous new collective intelligence looking out for the future.

Though New Westers seem insistent on more realistic visions of the West than have obtained in the past, they also show reluctance to forego much of its mythology and romance. That's understandable. They want it both ways. Native Americans in the West have always had it both ways, in a sense, with their immemorial beliefs interwoven with the mundane wisdom of their daily lives. Euro-Americans, on the other hand, have a more contingent situation. No longer Europeans and hardly Native Americans — since their ancestors emerged from ships, not, as the Pueblos believe concerning theirs, from a hole in the ground — they make do with a far less ancient body of powerful stories and a far more recently synthesized canon of values to connect them to the West. And make do they must; otherwise their realism would amount to nothing but a colorless, heritageless rationality. So, accepting the confusions that accompany their having it both ways, they love the West both because of and in spite of its mythology and romance —

though they may revise them. To borrow phrases from Joseph J. Wydeven, they betray "a desperate American hunger for heroic visions which require a tangible and imaginatively persistent location, a setting for hope in the recovery of lost values," but they also engage in "some effective thought which takes the real West seriously."[38] Like George P. Cosmatos's 1994 film *Tombstone*, they indulge in romance but self-consciously know it as such like never before — and complement it with historical sobriety. They're realists of a kind, but they nonetheless may believe that, to paraphrase Oscar Wilde, a United States map without Utopia on it ain't worth glancing at.

All of which is perhaps to say that current New Westering involves both a return to the American West and a return *of* the American West. As you move into it, it moves into you. When you inhabit the West, even if only in fantasy, its heritage, hard facts and happy fictions as well, inhabits you. You can't just take it straight: there's always some further activity of the imagination tangled in. As Robert Murray Davis notes, "The journey can be made only as a result of the act of invention, of discovering where one is *and* who one imagines oneself to be."[39] The journey to the West, back to the future and forth to the past: home and hope go hand in hand. Finally you wind up like Pea Eye after all the terrible doings in Larry McMurtry's *Streets of Laredo*: back on the farm, affirming a sweeter time ahead. Or you may already be, as the name of one of those Western-wear catalog companies has it, in The Last Best Place.

The poet-ecologist Gary Snyder has told us more than once of the need for all Americans to become "native" Americans, to make a genuinely sustainable bioregional home of where they live. Like others in other ways, many New Westers are dedicated to such a nativism. The movement they constitute is thus important as well as enjoyable, however merely amusing or irritating to anyone critical of it. New Westering has taken more than a decade to swell to its current proportions; its decay, if that ever really happens, also will be slow. New Westering will survive this century's end.

Much as a Taoist would say that the trail you can name isn't the Trail, so I would say that the end of the trail isn't the End of the Trail. It's been a good ride home. Let's tend to the horses, and I'll follow Texas Bix Bender's advice in *Don't Squat with Yer Spurs On! A Cowboy's Guide to Life*: "Never miss a good chance to shut up."[40]

Except for this: yeeeeehaaah!

He told the boy that although he was huérfano still he must cease his wanderings and make for himself some place in the world because to wander in this way would become for him a passion and by this passion he would become estranged from men and so ultimately from himself. He said that the world could only be known as it existed in men's hearts. For while it seemed a place which contained men it was in reality a place contained within them and therefore to know it one must look there and come to know those hearts and to do this one must live with men and not simply pass among them. — Cormac McCarthy, *The Crossing*

Notes

INTRODUCTION. WESTERING AGAIN

1. Tony Hillerman, "The Wild West Will Never Die," *Life*, 5 April 1993, p. 40.
2. Ibid., pp. 42, 46.
3. Ibid., p. 46.
4. Ibid.
5. Ibid., p. 49.
6. John Nichols, *On the Mesa* (Salt Lake City: Gibbs M. Smith, Peregrine Smith Books, 1986), p. 7.
7. Ibid., p. 9.
8. Ibid.
9. Ibid., p. 10.
10. "The Living Spirit of the Wild West," *Life*, 5 April 1993, p. 6.
11. Aristides [Joseph Epstein], "Such Good Taste," *American Scholar* 62 (1993): 167.

ONE. A VERTICAL RIDE

1. "Knock Wood," *Playboy*, April 1993, p. 104.
2. Asa Baber, "Shit-Kicker Redneck Women," *Playboy*, July 1992, p. 27.
3. *USA Weekend*, 14–16 May 1993, p. 7.
4. *Life*, 5 April 1993, pp. 5, 59, 69, 75.
5. David Dary, *Cowboy Culture: A Saga of Five Centuries* (Lawrence: University Press of Kansas, 1989), pp. xii, 336, 337–38.
6. Ibid., p. 338.
7. "Home on the Range," *Decorating*, Spring 1993, p. 14.
8. Ibid., pp. 14, 15.
9. Norman O. Brown, "Revisioning Historical Identities," in *Apocalypse and/or Metamorphosis* (Berkeley: University of California Press, 1991), p. 158.
10. Jane Garrett, "An Interview with Tom Averill," *Cottonwood* 47 (Fall 1992): 24.
11. Ibid.
12. Larry McMurtry, "An Introduction: The God Abandons Texas," in *In a Narrow Grave: Essays on Texas* (1968; reprint ed., New York: Simon and Schuster, Touchstone, 1989), pp. xxi, xxiii.
13. Jane Tompkins, *West of Everything: The Inner Life of Westerns* (New York: Oxford University Press, 1992), p. 14.
14. Richard White, *"It's Your Misfortune and None of My Own": A New History of the American West* (Norman: University of Oklahoma Press, 1991), p. 539.

15. Wallace Stegner, "Thoughts in a Dry Land," in *Where the Bluebird Sings to the Lemonade Springs: Living and Writing in the West* (New York: Penguin Books, 1992), pp. 48, 49–50.

16. Wallace Stegner, Foreword, *The Big Sky*, by A. B. Guthrie, Jr. (1952; reprint ed., New York: Bantam Books, 1972), pp. viii–ix.

17. Robert Frost, "The Gift Outright," in *The Poetry of Robert Frost*, ed. Edward Connery Lathem (New York: Holt, Rinehart and Winston, 1969), p. 348.

18. Stegner, "Thoughts in a Dry Land," p. 55.

19. Gerald Thompson, "Another Look at Frontier/Western Historiography," in *Trails: Toward a New Western History*, ed. Patricia Nelson Limerick, Clyde A. Milner II, and Charles E. Rankin (Lawrence: University Press of Kansas, 1991), pp. 94, 95.

20. Richard White, "Trashing the Trails," in *Trails*, ed. Limerick, Milner, and Rankin, pp. 35, 36.

21. White, *"It's Your Misfortune,"* p. 537.

22. Paige Rense, editor's note in "People Are the Issue," *Architectural Digest*, June 1993, p. 18.

23. Judith Thurman, "Portrait: Robert Redford: The Politics and Pleasures of Managing a Western Landscape," *Architectural Digest*, June 1993, p. 34.

24. Ibid., pp. 30, 34.

25. Steven M. L. Aronson, "Between a Rock and a Hard Place in Utah: Carving a Playful Hideaway from the Rugged Canyonlands Outside Moab," *Architectural Digest*, June 1993, pp. 92, 95.

26. Irene Borger, "Barn Raising in the Santa Ynez Valley: California Collectors Donna and Ken Fields Adapt Old Buildings to a New Setting," *Architectural Digest*, June 1993, p. 121.

27. Ramson Lomatewama, "Antiques: Kachina Dolls: Ceremonial Carvings That Evoke the Rich World of Hopi Culture," *Architectural Digest*, June 1993, p. 195.

28. Christopher Finch, "Antiques Notebook: Cowboy Memorabilia — Spirited Pieces of the American Past," *Architectural Digest*, June 1993, p. 40.

29. Ibid., pp. 43, 44.

30. Ibid., p. 44.

31. William C. Ketchum, Jr., Introduction, *Collecting the West: Cowboy, Indian, Spanish American, and Mining Memorabilia* (New York: Crown, 1993), p. 9.

32. Christine Mather and Sharon Woods, *Santa Fe Style* (New York: Rizzoli, 1986), p. 11.

33. John Ehrlichman, "The Southwest Spirit of Santa Fe," *Travel & Leisure*, June 1986, p. 84.

34. Jura Koncius, "New Macho Style Strikes '90s Furniture Designers," *New Mexican*, 22 November 1992, p. E–6.

35. Annie Woods, "Staying Power: Everyone Wants to Find Old Boots," *New Mexican*, 27 September 1992, pp. E–1, E–2.

36. Annie Woods, "Cowboy Style Garners Loyalty from Both Sexes," *New Mexican*, 27 September 1992, p. E–2.

37. Timothy Egan, "The Flannel Revolution," *Playboy*, June 1993, pp. 114, 112, 114, 116, 144.

38. Barry Lopez, *Arctic Dreams: Imagination and Desire in a Northern Landscape* (New York: Scribner's, 1986), pp. xxiii, 414.

39. Ann Wilson, "From the Editor," *West: The Spirit of the Frontier Home*, February 1994, p. 2.

40. Letters in "Mailbag," *Western Styles*, Fall 1993, pp. 6, 10, 9–10, 9.

41. Jordan Bonfante, "Sky's the Limit," *Time*, 6 September 1993, pp. 22, 26, 23, 25, 23.

TWO. MANIFEST DIVERSITY

1. Donald Worster, Preface, *Under Western Skies: Nature and History in the American West* (New York: Oxford University Press, 1992), p. viii.

2. Donald Worster, "Beyond the Agrarian Myth," in *Trails: Toward a New Western History*, ed. Patricia Nelson Limerick, Clyde A. Milner II, and Charles E. Rankin (Lawrence: University Press of Kansas, 1991), pp. 8, 9.

3. An informative collection of work about the historians who preceded New Western Historians is *Writing Western History: Essays on Major Western Historians*, ed. Richard W. Etulain (Albuquerque: University of New Mexico Press, 1991), which treats both pre- and post-Turnerian historians, including transition figures between Old and New Western History like Henry Nash Smith and Earl Pomeroy.

4. Ian Frazier, *Great Plains* (New York: Penguin Books, 1989), pp. 209–10.

5. Worster, "Beyond the Agrarian Myth," pp. 6, 7.

6. Gerald Thompson, "The New Western History: A Critical Analysis," *Continuity: A Journal of History* 17 (Fall 1993): 9, 13, 20.

7. See Gerald D. Nash, "Point of View: One Hundred Years of Western History," *Journal of the West* 32, no. 1 (January 1993): 3–4.

8. William W. Savage, Jr., "The New Western History: Youngest Whore on the Block," *AB Bookman's Weekly*, 4 October 1993, pp. 1244, 1245, 1242, 1245, 1246, 1245.

9. See Larry McMurtry, "How the West Was Won or Lost," *New Republic*, 22 October 1990, p. 38.

10. Worster, "Beyond the Agrarian Myth," pp. 12, 13.

11. Ibid., p. 15.

12. Ibid., pp. 15–16.

13. Ibid., pp. 16, 23, 24–25.

14. Richard White, "Trashing the Trails," in *Trails*, ed. Limerick, Milner, and Rankin, pp. 27, 29.

15. Ibid., pp. 31, 33, 32, 33, 35, 36, 37, 39.

16. Patricia Nelson Limerick, "The Unleashing of the Western Public Intellectual," in *Trails*, ed. Limerick, Milner, and Rankin, pp. 59, 61, 63.

17. Ibid., p. 67.

18. Ibid., p. 75.

19. Ibid., p. 77.

20. Patricia Nelson Limerick, "What on Earth Is the New Western History?" in *Trails*, ed. Limerick, Milner, and Rankin, pp. 85, 87.

21. Elliott West, "A Longer, Grimmer, but More Interesting Story," in *Trails*, ed. Limerick, Milner, and Rankin, pp. 103, 105.

22. Ibid., pp. 106, 108.

23. Ibid., pp. 108, 110, 111.

24. Brian W. Dippie, "American Wests: Historiographical Perspectives," in *Trails*, ed. Limerick, Milner, and Rankin, pp. 125, 114, 115, 117.

25. Ibid., pp. 128, 130, 135.

26. Ibid., pp. 135, 136.

27. Michael P. Malone, "Beyond the Last Frontier: Toward a New Approach to Western American History," in *Trails*, ed. Limerick, Milner, and Rankin, pp. 139, 140. Malone's citation of Howard Lamar is from the latter's "Much to Celebrate: The Western History Association's Twenty-fifth Birthday," *Western Historical Quarterly* 17 (1986): 397–416, originally an address to the WHA.

28. Malone, "Beyond the Last Frontier," pp. 144, 145, 147, 148.

29. Ibid., pp. 148, 149.

30. Ibid., pp. 150–51.

31. Ibid., pp. 153, 154. See Walter Nugent, "Frontiers and Empires in the Late Nineteenth Century," *Western Historical Quarterly* 20 (1989): 393–408.

32. Malone, "Beyond the Last Frontier," pp. 155, 157, 160.

33. William G. Robbins, "Laying Siege to Western History: The Emergence of New Paradigms," in *Trails*, ed. Limerick, Milner, and Rankin, pp. 183, 185, 191.

34. Ibid., pp. 192, 193, 194.

35. Ibid., pp. 194, 204, 202, 212, 213, 214.

36. Limerick, "Unleashing," pp. 75, 76. Interestingly enough, the foremost center for the scientific study of complexity in cultural and other systems, the Sante Fe Institute, is located in Santa Fe.

37. F. Scott Fitzgerald, *The Great Gatsby* (1925; reprint ed., New York: Scribner's, 1953), p. 1.

38. Robert F. Berkhofer, Jr., "Native Americans and United States History," in *The Reinterpretation of American History and Culture*, ed. William H. Cartwright and Richard L. Watson, Jr. (Washington, D.C.: National Council for Social Studies, 1973), pp. 47–48.

39. Reginald Horsman, "Recent Trends and New Directions in Native American History," in *The American West: New Perspectives, New Dimensions*, ed. Jerome O. Steffen (Norman: University of Oklahoma Press, 1979), pp. 129–30, 130, 128, 124, 131.

40. Ibid., pp. 142, 125. Have a look at two exemplary collections edited by José Barreiro: *Indian Roots of American Democracy* (Ithaca, N.Y.: Akwe

Kon Press, 1992) and *A View from the Shore: American Indian Perspectives on the Quincentenary* (Ithaca, N.Y.: Akwe Kon Press, 1992).

41. Worster, "Beyond the Agrarian Myth," p. 24.

42. Sandra L. Myres, *Westering Women and the Frontier Experience, 1800–1915* (Albuquerque: University of New Mexico Press, 1982), pp. xv, xvi (emphasis added).

43. Ibid., pp. xvi, xvii, 2, 4, 5, 11, 269–70.

44. Teresa Jordan, *Cowgirls: Women of the American West* (Garden City, N.Y.: Doubleday, Anchor Press, 1982), p. xii.

45. Ibid., pp. xxvi, xxii, xxxv.

46. Robbins, "Laying Siege," pp. 208, 209.

47. Peggy Pascoe, "Western Women at the Cultural Crossroads," in *Trails*, ed. Limerick, Milner, and Rankin, pp. 42, 43, 44, 46, 57, 53.

48. Dee Brown, *The Westerners* (New York: Holt, Rinehart and Winston, 1974), pp. 7, 8.

49. Ibid., pp. 260, 275.

50. Tom Mathews, "The Custer Syndrome: What's the Right Answer to 'Who Owns the West?' " *Newsweek*, 30 September 1991, p. 34.

51. Ibid., p. 35

52. Gene M. Gressley, "Regionalism and the Twentieth-Century West," in *American West*, ed. Steffen, p. 223.

53. Dippie, "American Wests," pp. 131–32. In this connection, see also William Cronon's "A Place for Stories: Nature, History, and Narrative," *Journal of American History* 78 (1992): 1347–76, in which he challenges historians to consider how manifoldly historiography itself consists of culture-driven stories.

54. Dippie, "American Wests," pp. 132, 133.

55. Kent Ladd Steckmesser, *The Western Hero in History and Legend* (Norman: University of Oklahoma Press, 1965), pp. vii, 242, 243, 245, 246, 247, 249, 252, 251, 255, 245.

56. William W. Savage, Jr., *The Cowboy Hero: His Image in American History and Culture* (Norman: University of Oklahoma Press, 1979), pp. 58, 60, 61, 62. Walter Prescott Webb's characterizing terms for Western history may be found in his essay "The American West: Perpetual Mirage," *Harper's Magazine*, May 1955, p. 31.

57. Richard White, *"It's Your Misfortune and None of My Own": A New History of the American West* (Norman: University of Oklahoma Press, 1991), p. 613.

58. Ibid., pp. 614–15, 617. The anecdote concerning Kit Carson may be found in Patricia Nelson Limerick, "Making the Most of Words: Verbal Activity and Western America," in *Under an Open Sky: Rethinking America's Western Past*, ed. William Cronon, George Miles, and Jay Gitlin (New York: Norton, 1992), pp. 167–68.

59. McMurtry, "How the West Was Won or Lost," p. 38.

60. Walter Nugent, "Western History, New and Not So New," *Magazine*

of History 9, no. 1 (Fall 1994): 5, 6. On the matter of anti-Turnerian excesses, see William Cronon, George Miles, and Jay Gitlin, "Becoming West: Toward a New Meaning for Western History," in *Under an Open Sky*, ed. Cronon, Miles, Gitlin, p. 6.

61. Nugent, "Western History," p. 6.

THREE. REWRITERS OF THE PURPLE SAGE, 1

1. Max Westbrook, Preface, *A Literary History of the American West* (Fort Worth: Texas Christian University Press, 1987), p. xx.

2. Michael Seidman, *Living the Dream: An Outline for a Life in Fiction* (New York: Carroll and Graf, 1992), pp. 35, 36, 37, 39.

3. Susan Porter, "Back in the Saddle Again," *Writer's Digest*, August 1993, p. 44.

4. Richard White, *"It's Your Misfortune and None of My Own": A New History of the American West* (Norman: University of Oklahoma Press, 1991), pp. 617, 618, 619.

5. Richard W. Etulain, "Western Fiction and History: A Reconsideration," in *The American West: New Perspectives, New Dimensions*, ed. Jerome O. Steffen (Norman: University of Oklahoma Press, 1979), pp. 152, 153, 154.

6. Ibid., p. 155.

7. Ibid., pp. 173, 155, 169.

8. Ibid., pp. 161, 170.

9. Wallace Stegner, *Angle of Repose* (1971; reprint ed., New York: Penguin Books, 1992), p. 277.

10. Etulain, "Western Fiction and History," pp. 167, 166, 170.

11. Jackson J. Benson, "Wallace Stegner, 1909–1993," *Western American Literature* 28 (1993): 51.

12. Wallace Stegner, Introduction, *Where the Bluebird Sings to the Lemonade Springs: Living and Writing in the West* (New York: Penguin Books, 1992), pp. xxii–xxiii.

13. Wallace Stegner, "Variations on a Theme by Crèvecoeur," in *Where the Bluebird Sings*, pp. 115–16.

14. Elliott West, "A Longer, Grimmer, but More Interesting Story," in *Trails: Toward a New Western History*, ed. Patricia Nelson Limerick, Clyde A. Milner II, and Charles E. Rankin (Lawrence: University Press of Kansas, 1991), pp. 110–11.

15. Stegner, Introduction, *Where the Bluebird Sings*, p. xxiii.

16. Harold P. Simonson, *Beyond the Frontier: Writers, Western Regionalism and a Sense of Place* (Fort Worth: Texas Christian University Press, 1989), pp. 2, 3–4.

17. Ibid., pp. 11, 12, 13, 14–15, 144, 147.

18. Larry McMurtry, "A Foreword," in *In a Narrow Grave: Essays on Texas* (1968; reprint ed., New York: Simon and Schuster, Touchstone, 1989), pp. xvi, xvii.

19. Jane Nelson, "Larry McMurtry," in *Literary History*, p. 619.

20. White, "*It's Your Misfortune*," pp. 629, 628, 629.

21. Lou Rodenberger, "Trends in Western Women's Writing," in *Literary History*, pp. 1178, 1179, 1180.

22. Barbara Howard Meldrum, Introduction, *Under the Sun: Myth and Realism in Western American Literature*, ed. Barbara Howard Meldrum (Troy, N.Y.: Whitston, 1985), pp. 1, 2, 3, 4, 5.

23. Ibid., pp. 5, 6, 7.

24. Max Westbrook, "Myth, Reality, and the American Frontier," in *Under the Sun*, ed. Meldrum, pp. 17, 18.

25. Madelon Heatherington, "Romance Without Women: The Sterile Fiction of the American West," in *Under the Sun*, ed. Meldrum, pp. 75, 76.

26. Ibid., pp. 76–77.

27. Ibid., pp. 77, 78, 80.

28. Ibid., pp. 80, 81.

29. Ibid., p. 82.

30. Ibid., pp. 86, 87.

31. Ibid., pp. 87–88.

32. Kathryn Hume, "Ishmael Reed and the Problematics of Control," *Publications of the Modern Language Association* 108 (1993): 508, 515.

33. Robert Murray Davis, *Playing Cowboys: Low Culture and High Art in the Western* (Norman: University of Oklahoma Press, 1992), pp. 132–34.

34. James C. Work, Introduction to Part 4: The Neowestern Period: 1915–Present, *Prose and Poetry of the American West*, ed. James C. Work (Lincoln: University of Nebraska Press, 1990), pp. 626, 627, 628, 629.

35. Ibid., p. 629.

36. Ibid., pp. 630, 631. See John R. Milton, *The Novel of the American West* (Lincoln: University of Nebraska Press, 1980), p. 324. His study throughout concerns the Western novel as a literature of the land.

37. Work, Introduction to Part 4, pp. 631, 632.

38. Russell Martin, Introduction, *New Writers of the Purple Sage: An Anthology of Contemporary Western Writing*, collected and with an introduction by Russell Martin (New York: Penguin Books, 1992), p. xix.

39. Ibid.

40. William T. Pilkington, Introduction to Section 2: The Southwest, in Part 2: Settled In: Many Wests, a *Literary History*, p. 511.

41. Gerald W. Haslam, Introduction to Section 1: Earth Tones: Ethnic Expression in Western American Literature, in Part 3: Rediscovering the West, *Literary History*, pp. 1035, 1036.

42. Gerald W. Haslam, Introduction to Section 2: Present Trends, in Part 3: Rediscovering the West, *Literary History*, pp. 1162, 1163, 1165, 1166, 1165, 1163.

43. William Kittredge, "Death of the Western," *Culturefront*, Summer 1993, p. 55.

44. Ibid., pp. 55, 80.

45. Ibid., p. 80.

46. Alexander Blackburn, "A Western Renaissance," *Western American Literature* 29 (1994): 62, 52, 62.

FOUR. REWRITERS OF THE PURPLE SAGE, 2

1. Mark Siegel, "Contemporary Trends in Western American Fiction," in *A Literary History of the American West* (Fort Worth: Texas Christian University Press, 1987), pp. 1182, 1183, 1184, 1187, 1188, 1192.

2. John R. Milton, *The Novel of the American West* (Lincoln: University of Nebraska Press, 1980), pp. xiv, xv.

3. Alan Prendergast, "The Last Man Alive," in *Writers of the Purple Sage: An Anthology of Recent Western Writing*, ed. Russell Martin and Marc Barasch (New York: Viking, 1984), pp. 223, 225.

4. Jan Roush, "The Developing Art of Tony Hillerman," *Western American Literature* 28 (1993): 99, 101.

5. Ibid., p. 102.

6. Charles Leerhsen, "A Rare Breed of Writer," review of *Last of the Breed*, by Louis L'Amour, *Newsweek*, 14 July 1986, p. 68.

7. Jane Tompkins, *West of Everything: The Inner Life of Westerns* (New York: Oxford University Press, 1992), pp. 207–8.

8. Pam Houston, "Cowboys Are My Weakness," in *Cowboys Are My Weakness* (1992; reprint ed., New York: Pocket Books, Washington Square Press, 1993), pp. 108, 123.

9. John Lewis Longley, Jr., "The Nuclear Winter of Cormac McCarthy," *Virginia Quarterly Review* 62 (1986): 749, 750, 746.

10. See ibid., p. 750.

11. Geoffrey O'Brien, "Cowboys and Nothingness," review of *Blood Meridian; or, The Evening Redness in the West*, by Cormac McCarthy, *Village Voice*, 15 July 1986, p. 48.

12. Tom Pilkington, "Borders of Destiny," *The World and I*, September 1992, pp. 378, 379.

13. Cormac McCarthy, *All the Pretty Horses* (New York: Knopf, 1992), p. 5. Speaking of horses — check out Robert F. Gish's *First Horses: Stories of the New West* (Albuquerque: University of New Mexico Press, 1993).

14. Pilkington, "Borders of Destiny," pp. 380–81, 382–83.

15. Richard Eder, "John's Passion," review of *All the Pretty Horses*, by Cormac McCarthy, *Los Angeles Times Book Review*, 17 May 1992, pp. 3, 13.

16. Kerry Ahearn, review of *All the Pretty Horses*, by Cormac McCarthy, *Western American Literature* 28 (1993): 183–84.

17. Milton, *Novel of the American West*, pp. 58, 59.

18. Siegel, "Contemporary Trends," pp. 1196, 1195.

19. William Lockwood, "Present Trends in Western Poetry," in *Literary History*, pp. 1202, 1207, 1208, 1217, 1218.

20. Ibid., pp. 1224, 1225, 1227, 1228.

21. Raymund A. Paredes, "Contemporary Mexican-American Literature, 1960–Present," in *Literary History*, pp. 1103, 1104.

22. Patricia Clark Smith, "Coyote's Sons, Spider's Daughters: Western American Indian Poetry, 1968–1983," in *Literary History*, pp. 1067, 1068.

23. Geary Hobson, "Buffalo Poem #1," in *The Remembered Earth: An Anthology of Contemporary Native American Literature*, ed. Geary Hobson (Albuquerque: Red Earth Press, 1979), p. 99.

24. Smith, "Coyote's Sons, Spider's Daughters," pp. 1068–69.

25. Ibid., pp. 1070–71.

26. Ibid., p. 1071.

27. Linda Hogan, "Heritage," "Red Clay," and "Calling Myself Home: Introduction," in *Red Clay: Poems and Stories* (Greenfield Center, N.Y.: Greenfield Review Press, 1991), pp. 21, 7, 1.

28. Stephanie Izarek Smith, "Joy Harjo" (interview), *Poets and Writers Magazine*, July–August 1993, pp. 23, 24.

29. Smith, "Coyote's Sons, Spider's Daughters," pp. 1073, 1074, 1075.

30. Andrea Millenson Penner, "At Once, Gentle and Powerful: Voices of the Landscape in the Poetry of Luci Tapahonso" (Master's thesis, Northern Arizona University, 1993), p. 4.

31. Luci Tapahonso, "Blue Horses Rush In," in *Sáanii Dahataał: The Women Are Singing* (Tucson: University of Arizona Press, 1993), p. 1.

32. "One with the Horse: New-Age 'Pokes Take Zen Path to Bronco Busting," *Lawrence Journal-World*, 11 October 1993, p. 10B.

33. Smith, "Coyote's Sons, Spider's Daughters," p. 1075.

34. Jim Harrison, "Poetry as Survival," in *Just Before Dark: Collected Nonfiction* (Livingston, Mont.: Clark City Press, 1991), pp. 294, 297–98.

35. Ibid., pp. 298–99.

36. Ibid., pp. 300, 301, 302, 303, 305, 304, 305.

37. Simon J. Ortiz, "The Significance of a Veteran's Day," "How Much Coyote Remembered," "Leaving America," and "I Tell You Now," in *Woven Stone* (Tucson: University of Arizona Press, 1992), pp. 108, 224, 97, 283.

38. Peter Wild and Frank Graziano, Introduction, *New Poetry of the American West*, ed. Peter Wild and Frank Graziano (Gettysburg, Pa.: Logbridge-Rhodes, 1982), pp. 10–11, 12, 13, 14.

39. Linda Hasselstrom, "The Poet Falls in Love with a Cowboy," "Goodbye," and "Medicine Rock Rodeo," in *Dakota Bones: Collected Poems of Linda Hasselstrom* (Granite Falls, Minn.: Spoon River Poetry Press, 1993), pp. 16, 120, 65.

40. George Venn, review of *Yellow*, by Anne Pitkin, and *All That Comes to Light*, by Lisa Malinowski Steinman, *Western American Literature* 25 (1990): 55–56.

41. Richard Dankleff, "Posse," in *Westerns* (Corvallis: Oregon State University Press, 1984), p. 11.

42. Hal Cannon, Introduction, *Cowboy Poetry: A Gathering*, ed. Hal Can-

non (Salt Lake City: Gibbs M. Smith, Peregrine Smith Books, 1985), pp. ix, x, xi.

43. Lawrence Clayton, review of *Roughstock Sonnets*, by Paul Zarzyski, *Western American Literature* 27 (1992): 190.

44. William Kittredge, *Hole in the Sky: A Memoir* (New York: Knopf, 1992), pp. 171, 172–73.

45. Hal Cannon, Introduction, *New Cowboy Poetry: A Contemporary Gathering*, ed. Hal Cannon (Layton, Utah: Gibbs Smith, Peregrine Smith Books, 1990), pp. vii, viii, ix, x.

46. Raymund A. Paredes, "Contemporary Mexican-American Literature, 1960–Present," pp. 1101–2.

47. Mark Busby, "Contemporary Western Drama," in *Literary History*, p. 1232.

48. Ibid., pp. 1239, 1242.

49. Jerry R. Dickey, " 'Myths of the East, Myths of the West': Shattering Racial and Gender Stereotypes in the Plays of David Henry Hwang," in *Old West — New West: Centennial Essays*, ed. Barbara Howard Meldrum (Moscow: University of Idaho Press, 1993), pp. 278–79, 277.

50. Ibid., p. 278.

51. Helen Lojek, "Reading the Myth of the West," in *Old West — New West*, ed. Meldrum, pp. 184, 185, 184, 185.

52. Ibid., pp. 186, 187, 188, 189.

53. Ibid., p. 190.

54. Mark Medoff, *The Majestic Kid* (New York: Dramatists Play Service, 1986), p. 8.

55. Lojek, "Reading the Myth," p. 190.

56. Ibid., pp. 191, 192.

57. Ibid., pp. 192, 193, 194, 195.

58. Ibid., p. 195.

59. Ann H. Zwinger, "What's a Nice Girl like Me Doing in a Place like This?" *Western American Literature* 27 (1992): 101.

60. Harold P. Simonson, *Beyond the Frontier: Writers, Western Regionalism and a Sense of Place* (Fort Worth: Texas Christian University Press, 1989), p. 141.

61. Glen A. Love, "*Et in Arcadia Ego*: Pastoral Theory Meets Ecocriticism," *Western American Literature* 27 (1992): 203.

62. See Tim Poland, " 'A Relative to All That Is': The Eco-Hero in Western American Literature," *Western American Literature* 26 (1991): 195–208.

63. Peter Wild, review of *Sky's Witness: A Year in the Wind River Range*, by C. L. Rawlins, *Western American Literature* 28 (1993): 147.

64. Thomas J. Lyon, "The Western Nature Essay Since 1970," in *Literary History*, p. 1246.

65. Ibid., pp. 1246–47.

66. Ann Ronald, *The New West of Edward Abbey* (Albuquerque: University of New Mexico Press, 1982), p. 1.

67. Edward Abbey, *The Monkey Wrench Gang* (New York: Avon Books, 1976), p. 211.

68. See Paul T. Bryant, "The Structure and Unity of *Desert Solitaire*," *Western American Literature* 28 (1993): 3–19.

69. David Copland Morris, "Celebration and Irony: The Polyphonic Voice of Edward Abbey's *Desert Solitaire*," *Western American Literature* 28 (1993): 21, 25, 27.

70. Lyon, "Western Nature Essay Since 1970," pp. 1252, 1253.

71. Barry Lopez, "The Bull Rider," in *Crossing Open Ground* (New York: Random House, Vintage Books, 1989), pp. 101–2.

72. William Kittredge, review of *Land Circle: Writings Collected from the Land*, by Linda Hasselstrom, *Western American Literature* 27 (1993): 377, 376.

73. Reg Saner, "Technically Sweet," in *The Four-cornered Falcon: Essays on the Interior West and the Natural Scene* (Baltimore: Johns Hopkins University Press, 1993), pp. 78–79.

74. Kathleen Norris, "The Beautiful Places" and "Weather Report: January 17," in *Dakota: A Spiritual Geography* (New York: Ticknor and Fields, 1993), pp. 3, 6, 8, 9, 10, 13.

75. Scott Russell Sanders, Preface and "House and Home," in *Staying Put: Making a Home in a Restless World* (Boston: Beacon Press, 1993), pp. xiii, xiv, xv, xvii, 27, 29, 35.

76. Scott Russell Sanders, "Settling Down," in *Staying Put*, pp. 104, 108, 109, 110, 111, 113, 114.

77. Dick Kirkpatrick, review of *Desierto: Memories of the Future*, by Charles Bowden, *Western American Literature* 27 (1992): 249.

78. See Kevin Breen, "Rick Bass" (interview), *Poets and Writers Magazine*, May–June 1993, pp. 18–25.

79. Michael L. Johnson, "An Epitaph for Wallace Stegner," in *Violence and Grace: Poems About the American West* (Lawrence, Kans.: Cottonwood Press, 1993), p. 44.

80. A. Carl Bredahl, Jr., *New Ground: Western American Narrative and the Literary Canon* (Chapel Hill: University of North Carolina Press, 1989), pp. 93, 98, 138, 140.

81. William Kittredge, "Falling" and "Paradise All Around," in *Hole in the Sky: A Memoir* (New York: Knopf, 1992), pp. 10, 11, 224, 237, 238.

82. Wallace Stegner, "Coming of Age: The End of the Beginning," in *Where the Bluebird Sings to the Lemonade Springs: Living and Writing in the West* (New York: Penguin Books, 1992), p. 141.

83. Marilynne Robinson, "My Western Roots," in *Old West — New West*, ed. Meldrum, pp. 171–72, 165–66.

84. See Malcolm Jones, "The Ghost Writer at Home on the Range," review of *Streets of Laredo*, by Larry McMurtry, *Newsweek*, 2 August 1993, p. 53.

85. James C. Work, "Who's Afraid of the Virginian's Wolf?" (past presi-

dent's address), Twenty-seventh Annual Meeting of the Western Literature Association, Reno, Nevada, 9 October 1992, pp. 9, 10–11, 12, 13, 2, 13, 1, 13.

FIVE. CROSSED OVER

1. Nancy Shoemaker, "Teaching the Truth About the History of the American West," *Chronicle of Higher Education*, 27 October 1993, p. A48.

2. William H. Truettner, "Ideology and Image: Justifying Westward Expansion," in *The West as America: Reinterpreting Images of the Frontier, 1820–1920*, ed. William H. Truettner (Washington, D.C.: Smithsonian Institution Press, 1991), p. 42.

3. William H. Truettner, "The West and the Heroic Ideal: Using Images to Interpret History," *Chronicle of Higher Education*, 20 November 1991, pp. B1, B2.

4. Bryan J. Wolf, "How the West Was Hung, Or, When I Hear the Word 'Culture' I Take Out My Checkbook," *American Quarterly* 44 (1992): 419, 420, 423, 428, 435, 431.

5. Eric Gibson, "Smithsonian Politics on Exhibit," *Washington Times*, 24 June 1991, p. C8.

6. Richard Slotkin, "Gunsmoke and Mirrors," *Life*, 5 April 1993, p. 63.

7. Ibid.

8. Ibid.

9. David Daly and Joel Persky, *The West and the Western*, a special issue of *Journal of the West* 29, no. 2 (April 1990): 13, 16.

10. Ibid., p. 20.

11. Michael T. Marsden and Jack Nachbar, "The Modern Popular Western: Radio, Television, Film, and Print," in *A Literary History of the American West* (Fort Worth: Texas Christian University Press, 1987), pp. 1266–67.

12. Ibid., pp. 1267, 1269.

13. Ibid., p. 1269.

14. Max Westbrook, "The Night John Wayne Danced with Shirley Temple," in *Old West — New West: Centennial Essays*, ed. Barbara Howard Meldrum (Moscow: University of Idaho Press, 1993), p. 60.

15. Daly and Persky, *West and Western*, p. 51.

16. Marsden and Nachbar, "Modern Popular Western," p. 1270.

17. Richard White, *"It's Your Misfortune and None of My Own": A New History of the American West* (Norman: University of Oklahoma Press, 1991), p. 626.

18. Marsden and Nachbar, "Modern Popular Western," p. 1270.

19. Ibid., pp. 1270, 1271.

20. Ibid., pp. 1271–72.

21. Ibid., pp. 1272, 1273.

22. Larry McMurtry, "Cowboys, Movies, Myths, and Cadillacs: An Excursus on Ritual Forms in the Western Movie," in *In a Narrow Grave: Es-*

says on Texas (1968; reprint ed., New York: Simon and Schuster, Touchstone, 1989), p. 23.

23. Ibid., pp. 24, 27–28.

24. Ibid., p. 28.

25. Marsden and Nachbar, "Modern Popular Western," p. 1273.

26. Rita Parks, *The Western Hero in Film and Television: Mass Media Mythology* (Ann Arbor, Mich.: UMI Research Press, 1982), p. 115.

27. Ibid., pp. 116, 120, 121, 123.

28. Marsden and Nachbar, "Modern Popular Western," pp. 1273–74.

29. Parks, *Western Hero*, p. 124.

30. A. Carl Bredahl, Jr., *New Ground: Western American Narrative and the Literary Canon* (Chapel Hill: University of North Carolina Press, 1989), p. 157.

31. Marsden and Nachbar, "Modern Popular Western," pp. 1274–75.

32. Ibid., p. 1275.

33. Robert Murray Davis, *Playing Cowboys: Low Culture and High Art in the Western* (Norman: University of Oklahoma Press, 1992), pp. 98, 118, 122–23. Robert Sheckley's "The Never-ending Western Movie" may be found in *Science Fiction Discoveries*, ed. Carol Pohl and Frederick Pohl (New York: Bantam, 1978), pp. 31–50.

34. Marsden and Nachbar, "Modern Popular Western," pp. 1275–76.

35. Ibid., p. 1276.

36. Daly and Persky, *West and Western*, p. 13. The quotation is from Thomas Schatz, "The Western," in *Handbook of American Film Genres*, ed. Wes D. Gehring (New York: Greenwood Press, 1988), p. 31.

37. Parks, *Western Hero*, pp. 155, 156, 157.

38. Brian Garfield, *Western Films: A Complete Guide* (New York: Rawson Associates, 1982), pp. 8, 6, 8.

39. Scot Haller, review of *Pale Rider*, dir. Clint Eastwood, *People Weekly*, 15 July 1985, p. 11.

40. Pauline Kael, review of *Pale Rider*, dir. Clint Eastwood, *New Yorker*, 12 August 1985, pp. 64–65, 64.

41. Richard Corliss, "Cuisinartistry," review of *Silverado*, dir. Lawrence Kasdan, *Time*, 22 July 1985, p. 77.

42. David Ansen, "Saddled Up and Rarin' to Go," review of *Silverado*, dir. Lawrence Kasdan, *Newsweek*, 15 July 1985, p. 54.

43. Michele Morris, *The Cowboy Life: A Saddlebag Guide for Dudes, Tenderfeet, and Cowpunchers Everywhere* (New York: Simon and Schuster, Fireside, 1993), p. 37.

44. Daly and Persky, *West and Western*, p. 61.

45. Richard Schickel, "Riding to Redemption Ridge," review of *Dances with Wolves*, dir. Kevin Costner, *Time*, 12 November 1990, p. 102.

46. Pauline Kael, review of *Dances with Wolves*, dir. Kevin Costner, *New Yorker*, 17 December 1990, p. 115.

47. David Ansen, "How the West Was Lost," review of *Dances with Wolves*, dir. Kevin Costner, *Newsweek*, 19 November 1990, pp. 67, 68.

48. William K. Everson, *The Hollywood Western: 90 Years of Cowboys and Indians, Train Robbers, Sheriffs and Gunslingers, and Assorted Heroes and Desperados* (New York: Citadel Press, 1992), pp. 278, 279, 280.

49. William W. Savage, Jr., *The Cowboy Hero: His Image in American History and Culture* (Norman: University of Oklahoma Press, 1979), pp. 161, 162.

50. Parks, *Western Hero*, pp. 151, 152, 153.

51. Ibid., p. 153.

52. Ibid., pp. 154, 153.

53. Gail Gilchriest, *The Cowgirl Companion: Big Skies, Buckaroos, Honky Tonks, Lonesome Blues, and Other Glories of the True West* (New York: Hyperion, 1993), pp. 141, 143.

54. Callie Khouri, quoted in Janice C. Simpson, "Moving into the Driver's Seat," *Time*, 24 June 1991, p. 55.

55. Ibid.

56. See Jane Tompkins, *West of Everything: The Inner Life of Westerns* (New York: Oxford University Press, 1992), pp. 103–4.

57. J. Frank Dobie, *The Mustangs* (Boston: Little Brown, 1934), pp. 185–86.

58. Scott Rosenberg, " 'Unforgiven': Eastwood's New Killing Fields," review of *Unforgiven*, dir. Clint Eastwood, *San Francisco Examiner*, 7 August 1992, p. B9.

59. Slotkin, "Gunsmoke and Mirrors," p. 68.

60. James Ryan, "Shoot-out at the P.C. Corral," *Vogue*, July 1993, pp. 68, 69.

61. Ibid., pp. 69, 70.

62. Ibid., p. 70.

63. Joseph Hooper, "Finally Cowgirls Get Their Due: New Thoughts on the Old West," *Harper's Bazaar*, August 1993, pp. 155, 156.

64. Ibid., p. 157.

65. Ivan Karp, "Dealing from New York," in *The Business of Art*, ed. Lee Evan Caplin (Englewood Cliffs, N.J.: Prentice-Hall, 1982), p. 270.

66. Patricia Janis Broder, *The American West: The Modern Vision* (Boston: Little, Brown, New York Graphic Society Books, 1984), p. 1.

67. Ibid., pp. 1, 2.

68. Ibid., p. 267.

69. Ibid., pp. 270, 275. Though Broder offers Baker as an example of "the *nouveau* Native American" (p. 270), what I know of him, from personal conversation, argues against that classification.

70. William H. Goetzmann and William N. Goetzmann, *The West of the Imagination* (New York: Norton, 1986), pp. 404–5.

71. Ibid., pp. 410, 413.

72. Ibid., pp. 419, 420, 421.

73. Broder, *American West*, pp. 329, 330, 331.

74. Charles A. Guerin, Introduction, *The New West* (Colorado Springs, Colo.: Colorado Springs Fine Arts Center, 1986), pp. 4, 5.

SIX. GARTH AND FRIENDS

1. Jimmy Guterman, "Origins of the Species: From the Singing Brakeman to the Judds," *New Country Music*, Fall 1993, p. 48.

2. Ibid., pp. 48–49.

3. Colin Escott, "Western Dreams and Nightmares: Putting the 'W' Back in 'C & W,' " *New Country Music*, Fall 1993, p. 50.

4. Ibid., pp. 50–51.

5. William W. Savage, Jr., *The Cowboy Hero: His Image in American History and Culture* (Norman: University of Oklahoma Press, 1979), p. 79.

6. Ibid., pp. 79–80, 80–81. The quotation from Dorothy Horstman is from her *Sing Your Heart Out, Country Boy* (New York: Dutton, 1975), p. 289.

7. Savage, *Cowboy Hero*, pp. 81, 82.

8. Ibid., p. 83.

9. Ibid., p. 84.

10. Ibid., pp. 85–86.

11. Ibid., pp. 87, 88.

12. Ibid., pp. 88, 89.

13. Ibid., pp. 89, 90, 91.

14. Ibid., p. 92.

15. Ibid., pp. 93–94.

16. George H. Lewis, "Duellin' Values: Tension, Conflict and Contradiction in Country Music," *Journal of Popular Culture* 24, no. 4 (Spring 1991): 103–4.

17. Ibid., pp. 104, 105, 106.

18. Ibid., p. 110.

19. Dwight Yoakam, "Guitars, Cadillacs," on *Just Lookin' for a Hit*, Reprise, 25989, 1989.

20. Lewis, "Duellin' Values," pp. 110, 111.

21. Ibid., pp. 112, 113, 114.

22. Bill C. Malone, "CMA Awards: Wins of Change?" *Journal of Country Music* 11, no. 1 (1986): 8, 9.

23. Gary Graff, "New Country Sends Old Stars to Pasture," *Las Vegas Review-Journal*, 25 June 1993, pp. 1C, 7C.

24. The Escape Club, "Wild, Wild West," on *Wild, Wild West*, Atlantic, 81871, 1988.

25. Jack Hurst, "Charting a Course: A Look at Nashville's Options for the '90s," *Chicago Tribune*, 20 March 1988, sect. 13, pp. 22, 23.

26. Susan Stewart, *On Longing: Narratives of the Miniature, the Gigantic, the Souvenir, the Collection* (Baltimore: Johns Hopkins University Press, 1984), p. 150.

27. Garth Brooks, "Cowboy Bill," on *Garth Brooks*, Liberty, 90897, 1989.

28. Charles Hirshberg, "He's Garth Brooks," *Life*, July 1992, p. 60.

29. James Bowen, quoted in Lisa Gubernick and Peter Newcomb, "The Wal-Mart School of Music," *Forbes*, 2 March 1992, p. 72.

30. Priscilla Painton, "Country Rocks the Boomers," *Time*, 30 March 1992, pp. 63, 64.

31. Susan Holly, "A Country Twist at Every Turn," *Nation's Business*, March 1993, pp. 33, 37.

32. Allen St. John, "Achy Breaky and Squeaky Clean," *Schwann Spectrum* 4, no. 2 (Spring 1993): 17–18, 17.

33. Sushil K. Dulai, "Always and Forever," *Western Styles*, Fall 1993, pp. 18, 20.

34. Gail Gilchriest, *The Cowgirl Companion: Big Skies, Buckaroos, Honky Tonks, Lonesome Blues, and Other Glories of the True West* (New York: Hyperion, 1993), pp. 154, 155.

35. Painton, "Country Rocks the Boomers," p. 68.

36. Gilchriest, *Cowgirl Companion*, pp. 156, 155.

37. Connie Schultz Gard, "Hooked on Country," *Cosmopolitan*, September 1993, p. 54.

38. Hurst, "Charting a Course," p. 23.

39. Tish Hinojosa, liner notes for her *Homeland*, A&M, 75021–5263, 1989.

40. Michele Morris, *The Cowboy Life: A Saddlebag Guide for Dudes, Tenderfeet, and Cowpunchers Everywhere* (New York: Simon and Schuster, Fireside, 1993), p. 243.

41. Ibid., p. 245.

42. Huck Talbot, "Huck Talbot's Neck o' the Woods: It's Awards Time Again!" *Countrygazette*, September 1993, pp. 8, 12.

43. Escott, "Western Dreams and Nightmares," p. 52.

44. Julie L. Semrau, "WestFest at Copper Mountain Resort," *Yippy-Yi-Yea*, Fall 1993, p. 24.

45. Escott, "Western Dreams and Nightmares," p. 51.

46. Talbot, "It's Awards Time Again!" p. 12.

47. Escott, "Western Dreams and Nightmares," p. 52.

48. Ibid., p. 53.

49. Ibid.

50. Guy Garcia, "Scoot Your Booty!" *Time*, 15 March 1993, pp. 60–61.

51. Elizabeth Tallent, "Why I Love Country Music," in *Writers of the Purple Sage: An Anthology of Recent Western Writing*, ed. Russell Martin and Marc Barasch (New York: Viking, 1984), p. 186.

52. Patsy Swayze, quoted in René E. Riley, "Kick and Pivot: Your Inside Guide to Today's Hot Country-Western Dance Styles," *Western Styles*, February 1994, p. 66.

SEVEN. THE NEW WEST

1. Susan Stewart, *On Longing: Narratives of the Miniature, the Gigantic, the Souvenir, the Collection* (Baltimore: Johns Hopkins University Press, 1984) pp. 150, 23, 139–40, 142, 143.

2. Ibid., pp. 145, 146.

3. Stephen Tatum, "Adventure in the Fashion System," *Western Humanities Review* 43, no. 1 (Spring 1989): 9, 14, 15.

4. Ibid., pp. 16, 17, 18.

5. Ibid., pp. 8, 13, 18, 19.

6. Leonard Lutwack, *The Role of Place in Literature* (Syracuse, N.Y.: Syracuse University Press, 1984), p. 27.

7. Ibid., pp. 142, 143, 144, 145, 144.

8. Ibid., pp. 147, 148, 149, 150, 151–52, 156, 160, 165, 166, 181.

9. Ibid., pp. 172, 229, 240.

10. Ibid., pp. 181, 245.

11. A. Carl Bredahl, Jr., *New Ground: Western American Narrative and the Literary Canon* (Chapel Hill: University of North Carolina Press, 1989), pp. 4–5, 31, 32.

12. Ibid., pp. 36, 39, 42.

13. Ibid., pp. 43, 48.

14. Dayton Duncan, *Out West: An American Journey* (New York: Viking, 1987), pp. x, xi.

15. Ibid., pp. 4, 7, 9, 12, 13–14, 414.

16. Jonathan Walters, "Hitch Your Wagon to History," *USA Weekend*, 23–25 July 1993, p. 8.

17. Michael L. Johnson, "Lumen Martin Winter's *The Great White Buffalo*," in *Violence and Grace: Poems About the American West* (Lawrence, Kans.: Cottonwood Press, 1993), p. 7.

18. Carolyn J. Mooney, "Finding a 'Sense of Place' in the Great Plains," *Chronicle of Higher Education*, 20 May 1992, p. A5.

19. Wes Jackson, "Becoming Native to This Place," Twenty-eighth Annual Meeting of the Western Literature Association, Wichita, Kansas, 8 October 1993.

20. Rex Buchanan, "Earthly Goods," *Kansas Alumni Magazine*, August–September 1993, p. 25.

21. Ibid., p. 26.

22. Gail Gilchriest, *The Cowgirl Companion: Big Skies, Buckaroos, Honky Tonks, Lonesome Blues, and Other Glories of the True West* (New York: Hyperion, 1993), p. 118.

23. Ibid., p. 35.

24. Jane Stern and Michael Stern, *Way Out West* (New York: HarperCollins, 1993), p. 229.

25. Larry McMurtry, "A Look at the Lost Frontier," in *In a Narrow Grave: Essays on Texas* (1968; reprint ed., New York: Simon and Schuster, Touchstone, 1989), p. 90.

26. Wallace Stegner, "Finding the Place: A Migrant Childhood," in *Where the Bluebird Sings to the Lemonade Springs: Living and Writing in the West* (New York: Penguin Books, 1992), p. 16.

27. Elizabeth Atwood Lawrence, *Rodeo: An Anthropologist Looks at the Wild and the Tame* (Knoxville: University of Tennessee Press, 1982), pp. 3, 4, 5.

28. Ibid., p. 7.

29. Ibid., pp. 7, 107–8, 228.

30. Ibid., pp. 93, 110, 112, 116, 250.

31. Ibid., pp. 263, 265.

32. Michael L. Johnson, "Tucson," in *Violence and Grace*, p. 8.

33. *Las Vegas Today*, 24 June 1993, p. 7.

34. F. Scott Fitzgerald, *The Great Gatsby* (1925; reprint ed., New York: Scribner's, 1953), p. 99.

35. Wallace Stegner, *Angle of Repose* (1971; reprint ed., New York: Penguin Books, 1992), p. 367.

36. Fitzgerald, *Great Gatsby*, p. 182.

37. Aaron Latham, "Attitude Cowboys," *Esquire*, August 1993, pp. 93, 94, 93, 94.

38. Ibid., pp. 94, 93, 94.

39. Ian Frazier, *Great Plains* (New York: Penguin Books, 1989), p. 117.

40. Jane Tompkins, *West of Everything: The Inner Life of Westerns* (New York: Oxford University Press, 1992), pp. 180, 183, 187, 188, 189.

41. Ibid., pp. 190, 194, 185.

42. Ibid., pp. 195, 194, 195, 197–98, 199.

43. Ibid., p. 200.

44. Raye C. Ringholz, *Little Town Blues: Voices from the Changing West* (Salt Lake City: Gibbs Smith, Peregrine Smith Books, 1992), p. 13.

45. Ibid., pp. 15, 17, 15, 16, 17, 18, 16.

CONCLUSION. STAYING PUT

1. A. B. Guthrie, Jr., *The Big Sky* (1947; reprint ed., New York: Bantam Books, 1982), p. 214.

2. Wallace Stevens, *Adagia*, in *Opus Posthumous*, ed. Milton J. Bates, rev., enl., and corrected ed. (New York: Knopf, 1989), p. 197.

3. William Kittredge, "The Last Safe Place," *Time*, 6 September 1993, p. 27.

4. Ibid.

5. Robert James Waller, *The Bridges of Madison County* (New York: Warner Books, 1992), p. 100.

6. William W. Savage, Jr., *The Cowboy Hero: His Image in American History and Culture* (Norman: University of Oklahoma Press, 1979), pp. 156, 157.

7. Lawrence Clayton, "Evolution of the Cowboy: Coping with Changes Without Losing Heart," in *The Catch-Pen: A Selection of Essays from the First Two Years of the National Cowboy Symposium and Celebration*, ed. Len Ainsworth and Kenneth W. Davis (Lubbock, Tex.: Ranching Heritage Center, 1991), p. 183.

8. Ernestine Sewell Linck, "Food, Fun, and Western Women," in *Catch-Pen*, ed. Ainsworth and Davis, p. 79.

9. Clay Reynolds, "Images of the Cowboy, For-real and Urban: The

Search for the Horseman," in *Catch-Pen*, ed. Ainsworth and Davis, pp. 187, 191, 194.

10. Ibid., p. 194.

11. Michael Stern, interview, *First Word* 1, no. 3 (1993): 2, 4.

12. Robert Murray Davis, Preface, *Playing Cowboys: Low Culture and High Art in the Western* (Norman: University of Oklahoma Press, 1991), p. xii.

13. Cynthia Heimel, "Sleepless in Sandusky," *Playboy*, October 1993, p. 32.

14. Sharman Apt Russell, *Kill the Cowboy: A Battle of Mythology in the New West* (Reading, Mass.: Addison-Wesley, 1993), pp. 11, 3.

15. Ibid., pp. 5, 6, 7.

16. Ibid., pp. 10, 11, 12, 13.

17. Ibid., p. 193.

18. Ibid., pp. 194, 195, 196, 197.

19. Jim Robbins, *Last Refuge: The Environmental Showdown in Yellowstone and the American West* (New York: Morrow, 1993), p. 12.

20. Ibid., pp. 12, 13.

21. Ibid., pp. 205, 207, 208, 212, 213.

22. Ibid., pp. 213–14, 215, 216, 219, 221.

23. Ibid., p. 221.

24. Ibid., p. 227.

25. Ibid., pp. 233, 234.

26. Ibid., pp. 236, 242, 251.

27. Ibid., pp. 257, 260, 265.

28. Ibid., pp. 265–66.

29. Ibid., p. 266.

30. Donald Worster, *Under Western Skies: Nature and History in the American West* (New York: Oxford University Press, 1992), pp. 238, 239, 253–54.

31. See William Stafford, "Written on the Stub of the First Paycheck," part 6 of "The Move to California," in *Stories That Could Be True: New and Collected Poems* (New York: Harper and Row, Perennial Library, 1977), p. 47.

32. Reg Saner, "Epilogue: What's to Become?" in *The Four-cornered Falcon: Essays on the Interior West and the Natural Scene* (Baltimore: Johns Hopkins University Press, 1993), pp. 281, 282–83.

33. A. Carl Bredahl, Jr., *New Ground: Western American Narrative and the Literary Canon* (Chapel Hill: University of North Carolina Press, 1989), p. 99.

34. See Rebecca Brown, "Annie," in *Annie Oakley's Girl* (San Francisco: City Lights, 1993), pp. 2–33.

35. David Daly and Joel Persky, *The West and the Western*, a special issue of *Journal of the West* 29, no. 2 (April 1990): 5.

36. Mary Catherine Harper, "Spiraling Around the Hinge: Working Solutions in *Always Coming Home*," in *Old West — New West: Centennial Es-*

says, ed. Barbara Howard Meldrum (Moscow: University of Idaho Press, 1993), pp. 241, 248, 254.

37. Richard White, *"It's Your Misfortune and None of My Own": A New History of the American West* (Norman: University of Oklahoma Press, 1991), p. 623.

38. Joseph J. Wydeven, review of *Visions of the American West*, by Gerald F. Kreyche, *Western American Literature* 27 (1992): 135.

39. Davis, *Playing Cowboys*, p. 151 (emphasis added).

40. Texas Bix Bender, *Don't Squat with Yer Spurs On! A Cowboy's Guide to Life* (Salt Lake City: Gibbs Smith, Peregrine Smith Books, 1992), p. 96.

Suggested Readings

The following selections may be of interest to readers who wish to pursue certain topics in more detail. Some I've mentioned or discussed in the text, but most titles are in addition to those already cited.

INTRODUCTION. WESTERING AGAIN

Nichols, John. *On the Mesa.* Salt Lake City: Gibbs M. Smith, Peregrine Smith Books, 1986.

Potter, Edgar F. "Frosty." *Cowboy Slang.* Phoenix, Ariz.: Golden West, 1986.

ONE. A VERTICAL RIDE

Baca, Elmo, and Elaine Markoutsas, contributing writer. *Southwest Expressions.* Lincolnwood, Ill.: Publications International, 1992.

Blomberg, Nancy J. *Navajo Textiles: The William Randolph Hearst Collection.* Tucson: University of Arizona Press, 1988.

Burciaga, José Antonio. *Drink Cultura: Chicanismo.* Santa Barbara, Calif.: Capra Press, Joshua Odell Editions, 1993.

Cameron, Sheila MacNiven. *The Best from New Mexico Kitchens.* Santa Fe, N.Mex.: New Mexico Magazine, 1978.

Fein, Judith. *Indian Time: A Year of Discovery with the Native Americans of the Southwest.* New York: Simon and Schuster, 1993.

Flood, Elizabeth Clair. *Cowboy High Style: Thomas Molesworth to the New West.* Salt Lake City: Peregrine Smith Books, 1992.

Friedman, Michael. *Cowboy Culture: Last Frontier of American Antiques.* Atglen, Pa.: Schiffer, 1992.

Ketchum, William C., Jr. *Collecting the West: Cowboy, Indian, Spanish American, and Mining Memorabilia.* New York: Crown, 1993.

Kusz, Natalie. *Road Song: A Memoir.* New York: HarperCollins, 1991.

Poulsen, Richard C. *The Landscape of the Mind: Cultural Transformations of the American West.* New York: Peter Lang, 1992.

Tanner, Clara Lee. *Indian Baskets of the Southwest.* Tucson: University of Arizona Press, 1983.

Tatum, Stephen. "Adventure in the Fashion System." *Western Humanities Review* 43, no. 1 (Spring 1989): 5–26.

Walker, Judy Hille. *Savory Southwest: Prize-winning Recipes from the Arizona Republic.* Flagstaff, Ariz.: Northland, 1990.

Williams, Jacqueline B. *Wagon Wheel Kitchens: Food on the Oregon Trail.* Lawrence: University Press of Kansas, 1993.

TWO. MANIFEST DIVERSITY

Armitage, Susan, and Elizabeth Jameson, eds. *The Women's West.* Norman: University of Oklahoma Press, 1987.

Athearn, Robert G. *The Mythic West in Twentieth Century America.* Lawrence: University Press of Kansas, 1986.

Beckstead, James H. *Cowboying: A Tough Job in a Hard Land.* Salt Lake City: University of Utah Press, 1991.

Billington, Ray Allen, ed. *Frontier and Section: Selected Essays of Frederick Jackson Turner.* Englewood Cliffs, N.J.: Prentice-Hall, 1961.

Bogart, Barbara Allen. *In Place: Stories of Place and Identity from the American West.* Glendo, Wyo.: High Plains Press, 1994.

Brown, Dee. *The American West.* New York: Scribner's, 1994.

Calloway, Colin G., ed. *New Directions in American Indian History.* Norman: University of Oklahoma Press, 1988.

Cronon, William. *Nature's Metropolis: Chicago and the Great West.* New York: Norton, 1991.

Limerick, Patricia Nelson. *The Legacy of Conquest: The Unbroken Past of the American West.* New York: Norton, 1987.

McMurtry, Larry. "Westward Ho Hum: What the New Historians Have Done to the Old West." *New Republic*, 9 October 1990, pp. 32–38.

Milner, Clyde A., II, Carol A. O'Connor, and Martha A. Sandweiss, eds. *The Oxford History of the American West.* New York: Oxford University Press, 1994.

Mullins, Reuben B. *Pulling Leather: Being the Early Recollections of a Cowboy on the Wyoming Range, 1884–1889.* Edited by Jan E. Roush and Lawrence Clayton. Glendo, Wyo.: High Plains Press, 1988.

Parman, Donald L. *Indians and the American West in the Twentieth Century.* Bloomington: Indiana University Press, 1994.

Riley, Glenda. *A Place to Grow: Women in the American West.* Arlington Heights, Ill.: Harlan Davidson, 1992.

Robinson, Forrest G. "The New Historicism and the Old West." In *Old West — New West: Centennial Essays*, edited by Barbara Howard Meldrum, pp. 74–96. Moscow: University of Idaho Press, 1993.

Schlissel, Lillian, Vicki L. Ruiz, and Janice Monk, eds. *Western Women: Their Land, Their Lives.* Albuquerque: University of New Mexico Press, 1988.

Schwantes, Carlos A. *The Pacific Northwest: An Interpretive History.* Lincoln: University of Nebraska Press, 1989.

Slatta, Richard W. *Cowboys of the Americas.* New Haven: Yale University Press, 1990.

Slotkin, Richard. *Gunfighter Nation: The Myth of the Frontier in Twentieth-Century America.* New York: Atheneum, 1992.

Stegner, Wallace. *Beyond the Hundredth Meridian: John Wesley Powell and the Second Opening of the West.* Boston: Houghton Mifflin, 1954.

_____. *The Gathering of Zion: The Story of the Mormon Trail.* New York: McGraw-Hill, 1964.

White, Richard, and Patricia N. Limerick. *The Frontier in American Culture: An Exhibit at the Newberry Library, August 26–November 26, 1994.* Edited by James R. Grossman. Berkeley: University of California Press, 1994.

Worster, Donald. *Under Western Skies: Nature and History in the American West.* New York: Oxford University Press, 1992.

_____. *An Unsettled Country: Changing Landscapes of the American West.* Albuquerque: University of New Mexico Press, 1994.

THREE. REWRITERS OF THE PURPLE SAGE, 1

Erisman, Fred. "Elmer Kelton's 'Other' West." *Western American Literature* 28 (1994): 291–99.

Lewis, Merrill, and L. L. Lee, eds. *The Westering Experience in American Literature: Bicentennial Essays.* Bellingham: Western Washington University, Bureau for Faculty Research, 1977.

Manfred, Frederick. *Lord Grizzly.* 1954. Reprint. New York: Signet, 1964.

Meldrum, Barbara Howard, ed. *Under the Sun: Myth and Realism in Western American Literature.* Troy, N.Y.: Whitston, 1985.

Robinson, Forrest G. *Having It Both Ways: Self-Subversion in Western Popular Classics.* Albuquerque: University of New Mexico Press, 1993.

Simonson, Harold P. *Beyond the Frontier: Writers, Western Regionalism and a Sense of Place.* Fort Worth: Texas Christian University Press, 1989.

Stegner, Wallace. *Angle of Repose.* Garden City, N.Y.: Doubleday, 1971.

Work, James C., ed. *Prose and Poetry of the American West.* Lincoln: University of Nebraska Press, 1990.

FOUR. REWRITERS OF THE PURPLE SAGE, 2

Baker, Alison. *How I Came West, and Why I Stayed: Stories.* San Francisco: Chronicle Books, 1993.

Barnes, Kim, and Mary Clearman Blew, eds. *Circle of Women: An Anthology of Contemporary Western Women Writers.* New York: Penguin Books, 1994.

Bass, Rick. *In the Loyal Mountains.* New York: Houghton Mifflin, 1995.

Briggs, Joe Bob. *Iron Joe Bob.* New York: Atlantic Monthly Press, 1992.

Clow, Deborah, and Donald Snow, eds. *Northern Lights: A Selection of New Writing from the American West.* New York: Random House, Vintage, 1994.

Davidson, Arnold E. *Coyote Country: Fictions of the Canadian West.* Durham, N.C.: Duke University Press, 1994.

Doig, Ivan. *Heart Earth.* New York: Atheneum, 1993.

Ehrlich, Gretel. *The Solace of Open Spaces.* New York: Viking, 1985.

Erdrich, Louise. *Baptism of Desire: Poems.* New York: Harper and Row, 1989.

Evans, Max. *Bluefeather Fellini.* Niwot: University Press of Colorado, 1993.

Fox, William L., ed. *TumbleWords: Writers Reading the West.* Reno: University of Nevada Press, 1995.

Galvin, James. *The Meadow.* New York: Henry Holt, 1992.

Gish, Robert Franklin. *When Coyote Howls: A Lavaland Fable.* Albuquerque: University of New Mexico Press, 1994.

Hansen, Ron. *The Assassination of Jesse James by the Coward Robert Ford.* New York: Norton, 1983.

Harris, Jana. *Oh How Can I Keep on Singing? Voices of Pioneer Women.* Princeton, N.J.: Ontario Review Press, 1993.

Hinojosa, Rolando. *Dear Rafe.* Houston: Arte Público Press, 1985.

Hogan, Linda. *Mean Spirit.* New York: Ivy Books, 1990.

Johnson, Michael L. *Violence and Grace: Poems About the American West.* Lawrence, Kans.: Cottonwood Press, 1993.

Jordan, Teresa. *Riding the White Horse Home: A Western Family Album.* New York: Pantheon, 1993.

_____, ed. *Graining the Mare: The Poetry of Ranchwomen.* Layton, Utah: Gibbs Smith, Peregrine Smith Books, 1994.

Kimball, Philip. *Harvesting Ballads.* 1984. Reprint. Norman: University of Oklahoma Press, 1994.

King, Thomas. *Green Grass, Running Water.* New York: Houghton Mifflin, 1993.

Momaday, N. Scott. *In the Presence of the Sun: Stories and Poems.* New York: St. Martin's Press, 1992.

Morris, Gregory L. *Talking Up a Storm: Voices of the New West.* Lincoln: University of Nebraska Press, 1994.

Nelson, Robert M. *Place and Vision: The Function of Landscape in Native American Fiction.* New York: Peter Lang, 1993.

Owens, Louis. *Other Destinies: Understanding the American Indian Novel.* Norman: University of Oklahoma Press, 1992.

_____. *The Sharpest Sight.* Norman: University of Oklahoma Press, 1992.

Ronald, Ann, and Stephen Trimble. *Earthtones: A Nevada Album.* Reno: University of Nevada Press, 1995.

Silko, Leslie Marmon. *Almanac of the Dead.* New York: Simon and Schuster, 1991.

Simmen, Edward, ed. *North of the Rio Grande: The Mexican-American Experience in Short Fiction.* New York: Penguin, NAL/Dutton, 1992.

Thomas, James, and Denise Thomas, eds. *The Best of the West 4: New Stories from the Wide Side of the Missouri.* New York: Norton, 1991.

Tisdale, Sallie. *Stepping Westward: The Long Search for Home in the Pacific Northwest.* New York: HarperPerennial, 1992.

Vizenor, Gerald. *Dead Voices: Natural Agonies in the New World.* Norman: University of Oklahoma Press, 1992.

Walters, Anna Lee, ed. *Neon Pow-Wow: New Native American Voices of the Southwest.* Flagstaff, Ariz.: Northland Publishing, 1993.

Welch, James. *Fools Crow.* New York: Penguin Books, 1987.

Widmark, Anne Heath, ed. *Between Earth and Sky: Poets of the Cowboy West.* New York: Norton, 1995.

Wild, Peter, ed. *The Desert Reader.* Salt Lake City: University of Utah Press, 1991.

Wilkinson, Charles F. *The Eagle Bird: Mapping a New West.* New York: Pantheon, 1992.

FIVE. CROSSED OVER

Abbott, Lawrence, ed. *I Stand in the Center of the Good: Interviews with Contemporary Native American Artists.* Lincoln: University of Nebraska Press, 1994.

Broder, Patricia Janis. *The American West: The Modern Vision.* Boston: Little, Brown, New York Graphic Society Books, 1984.

Eaton, Linda B., and J. J. Brody, consultant. *Native American Art of the Southwest.* Lincolnwood, Ill.: Publications International, 1993.

Engel, Len. "Rewriting Western Myths in Clint Eastwood's New 'Old Western.' " *Western American Literature* 29 (1994): 261–69.

Everson, William K. *The Hollywood Western: 90 Years of Cowboys and Indians, Train Robbers, Sheriffs and Gunslingers, and Assorted Heroes and Desperados.* New York: Citadel Press, 1992.

Herd, Stan. *Crop Art and Other Earthworks.* New York: Harry N. Abrams, 1994.

Manchester, Ellen. *Arid Waters: Photographs from the Water in the West Project.* Edited by Peter Goin. Reno: University of Nevada Press, 1992.

Truettner, William H., ed. *The West as America: Reinterpreting Images of the Frontier, 1820–1920.* Washington, D.C.: Smithsonian Institution Press, 1991.

SIX. GARTH AND FRIENDS

Bufwack, Mary A., and Robert K. Oermann. *Finding Her Voice: The Saga of Women in Country Music.* New York: Crown, 1993.

Malone, Bill C. *Country Music, U.S.A.* Rev. ed. Austin: University of Texas Press, 1985.

Savage, William W., Jr. *The Cowboy Hero: His Image in American History and Culture.* Norman: University of Oklahoma Press, 1979.

———. *Singing Cowboys and All That Jazz: A Short History of Popular Music in Oklahoma*. Norman: University of Oklahoma Press, 1983.

Stewart, Susan. *On Longing: Narratives of the Miniature, the Gigantic, the Souvenir, the Collection*. Baltimore: Johns Hopkins University Press, 1984.

Tichi, Cecelia. *High Lonesome: The American Culture of Country Music*. Chapel Hill: University of North Carolina Press, 1994.

SEVEN. THE NEW WEST

Frazier, Ian. *Great Plains*. New York: Penguin Books, 1989.

Gallagher, Winifred. *The Power of Place: How Our Surroundings Shape Our Thoughts, Emotions, and Actions*. New York: Poseidon Press, 1993.

Jackson, Wes. *Becoming Native to This Place*. Lexington: University Press of Kentucky, 1994.

Kilgore, Eugene. *Ranch Vacations: The Complete Guide to Guest and Resort, Fly-Fishing, and Cross-Country Skiing Ranches*. 2d ed. Santa Fe, N.Mex.: John Muir, 1991.

Lutwack, Leonard. *The Role of Place in Literature*. Syracuse, N.Y.: Syracuse University Press, 1984.

Norbury, Rosamond. *Behind the Chutes: The Mystique of the Rodeo Cowboy*. Missoula, Mont.: Mountain Press, 1994.

Rhodes, Richard. *The Inland Ground: An Evocation of the American Middle West*. Rev. ed. Lawrence: University Press of Kansas, 1991.

CONCLUSION. STAYING PUT

McPhee, John. *The Control of Nature*. New York: Farrar Straus Giroux, 1989.

Plant, Judith, and Christopher Plant, eds. *Turtle Talk: Voices for a Sustainable Future*. Philadelphia: New Society, 1990.

Rifkin, Jeremy. *Beyond Beef: The Rise and Fall of the Cattle Culture*. New York: Dutton, 1992.

Udall, Stewart L., Patricia Nelson Limerick, Charles Wilkinson, John Volkman, and William Kittredge. *Beyond the Mythic West*. Edited by Stewart L. Udall. Salt Lake City: Gibbs Smith, Peregrine Smith Books, 1990.

Whitley, Glenna. "Range War." *Western Styles*, June 1994, pp. 78–84.

Wilson, Edward O. *Biophilia*. Cambridge, Mass.: Harvard University Press, 1984.

Zeveloff, Samuel I., L. Mikel Vause, and William H. McVaugh, eds. *Wilderness Tapestry: An Eclectic Approach to Preservation*. Reno: University of Nevada Press, 1992.

Index

Abbey, Edward, vii, 15, 115, 127, 141, 180, 189, 225; myth and, 126; as radical ecologist, 181–83
Academy of Country Music (ACM), 276, 280, 300
Achievement of Cormac McCarthy, The (Bell), 143
Achy Breaky Heart (Cyrus), 298
Acosta, Oscar Zeta, 190, 191
Across the Wide Missouri (DeVoto), 27
Acuff, Roy, 264
Adams, Ansel, 188, 250
Adams, Ramon, on myth, 93
African Americans: historiography of, 81; New West and, 161–64, 174, 347; Westerns and, 208, 212–13, 244, 308–9
"A Funnie Place, No Fences": Teenagers' Views of Kansas, 1867–1900 (Haywood and Jarvis), 85
Ahearn, Kerry, 147–48
Alarcón, Francisco X., 151
"Albert Bierstadt: Art and Enterprise," 201
Albuquerque (Anaya), 128, 141
Alcosser, Sandra, 162
Aldrich, Robert, 215
Alexie, Sherman, 152
All but the Waltz: Essays on a Montana Family (Blew), 191
Allen, Paula Gunn, 156
Allmendinger, Blake, 78
All the Pretty Horses (McCarthy), 141, 144–48
Alter, Judy, 197
Altman, Robert, 28, 216, 227
Always Coming Home (Le Guin), 359
Amazing Rhythm Aces, 268, 278
American Country West: A Style and Source Book (Emmerling), 42
American Cowboy, 53
American Progress (Gast), 58(illus.)
American West, The (Brown), 79
American West: A Twentieth-Century History (Malone and Etulain), 72, 76, 77
Anaya, Rudolfo, vii, 111, 128, 130, 131, 141
Anderson, Broncho Billy, 206
Anderson, Lindsay, 230
And Stood There Amazed (Tyson), 295
Angle of Repose (Stegner), 107–11, 121, 335
Anglos and Mexicans in the Making of Texas, 1836–1986 (Montejano), 81
Animal Dreams (Kingsolver), 139
"Annie" (Brown), 358
Annie Oakley, 235
Ansen, David, 226–27, 229
Antiques, 34–35, 304–5
Anti-Westerns, 215–18, 227, 236–37
Antonio, Lou, 240
Anything for Billy (McMurtry), 139
Anzaldúa, Gloria, 191
Apaches, 234–35, 245; Carson and, 98–99
Apple, Max, 131
Apted, Michael, 246
Arctic Dreams (Lopez), 50
Arness, James, 234
Asian-Americans: historiography of, 81; New West and, 347
Assimilation, 95–96, 229
Association for the Study of Literature and Environment (ASLE), 118
Athearn, Robert G., 92
Attack on an Emigrant Train (Wimar), 202
Austin, Mary, 178
"Austin City Limits," 233, 296
Autobiography of a Brown Buffalo, The (Acosta), 190
Autry, Gene, 207, 264, 265, 267, 296
Averill, Charles, 98
Averill, Tom, 21–22
Avery, Milton, 250

Babbs, Ken, 148
Baber, Asa, 15
Baca, Jimmy Santiago, 127, 128, 151
Backes, Clarus, 87
Bad Girls, 246
Baker, Joe, 252–53, 254, 257
Ballad of Gregorio Cortez, The, 224
Ballad of Little Jo, The, 248
Bankers and Cattlemen (Gressley), 78, 89
Barasch, Marc, 129
Barbara Blackburn's Old West Cookbook, 47
Bare, Bobby, 264
Barker, S. Omar, 166
Barney, William, 150
Barth, John, 116
Bass, Rick, 189
Battle for Butte: Mining and Politics on the Northern Frontier, 1864–1906, The (Malone), 89

Battle of Mythology in the New West, A (Russell), 348
Beard, Tyler, 46
Beard, The (McClure), 173
Becoming Native to This Place (Jackson), 315
Bedichek, Roy, 131
Bell, Vereen M., 143
Bender, Texas Bix, 362
Benson, Jackson J., 110
Beres, Al, 45
Berger, Thomas, 122, 125
Berkhofer, Robert F., Jr., 79
Berry, Chuck, 262, 263
Berry, Wendell, 180, 315
Best Little Whorehouse in Texas, The (King and Masterson), 173
"Best of Country '92: Countdown at the Neon Armadillo," 233, 276, 300(illus.)
Betts, Doris, 1, 138
Beyond the Frontier: Writers, Western Regionalism, and a Sense of Place (Simonson), 75, 113–14
Bierstadt, Albert, 201, 202, 205
Big Sky, The (Guthrie), 24, 27, 120, 191
"Big Wind Conference: A Gathering of Writers and Rivers," 132
Billington, Ray Allen, 67, 72
Billy the Kid, 173, 200, 212, 214, 248, 285, 293; myth of, 93, 94, 106, 139, 215; portrait of, 206
Billy the Kid: A Short and Violent Life (Utley), 70
Biophilia (Wilson), 357
Bite the Bullet, 223
Black, Baxter, 165, 166, 168
Black, Clint, 273, 276, 297
Blackburn, Alexander, 134
Black Elk Speaks (Neihardt), 174
Black West, The (Katz), 161
Blazing Saddles, 222, 233
Blessing Way, The (Hillerman), 137
Bless Me, Ultima (Anaya), vii, 128
Blew, Mary Clearman, 134, 191
Blind Side, 248
Blood Meridian (McCarthy), 141, 143, 144, 145
Blood Trails (Jones and McQueary), 168
Blue Highways (Least Heat-Moon), 190
Bly, Robert, 148, 149
Bogdanovich, Peter, 218
Bogguss, Suzy, 272, 276, 287, 287(illus.)
"Bonanza," 34, 210, 211, 233
Bonfante, Jordan, 53–54
Book of Kids Songs 2: Another Holler-Along Handbook, The (Cassidy and Cassidy), 296
Boomtown Blues: Colorado Oil Shale, 1885-1985 (Gulliford), 89
Boorstin, Daniel J., 204
Boosterism, 27, 200–201
Boots, 46–47, 328
Borderlands/La Frontera: The New Mestiza (Anzaldúa), 191
Border Music (Waller), 344
Border stories, postmodern, 358–59
Born to This Land (Steagall), 292
Bowden, Charles, 188
Bowen, James, 283
Boyle, Peter, 344–45
Brand, Max, 108, 136
Brando, Marlon, 145, 241, 345
Brautigan, Richard, 195
Brave Cowboy: An Old Tale in a New Time, The (Abbey), 181
Bravo 20: The Bombing of the American West (Misrach), 256
Bredahl, A. Carl, Jr., 191, 221, 310, 311, 358
Bridges of Madison County (Waller), 344
Britt, Elton, 267
Broder, Patricia Janis, 251, 252; on New Western art, 250, 255, 256–57
Bronco Billy, 223
Brooks, Garth, 249, 264, 266, 276, 282(illus.), 284, 293, 299, 301, 318; albums by, 239, 278–79; New West and, 261–62, 263; success of, 274, 279–82, 283
Brooks, Gwendolyn, 161
Brooks, Mel, 222
Broun, Elizabeth, 201
Brown, Dee, 64–65, 78–79, 86–87, 91
Brown, Norman O., 21
Brown, Rebecca, 358
Broyhill, J. Edgar, 42
Bruce, Ed, 268, 269
Bruchac, Joseph, 159
Brynner, Yul, 222
Bucco, Martin, 194
Buchanan, Rex, 315, 316
Buck and the Preacher, 223
Buckaroo Poet (Mitchell), 292
Buckaroo: Visions and Voices of the American Cowboy (Cannon and West), 168
Buffalo Bill and the Indians, 28
Buffalo Bill Historical Center, 338
Buffalo Girls (McMurtry), 139
"Buffalo Poem #1" (Hobson), 153
Buffalo soldiers, 161
Buffalo Soldiers (movie), 246
"Bull Rider, The" (Lopez), 184
Bull riding, 326, 327(illus.)
Buntline, Ned, 124
Burke, L. D., III, 329(illus.)
Burns, Ric, 232–33

Burroughs, John, 178
Bury My Heart at Wounded Knee (Brown), 109
Busby, Mark, 173, 174
Bus to Veracruz, The (Lockwood), 150
Butch Cassidy and the Sundance Kid, 32, 223, 236
Butterfield, Deborah, 257
Byrd, Tracy, 285

Cadillac Desert: The American West and Its Disappearing Water (Reisner), 90
Cahill, United States Marshal, 214
Cain, Christopher, 227–28
Calamity Jane, 70, 139
Campbell, Joseph, 126
Canciones de Mi Padre (Ronstadt), 289
Candyland (McMurtry), 344
Cannon, Hal, 168, 170–71, 296–97; cowboy poetry and 164–65, 171
Cannon, T. C., 251, 254
Can Poetry Matter? Essays on Poetry and Culture (Gioia), 170
Captive, The (Couse), 202
Carlile, Clancy, 244
Carpenter, Mary-Chapin, 286, 287, 288, 301
Carroll, Lenore, 197
Carson, Kit, 80, 94, 98–99
Carter, Carlene, 286
Carter, June, 263
Carver, Raymond, 112
Cash, Johnny, 263, 283
Casinos, 334, 351
Cassidy, Butch, 103
Cassidy, Nancy and John, 296
Castro, Michael, 195
Cat Ballou, 217, 235
Cather, Willa, 24, 107, 118, 125
Catlin, George, 86, 202, 204, 208
Catlin and His Contemporaries: The Politics of Patronage (Dippie), 204
Cattle Kate, 3(illus.), 44
Cattle Towns: A Social History of the Kansas Cattle Trading Centers, The (Dykstra), 78
Caudill, Boone, 24, 191, 342
Cervantes, Lorna Dee, 151
Chan, Sucheng, 81
Charlie Daniels Band, 266
Chase, Richard, 107
Chase, The (Brooks), 279
Chato's Land, 222
Chatwin, Bruce, 188
Chávez, César, 172
Cheever, Susan, 31
Cheney, Thomas Edward, 193
Chestnutt, Mark, 288, 290
Cheyenne Autumn, 213
Chickencoop Chinaman, The (Chin), 127
Chief Thunderfoot Takes a Dip (Baker), 253, 253(illus.)
Chin, Frank, 127, 173
Chisum, John, 98, 164
Cimarron (movie), 229
Cimarron Cutoff, 320–21
Cimino, Michael, 224
Cirillo, Dexter, 38
City Slickers, 5, 194, 235–36, 238, 239, 247, 249, 284, 296, 317
Clark, Walter Van Tilburg, 119, 120, 128
Clark, William, 86, 127, 312
Clayton, Lawrence, 168, 345
Clift, Montgomery, 209
Cline, Patsy, 286
Clothes, Western, 2, 12, 34, 38, 43–47, 50, 276, 305, 306, 317
Coalition for Western Women's History, 81
Cody, William F. ("Buffalo Bill"), 30, 58, 96, 124, 200, 207, 293; myth of, 10, 28–29, 338–40; poster of, 339(illus.)
Coe, David Allen, 121, 269
Cohlene, Terri, 132
Coldsmith, Don, 127
Coleman, Jane Candia, 164
Collectibles, 28, 34–35, 37, 39
Collecting the West: Cowboy, Indian, Spanish American, and Mining Memorabilia (Ketchum), 35
Comes a Horseman, 223
Coming of the Kid, The (Hall), 126
Common Thread: The Songs of the Eagles, 276–77
Conagher, 243
Conrad, Joseph, 143
Cook, Don, 7
Cooper, Gary, 225, 239
Cooper, James Fenimore, 112, 123, 205
Cooper, Roy, 326
Copas, Cowboy, 267
Coppola, Francis Ford, 143
Corliss, Richard, 226
Cosmatos, George P., 246, 361
Costner, Kevin, 200, 229, 230
Country music, 282, 298; conservatism of, 280–81; development of, 261–77, 278, 283, 286, 290–91; multi-culturalizing, 288–90; new image for, 273–74, 284–85; rodeo and, 331; western music and, 264, 266, 290–97, 359
Country Music Association (CMA), 273, 277
Country Music Television, 276
Couse, Irving, 202

Cowboy: Representations of Labor in an American Work Culture, The (Allmendinger), 78
Cowboy Artists of America, 255
Cowboy Boot Book, The (Beard), 46
Cowboy Christmas (Murphey), 52
Cowboy culture, 17–18, 22
Cowboy Culture: A Saga of Five Centuries (Dary), 17
"Cowboy Curmudgeon, The," and Other Poems (McRae), 168
Cowboy Has to Sing, A (Murphey), 295
Cowboy Hero, The (Savage), 264–65
Cowboy Life: A Saddlebag Guide for Dudes, Tenderfeet, and Cowpunchers Everywhere, The (Morris), 228
Cowboyography (Tyson), 295
Cowboy poetry, 2, 104, 164–71, 226
Cowboy Poetry: A Gathering (Cannon), 164
Cowboy Poetry Cookbook: Menus and Verse for Western Celebrations (McMullen and McMullen), 169
Cowboy Real (Russell), 295
Cowboys: myth of, 346–47; playing, 332–33; revised image of, 277–82; rodeo, 325, 331
Cowboys (Shepard), 125, 173
Cowboys, The (movie), 214
Cowboys & Indians, 53
Cowboys Are My Weakness (Houston), 139–40
Cowboy Slang (Potter), 2
Cowboys of the Americas (Slatta), 78
Cowboy songs, 170, 266, 289, 291, 292
Cowboy Songs (Murphey), 7, 260, 293, 294
Cowboy Way, The, 249, 296
Cowgirl Companion: Big Skies, Buckaroos, Honky Tonks, Lonesome Blues, and Other Glories of the True West, The (Gilchriest), 235
Cowgirl Hall of Fame, 276
Cowgirls, 247–48, 350; country music and, 288; rodeos for, 325
Cowgirls: Women of the American West (Jordan), 82–83
Coyote Waits (Hillerman), 103, 137
Crane, Stephen, 119
Crawford, Joan, 235
Crawford, Mark, 256
Crazy Horse, 60, 337
Crichton, Michael, 222
Crockett, Davy, 243
Cronon, William, 76–77, 98, 100; New Western History and, 75–76
Crossing, The (McCarthy), 141–42, 147, 363
Crybaby Ranch (Denver, Colo.), 18–21
Crystal, Billy, 5
Cultural issues, 80, 194, 356
Culture Swing (Rounder), 290
Curtin, R. L., 340
Custer, Elizabeth, 81
Custer, George Armstrong, 88–89, 93–94, 215
Custer Died for Your Sins: An Indian Manifesto (Deloria), 64
Custer's Last Fight, 207
Custer's Last Stand: The Anatomy of an American Myth (Dippie), 94
Cyrus, Billy Ray, 298

Dakota: A Spiritual Geography (Norris), 186
Dakota Bones: Collected Poems of Linda Hasselstrom (Hasselstrom), 162
Dallas, Claude, Jr., 136
Dalton, Emmett, 207
Daly, David, 208, 209, 358; on Westerns, 212–13, 224, 228
Dance clubs, dress at, 301–2
Dances with Wolves, 42, 200, 229–31, 234, 235, 243, 245, 246
Dancing, 2, 297–302, 301(illus.)
Daniels, Douglas Henry, 81
Daniels, John, 111
Dankleff, Richard, 163–64
Dary, David, 17–18, 21, 22, 91
Davis, Geena, 237
Davis, Kenneth W., 168
Davis, Robert Murray, 126, 194–95, 222, 347, 361
Dawson, Robert, 256
Day, A. Grove, 131
Day, Robert, 231
Day of the Locust, The (West), 114
Day the Cowboys Quit, The (Kelton), 139
Deadly Companions, The, 219
Dean, Billy, 285
De Aragon, Ray John, 205–6
Death Comes for the Archbishop (Cather), 125
Death of a Gunfighter, 220
De Leon, Arnoldo, 88
Deloria, Vine, 64, 78–79
De Maria, Walter, 255
DePaola, Tomie, 132
Desert Rose, The (McMurtry), 138
Desert Solitaire: A Season in the Wilderness (Abbey), vii, 181, 182–83
Desert Wood: An Anthology of Nevada Poets (Griffin), 162
Desierto: Memories of the Future (Bowden), 188
Destry Rides Again, 248
Deutsch, Sarah, 85

Development, 303, 308, 309
DeVoto, Bernard, 27
De Wilde, Brandon, 217
Dickey, Jerry R., 174
Diebenkorn, Richard, 250
Dietrich, Marlene, 248
Di Novi, Denise, 247
Dinsmoor, S. P., 319
Dippie, Brian W., 73, 79, 94, 204; on myth, 93; on Western history, 70–71
Dirty Little Billy, 215
Dixie Chicks, 286
Dmytryk, Edward, 212
Dobie, J. Frank, 131, 238
Doc, 215
Dodd, Elizabeth, 162
Dodge and Montague Shake (Russell), 202, 204(illus.)
Doig, Ivan, 111, 112, 115, 134, 191
Doing a Good One for the Red Man: A Red Farce (Medoff), 173
Donner Party, The, 232–33
Dorn, Ed, 125
Douglas, Kirk, 181
Doyle, Don, 301(illus.)
Dramas of Kansas, The (Phifer), 149
Dream-vision, 153
Driving to Vegas: New and Selected Poems, 1969–87 (Robertson), 334
Duigan, John, 246
Dulai, Sushil K., 285
Duncan, Dayton, 190, 311–13
Duvall, Robert, 221, 228
Dykstra, Robert R., 78

Eakins, Thomas, 251
Earp, Wyatt, 28, 93, 95, 207, 216, 249, 320
Eastlake, William, 136
East Meets West (Russell), 202, 204(illus.)
Eastwood, Clint, 31, 42, 226, 227, 247, 344; *Unforgiven* and, 240–43; Westerns and, 212, 214–15, 216
Ecoliterature, 118, 195, 197
Ecological issues, 15, 65, 88, 194, 355
Eddis, Craig "Harley," 26(illus.)
Eder, Richard, 147
Edison, Thomas, 206
Edwards, Don, 291, 292
Egan, Timothy, 49, 50, 188
Ehrlich, Gretel, 111, 115, 130, 180
Ehrlichman, John, 40
8 Seconds, 249, 276, 281
Eiseley, Loren, 181, 183
Eisenhower, Dwight, 213
Electric Horseman, The, 216, 223
Elements of San Joaquin, The (Soto), 151
Eliot, T. S., 304
Emery, Steven, 290
Emigrants Crossing the Plains (Bierstadt), 202
Emmerling, Mary, 42–43
Emplumada (Cervantes), 151
End of Nature, The (McKibben), 356
Environment, 10, 41, 184, 259; concern about, 89, 171, 343–44, 349, 353, 355; humankind and, 310; ranchers and, 349–50
Epstein, Joseph, 11–12
Erdrich, Louise, 111, 113, 134, 138, 156, 160
Ernst, Max, 250
Escott, Colin, 264, 290, 292; on Western music, 294–95, 296
Ethnocriticism: Ethnography, History, Literature (Krupat), 195
Ethnography, 87, 195
Etulain, Richard W., 72, 76, 106; New Historicism and, 109; on western literature, 107–8
Evans, Dale, 104, 235, 247, 346
Evans, Max, 6
Even Cowgirls Get the Blues (Robbins), 121, 126–27, 246
Even Cowgirls Get the Blues (movie), 247
Everson, William K., 150, 229–30
Exalted One, The (Wallis), 166

Far and Away, 200, 242, 243
Farmington Pro Rodeo and Western Trade Show, 165
Far Side, 258(illus.), 259
Fatal Environment: The Myth of the Frontier in the Age of Industrialization, 1800–1890, The (Slotkin), 92
Faulkner, William, 141, 142
Fear and Loathing in Las Vegas: A Savage Journey to the Heart of the American Dream (Thompson), 190, 334
Female Frontier: A Comparative View of Women on the Prairie and the Plains, The (Riley), 85
Ferril, Thomas Hornsby, 127
Fiedler, Leslie, 71, 112
Fight for the Water Hole (Remington), 202, 203(illus.)
Filmmaking, Western, 209, 211, 225–30, 232, 245, 247–49
Finch, Christopher, 34, 35
Fincher, John, 255, 257
Finkhouse, Joseph, 256
Fisher, James J., 313

Fisher, Vardis, 107
Fistful of Dollars, A, 215–16
Fitting Death for Billy the Kid, A (Adams), 93
Fitzgerald, F. Scott, 78
Fogelberg, Dan, 262
Folk music, 105–6, 290
Fonda, Henry, 212, 215
Fonda, Jane, 235
Fonseca, Henry, 254
Foods, Western, 47–48
Foote, Cheryl J., 85
For a Few Dollars More, 216
Forché, Carolyn, 150
Ford, John, 207–9, 212–13, 215, 216, 219–21, 229
Fort Apache, 212
Foster, Gus, 257
Four-cornered Falcon: Essays on the Interior West and the Natural Scene, The (Saner), 185
Fowles, John, 350
Frazier, Ian, 59, 61, 86, 87, 190, 337
Freeman, Morgan, 241
Frémont, John C., 311
From the Cables of Genocide: Poems on Love and Hunger (Cervantes), 151
Frontier, myth of, 71, 113–14
Frontier in American History, The (Turner), 67
Frontier Women: The Trans-Mississippi West, 1840–1880 (Jeffrey), 81
Frost, Lane, 249
Frost, Robert, 27
Frye, Northrop, 117, 135, 217
Furniture, Western, 42–43, 52

Galvin, James, 134
Garcia, Guy, 298
Garcia, Mario T., 81
Garfield, Brian, 225
Garner, James, 16
Garrard, Lewis, 311
Garth Brooks (Brooks), 274
Garver, James, 262
Gast, John, 58
Geiogamah, Hanay, 173, 234
Georgia O'Keeffe: A Life (Robinson), 87
Geronimo, depiction of, 243, 245, 246
Geronimo (movie), 234, 235, 245
Geronimo: An American Legend (movie), 245, 246
Gerrard, Roy, 132
Ghiselin, Brewster, 163
Ghostway, The (Hillerman), 137
Giants in the Earth (Rølvaag), 114
Gibbs Smith (publisher), 104, 169, 296
Gibson, Eric, 205
Gilchriest, Gail, 235, 236, 248; on Dixie Chicks, 286; on Homestead Ranch, 316–17
Gill, Vince, 288
Gilmore, Jimmie Dale, 285
Gioia, Dana, 170
Gish, Robert F., 188
Glover, Danny, 227
God's Dog (Ryden), 184
Goetzmann, William H. and William N., 231, 342; on New Western art, 253, 254, 255
Goin' Back to Texas (Edwards), 292
Going to See the Elephant (Hensel), 174
Goin' South, 223
Good, the Bad, and the Ugly, The, 216
Goodbye to a River (Graves), 181
Goodnight, Charles, 63, 86, 99–100
Good Old Boys, The, 246
Good Rain: Across Time and Terrain in the Pacific Northwest, The (Egan), 49
Gorman, R. C., 251
Graff, Gary, 273, 274
Gragg, Rod, 91
Grand Canyon, 240
Grandmother's Adobe Dollhouse (Smith), 132
Graves, John, 99, 181
Gray, Otto, 265
Graziano, Frank, 161
Greater Yellowstone Coalition (GYC), 354
Great Northfield, Minnesota Raid, The, 221
Great Plains (Frazier), 59, 190
Great Train Robbery, The, 206
Great White Buffalo, The (Winter), 314
Green, Jack N., 241
Greener Pastures Institute, 353
Greenwald, Maggie, 248
Green woman, 350–51
Gressley, Gene M., 78, 89, 90, 91–92
Grey, Zane, 25, 28, 108
Griffin, Shaun T., 162
Growing Up Western (Backes), 87
Growing Up with the Country: Childhood on the Far Western Frontier (West), 69, 85
Gubernick, Lisa, 283
Guerin, Charles A., 257
Guerrero, Salvador, 88
Gulliford, Andrew, 89
Gunfighter, The, 212, 217, 218
Gunfighter Nation: The Myth of the Frontier in Twentieth-Century America (Slotkin), 92

Gunn, Thom, 150
"Gunsmoke," 208, 209–10, 233
Guterman, Jimmy, 263
Guthrie, A. B., Jr., 24, 87, 107, 120, 128, 191
Guts & Glory: Legends of Rodeo, 326
Gwyn, Woody, 255, 257

Hackman, Gene, 241
Haggard, Merle, 271
Haines, John, 149, 161
Hall, Oakley, 126, 127, 195, 212
Haller, Scot, 226
Hamblin, Louisa Medina, 171
Hammerbeck, Wanda, 256
Hampsten, Elizabeth, 85
Hands Up! (Dorn), 125
Hannie Caulder, 223
Hard Times in Paradise: Coos Bay, Oregon, 1850–1986 (Robbins), 89
Harjo, Joy, 128, 155, 156, 157–58
Harnett, William M., 251
Harper, Mary Catherine, 359
Harper's Anthology of 20th Century Native American Poetry (Niatum), 159
Harris, Emmylou, 272, 297
Harris, Richard, 241
Harrison, Jim, 170, 189; on Native American poetry, 158–60, 161
Hart, William S., 207
Harte, Bret, 127
Hartford, John, 270
Hartley, Marsden, 250
Haruf, Kent, 113
Haslam, Gerald W., 131
Hasselstrom, Linda, 162–63, 184–85
Hats, symbolism of, 328, 329(illus.)
Hawks, Howard, 5, 208, 209
Hayes, Isaac, 244
Haynes, I. J., 8–9, 10
Haywood, C. Robert, 85
Heading West (Betts), 1, 138
Heart of the Land, The (McGuane), 141
Heatherington, Madelon, 148; Western fiction and, 120–21, 122–23, 124
Heaven's Gate, 224, 230
Heimel, Cynthia, 347–48
Heizer, Michael, 255
Henley, Patricia, 112–13
Hensel, Karen, 174
Herd, Stan, 255, 255(illus.)
Hickok, Wild Bill, 94, 95, 243, 315
High Noon, 208, 214, 223, 225, 243, 267
High Plains Drifter, 215, 243
Hill, Walter, 243, 245–46
Hillbilly music, 265, 266
Hillerman, Tony, 5–6, 7, 8, 10, 103, 131, 136, 137
Hillman, James, 148
Hinojosa, Tish, 289–90, 289(illus.)
Hinojosa-Smith, Rolando, 131
Hirshberg, Charles, 279
Historians and the American West (Malone), 72
History of New Mexico (Pérez de Villagrá), 103
Hobson, Geary, 152–54
Hockney, David, 255
Hofstadter, Richard, 63
Hogan, Linda, 154–55, 156
Holden, William, 220
Hole in the Sky (Kittredge), 191, 192–93
Holliday, Doc, 93, 215, 249, 332
Holly, Susan, 284
Holthaus, Gary, 360
Hombre, 215
Homeland (Hinojosa), 289–90
Homestead Act (1862), 83
Homestead Ranch, 316–17
Home theme, 124, 129–31, 141, 145–46, 246–47
Hood, Rance, 251
Hooks, Robert, 244
Hooper, Joseph, 14, 247, 248
Hopper, Edward, 250
Horseman, Pass By (McMurtry), 216
Horsing Around: Contemporary Cowboy Humor (Clayton and Davis), 168
Horsman, Reginald, 79
Horstman, Dorothy, 265
Hour of the Gun, 215
Housekeeping (Robinson), 134, 196
House Made of Dawn (Momaday), 138
Houser, Allan, 257
Houston, Pam, 16, 139–40, 140(illus.)
Houston, Randy, 168
Houston, Velina Hasu, 173
Howard, Ron, 242
Howell-Sickles, Donna, 255
"How the West Was Lost," 80, 233
How the West Was Won, 216, 217
Hoy, Jim, 193
Hud, 216, 217, 218, 218(illus.)
Huerta, Jorge, 172
Hughes, Langston, 161
Hugo, Richard, 112, 149
Hume, Kathryn, 125–26
Hunger of Memory: The Education of Richard Rodriguez (Rodriguez), 191
Hurst, Jack, 274
Huston, John, 212, 214, 217
Hwang, David Henry, 173, 174, 175

In a Narrow Grave: Essays on Texas (McMurtry), 23, 64, 116
Ince, Thomas H., 207
Indian Market (Santa Fe, N.M.), 40(illus.)
Indians (Kopit), 28
Indian with Beer Can (Scholder), 251, 252(illus.)
Individualism, 17, 27, 90, 123, 135, 247, 257
Inge, William, 171
Ingram, Jerry, 251
In Mad Love and War (Harjo), 155
In Pieces (Brooks), 279
Institute of American Indian Arts (IAIA), 253, 254, 257
International Rodeo Association, 327
Into the West, 248
Inventing Billy the Kid: Visions of the Outlaw in America, 1881–1981 (Tatum), 93
Iron Horse, The, 207
Isern, Tom, 193
"It's Your Misfortune and None of My Own": A New History of the American West (White), 65–66, 76, 97

Jackson, Alan, 276, 277
Jackson, Wes, 315, 316, 355
Jacobs, Marc, 45
James, Jesse, xi, 222, 248, 293, 313
Jameson, Jerry, 233
Jarvis, Sandra, 85
Jeffers, Robinson, 162, 189
Jeffrey, Julie Roy, 81
Jennings, Waylon, 268, 269, 272, 280
Jeremiah Johnson (Pollack), 189, 222
Jibbenainosay, The (Hamblin), 171
Jimenez, Luis, 254, 255, 257
Jimenez, Santiago, Jr., 290
Johnny Guitar, 216, 235
Johnson, Ben, 233
Johnson, Liver-eating, 70
Jones, Bill, 168
Jones, George, 271, 283
Jones, Preston, 173
Jones, Tommy Lee, 246
Jordan, Teresa, 82–83
Journal of Popular Culture, 106
Journal of the Gun Years (Matheson), 139
Junior Bonner, 220

Kael, Pauline, 226, 229
Kaplan, Jonathan, 246
Kapoun, Robert W., 38
Karp, Ivan, 249–50, 259
Kasdan, Lawrence, 226, 227, 240
Katz, William L., 161
Kaufman, Philip, 221–22
Kaufmann, Theodor, 202
Keitel, Harvey, 238
Keith, Toby, 276, 288
Kellogg, Steven, 132
Kelton, Elmer, 139, 168, 246
Kennedy, John F., 18
Kerouac, Jack, 190
Kesey, Ken, 122, 148
Ketchum, Hal, 293
Ketchum, William, Jr., 35
Khouri, Callie, 237, 238
Kill the Cowboy: A Battle of Mythology in the New West (Russell), 186, 348
Kilmer, Val, 249
King, Henry, 209, 212
King, Larry, 173
Kingsolver, Barbara, 139
Kit Carson, Prince of the Gold Hunters (Averill), 98
Kittredge, William, 88, 111, 112, 113, 130, 180, 185, 189, 191, 192–93, 351, 352; on cowboy poetry, 169; on environmentalists, 343–44; New Western literature and, 134, 135; on Westerns, 132–33
Kleppner, Paul, 72
Kline, Kevin, 227
Klotz-Reilly, Suzanne, 257
Koger, Jane, 316, 317
Koncius, Jura, 41, 42
Kopit, Arthur, 28
Kramer, Jane, 98
Krupat, Arnold, 195
Kubrick, Stanley, 230
Ku Klux Klan, 243, 244

Lakota Woman: Siege at Wounded Knee, 234
Lamar, Howard, 72
L'Amour, Louis, 25, 100, 104, 112, 128, 132, 138–39, 148, 230
Land Circle: Writings Collected from the Land (Hasselstrom), 185
Land Institute, 315, 316, 355
Land Use, Environment, and Social Change: The Shaping of Island County (White), 89
lang, k. d., 247, 286
Language of the Robe: American Indian Trade Blankets (Kapoun and Lohrmann), 38
Larson, Gary, 259
Last Cattle Drive, The (Day), 231
Last Command, The, 211
Last Cowboy, The (Kramer), 98
Last Go Round (Kesey), 148

Last Hunt, The, 211
Last of the Breed (L'Amour), 138–39
Last of the Comanches, 211
Last of the Fast Guns, The, 211
Last Picture Show, The, 218
Last Posse, The, 211
Last Prostitute, The, 240
Last Refuge: The Environmental Showdown in Yellowstone and the American West (Robbins), 351
Last Sunset, The, 212
Last Train from Gun Hill, 212
Las Vegas, Nev.: New West and, 333–36
Latham, Aaron, 336, 337
Lawrence, D. H., 322
Lawrence, Elizabeth Atwood: on rodeo, 326–27, 328, 331–32
Least Heat-Moon, William, 21–22, 190
LeDoux, Chris, 262, 279, 291, 292, 293
Left-handed Gun, The, 212, 214
Legacy of Conquest: The Unbroken Past of the American West, The (Limerick), 67, 68–69, 73
Legend of the Indian Paintbrush, The (DePaola), 132
Legends of the Fall, 249
Le Guin, Ursula K., 359
Leonard, Zenas, 164
Leone, Sergio, 144, 215–16, 217, 242
Leopold, Aldo, 181
Lesley, Craig, 113
Leslie, Wade, 326
Lessinger, Jack, 354
LeSueur, Meridel, 118
Lewis, George H., 279; on country music, 269–71, 272
Lewis, Janet, 162
Lewis, Meriwether, 86, 127, 311–12
Liberty Records, 279, 283
Lichtenstein, Roy, 250
Life and Times of Judge Roy Bean, The (Huston), 217
Life magazine, 5–6, 10, 16
Lightning Jack, 249
Limerick, Patricia Nelson, 55, 57, 71–75, 98, 109, 199, 360; New Western History and, 66–69, 78, 90; Old Western History and, 69, 77
Linck, Ernestine Sewell, 345
Linderman, Earl, 257
Listening Woman (Hillerman), 137
Literary criticism, 193–94, 196
Literary History of the American West, A, 103, 131, 136
Little America (Swigart), 127
Little Big Man (Berger), 122, 125
Little Big Man (movie), 214, 215, 217
Little Town Blues: Voices from the Changing West (Ringholz), 340–41
Living the Dream: An Outline for a Life in Fiction (Seidman), 103–4
Lochsa Road: A Pilgrim in the West (Stafford), 190
Lockwood, William, 149–50
Lohrmann, Charles J., 38
Lojek, Helen, 175–76, 177, 178
Lomatewama, Ramson, 33, 34
Lomax, John A., 165
Lonely Are the Brave, 181, 214, 216, 217, 218
Lone Ranger, xi, 104, 123, 207
Lonesome Dove (McMurtry), 117, 138, 141, 217, 226, 228, 234, 243
Lonesome Dove (movie), 228, 234, 243
Longley, John Lewis, Jr., 143, 144
Long Riders, The, 223
Lopez, Barry, 50, 127, 180, 183, 184
Louis L'Amour Western Magazine, 104
Love, Glen A., 180
Loveless, Patty, 272, 287, 301
Love Medicine (Erdrich), 138
Lovendahl, Nancy, 257
Lovett, Lyle, 15, 276, 285
Lusty Men, The, 223
Lutwack, Leonard, 306–9
Lynch, David, 48
Lynn, Loretta, 121, 271
Lynne, Shelby, 285
Lyon, Thomas J., 181, 182, 184, 189

McCabe and Mrs. Miller, 216
McCanless, Allen, 166
McCarthy, Cormac, 134, 141–46, 142(illus.), 178, 230, 363; New Western History and, 143, 145, 147
McClure, Michael, 173
McCoy, Tim, 166
McCrea, Joel, 219
McDonald, Walter, 163
Macdonnell, Norman, 209
McEntire, Reba, 272, 273, 276, 287, 288
McGraw, Tim, 288
McGuane, Thomas, 140, 141
McKibben, Bill, 356
Maclean, Norman, 111, 112, 115
MacLeish, Archibald, 175
McLuhan, Marshall, 274, 358–59
McMullen, Cyd and Anne Wallace, 169
McMurphy, Randle Patrick, 122
McMurtry, James, 344
McMurtry, Larry, 23, 24, 64, 76, 99, 139, 141, 147–48, 196, 216, 217, 218, 226, 228, 321, 344, 361; myth and, 116–17;

McMurtry, Larry, *continued*
on New Western Historians, 63; Pulitzer for, 138; West and, 25
McQueary, Rod, 168
McRae, Clinton, 168
McRae, Wallace, 168
Mad Dog McCree (arcade game), 4(illus.)
Maddox, Lucy, 195
Madonna of the Trail (statue), 83, 84(illus.)
Mahan, Larry, 326
Majestic Kid, The (Medoff), 175, 176–77
Major Dundee, 219
Major Problems in the History of the American West (Milner), 77
Malden, Karl, 241
Malone, Bill C., 273
Malone, Michael P., 72–75, 76, 89
Man Called Horse, A, 222
Manfred, Frederick, 107, 119
Manifest Destiny, 55–56, 58(illus.), 192, 202
Mann, Anthony, 213
Man Who Killed the Deer, The (Waters), 125
Man Who Rode Midnight, The (Kelton), 139
Man Who Shot Liberty Valance, The, 218–19, 242
Marsden, Michael T., 210, 220, 221; on Westerns, 211–12, 213, 214, 216, 223–24
Martin, Russell, 102, 129, 130–31
Martín and Meditations on the South Valley (Baca), 151
Marvin, Lee, 217, 219
Masterson, Peter, 173
Mather, Christine, 39–40, 41, 45, 52
Matheson, Richard, 139
Mathews, Tom, 88–89
Mattea, Kathy, 288
Matthews, William, 169
Maverick (movie), 249
Maynard, Ken, 265
Meade, Michael, 148
Mechanical bulls, 25, 26(illus.), 299
Medoff, Mark, 173, 175, 176–77
Meldrum, Barbara Howard, 119, 195
Memorias: A West Texas Life (Guerrero), 88
Meston, John, 209
Metcalf, P. Richard, 79
Metzger, Fran, 257
Midnight Cowboy, 216
Milagro Beanfield War, The (Nichols), 8, 32
Miles, Vera, 219
Miller, Bill, 293, 296
Milner, Clyde A., II, 57, 77
Milton, John R., 129, 177; on Eastern/Western fiction, 148; New Western literature and, 136; Westerns and, 137
Mink, Ben, 247
Misfits, The, 214, 248
Misrach, Richard, 256; photo by, 256
Mitchell, Waddie, 166, 292
Mix, Tom, 207, 249
Mizrahi, Isaac, 45
Momaday, Al, 251
Momaday, N. Scott, 111, 127, 128, 130, 131, 138, 153
Monacelli, Greg, 15
Monkey Wrench Gang (Abbey), 126, 181
Monroe, Marilyn, 248
Montana, Patsy, 286
Montana, Ruby, 21
Montana Slim, 267
Montejano, David, 81
Monte Walsh, 220
Montoya, José, 131
Mooney, Carolyn J., 314
Morris, Michele, 228, 291, 295
Morris, Wright, 119
Morton, Carlos, 173
Mose, Allen, 15
Muir, John, 9, 65, 178, 181
Multiculturalism, 30, 40, 85, 245
Munson, Eve Stryker, 360
Murphey, Michael Martin, 260, 266, 291, 292–94, 294(illus.), 296; albums by, 7, 52, 294–95; cowboy poetry and, 165–66
Murphy, Geoff, 248
Murray, Marie, 206
Murray, Ty, 325
Museum Pieces (Tallent), 138
Mustangs, The (Dobie), 238
My Ántonia (Cather), 24
My Darling Clementine, 216
Myerson, Alan, 344
Myres, Sandra L., 81–82
Myths, 91–97, 116, 351; durability of, 199–200; movies and, 205–6, 208; realism and, 120; romantic, 107, 121; Western, 99, 120, 121, 126–27, 171, 177, 224, 349; women and, 117, 118–19
Mythic West in Twentieth-Century America, The (Athearn), 92

Nachbar, Jack, 210, 220, 221; on Westerns, 211–12, 213, 214, 216, 223–24
Naked Spur, The, 213
Names on the Land: A Historical Account of Placenaming in the United States (Stewart), 193
Nash, Gerald D., 62, 63, 127
Nashville Network, 273, 276, 277, 296

National Cattlemen's Association, 355
National Cowboy Hall of Fame and Western Heritage Center, 165, 318
National Cowboy Symposium and Celebration, 321
Native America: Arts, Traditions, and Celebrations (Mather), 39
Native Americans: An Illustrated History, The, 234
Native Americans: art of, 252, 257; historiography of, 80–81; New West and, 78–79, 152–61, 347; rodeo and, 331, 332; stereotypes of, 28, 202; vision of, 360; writing of, 104, 128–29
Native American Theater Ensemble, 173
Nature Conservancy, 318
Necessary Theater: Six Plays About the Chicano Experience (Huerta), 172
Neihardt, John, 174
Nelson, Jane: on McMurtry, 116–17
Nelson, Willie, 269, 285
Neotraditionalism, 272–76, 281, 284, 285, 346; rise of, 277–78
Neowesternism, 13, 127–29, 246
New Agers, 40, 50, 322
Newcomb, Peter, 283
New Cowboy Poetry: A Contemporary Gathering (Cannon), 165, 170–71
Newell, Mike, 248
Newman, Paul, 29, 215, 218(illus.)
New Poetry of the American West (Wild and Graziano), 161
"New Significance: Re-envisioning the History of the American West," 77
New West: fashionability of, 30; marketing, 18–19; Old West and, 11, 12, 23, 69; past/future of, 358–59; style of, 19–20; wisdom of, 6–7
New West, The (catalog), 257
New Western Historians, 61, 70, 71–72; criticism of, 62–63, 66; myths and, 91–92, 96–97, 99; national self-explanation and, 100–101; on New Westers, 94; Old Western Historians and, 65–66; Turner thesis and, 58–59; Westerns and, 243
New Western History, 29, 57, 101, 109, 267; anti-myth of, 71; criticism of, 64; diverse complexity and, 77; goals of, 86; as industry, 90; literature and, 107, 179; poetry and, 155
New Western literature, 102–3, 135, 141, 226; arrival of, 124–27; feminine place in, 120; future of, 196–97, 198; Old Western literature and, 111, 136; synthesis by, 114–15
New Westers, 13, 90, 94, 171, 361; attitudes of, 5–6, 7; credo for, 350–51; Old Westers and, 7–8, 10–12, 232; skills of, 347–48; threat of, 343; vision of, 360; Western lifeway and, 346, 360
New West of Edward Abbey (Ronald), 195
New Writers of the Purple Sage: An Anthology of Contemporary Western Writing (Martin), 102, 130
Niatum, Duane, 159
Nichols, John, 8–10, 32
Nichols, Roger, 93
Ninemile Wolves, The (Bass), 189
No Fences (Brooks), 278–79
Nolan, Bob, 264
No Roof but Sky: Poetry of the American West (Coleman), 164
Norris, Kathleen, 186–87
Northwest, New West and, 48–50
No Separate Refuge: Culture, Class, and Gender on an Anglo-Hispanic Frontier in the American Southwest, 1880–1940 (Deutsch), 85
Nostalgia, vii, 32, 101, 304–5
Nothing but Blue Skies (McGuane), 140
Novel of the American West, The (Milton), 148
Nugent, Walter, 72, 74, 100, 101

Oakley, Annie, 358
O'Brien, Geoffrey, 144
O'Connor, Flannery, 141
Of Wolves and Men (Lopez), 184
O.K. Corral, 93, 332
O'Keeffe, Georgia, 250, 255
Oklahoma!, 171, 173
Oklahoma Cowboy Poetry Gathering, 165
Oklahoma Cowboys, 265, 266
Old-Time Cowboy Songs (Cannon), 296–97
Old Tucson, 332, 333(illus.)
Old West: New West and, 12, 23, 69, 192; transforming, 2, 5, 31; wisdom of, 6–7
Old Western Historians, 63; criticism of, 66, 78; New Western Historians and, 65–66; Turner thesis and, 59
Old Western History, 57–58, 80; criticism of, 59, 62; myth of, 71; restored, 67–68, 77
Old Western literature, 115; New Western literature and, 111, 136
Old Westers, 5–6; cowboy poetry and, 171; New Westers and, 7–12, 232
Old West–New West: Centennial Essays (Meldrum), 195
Old West Quiz and Fact Book (Gragg), 91
Once upon a Time in the West, 216
One-eyed Jacks, 241, 345, 214

On Longing: Narratives of the Miniature, the Gigantic, the Souvenir, the Collection (Stewart), 278, 304
On Nature's Terms: Contemporary Voices (Lyon and Stine), 189
On the Mesa (Nichols), 8
On the Road (Kerouac), 190
Oregon Trail, The (Parkman), 311
Original Cowboy Movie Fantasy Camp, 332–33
Ortiz, Simon, 152, 156, 158, 160–61
Oslin, K. T., 272, 288
O'Sullivan, John L., 55–56
Outland, 223
Outlaw Josey Wales, The, 215
Outlaws, 246
Out West: An American Journey (Duncan), 190, 312
Owen, Randy, 276
Owens, Louis, 16, 195
Owen Wister out West: His Journals and Letters (Wister), 105
Ox-Bow Incident, The (Clark), 119

Painton, Priscilla, 283, 286
Palance, Jack, 133, 317
Pale Rider, 226, 227
Palomino (Steel), 115–16
Paredes, Raymund A., 151, 172
Parikhal, John, 274–76, 288
Parks, Rita, 219–21, 228, 231; on Westerns, 224, 232
Parnell, Peter, 174
Parton, Dolly, 270, 272
Pascoe, Peggy, 85
Pat Garrett and Billy the Kid, 214
Peck, Gregory, 212
Peckinpah, Sam, 74, 144, 219–20, 221, 227, 242
Pecos Bill (Kellogg), 132
Penn, Arthur, 212
Penner, Andrea Millenson, 157
Penturbia: Where Real Estate Will Boom After the Crash of Suburbia (Lessinger), 354
People for the West!, 355
Peoples, David Webb, 241
Peoples of Color in the American West (Chan, Daniels, Garcia, Wilson), 81
Pérez de Villagrá, Gaspar, 103
Perry, Luke, 281
Persky, Joel, 208, 209, 358; on myth, 228; on Westerns, 212–13, 224
Peters, Pete, 313
Petersen, Gwen, 166
Petticoat County, lingerie by, 50, 51(illus.)
Peyote Song (Hood), 251
Phifer, Lincoln, 149
Pilkington, Tom, 131, 148; on McCarthy, 144–45; on *Pretty Horses*, 146–47
Pioneer Women: Voices from the Kansas Frontier (Stratton), 81
Pitkin, Anne, 163
Place, 74, 112, 129, 221, 309
Plains Folk: A Commonplace of the Great Plains (Hoy and Isern), 193
Plains Woman: The Diary of Martha Farnsworth, 1882–1922 (Springer and Springer), 85
Playing Cowboys: Low Culture and High Art in the Western (Davis), 194–95
Poetry: African-American, 161–64; cowboy, 2, 104, 164–66, 168–71, 226; Hispanic-American, 150-51; Native American, 152–61; New Western, 149–51, 161–62, 169–71; performing competitions for, 170; voice, 164
Poets West: Contemporary Poems from the Eleven Western States (Spingarn), 161
Pollack, Sidney, 189, 216, 222
Pollard, Michael J., 215
Pollock, Jackson, 250
Pomeroy, Earl, 63, 71, 73
Pontiac (Lovett), 15
Pony Express National Memorial, 313
Popular Culture Association, 106
Porter, Edwin S., 206
Porter, Susan, 104
Portrait of Saginaw Grant (Herd), 255(illus.)
Posse, impact of, 243–44, 245
Potter, Jack, 123
Powell, John Wesley, 127, 356
Prairie Women Adventures and Retreat, 317
PrairyErth: (A Deep Map) (Least Heat-Moon), 190
Prendergast, Alan, 136
Pride, Charley, 288
Professional Rodeo Cowboys Association (PRCA), 324, 327, 331
Professionals, The, 222
Progress II, 254
ProRodeo Hall of Fame and Museum of the American Cowboy, 326
Prose and Poetry of the American West (Work), 127
Proust, Marcel, 309
Pueblo Nations: Eight Centuries of Pueblo Indian History (Sando), 79

Quammen, David, 113
Quick and the Dead, The, 249
Quigley Down Under, 228–29
Quillworker: A Cheyenne Legend (Cohlene), 132

Radio programs, 207–8, 296
Rag and Bone Shop of the Heart, The: Poems for Men (Bly, Hillman, and Meade), 148
Rains, Chick, 7, 293
Ramsey, Buck, 166
Ranching Heritage Center, 321
Rancho Hollywood (Morton), 173
Rankin, Charles E., 57
Ranney, William, 202–3
Rattlesnake in a Cooler (South), 175
"Rawhide," 210, 228, 234
Rawlins, C. L., 180
Ray, Nicholas, 216
Real Bird, Hank, 166
Reckling, Genevieve, 257
Red Earth Festival, 318
Redford, Robert, 31–33, 89
Red Headed Stranger (Nelson), 269
Red River, 5, 208, 209, 228
Red Star, Kevin, 252
Reed, Ishmael, 125–26, 161
Refuge: An Unnatural History of Family and Place (Williams), 188
Regeneration Through Violence: The Mythology of the American Frontier, 1600–1860 (Slotkin), 92, 176
Regionalism, 30, 73, 90, 115, 116, 121
Reid, Ace, 168
Reis, Dennis, 158
Reisner, Marc P., 90
Relations of Rescue: The Search for Female Moral Authority in the American West, 1874–1939 (Pascoe), 85
Remembered Earth, The (Hobson), 152
Remington, Frederic, 199, 202, 208, 249, 254–55, 338; painting by, 203(illus.)
Removals: Nineteenth-Century American Literature and the Politics of Indian Affairs (Maddox), 195
Rense, Paige, 31
"Returning the Gift: Southwest Native American Voices," 132
Return to Lonesome Dove, 226, 233, 234
Reynolds, Clay, 345
Ricky Lynn Gregg (Gregg), 290
Riders in the Sky, 266, 296
Ride the High Country, 219, 220, 221
Riley, Glenda, 85
Riley, René E., 302
Ringholz, Raye C., 340–41, 351
Ritt, Martin, 216
Ritter, Tex, 177, 267, 296
River Runs Through It, A (Maclean), 32, 134, 243, 343
Rivers of Empire: Water, Aridity, and the Growth of the American West (Worster), 73, 90
River Too Far: The Past and Future of the Arid West, A (Finkhouse and Crawford), 256
Robbins, Jim: on GYC, 354; on Old/New West, 351–52, 355–56; on tourism, 351–52
Robbins, Marty, 267, 272, 292, 293, 296
Robbins, Tom, 121, 126–27, 136, 246
Robbins, William G., 75, 76, 85, 89
Robertson, Kirk, 334
Robinson, Marilynne, 134, 196
Robinson, Roxana, 87
Rodenberger, Lou, 118
Rodeo, 324–28; armchair, 25; cowgirl, 325, 332; frontier spirit of, 324, 328; Native American, 331, 332; symbols of, 331
Rodeo: An Anthropologist Looks at the Wild and the Tame (Lawrence), 326–27
Rodgers, Jimmie, 263
Rodman, Charmayne, 325
Rodriguez, David, 290
Rodriguez, Richard, 191
Roethke, Theodore, 115, 149
Rogers, Kenny, 280
Rogers, Roy, 19, 104, 200, 207, 264, 265, 267–68, 346
Rogers, Will, 7, 346
Role of Place, The (Lutwack), 307
Rolling Stone, cover of, 282(illus.)
Rølvaag, Ole, 107, 114
Romance, vii, 28, 107, 121–24, 128, 197, 307–8
Romance Language (Parnell), 174
Ronald, Ann, 182, 195
Ronstadt, Linda, 289
Roosevelt, Theodore, 28, 87, 92, 338
Ropin' the Wind (Brooks), 239, 279
Rosenberg, Scott, 242
Rosie and the Rustlers (Gerrard), 132
Roth, Bobby, 300
Roughing It (Twain), 310
Roughstock Sonnets (Zarzyski), 168
Rounders, The (Evans), 6, 98
Roush, Jan, 137
Roy Bean: Law West of the Pecos (Sonnichsen), 91
Royce, Josiah, 59
Rubinek, Saul, 241

Ruggles, Wesley, 229
Ruiz, Vicki, 85
Run, River, Run: A Naturalist's Journey down One of the Great Rivers of the West (Zwinger), 183–84
Runningfox, Joseph, 234
Russell, Andrew Joseph, 202, 204(illus.)
Russell, Sharman Apt, 186, 351; on green woman, 350; on Old/New West, 348, 350; on ranchers/environmentalists, 349–50
Russell, Tom, 295
Rutsala, Vern, 149
Ryan, James, 245, 246, 247
Ryan, Robert, 220
Ryden, Hope, 127, 183, 184

Sáanii Dahataał: The Women Are Singing (Tapahonso), 156
Saarinen, Eero, 312
St. John, Allen, 284
Sanders, Scott Russell, 187–88
Sando, Joe, 79
Sandoz, Mari, 117–18, 127
Saner, Reg, 161, 185, 357–58
Santa Fe, N.M.: art in, 39; fashion in, 38; multiculture of, 40; refugees in, 353; rodeo in, 39, 324
Santa Fe Christmas (Mather), 52
Santa Fe Style (Mather and Woods), 39–40, 41
Sarandon, Susan, 237
Savage, William W., Jr., 277, 344; on country music, 264–69; on cowboy underground, 231; on fantasy, 95–96; on New Western Historians, 62
Schaare, Harry, 16
Schatz, Thomas, 224
Schickel, Richard, 229
Schlesinger, John, 216
Scholder, Fritz, 250, 251, 257; on Native Americans/American art, 254; painting by, 252(illus.)
Schultz Gard, Connie, 288
Schwann Publications, 284
Science fiction, Western, 125–26, 136
Scorsese, Martin, 230
Scott, Marci Haynes, 255
Scott, Randolph, 219
Scott, Ridley, 235, 236, 238
Seals, Dan, 272
Searchers, The, 213, 214
Seeking Awareness in American Nature Writing (Slovic), 195
Seidman, Michael, 103–4
Semrau, Julie L., 293
Sergeant Rutledge, 212–13, 214
Sergel, Christopher, 174
Service, Robert, 165
Settlers' Children: Growing Up on the Great Plains (Hampsten), 85
Shafer, Billy Joe, 272
Shane, 208, 214, 217, 218, 226
Sheckley, Robert, 222
She Had Some Horses (Harjo), 155
Shelton, Jim, 165
Shelton, Richard, 150
Shepard, Sam, 42, 125, 173
Sheplers, 2, 21, 38, 317, 318; clothing by, 43(illus.)
Shine, Ted, 174
Shoemaker, Nancy, 199–200
Shootist, The, 132, 220
Short, Luke, 108, 136
Shoulders, Jim, 326
Siegel, Bugsy, 334
Siegel, Don, 242
Siegel, Mark, 136, 148
"Significance of the Frontier in American History, The" (Turner), 58
Silko, Leslie Marmon, 134
Silver, Joel, 246
Silverado, criticism of, 226–27
Silverstar, George, 155
Simonson, Harold P., 75, 77, 113–14, 120; American exploration and, 114–15; on nature writers, 180
Sitting Bull, 60, 70, 86
Skaggs, Ricky, 272, 273
Sketches for a New Mexico Hill Town (Lockwood), 150
Skinwalkers (Hillerman), 137
Sky Clears, The (Day), 131
Sky's Witness: A Year in the Wind River Range (Rawlins), 180
Slatta, Richard W., 78
Slinger (Dorn), 125
Slotkin, Richard, 97, 176, 206, 207, 208, 209, 244; on myth, 92, 348
Slovic, Scott, 195
Smedley, Agnes, 118
Smith, Henry Nash, 58, 63, 106, 248
Smith, Jaune Quick-to-See, 252
Smith, MaryLou M., 132
Smith, Patricia Clark, 154; on Native American poets, 152, 153, 156, 158
Smith, Sherry L., 61, 62
Smith, Stephanie Izarek, 155
Smithsonian Institution's National Museum of American Art, 201, 205
Smittle, Betsy, 262
Snyder, Gary, 361
Society to Match the Scenery: Personal

Visions of the Future of the American West, A (Holthaus, Limerick, Wilkinson, and Munson), 360
Sodowsky, Roland, 193
Soldier Blue, 215
Songlines, The (Chatwin), 188
Songs from an Aging Sex Bomb (Oslin), 288
Songs from This Earth on Turtle's Back (Bruchac), 159
Songs of My Hunter Heart (Gish), 188
Songs of the Fluteplayer (Russell), 186
Songs of the Silver Screen (Murphey), 295
Songs of the Trail (Edwards), 292
Songs of the West (Harris), 297
Sonnichsen, C. L., 91
Sons of the Pioneers, 264, 267, 294, 295
Sons of the San Joaquin, 291, 294–95
Sosa, Pam, 301(illus.)
Soto, Gary, 131, 151
Sound of Mountain Water, The (Stegner), 183
South, Frank, 175–76, 177–78
Southwest, New West and, 87–88, 141
Southwestern American Literature, 106
Southwestern Indian Jewelry (Cirillo), 38
Southwestern Literature Association, 106
Southwest Indian Foundation, 38
Southwest Trails Blankets, ad for, 36(illus.)
Spencer, Tim, 264
Spingarn, Lawrence P., 161
Springer, Marlene and Haskell, 85
Stafford, Kim R., 190
Stafford, William, 127, 149, 161, 163, 357
Stagecoach, 207, 215
Stanford, Ann, 162
Stanwyck, Barbara, 210, 235
Starr, Belle, 164, 293
Starr, Henry, 207
Staying Put: Making a Home in a Restless World (Sanders), 187
Steagall, Red, 291, 292, 296
Steckmesser, Kent Ladd, 94
Steel, Danielle, 115–16
Steelyard Blues, 344
Stegner, Wallace, 87, 107–8, 110(illus.), 126, 136, 142, 183, 186, 193, 303, 323, 351, 356; influence of, 189; Las Vegas and, 335; New West and, 111, 347; on place, 112; preservationist position of, 111; stereotypes and, 128; tribute to, 109–10; West and, 25, 27, 109
Steinbeck, John, 190
Steinman, Lisa Malinowski, 163
Stern, Jane and Michael, 319, 346–47
Stevens, George, 208, 209
Stevens, Ted, 204
Stevens, Wallace, 342
Stewart, George R., 193
Stewart, James, 219
Stewart, Sharon, 256
Stewart, Susan, 278, 304, 305, 306, 338
Sticker writing, 112, 113
Stine, Peter, 189
Storms of Life (Travis), 273
Strait, George, 262, 272, 273, 276, 290, 291, 292
Stratton, Joanna L., 81
Streets of Laredo (McMurtry), 141, 226, 361
Strode, Woody, 244
Studi, Wes, 245
Stuntmen, 333(illus.)
Sundance, Utah, 31–32, 33
Sunset Indian (Scholder), 251
Super Indian No. 2 (Scholder), 251
Swayze, Patsy, 302
Swigart, Rob, 127
Swimmer, Eddie, 24

Take a Hard Ride, 223
Talbot, Huck, 292, 295
Tallent, Elizabeth, 138, 298–99
Taos Pueblo, 322, 322(illus.); Powwow, 323
Tapahonso, Luci, 128, 155–56, 157(illus.), 158
Tatum, Stephen, 93, 135, 305, 306, 338
Tavernier, Bertrand, 230
Taylor, James, 262
Teatro Campesino, 128, 172, 173
Teatro de la Esperanza, 173
Tell Them Willie Boy Is Here, 222
Terry, Megan, 174
Texas Playboys, 266
Texas Tornados, 296
Texasville (McMurtry), 218
Thank Heavens for Dale Evans (Dixie Chicks), 286
Theater, Western, 171–78
Thelma & Louise, 235–40, 243, 247
There Was a Crooked Man, 215
Thiebaud, Wayne, 250
This House of Sky: Landscapes of a Western Mind (Doig), 191
This Is Garth Brooks, 261
This Time (Yoakam), 292
Thompson, Anna, 241(illus.)
Thompson, Gerald, 29–30, 62, 101
Thompson, Hank, 286
Thompson, Hunter S., 120, 141, 190, 334
Thorp, N. Howard, 165
Three Rivers Rodeo Association, 165
Thunderheart, 246
Thurman, Judith, 32–33

Thurman, Roxanne, 19, 20–21
Tibbs, Casey, 326
Tillis, Pam, 287
Tombstone (movie), 249, 361
Tom Horn, 220
Tompkins, Jane, 24–25, 148, 194, 195, 238; on Buffalo Bill, 338–40; on L'Amour, 139; on Plains Indians, 338
Tonto, xi, 104
Too Long in the Wasteland (McMurtry), 344
Tourism, 303, 305–6, 308–9, 355; dangers of, 340–41, 351–52
Track of the Cat, The (Clark), 120
"Trails Through Time," 57, 60(illus.), 67, 76, 77, 201
Trails: Toward a New Western History (Limerick, Milner, and Rankin), 57
Trapper's Last Shot (Ranney), 202–3
Travels with Charley in Search of America (Steinbeck), 190
Travis, Randy, 273, 285, 290
Travolta, John, 223
Tritt, Travis, 297
True Grit, 223
True Tales of Old-Time Kansas (Dary), 91
Truettner, William H., 201, 202, 205
True West (Shepard), 173
True West: Arts, Traditions, and Celebrations (Mather), 39, 41, 45
Trumbo, Dalton, 181
Trusky, Thomas, 162
Tucker, Tanya, 297
Turner, Frederick Jackson, 49, 50, 65–68, 70, 75, 77, 80, 92, 199; thesis of, 58–60, 62, 63, 83, 100–101
Turner, Ted, 234
Twain, Mark, 127, 182, 310
Tyson, Ian, 291, 293, 295

Ulzana's Raid, 215
Under the Sun (Meldrum), 118–19
Under Western Skies (Worster), 56–57, 356
Underwood, Ron, 5
Un-Due West (Sodowsky), 193
Unforgiven, 31, 212, 240–43, 241(illus.)
Unforgiven, The, 212
Unger, Douglas, 112
Unspoken Hunger: Stories from the Field, An (Williams), 188
Urban Cowboy, 48, 223, 277, 283, 298, 336
Utah Place Names (Van Cott), 193
Utley, Robert, 70, 93, 206

Valdez, Luis, 172, 173
Vale, Thomas R. and Geraldine R., 190
Van Cott, John W., 193
Vanishing American: White Attitudes and U.S. Indian Policy, The (Dippie), 79
Van Peebles, Mario, 199, 243–44
Van Sant, Gus, 235, 246, 247
Van Shelton, Ricky, 273
Van Zandt, Townes, 272, 285
Venn, George, 163
Vidal, Gore, 212
View from Officers' Row: Army Perceptions of Western Indians, The (Smith), 62
Village with Bomb (Cannon), 251
Violence and Grace: Poems About the American West (Johnson), 164
Virginian, The (movie), 225
Virginian: A Horseman of the Plains, The (Wister), 105, 123, 197–98, 206, 240
Virgin Land: The American West as Symbol and Myth (Smith), 58, 61, 106, 248
Visual arts, Western, 249–57, 259
Vizenor, Gerald, 195
Vliet, R. G., 141
Voice in the Margin, The: Native American Literature and the Canon (Krupat), 195
Voices from the Bottom of the Bowl: A Folk History of Teton Valley, Idaho, 1823–1952 (Cheney), 193
"Voices of the New West: Multicultural Issues and the Western Story," 77

Wagoner, Porter, 266
Wah-to-yah and the Taos Trail (Garrard), 311
Walker, Jerry Jeff, 121
Wallace, Henry A., 18
Waller, Robert James, 344
Wallis, Sue, 166
Ware, Eugene, 166
Warhol, Andy, 250
Waters, Frank, 87, 125, 129
Wayne, John, 34, 42, 73, 98, 132, 158, 200, 207, 213–17, 219, 223, 242, 265, 332; image of, 5, 122
Way Out West (Stern and Stern), 319, 346
Webb, Walter Prescott, 59, 66, 71, 75, 95, 96
Webster, Daniel, 359
Weide, David, 336
Welch, James, 111, 112, 115, 134, 160
Welch, Kevin, 285
Welch, Raquel, 223
Welcome to Hard Times, 216, 217
Wells, Kitty, 286

West: "actual," 105; boundaries of, 23–24; as comedy/tragedy, 90–91; complexity of, 66; cultural image of, 29–30, 98; destruction of, 22–23; fashionability of, 15–18, 22, 30; hope in, 312–13; images of, 128, 310; myth of, 24, 91–92, 95–98, 119–21, 200, 233; as region, 72–74; reinterpretation of, 201–3; return to/of, 361; threats to, 343–44
West, Elliott, 69, 85, 109, 112
West, Nathaniel, 114
West, Richard, 188
West, Thomas, 168
West and the Western, The (Daly and Persky), 358
"West as America: Reinterpreting Images of the Frontier, 1820–1920, The," 239; controversy over, 201–5
Westbrook, Max, 103, 120, 150, 212
Westering Women and the Frontier Experience, 1800–1915 (Myres), 81
Western American Literary Criticism (Bucco), 194
Western American Literature, 106, 110
Western Association of Women Historians, 81
Western Beat (Overtones), 285
Westerner, The, 225
Westerners, The (Brown), 86
Western Folklife Center, 166
Western Heritage Center, 318
Western Hero in History and Legend, The (Steckmesser), 94
Western Historical Quarterly, 57
Western History Association (WHA), 57, 63, 76–77
Western Images, Western Landscapes: Travels along U.S. 89 (Vale and Vale), 190
Western literature, 196, 267, 358; provincial/colonial culture and, 106; Western history and, 103, 107–9
Western Literature Association (WLA), 106, 118, 132, 196
Western music, 264–65, 284–85; country music and, 264, 266, 290–97, 359
Western Music Association (WMA), 296
Western Performers Hall of Fame, 318
Westerns, xi, 138; adult, 104; African Americans and, 208, 212–13, 244; borscht, 249; death of, 132–33; movie, 205–6, 209, 249; radio, 207–8; science-fiction, 125–26; soap opera, 232; spaghetti, 215–16; television, 211, 230–31, 235, 249; traditional, 214–15
Westerns (Dankleff), 163
Western Styles, 53
Western Writers of America (WWA), 7, 196
WestFest, 166, 293, 294
West of Everything: The Inner Life of Westerns (Tompkins), 194
West of the Imagination, The (Goetzmann and Goetzmann), 230–31, 253
West: Spirit of the Frontier Home, 38
West that Never Was, The (Thomas), 230–31
Westward the Star of Empire (Kaufmann), 202
Westworld, 222
Wettstein, Earl, 332
Whatcha Gonna Do with a Cowboy (LeDoux), 279
What Kansas Means to Me: Twentieth Century Writers on the Sunflower State (Averill), 21
Wheeler, Edward, 125
When It's Peach Pickin' Time in Georgia, It's Apple Pickin' Time at the B.I.A. (Cannon), 251
When the Legends Die, 220
When You Comin' Back, Red Ryder? (Medoff), 173
Where the Bluebird Sings to the Lemonade Springs (Stegner), 111, 183
White, Richard, 49, 76–77, 89, 98–99; on imagined West, 117, 359; local legends and, 105–6; on McCarthyism, 213–14; myth/history and, 97; on New Western Historians, 65–66; Pacific Rim and, 75; West and, 25, 30
White Buffalo Calf Woman, 187
Whitelaw, Ed, 56
Wild, Peter, 161, 180
Wild Bill, 249
Wild Bunch, The, 219, 220
Wilde, Oscar, 361
Wilder, Laura Ingalls, xi, 118
Wilderness, vii, 309, 350
Wild Horse Ranch, 332
Wild West, 178; early, 10–11; myth of, 70–71
"Wild West Yesterday and Today, The" *(Life)*, 5–6
Wilkinson, Charles F., 360
Williams, Hank, 288
Williams, Jeanne, 128
Williams, Terry Tempest, 134, 188
Will Penny, 220, 228
Will Rogers Follies, The, 346
Wills, Bob, 266, 285
Wills, Chill, 98
Wilson, Ann, 52
Wilson, Edward O., 357

Wilson, Keith, 150
Wilson, Terry P., 81
Wimar, Carl, 202
Wincer, Simon, 228–29
Winchell, Sandy, 34
Winchell, Terry, 34–35
Windbreak: A Woman Rancher on the Northern Plains (Hasselstrom), 185
Wind in the Wire (movie), 285
Wind in the Wire (Travis), 290
Windwalker, 223
Winter, Lumen Martin, 314
Winter: Notes from Montana (Bass), 189
Winters, Yvor, 149
Wister, Frances Kemble, 105
Wister, Owen, 25, 28, 123, 195, 197–98, 240
Wolf, Bryan J., 205
Women: African-American, 82; country music and, 286–88; feminist stereotypes of, 82; movies and, 208, 235–30; myth and, 117, 118–19; New Western, 139–41, 347; outlaw, 237; place of, 117; Western history and, 81–83, 85; writers, 118–19
Women of the New Mexico Frontier, 1846–1912 (Foote), 85
Women Poets of the West: An Anthology, 1850–1950 (Trusky), 162
Wondrous Times on the Frontier (Brown), 91
Wood, Nicole, 15
Woods, Annie, on boots, 46–47
Woods, Sharon, 39–40
Woolvett, Jaimz, 242
Work, James C., 127, 129, 197–98, 246
Worster, Donald, 56–57, 63, 66, 69–70, 82, 90, 356–57; minority history and, 80; New Western Historians and, 61, 65, 75; on Western history, 57–58, 59, 64–65, 67–68; at WHA meeting, 76–77
Wounded Knee, 70, 337
Woven Stone (Ortiz), 156, 161
Writers of the Purple Sage: An Anthology of Recent Western Writing (Martin and Barasch), 130
Writing: New Western, 124, 130–31, 189–96; Old Western, 108–9
Wyatt Earp, 209, 249
Wydeven, Joseph J., 360
Wynette, Tammy, 276

Yearwood, Trisha, 287
Yeats, William Butler, 148
Yellow Back Radio Broke-Down (Reed), 125
Yellowstone National Park, 351
Yellowstone Tomorrow, 354
Yoakam, Dwight, 271, 272, 274, 275(illus.), 292, 301
Young, Robert M., 224
Younger, Cole, xi, 222, 293
Young Guns, 200, 227–28

Zarzyski, Paul, 166, 167(illus.), 168
Zinnemann, Fred, 208
Zoot Suit: A New American Play (Valdez), 172
Zwinger, Ann H., 127, 179–80, 183–84